# *Social Work Practice with Families*

# Also Available from Lyceum Books, Inc.

Advisory Editors: Thomas M. Meenaghan, *New York University*
Ira C. Colby, *University of Houston*

ETHICS IN END-OF-LIFE DECISIONS FOR SOCIAL WORK PRACTICE,
by Ellen Csikai and Elizabeth Chaiten

A PRACTICAL GUIDE TO SOCIAL SERVICE EVALUATION,
by Carl F. Brun

ENDINGS IN CLINICAL PRACTICE: EFFECTIVE CLOSURE IN
DIVERSE SETTINGS, 2E,
by Joseph Walsh, foreword by Thomas M. Meenaghan

SECONDARY TRAUMATIC STRESS AND THE CHILD WELFARE PROFESSIONAL,
by Josephine G. Pryce, Kimberly K. Shackelford, and David H. Pryce

STRAIGHT TALK ABOUT PROFESSIONAL ETHICS,
by Kim Strom-Gottfried

THE ETHICS OF PRACTICE WITH MINORS: HIGH STAKES, HARD CHOICES,
by Kim Strom-Gottfried

WHAT IS PROFESSIONAL SOCIAL WORK?,
by Malcolm Payne

EVIDENCE-BASED PRACTICES FOR SOCIAL WORKERS,
by Thomas O'Hare

SHORT-TERM EXISTENTIAL INTERVENTION IN CLINICAL PRACTICE,
by Jim Lantz and Joseph Walsh

CLINICAL ASSESSMENT FOR SOCIAL WORKERS: QUALITATIVE AND
QUANTITATIVE METHODS, 2E,
edited by Catheleen Jordan and Cynthia Franklin

# Social Work Practice with Families

## A Resiliency-Based Approach

Mary Patricia Van Hook
*University of Central Florida*

LYCEUM
BOOKS, INC.

Chicago, Illinois

© Lyceum Books, Inc., 2008

Published by
LYCEUM BOOKS, INC.
5758 S. Blackstone Ave.
Chicago, Illinois 60637
773+643-1903 (Fax)
773+643-1902 (Phone)
lyceum@lyceumbooks.com
http://www.lyceumbooks.com

6 5 4 3 2 1   08 09 10 11

ISBN 978-1-933478-16-6


Library of Congress Cataloging-in-Publication Data

Van Hook, Mary.
　　Social work practice with families : a resiliency-based approach / Mary Van Hook.
　　　p. cm.
　　Includes bibliographical references and index.
　　ISBN: 978-1-933478-16-6
　　1. Family social work. I. Title.
　HV697.V36 2008
　362.82′53—dc22

2007042188


Material on pp. 53–54 is used with permission from Wiley-Blackwell.

*For my husband, Jay Martin Van Hook, and my children, Carrie, Stephen, Suzanne, and John, and their families who taught me important lessons about families and have given their ongoing support*

# Contents

# Preface

Early in my social work career I was working at a major New York City teaching psychiatric hospital on the children's services unit. In the course of arranging with a local foster care agency to place one of the children, we met the prospective foster father, a compassionate and responsible family man and father of two children. He and his wife were willing to open their home to a five-year-old boy from our program. He told his own childhood story of going from foster home to foster home until he grew too old for the foster-care system. During these years he developed the goal of providing a stable foster home to protect other children from his own experience. The time had now come to fulfill this commitment and he and his wife agreed to accept this little boy into their home. After meeting with this prospective foster father, the staff of the children's services discussed our own limitations in understanding the emotional and interpersonal strength of this man. If he had been a patient in the hospital and we had been asked to explain why he was in the hospital and unable to function or relate effectively with other people, we would have had no difficulty explaining his illness. We would have talked about attachment problems, ego deficits, and other contributing factors. We recognized that our theoretical tools had no answers for why he was the caring, responsible man that he currently was. We were humbled at the complex nature of human beings and the presence of strength despite great odds.

Several years ago a colleague and friend of mine received a major award for his contributions to the field of mental health. He had been responsible for creating some important changes in mental health services and had developed and administered several important mental health programs. In his acceptance speech, he described the source of his commitment to making a difference in the services offered. When he was a child, his father, a volunteer fireman, had died rushing to respond to a fire. He and his brothers were then raised by their mother, a fragile woman with many serious mental health problems. She was in and out of hospitals and the boys experienced the stigma of family mental illness in their small community with very limited resources to help the family. As a result, he grew up dedicated to ensuring that other families would receive the help they needed—help that had not been available to him and his family. He became a committed and effective leader in the field of mental health, especially to providing care to those in underserved areas. When I described my friend's background to my students and asked for their description of his current situation, their stories were replete with pathology—inability to hold down a job, problems in relationships, perhaps substance abuse. They were surprised and rather skeptical when I described instead a caring husband and father, respected in the mental health field, and a good friend to those around him. Perhaps if we had met his two older brothers, both of whom grew up to be dedicated public servants, we would have had some clue as to the source of his resiliency.

In the media we hear and read of children caught up in crime and drugs within their troubled neighborhoods. Many of these children join the case rolls of social workers and other counselors. Their stories reveal the trauma and ongoing dysfunction in the lives of the people involved. But receiving less attention are the children who somehow manage to forge productive and satisfying lives despite living in the same areas. We live in a world in which people must contend with the aftermath of accidents, violent actions, or severe illness that leaves families without a parent or partner. Other families face problems of poverty, political, or social oppression. Families experience the loss of children through illness or accidents. No family is immune to at least some of these adverse life events and many of the families that we see in social work have experienced several of them.

Social workers and related professionals realize that while discovering and identifying why people develop problems and disabilities are important, this information is inadequate for the assessment and treatment process. It is essential to find answers to how people manage to endure, cope, and even sometimes thrive under the troubles that can be part of the human condition. It is further important to identify the specific aspects of a person's life that make such coping possible (Blundo, 2002). The strengths perspective reminds us that such answers are critical in the design and implementation of prevention and treatment efforts and can promote the healing process (Saleeby, 2000). McQuaide (2000) in writing about women's resiliency at midlife goes even further. She describes assessment and treatment that is vulnerability and pathology based as participating "in the process of subjugation—the subjugation of the resilient selves" (p. 74).

In recognition of the importance of identifying sources of strength, vitality, and effective coping in our work with families, this book draws upon the theoretical framework and empirical literature regarding resiliency to examine the nature of the concept and the empirical basis of factors that promote resiliency in individuals and families. The book is organized to help the reader understand the concept of resiliency and the related concepts of risk and protection as well as individual, family, and community factors that promote resiliency. Subsequent chapters discuss resiliency from the perspective of families belonging to different racial or ethnic and community groups and with diverse family structures who are facing certain problem events. The book presents a model of assessing families using a resiliency framework. The book describes ways to join families using a resiliency approach. The understanding of what aspects of family life can either threaten or contribute to resiliency can guide the social worker in selecting intervention approaches that could be useful in strengthening a particular family with its unique set of current circumstances. Based on this discussion, the book links the concepts of resiliency with some of the family therapy approaches in terms of ways in which they can be used to promote the welfare of the family and its members.

Part I of the book introduces the reader to the concepts of resiliency and ways they can be incorporated into the basic social work practice with families. Chapter 1, The Nature and Sources of Resiliency, describes the meaning of the concept of resiliency and related concepts organized around risk and resiliency. It also presents findings regarding what contributes to resiliency for individuals and families and the process that influences how families are able to cope with potentially stressful life events. Recognizing the critical role that culture plays in how people experience and cope with life events, chapter 2, Cultural Issues and Family Resiliency, describes some of the risk and protective factors that have been identified with selected ethnic and racial groups, as well as rural, military, and gay and lesbian families. The next two chapters, chapter 3, Setting the Stage for Work with Families: Development of the Therapeutic Alliance and chapter 4, Assessing Families, discuss these two essential phases of social work with families from a resiliency-based perspective. Chapter 4 makes the bridge between assessment and the link to the selection of intervention approaches. Resiliency theory thus becomes one of the tools that can be used by social workers in guiding their clinical judgments in working with families. This book is based on the premise that it is important to match the intervention approach to the family and its unique set of circumstances.

Part II discusses several of the traditional family counseling approaches from a resiliency-based perspective. Resiliency-based practice can draw upon various counseling strategies with the joint goals of reducing the risks facing families and enhancing the protective aspects of families and their environment. The part opens with chapter 5, Social Learning/Cognitive Approaches to Family Counseling; chapter 6, Structural Family Therapy; chapter 7, Solution-Focused Approach to Counseling with Families; chapter 8, Narrative Family Therapy; chapter 9, Psychoeducational Models of Family Counseling; chapter 10, Multisystems Models of Family Therapy; and chapter 11, Object Relations Family Therapy, which discuss specific models of interventions with families. The chapters regarding specific models include one or more case illustrations of the use of this approach, a discussion of the theoretical background, major tenets, goals of treatment, role of the social worker, and an evaluation of the theory. Several chapters include information about adaptations of the approach for specific cultural groups or problems facing families. The part ends with chapter 12, Spirituality and Family Resiliency.

Unlike the preceding chapters that address specific models of practice, spirituality does not represent such a model but instead is an important aspect of life that can play a role in a variety of approaches.

Part III includes chapter 13, Families Coping with Difficult Life Events, that discusses the literature in terms of risk and protective factors for families that are facing a variety of difficult life events. Recognizing that the families seeking social work help tend to be struggling with one or more difficult life events, this chapter reviews literature in terms of valuable supports for families facing selected problems. Some of the topics include illness (both physical and mental health related), sexual abuse, divorce, trauma, and childhood behavior problems. With the essential caveat that information related to the problems facing families must be paired with an assessment of individual families and their context, each of the sections also includes a discussion regarding implications for treatment approaches. Chapter 14, Conclusion, includes a brief summary of the elements of a resiliency-based approach to social work practice with families and a discussion of the important aspects of this approach in strengthening families.

# Acknowledgments

Many people have helped make this book possible. The families I have had the privilege to work with during my years of clinical practice have provided essential insights into the challenges facing families and the sources of resiliency. A draft version of this manuscript was used with social work graduate students at the University of Central Florida. The feedback provided by these students and their faculty members Drs. Michael Rothenberg and Mary Beth Harris was invaluable. My husband's editing skills were essential. I am also deeply endebted to my mentor Dr. Sallie Churchill, professor emerita, of the University of Michigan School of Social Work, whose clinical wisdom has encouraged me to think in terms of resiliency. I would also like to thank Bruce Friedman, Mary Helen Hayden, Shelley Cohen Konrad, Marian Mattison, Fred McKenzie, Tom Meenaghan, Renee Pogue, William Powell, Pat Sickinger, Wendy Smith, and Martha Wilson, whose reviews of earlier versions of the manuscript provided invaluable probing questions and insights.

# About the Author

Mary Patricia Van Hook is professor emerita of the University of Central Florida School of Social Work and a research associate with the Center for Community Partnerships of UCF. She was director of the University of Central Florida School of Social Work and taught research and practice social work courses at University of Central Florida, the University of Michigan, Grand Valley State University, and Northwestern College. She was also a clinical social worker and administrator for mental health and family agencies in New York, Maryland, and Iowa. She has written extensively in the areas of families, rural mental health, spirituality, and women's issues both domestically and internationally. She received the Howery Award for outstanding contributions to rural mental health. She earned her PhD in social work from Rutgers University, her MS from Columbia University School of Social Work, and her BA from Calvin College.

# Part I

# *Introduction to Resiliency-Based Practice*

# 1

# *The Nature and Sources of Resiliency*

## WHAT IS RESILIENCY?

The term resiliency has been used to describe the process by which people manage not only to endure hardships but also to create and sustain lives that have meaning and contribute to those around them. The phrase "success against odds" is often used to capture the essence of resiliency. Resiliency thus involves being successful in life despite exposure to high risks. It also includes the ability to recover successfully from trauma (Fraser, Kirby, & Smokowski, 2004; Greene & Conrad, 2002). Resilient individuals are able to draw upon their own internal resources and potential ones in their environment to cope with challenges. McCubbin, Thompson, Thompson, and Fromer (1998) define resiliency in terms of behavior: "The positive behavioral patterns and functional competence individuals and families demonstrate under stressful or adverse circumstances" (p. xvi). Resiliency moves beyond the absence of pathology to the ability to cope, to find meaning, and continuity in the presence of adversity (Green & Conrad, 2002).

The characteristics that contribute to resiliency are multifaceted and interact in important ways throughout the life cycle as the challenges facing individuals and their potential resources vary during the life cycle. Acknowledging the developmental and contextual nature of resiliency, Stewart, Reid, and Mangham (1997) describe it as "the capacity of individuals to cope successfully in the face of significant change, adversity, or risk. This capacity changes over time and is enhanced by protective factors in the individual and the environment" (p. 22). Although having to cope with difficult life events can create a burden, the process of coping successfully leads to increased confidence and self-efficacy and enhances resiliency (Gutheil & Congress, 2000; Masten & Garmezy, 1984). Resiliency is thus described as a process (Greene, 2002; Walsh, 1998) "woven in a web of relationships and experiences over the course of a life lived from birth through death" (Walsh, 1998, p. 12).

3

# TYPES OF RESILIENCY

Fraser, Kirby, and Smokowski (2004) describe three types of resiliency: overcoming the odds, sustained competence under stress, and recovery from trauma (p. 23). Overcoming the odds is defined as the attainment of positive outcomes despite high-risk status, for example a preterm baby who does not experience negative outcomes or a child who grows up in a very high-risk neighborhood to become a contributing adult. Sustained competence under stress refers to the ability to cope despite ongoing difficult circumstances. People who either struggle with serious chronic illnesses or who care for such individuals can demonstrate this type of resiliency. Recovery from trauma is reflected in individuals who function well after a highly stressful event (e.g., war, violence, accidents).

# RISK, VULNERABILITY, AND PROTECTIVE FACTORS

Several related concepts help in understanding resiliency: risk factors, vulnerability factors, and protective factors. These factors interact in the process of stress and resiliency and vary over the life course as well as from individual to individual.

Risk factors include those aspects of life that increase the likelihood of a negative outcome. Risk factors can be characterized in terms of specific events (e.g., loss of a job, death of a parent, reading problems) or cumulative/additive risk factors by which a cluster of individual events contributes to the likelihood of this outcome (Fraser & Galinsky, 2004; Fraser, Kirby, & Smokiwski, 2004; Greene & Norman, 2002). The concept of cumulative/additive risk factors has received increased attention with recognition of "there is no single path to many social problems" (Fraser, Richman, & Galinsky, 1999, p. 13). A study of African American children living in single-mother households revealed the increased stress as the risk factors increased from three to four factors (Jones, Forehand, Brody, & Armistead, 2002). In an earlier study conducted with rural families who had suffered from the economic problems associated with the farm crisis, it was the number and extent of such problems rather than the nature of specific problems that emerged as the best predictor of the presence of symptoms (Van Hook, 1990b). Many of the families social workers work with are experiencing a combination of factors both currently and in their life span, for example, loss of a job, followed by illness of a child and then marital strain.

Risk factors can also be characterized in terms of their relative closeness to the individual's immediate environment. Proximal risk factors are closer to the individual (e.g., homelessness) than are distal risk factors (e.g., the economy in the community) (Greene & Conrad, 2002). Distal risk factors frequently increase stress by influencing proximal risk factors, for example, community poverty that negatively affects the child by diminishing the parent-child relationship or making it more likely that a family will be homeless, or a war in Iraq that leads to a family member's being called up to active duty with subsequent stress on all the family members. Therefore, it is important to understand the nature of the distal risk factors facing a family and the ways in which these factors influence the family members in more direct ways.

The process by which risk factors influence people needs to be viewed as a dynamic one depending on the individual, the developmental stage of the individual, and the life context (Greene & Conrad, 2002). While the emphasis in this discussion is on ways to promote resiliency, a careful assessment of risk factors is also necessary to identify the needs of individuals and to select appropriate intervention strategies.

Vulnerability factors refers to the concept that some people with risk factors are more likely than others to develop a negative outcome. "A vulnerability factor is a characteristic of an individual that makes that person more susceptible to a particular threat to development" (Masten, 1994, p. 7, cited in Greene & Conrad, 2002, p. 33). Vulnerability can take many forms involving the biological, psychological, developmental, and social aspects of the person, and no one is immune to being wounded by life events. Although one can talk about resiliency, the use of the term "invulnerable" is misleading (Garmezy, 1993, cited in Greene & Conrad, 2002).

Protective factors are the aspects of life that buffer the negative impact of risk factors. Protective factors can be internal to the person (e.g., intelligence, sense of self-efficacy), part of the supportive family context (e.g., loving parents), or the larger social context that is supportive (e.g., an interested youth leader, good schools, job opportunities) (Greene & Conrad, 2002; Norman, 2000).

Protective factors can be characterized in terms of playing one of three roles. Protective factors can buffer risk factors so that they cushion the negative impact of aversive life experiences. In the moving book, *Tuesdays with Morrie,* Morrie describes the important role played by a warm and loving stepmother in the lives of two boys left bereft by the death of their mother and an emotionally detached father (Albom, 1997). Protection can also occur through interrupting the risk chain, so that the protective factors eliminate the link between the aversive circumstances and the negative result (e.g., parents can receive help from a counselor dealing with the stress associated with economic strain). This service can potentially interrupt the risk chain because family conflict generated by these economic problems can be reduced and thus the chain of risk between economic problems and the negative impact on the children is reduced. Protection can also prevent the initial occurrence of a risk factor by changing the situation (e.g., a caring grandparent can give a child a sustaining relationship during the illness of a parent who is unable to care for the child). The presence of this grandparent thus changes the situation for the child (Fraser, Kirby, & Smokowski, 2004, pp. 32–33).

Resiliency thus represents a dynamic process during the life cycle of the individual and the family during which the multiple stresses of life are balanced by the ability to cope. Context influences the nature of the risk factors as well as potential means of coping. The family's resiliency is tested especially in times of transition. The experience of being successful in coping with difficult life events increase an individual's or a family's sense of competence.

Resiliency can be viewed as a continuum that varies by degree depending not only on individuals but also on their developmental stage of life and the life event facing them. As a result, individuals can differ in their ability to cope effectively depending on the developmental issues involved and the nature of the problem (Greene & Conrad, 2002).

## *Life Events and Resiliency*

Life events can demand very different coping and adaptive capacities. Greene and Conrad (2002) describe several ways to categorize life events. Events can be categorized in terms of either nonnormative events that are idiosyncratic to the individual or a small number of people (e.g., the birth of a child with serious developmental disabilities) or normative events that are influenced by social definitions of the stage of life (e.g., loss of a spouse, retirement) or cohort events that are common to people who are part of a cohort of individuals (e.g., the Great Depression, Vietnam War, political shifts within a country such as war in Iraq, fall of Communism in Eastern Europe, split of Korea into North and South Korea).

Events can also represent major traumatic life events that can readily overwhelm an individual's coping capacity. Examples include natural events such as tornadoes or hurricanes, human-induced events such as the terrorist attack on the World Trade Center, and accidents such as a plane crash or a major earthquake (Greene & Conrad, 2002).

The dynamic nature of resiliency presented in both the preceding and following discussion highlights the roles that social workers and other helping professionals can play in enhancing and supporting resiliency within families. While genetic characteristics and certain background factors of individuals may be givens in the situations, resiliency is a dynamic process influenced by the ongoing interplay between life events and individuals and families. Social workers and other helping professionals can enhance the ability of families to cope, to overcome adversity, and to move toward a more fulfilling future. Counselors' efforts to address contextual issues and the social support system in the design of prevention and treatment approaches can also enhance resiliency. Given the developmental nature of resiliency, such efforts not only help families cope with the present situation but can also enable them to gain a sense of self-efficacy and skills that can then enable them to cope more effectively with future life demands.

## HISTORICAL BACKGROUND

Early studies in the 1970s–1980s regarding resiliency in individuals recognized that despite difficult circumstances, some children were able to develop into relatively well-adjusted people who coped effectively with life. Families were also able to weather major problems, find a sense of meaning in these events, and forge ahead. These findings indicated that mechanistic views of life based on deterministic models that assume a certain set of problems (risk factors) inevitably create an accompanying list of maladaptive responses were inaccurate and unduly pessimistic. They pointed out the need to examine not only the factors that contribute to maladjustment (risk factors) but also the characteristics that contribute to this resiliency (protective factors). The emphasis on risk factors was balanced with a focus on the protective factors that enable people to adapt and cope effectively (protective factors). While appreciating the pain and possible damage to individuals and families created by difficult life events, there is also a respect for the potential strength resiliency present within individuals and families. Resiliency from this perspective is a strength-affirming perspective that believes it is worthwhile to look for the competencies and abilities within families.

## INDIVIDUAL RESILIENCY

Studies regarding resiliency of youth have identified three basic themes that promote resiliency: personality characteristics such as self-esteem, easygoing personality, or intelligence; nurturing family environments; and support systems external to the family system that offer opportunities for personal growth and mentoring (Conger & Elder, 1994; Elder & Conger, 2000; Fraser, Kirby, & Smokowski, 2004).

A landmark longitudinal study conducted by Werner and colleagues in Hawaii with children who grew up in high-risk environments revealed the importance of these individual traits as well as family and interpersonal relationships. The results were also encouraging because even the majority of youth who had juvenile criminal backgrounds became productive adults, especially those who were able to gain important educational and vocational skills, to create constructive social connections, and to develop a sense of spirituality (Werner & Smith, 1992). Similar patterns emerged in a small qualitative study conducted with African Americans who had made it against the odds. Factors promoting resiliency included individuals' traits (efforts related to prosocial goals, a sense of autonomy [locus of control], spiritual connections), sustaining interpersonal relationships in the course of their development, and positive meanings of life events (Gordon & Song, 1994, cited in Greene, 2000). These studies indicate the need to understand resiliency and individuals from a broader ecological perspective rather than traits limited to the individual.

The preceding discussion regarding resiliency illustrates the nature of a family as a living system occurring over time within an ecological framework. As a living system, the family has ongoing information and energy exchanges with its individual members, the family as a unit, and its larger context. The family is composed of individual members with their unique developmental history and individual characteristics that are both shaped by the family and its larger context and in turn influence the family and its context. The family as a unit also has a developmental history and organizational structures that in turn are influenced by individual members, life cycle issues, and the larger context. The family operates within and is shaped by a larger cultural and community context (e.g., neighborhood, employment and educational organizations, faith-based or other voluntary organizations) that in turn is influenced by family units. As a result, it is important to understand risk and resiliency factors from the perspective of individuals, family units, and the larger community context. As an example of this ongoing systematic interaction, the serious chronic illness of child within a family has an important impact on all the members of the family as well the nature of the demands on the family unit. The illness of the child potentially creates emotional strain for all the family members, makes demands on parental time and attention, forces the family to make potentially difficult decisions regarding parental employment and viable day care arrangements, and requires additional funds to pay for the treatment of the child. The child and her illness in turn are influenced by the interpersonal and economic resources of the nuclear and extended family—the ability of family members to provide adequate physical and emotional care, the nature of the marital/parental relationship and what effect does this strain make on the relationship, extended family members who can provide respite care, adequacy of the family's medical insurance or other economic resources. The nature of the community health-care system and social policies regarding payment of health care are critical for this family life. These policies in turn are potentially shaped by parent organizations who advocate for the needs of children with this illness, the nature of available community resources, and larger societal views regarding the role of health care.

These findings give support to a living system model in which individuals, the family unit, and the larger context interact on an ongoing basis. Fraser, Kirby, and Smokowski (2004) use an ecological approach to organize risk and protective factors in terms of these three system levels: (1) broad environmental conditions, including neighborhood and school, (2) family conditions, and (3) individual (psychosocial and biological). Based on an extensive review of the literature, they identify the following risk and protective factors.

### Environmental Level

Risk factors include few opportunities for education and employment, racial discrimination and injustice, and poverty.

Protective factors include many opportunities for education, employment, growth, and achievement; collective efficacy, and presence of caring adults (e.g., caring teachers, youth leaders, social workers, and other supportive community members).

### Family Level

Risk factors include child maltreatment, parental conflict, parental psychopathology, and harsh parenting.

Protective factors include positive parent-child relationships and effective parenting.

### Individual Level

Risk factors include biomedical problems (including genetic liability)

Protective factors include "easy temperament as an infant, self-esteem and hardiness, competence in normative roles, self-efficacy, and high intelligence (p. 36).

## *Interpersonal Relationships*

Positive and caring relationships within the family or other intimate environments support resiliency (Masten, Best, & Garmezy, 1991; Masten & Coatworth, 1998). Drawing from theoretical perspectives regarding development, these relationships foster development in several ways. In terms of object relations theory, Winnicott described the importance of "good enough mothering" or a "holding environment" that provides what the child needs at various developmental stages and in turn enables the child to develop an integrated sense of the self who can have genuine relationships with others (Goldstein, 1995; Kilpatrick, Kilpatrick, & Callaway, 2000). Attachment theory stresses the importance of someone that a young child can feel connected to and is able to trust his or her accessibility and responsiveness. Attachment theory studies have identified the following patterns as supportive of personal maturity: "mutual trust and approval between the child and his parents" (including acceptance, trust, open communication, encouragement of wider social relationships, and congenial parental relationships) and "consistency of family life" (including regular routines, consistency of parenting, participation of members in family activities) (Bowlby, 1973, p. 335). Nurturing relationships help build healthy brain architecture in young children and buffer the impact of stress of the development process (Shonkoff, 2005).

When such positive relationships are not found within the immediate family, individuals have been able to find someone within the extended family, teachers, neighbors, church members, and others within the community to establish these connections. Similar to the language of attachment theory, Norman (2000) describes these persons as offering "a safe harbor promoting autonomy and competence" (p. 9). While such relationships are important, recent research with economically troubled farm families points out the limitations of such relationships for teenagers when, for example, economic distress engenders harsh parenting by parents (Conger & Elder, 2000). Resiliency is also promoted when the child has relationships with others who hold positive and realistic expectations of the child (Norman, 2000, p. 10).

## *Personality Characteristics*

Key personality and related interpersonal characteristics that support resiliency in individuals include self-efficacy, a realistic appraisal of the environment, social problem-solving skills, a sense of direction or mission, empathy, humor, androgynous sex role behavior, and adaptive distancing—the ability to avoid being enmeshed into the problems and dysfunctional patterns of the family while at the same time remaining connected to the persons involved (Norman, 2000).

Self-efficacy includes both "a sense of self-worth or self-esteem, and a sense of mastery of one's self and the external environment (sometimes called an internal locus of control)" (Norman, 2000, p. 5). Self-efficacy is specific to context. Self-efficacy can take several different forms that contribute to resiliency in different contexts; for example, academic efficacy (ability to learn), social efficacy (social relationships), and self-regulatory efficacy (ability to resist pressure from peers and others) (Fraser, Kirby, & Smokowski, 2004).

Self-efficacy is enhanced by the ability to appraise one's environment in a realistic manner. This includes a realistic understanding of the nature of the situation and what one can do to change it. The ability to draw upon appropriate problem-solving skills also enhances self-efficacy. Individuals need a range of problem-solving skills to address the variety of situations they will face over time (Walsh, 1998). Self-efficacy with the accompanying actions to take control of one's life emerged as an important factor in supporting resiliency in studies including the Hawaiian cohort of Werner (1992), high-risk children (Rutter, 1984), the offspring of mentally ill parents (Garmezy, 1985, as cited in Norman, 2000), and the street children of Columbia (Felsman, 1989, as cited in Norman, 2000, p. 5).

Sense of direction or mission has been identified in groups ranging from concentration camp survivors (Moskowitz, 1983) to civil rights workers (Beardsley, 1989), and the young people from Hawaii (Norman, 2000; Werner & Smith, 1992). Ruby Bridges, the young girl who integrated her

New Orleans elementary school, was able to walk the gauntlet of threats while praying for those who threatened her, and survived this experience as a strong and happy person (Coles, 1964).

Self-regulation is important in developing competence in a variety of spheres associated with effective development. It is supported by means of loving but firm parenting efforts (Masten & Coatsworth, 1998). Such self-regulation enables individuals to draw upon effective coping strategies in a planned manner.

## *FAMILY RESILIENCY*

Walsh (1998) describes family resilience as "the coping and adaptational processes in the family as a functional unit. . . . How a family confronts and manages a disruptive experience, buffers stress, effectively reorganizes itself and moves forward with life" will influence how the family and its members adapt and survive in the immediate and long term (p. 14). Resiliency does not refer to a family that is problem-free, but rather a family that is able to absorb the shock of problems and discover strategies to solve them while finding ways to meet the needs of family members and the family unit. The challenge of social workers is to find ways to empower families to cope in this manner with the myriad of problems that are part of the ongoing life experience of families, for example, illness, loss of jobs, or death of members.

Key factors that promote resiliency of individuals or represent risks point to the important role of the family and thus the value of supporting the key factors that promote resiliency and finding ways to address risk factors. From the perspective of various studies and theoretical frameworks, caring and stable relationships within the family are identified as protective factors while conflictual family relationships are identified as risk factors. The presence of caring adults emerge as the "most important and consistent protective factor" in terms of dealing with multiple types of stress (Masten, Best, & Garmezy, 1991, p. 431). The development of competence that supports resiliency is nourished within an interpersonal context. Family members also respond in ways that encourage the sociability and sense of competence of the child—"the child and parent dance." Relationships set the stage for how events and potential resources are perceived. For example, depending on culture and individual family circumstances, families can value quite different traits for their children. For one family, academic excellence might be highly valued while in another family athletic prowess is honored. Within the family, children can also be valued for different reasons—one child might be valued for academic achievement while another for artistic or athletic ability.

Because families play crucial roles in the lives of their members and in supporting the ability of children to become resilient, it is important to understand the aspects within the family and the broader community that support families and promote family resiliency. Knowledge of these elements can help in the design of prevention and healing approaches that support resiliency both within families and individuals. While the specific forms of family units may change (e.g., extended families in some cultures compared to nuclear families in others, larger numbers of single parents, divorced and blended families, and gay and lesbian couples raising children), the family unit remains the key institution for providing children with the essential physical and emotional nourishment needed. The family unit gives its members a key sense of identity. Family members can turn to each other for companionship and ongoing social support in good and trying times. Families develop meaning systems that help members interpret the world around them and life events. These interpretations help in coping or contribute to ongoing struggles.

An emphasis on family resiliency also influences the basic nature of the relationship between the family and the helping professional. Using a collaborative relationship between the counselor and the family members is most effective when it identifies sources of resiliency and encourages the family's efforts in recovery and growth. Such an approach empowers people and enables them to cope with the current problem and prepares them to address the challenges of the future. As Walsh (1998) asserts, it "affirms the family's potential for self-repair and growth out of crisis and challenge" (p. 16). Research in the area of resiliency provides empirical grounding for assessment and treatment intervention strategies. While the specific focus of this book is on counseling approaches in working with families, evidence regarding resiliency points out the additional need for interventions in the areas of social and economic policies that address aspects of life that have a profound impact on families.

Research regarding family resiliency has grown out of two basic streams of research and thought: the nature of healthy family processes and family response to stressors and related family crisis theory. There is considerable overlap in the family and contextual characteristics that influence resiliency identified within these traditions. The following discussion is organized first in terms of the factors that have been identified that enhance resiliency within families, and second the process that occurs when families attempt to cope in terms of ways that promote resiliency or lead to further distress.

### *Principles of Family Resiliency*

In her excellent discussion of healthy family processes and resiliency, Walsh (1998) uses a family system approach to describe the interaction between individuals, families, and the wider context. The health of the family and the hardiness of individuals are influenced by the interaction between individuals, families, and their context. Crisis events affect the family as a whole as well as individual family members. While maladaptive responses increase vulnerability and distress, protective processes that buffer stress promote resiliency. The outcome of potential crisis events is influenced by family processes. Walsh offers a strength-affirming stance, "All families have the potential for resiliency, and we can maximize that potential by encouraging their best efforts and strengthening key processes" (p. 24).

## Key Factors of Family Resiliency

The keys to family resiliency can be understood in terms of three important family elements: belief systems, organizational patterns, and communication processes (Walsh, 1998, p. 24). These elements are further influenced by the social support system of the family, the community, and cultural context and reactivation of past issues that heighten positive or negative aspects of family members. The presence of several risk factors increases the vulnerability of families. Table 1 summarizes risk and protective factors identified in the family strengths and family crisis traditions. The following section discusses ways in which these factors contribute to either vulnerability or resiliency within families.

### Belief Systems

Family belief systems are the product of the historical and cultural context of families as well as the unique experiences of the extended and immediate family members. Families develop paradigms (organized belief systems about the world and individuals' relationship to it) that influence how they view the world and appropriate survival responses (Reiss, 1981). These belief systems provide a sense of coherence to family life events. Adversity in one form or another is part of the life journey for members of all families. Even if family members should be fortunate enough to escape economic and major interpersonal problems, loss is an inevitable part of the family life cycle. How family members interpret these events is critical in influencing how families are able to cope. Walsh (1998) asserts the importance of families creating meaning out of adversity and the value of sharing a sense of meaning by family members.

The family's definition of the nature of life events influences the strategies that family members employ to address problems and the preferred solutions (Hill, 1949; McCubbin, Thompson, Thompson, & Fromer, 1998; Reiss, 1981; Robinson, 2000; Walsh, 1998). These definitions influence, for example, whether or not the family can deal with it through its own internal resources, if it is appropriate to seek help from others outside of the family and what type of help to seek. When problems or issues are identified as something that the family is ashamed of, family members may be reluctant to seek help from those outside the family circle. A potential resource within

**TABLE 1.** Family Risk and Protective Factors

| Risk Factors | Protective Factors |
|---|---|
| **Belief Systems** | |
| Lack of sense of "we" in terms of the family | Relational perspective |
| Lack of trust | Trust of family, loyalty, affection |
| Lack of self-efficacy | Self-efficacy, mastery |
| Negative cultural beliefs | Appropriate cultural beliefs |
| Lack of developmental perspective | Developmental perspective |
| Demoralization | Sense of coherence |
| Fatalist views | Hope, courage, perseverance |
| Blaming and scapegoating | Recognition of complex patterns |
| All or nothing thinking | Recognition of what is possible |
| Negative aspects of spirituality | Transcendent beliefs that promote meaning |
| **Role Models** | |
| Ineffective role models | Role models of strength |
| **Organizational Patterns** | |
| Lack of cohesion, rigidity | Cohesion, flexibility |
| Lack of effective leadership, chaotic or abusive power | Effective leadership |
| Ineffective communication | Clear, open communication |
| Conflict | Positive interactions, trust |
| Ineffective problem-solving/coping strategies | Effective problem-solving and coping strategies |
| Lack of sense of humor | Humor |
| **Social Support System** | |
| Lack of social support | Social support |
| **Economic Resources** | |
| Poverty | Adequate resources |
| **Community Context** | |
| Poverty, lack of economic and educational opportunities | Economic and educational opportunities |
| **Reactivation of Past Events** | |
| Evidence of weakness and unresolved conflict | Evidence of strength and family support |

the community is not a resource to the family unless defined so by the family and the family is able to access this resource (Karpel, 1986).

Cultural messages shape perceptions of the meaning of life events, for example, the relative value of possessions, family ties, family honor and history. They influence how people view what contributes to success or difficulties in life and how to address problems (Falicov, 1999; McGolderick

& Giordano, 1996; McCubbin, McCubbin, Thompson, & Thompson, 1998). As an example, when my daughter was serving as a Peace Corps volunteer in a small village in the African country of Chad, a land stricken by poverty and decimated by a recent war and other problems, she was surprised to see how happy the people were despite having nothing in terms of the usual sense of belongings from a middle-class American standard of living. While from our perspective these people were extremely poor, they had close family and relational ties that made life meaningful. When it was time for her assignment to end after two years, some people were surprised that she would actually leave "the best place on earth to live." When my other daughter (also in her early twenties) joined the Peace Corps, she lived with a family during her training period in the Cameroons. The wife in this family was a lovely young woman who did not leave the family compound (the buildings that composed the home) without her husband's permission. The family was economically quite well off and she was able to send others to the market to get the daily needs of the family. This woman felt fortunate to be cared for in this way and worried about my daughter, who had no one to take care of her. The life circumstances and cultures of each of these young woman had led them to value quite different aspects of life—security/adventure.

Relevant cultural messages influence how family members view events and the appropriate types of help. Members of some cultures turn to folk healers while others might see solutions in terms of medical doctors or financial advisors. HIV/AIDS represents a critical global health problem with painful social and family definitions that have impeded people from seeking or receiving help because of the stigma involved. Advocates in the field of mental health have fought and are continuing to fight a battle against the stigma that has prevented people from receiving help.

*Relational Perspective.* The belief that we face problems together, that the situation represents a shared challenge, provides relational resilience (Walsh, 1998, p. 52). Families are strengthened by a sense of closeness as they tackle problems together (Beavers & Hampson, 1990; Walsh, 1998).

This sense of relational resilience is illustrated by a junior high boy who said when asked why his family that was experiencing major financial problems and related interpersonal ones had come for counseling, "Our family is having some hard times and *we* are here to find out ways that *we* can make things better in our family." The emphasis on the "we" made it clear that he viewed the job of solving the family problem as belonging to the entire family unit.

*Trust.* A sense of trust encourages this relational perspective and further strengthens families. This sense of trust enables family members to turn to others within the family for help and collaboration (Beavers & Hampson, 1990; Walsh, 1998). Krasner (1986) describes trustworthiness as the primal family resource.

Family trustworthiness occurs within the realistic complexity of family relationships with the inevitability of unfair expectations, doubts, and misunderstandings along with the possibilities of attachment, caring, and support. Family members are able to look beyond the negative aspects to the enduring elements of trust within relationships. Supporting family trustworthiness are valuable relational rules of respect that communicate that others are valued, reciprocity that entails fairness and give and take among members, reliability that enables people to count and trust each other, and repair that involves efforts to make up for damage done in relationships (Karpel, 1986, p. 186).

*Self-Efficacy and Competence.* Meanings are influenced by past life events within the extended family circle. These events create fundamental views about the nature of the world and the family's place in it (Reiss, 1981). Families who view themselves as having overcome difficult events in the past are most likely to have confidence in their ability to cope with the current event (McCubbin et al., 1998; Robinson, 2000).

As White and Epston (1990) stress in narrative family therapy, individuals and families have a variety of stories (narrative interpretations of life events) available to them that influence how life events are experienced. While some stories promote a sense of competence and strength and facilitate healing, others stories disqualify and are demeaning to the persons involved. The nature of these stories is important in promoting resiliency. As some family members said in a study with financially troubled farm families, "we got through tough times in the past and will do so again" (Van Hook, 1990b). Such an interpretation contributes to self-efficacy and an important sense of competence.

*Developmental Perspective.* The ability to take a life cycle, a developmental perspective, so that issues that arise are viewed as part of the rhythms of life further strengthens families. This perspective permits families to view change as developmental challenges rather than threats to the family (Walsh, 1998). Such a perspective can be especially helpful since threats to resiliency are especially likely to occur during times of family transition. Families are able to recognize the growing pains of adolescence or response to changes within the family. As family members grow up and marry, the resilient family is able to incorporate new members rather than to focus on the loss of connection.

In the insightful musical, *The Fantastiks*, the fathers seek to protect and script a happy life for their children (Jones & Schmidt, 1960). As both the parents and the young people discover, however, depth of character and a genuine relationship between the two young people are forged through pain and adversity, not through the father's protective activities.

*Coherence.* A sense of coherence—that life is comprehensible and meaningful—also supports resiliency (Antonovsky, 1998; McCubbin, Thompson, Thompson, & Fromer, 1998; Walsh, 1998). Such an orientation to life promotes confidence in the ability to clarify the nature of problems so that they are understandable and predictable. This orientation is related to the self-efficacy identified earlier in terms of resiliency in individuals but goes beyond it to include issues of meaning and purpose of life. Family members are able to view problems, for example, as ways that the family will be strengthened in the long way or as opportunities for growth for family members.

*Recognition of Complex Patterns.* Effective families are able to recognize that events are products of complex patterns and to explain life events accordingly rather than to blame individual family members. Poorly functioning families, on the other hand, tend to lock onto one explanation for a problem and to be organized in terms of blaming and scapegoating (Beavers & Hampson, 1986, 1990). These are the families whose members are either so busy trying to point the figure of blame or defending against blame that they have little energy left to work together to solve their problems.

*Views of the Future.* Family views about the future also influence resiliency. The efficacious belief that family members can have a positive impact on what happens to them strengthens them and gives them the impetus to continue to try. They in turn suffer when family members hold fatalist views that nothing can be done or expect that one person should be able to control everything (Walsh, 1998).

Several important elements contribute to a positive outlook. These include perseverance, courage and encouragement, hope and optimism, and mastery of the art of the possible (Walsh, 1998).

Perseverance—the ability to struggle well and persist in the face of overwhelming adversity—is a key element in resilience. It enables family members to continue to struggle despite odds (Walsh, 1998). In the many accounts of ways in which families have coped with the difficult life events created by the tragedy of September 11, 2001, a key theme has been the family's determination and ability to continue to move forward as a family despite terrible losses and pain. Families who struggled to find new lives for their families following the Katrina disaster in New Orleans and other Gulf Coast communities also demonstrated such persistence.

The courage of family members to cope, especially combined with the support of others further supports resiliency (Walsh, 1998). Courage can be manifested in facing dramatic life events as well as the daily efforts to move ahead despite difficulties. An individual who runs into a burning building to save a child demonstrates courage—so does the daily act of holding down two difficult jobs while also meeting the many needs of the family members or caring for family members despite ongoing severe health problems. The latter type of courage is frequently not identified as such by the parties involved but are manifested in many of the families seen by social workers and other counselors.

Hope promotes resiliency by enabling people to look to a brighter future despite the bleak past and present and thus to persevere. Resilient families have an "optimistic orientation in dealing with stress and crisis" (Walsh, 1998, p. 63). These views enable family members to think about ways that they can contribute to the solution. As counselors recognize, one of the key elements in any effective counseling endeavor is the ability to engender hope for the future that enables individuals and families to mobilize their efforts to meet their goals.

Hopefulness is supported by beliefs and mind-sets. The family's belief that they have the ability to match the current challenge promotes hope (Friedman, 1986). There is an ongoing interaction between belief systems and life experiences. This positive mind-set needs to be reinforced by experiences that give evidence of success and a context that is supportive. Such experience encourages the sense of self-efficacy described earlier. Positive illusions contribute by enabling people to hold to the possibility of optimistic outcomes (Walsh, 1998, p. 62). Such hopeful mind-sets encourage families and individuals to maintain the efforts to cope and address difficult life events in contrast to a sense of helplessness that discourages efforts to try.

Interpretations about success and failure also influence resiliency. Resilient families are more likely to view mistakes or failure as experiences from which to learn rather than occasions of defeat. They view difficult life events as possibilities for growth and strengthening of the family. Such life events are viewed as opportunities to reassess life and even "to be seen as a gift that opens a new phase of life or new opportunities" (Walsh, 1998, p. 76).

*Mastery of the Art of the Possible.* Resilient families are able to assess what is possible to accomplish in a situation and to organize their efforts accordingly rather than being governed by all or nothing thinking. Families can thus direct their attention to these steps. Such successful efforts provide confidence about future success or opportunities for learning for future actions (Walsh, 1998, p. 124).

Culture influences what success means in this context. Walsh (1998), for example, contrasts the orientation of control and of mastery of people from Western backgrounds to that of living in harmony of families from Eastern and Native American traditions. Regardless of the tradition, families need to be able to identify what are the steps that enable the family to work toward these cultural goals. Related to this is the ability of family members to use their creative imagination to envision new possibilities for the family (Walsh, 1998).

*Transcendent Beliefs and Spirituality.* These beliefs enable family members to cope with difficult life experiences by providing a link to the transcendent and providing a sense of meaning. This transcendent value system enables people to define their lives as meaningful and significant (Walsh, 1998, 1999). Families can especially need such a sense of meaning when tragedy and hardship strikes (Wright, 1999). Studies drawn from a variety of traditions suggest ways in which religion can potentially provide a sense of meaning and support for families as well as some of the risk factors that religion can pose. (Falicov, 1999; Van Hook, Hugen, & Aguilar, 2001; Walsh, 1999).

### Role Models

Role models can be viewed in terms of the organization of the family as well as the belief systems that are created. Images of strength and new possibilities can be drawn from role models of strength within the family or the larger context. Such strength can be identified in response to the big challenges of life as well as to ongoing efforts to address the ongoing challenges of life. Social workers regularly encounter family members who demonstrate such strength as they care for family members with disabilities, raise children in dangerous neighborhoods, and work in difficult and dangerous conditions to support their families. These role models within the family can be the source of powerful messages that create beliefs systems of hope and strength that support resiliency.

### Organizational Patterns

Research from the traditions of normal family processes, family resources, and family crisis identify specific organizational patterns that contribute to family resiliency.

*Flexibility and Connectedness (cohesion).* These two concepts are important because they enable families to respond to the changes and vicissitudes of life while maintaining an essential sense of relatedness and support within the family. Walsh (1998) describes these characteristics as family shock absorbers (p. 80). Optimally families require a balance of these characteristics so that flexibility is within the context of some stability and connection permits individual family members their own individuality (Beavers & Hampson, 1990; Olson, 1993).

Families need to be flexible to respond to a variety of positive and negative changes. When one parent can no longer carry out her/his accustomed family role due to illness, death, or change in the economic situation, other family members must be able to rise to the challenge and take over these responsibilities in some form or another (Beavers & Hampson, 1990; McCubbin & Patterson, 1983; Robinson, 2000; Walsh, 1998).

Families also need a degree of stability and consistency that helps give life a sense of predictability (Olson, 1993). Cohesion or connectedness supports family resiliency by enabling families to experience the strength of drawing together to deal with difficult life circumstances (McCubbin & Patterson, 1983; Walsh, 1998; Van Hook, 1990). This experience further strengthens the mutual respect and sense of trustworthiness within families. The challenge is to balance change with stability. Too many demands for change on the family can result in a state of crisis.

*Leadership.* Families need leadership within the family to mobilize its resources appropriately (Friedman, 1986). Friedman (1986) describes effective family leadership as occurring "when a family member has the capacity to maintain enough distance from the surrounding emotional whirlwinds so as to be able to keep his or her own life's goals (maintain his or her own horizons an integrity) and can articulate them and follow them despite the family's crisis, and can as a result of this capacity maintain a nonanxious presence in the system" (p. 77). Families need leadership to provide for nurturing, protecting, and guiding of children and care of older adults and other vulnerable family members. Collaborative efforts among family leaders are important. While warmth remains an important element of family leadership, the relative firmness required depends on the context and the developmental life stage of family members (Walsh, 1998). Parents with very young children, for example, need to exercise leadership in a different manner than those with adolescents and young adults. Parents of families living in potentially dangerous settings may need to exercise greater firmness than those living in more safe environments. Family leaders within the immediate and extended families provide mentoring opportunities.

Identifying and strengthening such potential for leadership within the family is a key element in successful therapy with families. Such efforts require sensitivity to cultural nuances in terms of gender roles and other messages in terms of appropriate family leadership. Cultural gender issues can become especially sensitive in working with families dealing with cultural change between generations or differences in cultural expectations from their own backgrounds and current community expectations (McGolderick, Giordano, & Pearce, 1986; Walsh, 1998).

*Communication.* Three aspects of communication contribute to effective communication: clarity, open emotional expression, and collaborative problem solving (Walsh, 1998, p. 107). Clarity enables family members to communicate accurately in terms of the nature of relationships, family rules, and information. Clear communication during times of crisis is important in enabling families to manage life events in an honest manner. Emotional sharing involves the ability of families to express, encourage, and accept a range of emotions, to demonstrate an empathic understanding of the feelings of other family members, to accept differences within the family, and to take ownership for their own emotions (Robinson, 2000; Walsh, 1998, pp. 109–110). Cultural patterns strongly shape the specific form that emotional expression takes within families. Collaborative problem solving is critical in identifying effective strategies and mobilizing the appropriate family resources. Such communication rests within the context of mutual respect and trust identified earlier so that family members can feel safe in doing so.

While family members may be secretive with the goal of protecting other family members, such efforts sometimes lead to additional stress within the family. A seven-year-old boy was referred to me for nightmares, fears of monsters, and excessive worry when his mother became ill. I learned from the mother that the father had been married before and his first wife and mother of several now grown children had died. When the father remarried and two children were born of the second marriage, the entire family colluded to protect the children from fear of losing their mother. They created a fictitious story about the person whose grave they visited and led the children to believe that all of the children were from the current mother and father. The boy told me his view of what had happened within the family. It was a much more frightening version than the actual family events. When the parents were encouraged and helped to tell the children what had really happened, the boy became markedly less anxious as evidenced by the absence of nightmares and his relaxed response to his mother.

*Positive Interactions.* As family members struggle to cope, finding ways in which family members can enjoy each other, can express positive feelings toward each other, and find pleasure in their company and activities are important in enabling families to be successful (Karpel, 1986). These positive interactions buffer stress and help provide an important foundation for the family. When interviewing youth about ways in which their families coped and survived the difficult economic times of the farm crisis, one thirteen-year-old answered immediately that he knew how they had coped and what was important to him—they had gone out and done things as a family. His mother reported that they did so to avoid the bill collectors and was surprised at the meaning these events had on their son—but now intended to do so intentionally to help strengthen the family.

*Collaborative Problem Solving.* As families face inevitable difficult life events, the ability of family members to work together to problem solve supports resiliency (Orthner, Jones-Sanpei, & Williamson, 2004; Robinson, 2000; Walsh, 1998). Collaborative problem solving is enhanced by the ability to family members to communicate in assessing the problem, identifying and implementing appropriate coping strategies, and drawing on the resources available to the family to address the problem. Effective negotiation strategies enable family members to recognize their differences and find ways to work together toward the mutual goals of the family. Such efforts transcend win-and-lose mind-sets to look at what the family unit needs. Gender differences can complicate such a process in the family (Walsh, 1998). Allied with this are effective conflict resolution skills that support family resiliency. Both conflict avoidance and uncontrollable conflict undermine the family unit (Walsh, 1998).

*Humor.* Humor is an important family asset that enables family members to accept the limitations of family members and their efforts. It can also communicate acceptance and enables interactions to go more smoothly (Beavers & Hampson, 1993; Karpel, 1986; Walsh, 1998).

### Social Support System

Resiliency is supported by adequate social support in the form of instrumental assistance as well as emotional support and a sense of meaning (Fraser, 2004; Fraser, Kirby, & Smokowski, 2004; Greene, 2002; Orthner,

Jones-Sanpei, & Williamson, 2004; Walsh, 1998; Werner & Smith 1992). Social resources are only effective if family members feel comfortable in accessing them. Families thus need to be able to trust their social support network and to feel comfortable in seeking this help. In the process of interviewing rural families who had suffered great losses during the farm crisis of the 1980s, for example, it became very clear that while family, church, and community social support systems were viewed as potential sources of help by some family members, they were viewed as sources of blame and criticism by others (Van Hook, 1990b).

Cultural traditions regarding the nature of available and acceptable social support strongly influence the resources available for people. Cultural prescriptions influence, for example, the roles of folk healers, clergy, extended family members, and mental health professionals (McGolderick, Giordano, & Pearce, 1986).

### Economic Resources

Adequate family resources are important in promoting family resiliency. Families that are on the edge financially or must struggle from day to day to meet the basic needs of the family face additional odds in coping with a variety of life problems. Poverty creates a situation of multiple stressors and inadequate resources to meet family needs (Fraser, Kirby, & Smokowski, 2004). Many of the families seen by social workers are struggling with the pressures of major financial pressures due to low wages, unemployment, or financial pressures due to illness or other catastrophic expenses. Such financial problems contribute to the pileup of stressors identified as very stressful for families.

Conger and Elder (1994), in their extensive study of rural families experiencing financial crisis, document the negative impact of such economic problems on the marital and parent-child relationships. The cushion of a safe place to live, money to hire a babysitter when the pressure gets too intense, resources for adequate food and medical care can make a profound difference in the ability to families to cope with the ongoing challenges of life. I volunteer at a program for homeless families and watch these parents (usually mothers) try to raise their children in a setting where they must pack up and move to a different place every week. This is such a contrast to the world of my grandchildren with the security and sense of place of their own beds and special stuffed animals.

### Community Context

Family poverty also typically occurs within the context of neighborhoods that are disadvantaged in terms of employment opportunities, crime, violence, residential mobility, cultural conflict, broken families, and limited access to resources. Fraser, Kirby, and Smokowski (2004) assert the importance of looking at how poverty impacts the individual, the family, the school, and the neighborhood risk factors that disadvantage children. As a result, families face a compounding of family and community economic risk factors.

### *Reactivation of Past Events*

As discussed in greater detail in chapter 4, reactivation of past events can influence the family's ability to handle the current situation. Past events can represent evidence of the family's ability to handle difficult times and thus increase current self-efficacy. They can also bring back memories that erode confidence by reminding people of their ability to cope in the past as well as potentially eroding the family members' trust in other family members.

## *IMPLICATIONS FOR FAMILY ASSESSMENT AND INTERVENTIONS*

Based on the proceeding discussion, approaches that enable families to cope with the demands of life are likely to include the following: addressing the meaning systems created by families that enhance a sense of hopefulness and purpose; supporting organizational structures that provide effective leadership and a balance of flexibility and stability; promoting clear, empathic, and supportive communication patterns; enhancing the positive relationships between family members, promoting the problem-solving ability of family members; improving the social support system accessible to the family; and enhancing the community and economic resources available to the family. Such efforts draw upon a multisystems and multilevel approach to families. The assessment process requires an understanding of the demands placed on the family, the specific elements that are important at this particular time in the life of the family, developmental issues, the nature of the particular family, and the context in identifying both stressors and resources to support the resiliency of the family.

## *FAMILY CRISIS AND RESILIENCY MODELS*

Family crisis theory and related resiliency models offer valuable frameworks for understanding family resiliency and ways to promote it. They also identify the importance of family appraisals, family coping strategies, and resources within the larger community. Many of the family and community protective factors identified within this tradition reflect those previously described within the family strengths tradition and were thus incorporated into the earlier preceding discussion. The emphasis in these family crisis models is on the process that influences how families respond to events, how families become overwhelmed by difficult events, or manage to forge effective ways to respond to them.

The family crisis model for coping and resiliency grew out of the early work by Rubin Hill and colleagues that examined how families coped with potentially stressful life events in terms of what created disabling crises or enabled families to cope. Hill's model (Family ABCX model) identified the role that A (stressor events), B (family resources), C (family definition of the stressor), and X (crisis) factors played in mediating how families respond to difficult life events (Hill, 1949).

The subsequent double ABCX family crisis model was built on this foundation and highlighted the need to look at how the family's response to the first set of stressor events can in turn affect the family by creating a second round of stressors, resources, and definitions (McCubbin & Patterson, 1983). The family that deals with high medical bills due to the illness of a family member by having one of the parents assume extra work hours can experience stress as the parents find themselves stretched to meet the other needs of family members.

Two additional models were developed to address the complexities and patterns in buffering against stress as families adapt to stressful situation: the FAAR (Family Adjustment and Adaptation and Response) Model A and a subsequent model—the Typology Model of Family Adjustment and Adaptation (McCubbin, McCubbin, Thompson, & Thompson, 1998). These models emphasize the importance of the balance of demands and resources and the patterns of functioning of the families—the typologies—used to buffer against family dysfunction and as targets for change as the family adapts to a crisis.

More recently McCubbin and McCubbin (1998) developed the Resiliency Model. It emphasizes the family's relational processes of adaptation and the family's appraisal processes that involve ethnicity and culture and that facilitate the ability to institute new patterns of functioning and achieve harmony while promoting the well-being and development of its members. The Resiliency Model focuses on family change and adaptation over time to understand how the family adapts after the period of potential crisis is completed. While McCubbin and McCubbin (1998) describe this model in terms of ethnic families, all families develop a culture that influences how they experience the world. As a result, although the meaning of these elements for specific families will vary, the framework is useful as a basic outline of the processes and elements involved.

The Resiliency Model has two discernible phases: adjustment (minor changes) and adaptation (more major changes). The following information is drawn from the work of McCubbin, McCubbin, Thompson, and Thompson (1998) in their introduction to research on the resiliency of Native American and other immigrant families.

## *Adjustment Phase*

The emphasis of the adjustment phase is upon the minor changes that the family institutes to address stressful life events and the series of interacting components involved (McCubbin et al., 1998). The actions of the family can result in outcomes that vary along a continuum from positive bonoadjust-ment, in which established patterns of functioning are maintained, to the extreme of maladjustment, a family crisis that demands changes in the es-tablished pattern of functioning (McCubbin et al., 1998, p. 5). The nature of the outcome depends on the nature of the event, family circumstances that influence vulnerability, the organizational pattern of families, the belief sys-tems of family members, and the coping strategies of families. The following outlines these elements that influence the adjustment phase.

First, the stressor (A) places demands on the family. The severity of this stressor depends on the extent to which it threatens the family unit stability, disrupts the ways in which the family unit functions, or places major de-mands on and depletes the family resources (McCubbin et al., 1998).

Second, family vulnerability (V) piles up and family life cycle changes. Vulnerability is the fragile interpersonal and organizational condition of the family system. A pileup of stressor events (e.g., loss of a job, unwanted move) or difficulty associated with life cycle changes can increase the fam-ily's vulnerability (McCubbin et al., 1998). A family might be experiencing the challenge of the loss of a job while needing to assume greater financial responsibility and care for an older parent with serious health problems or a heart attack by the husband while the wife is dealing with the health problems of her parents.

Third, family typology of established patterns of functioning (T) rep-resents the predictable pattern by which the family copes. Families whose patterns include a balance of flexibility and cohesion (family bonding) are best able to handle difficult life events (McCubbin et al., 1998).

Fourth, family resistance resources (B) include capabilities and strengths. These resources enable the family to manage the stressor without creating major changes in the patterns of functioning. Important family resources were described in the preceding discussion and are included in table 1 (Mc-Cubbin et al., 1998, p. 8).

Fifth, family appraisal of the stressor includes the family's definition of the stressors in terms of the seriousness of the stressor for the family. Fam-ily's schemes of life strongly influence how they perceive specific events. As a result, the meaning to the individuals involved can be quite different from what an outsider might imagine the stress would be. When interviewing farm families who had gone through difficult times during the farm crisis of the 1980s in Iowa, one question related to how much change they had experi-enced. One farmer who was still living on the same family century farm and raising hogs, but now under contract rather than independently, described his situation as representing the highest change possible. Another man who had given up his farm, moved to another state and was now managing the mechanical equipment of the science building at a college, described the change he had experienced at a very low level. The second man described his work in both settings as that of a manager. As would not be surprising, the level of current stress reported by both men also reflected the change that they had experienced with the symptoms of stress for the first man much higher than for the second man.

Sixth, family problem solving and coping (PSC). Problem solving is a critical step. Some important abilities that can help families include: organizing a stressor into manageable components, identifying alternative courses of action to deal with each of these components, to initiating steps to resolve the issues involved, developing and cultivating the patterns of problem solving communication needed to solve the family problems. Coping refers to a wide range of behaviors that the family uses to cope. Some of the tasks include "maintaining and strengthening the family as a whole, maintaining the emotional stability and well-being of members, obtaining or using family and community resources to manage the situation, and initiating efforts to resolve family hardships created by the stressor" (McCubbin et al., 1998, p. 9). Given the many different threats potentially facing families, families benefit from developing a rich repertoire of coping strategies (Friedman, 1986).

Family hardiness helps to mitigate the impact of stress on families. Hardiness is "characterized by a sense of control over the outcome of life events and hardships, a view of change as beneficial and growth producing, and an active rather than passive orientation in adjusting to and managing stressful situations" (McCubbin, Thompson, Thompson, Elver, & McCubbin, 1998, p. 54). Family problem solving, communication and available community social support contribute to family hardiness (McCubbin et al., 1998).

A family can respond to these series of stressors, family patterns, resources, appraisals, and problem-solving efforts in ways that promote effective coping (bonoadjustment) or that create potential tension, stress, and distress (maladjustment). When a family experiences an imbalance in the demands placed on the family compared with the available resources, a family experiences stress, eventually reaching the point of disorganization and a crisis for the family (X). Families experience a crisis when they are unable to restore their stability and experience a state of disorganization within the family system. Families initially seek to cope by making small adjustments; however, when these are not adequate to address the situation, major changes in the family patterns can be required at this stage in the process (McCubbin et al., 1998). Efforts to begin to make these changes marks the beginning of the adaptation phase.

## Family Adaptation Phase

Family adaptation refers to the important changes that a family may need to make to cope with the demands facing it. The Family Adaptation phase of the Resiliency model examines how the family seeks to cope following the crisis (McCubbin et al., 1998). Similar to the double ABCX family crisis model, these processes include a second round of life events, appraisals, family and community resources, and coping behaviors. The family's response to the crisis is influenced by the interaction among a series of components: The pileup (AA) of demands on the family system created by the situation, the family life cycle, or unresolved strains in interaction with the family's new way of functioning. These interact with the family resources (BB) that can include support from the extended family and community and the family's appraisal and coping strategies.

## Family Appraisal Process

Several layers influence how family members interpret an event. The family begins by appraising the situation (CC) in terms of the available resources and demands (e.g., does the family have adequate medical insurance to cover the cost of a needed surgery for the parent). Such appraisal interacts with the family's more general paradigms (CCC)—basic beliefs pertaining to a specific area of life (e.g., health is all important and the families do everything that they can do to help). These paradigms are shaped by the family's sense of coherence (CCCC), a worldview that gives a sense of order to life, (e.g., there is a purpose for everything that happens in life) (McCubbin et al., 1998). The family also appraises the situation in terms of the family's schema (CCCCC)—the shared values, beliefs, and expectations of the family. These beliefs legitimate family coping efforts and are very difficult to change (e.g., the entire extended family bands together when one person in the family has a need). These appraisals interact with "the family's problem-solving and coping repertoire (PSC)" to influence how the family adapts to the crisis situation (p. 12) (e.g., asking for help from members of the extended family to help pay for this surgery). The cultural heritage of families profoundly influences this appraisal process by shaping the meaning of life events, the legitimate ways to cope, and the nature of the coping repertoire of families. It can also give a sense of meaning to life events.

### Demands

Pileup of demands (AA) recognizes that families are frequently facing more than one stressful event—the additive events described earlier. These events can relate to the current situation, issues of life transitions, earlier life experiences, long-standing family strains, family efforts to cope, and lack of clarity regarding how to cope (McCubbin et al., 1998, p. 14). Such a pileup of stressful life events is certainly common in the families seeking help from social workers. These families might be struggling simultaneously with economic loss, difficulties in housing, and the school adjustment problems of a child or persons in caregiver roles might themselves be contending with health problems of their own.

Family resources (BB) can belong to the family unit, individual family members, and the community. Some personal resources of individual family members include traits identified earlier: intelligence, appropriate knowledge and skills, personality characteristics (e.g., sense of humor), physical, spiritual and emotional health of members, sense of mastery, self-esteem, and ethnicity and cultural identity (McCubbin et al., 1998, pp. 18–19). In contrast, weakening of self-esteem can be a source of vulnerability of family members facing a pile up of stress that threatens mastery (p. 19), and the challenges of this situation can also erode the self-esteem of family members.

Family system resources are listed in table 1 and in the discussion regarding family protective factors. Family hardiness here refers to the "internal strengths and durability of the family unit. It is further characterized by a sense of control over the outcome of life events and hardships, a view of change as beneficial and growth producing, and active orientation in responding to stressful situations" (p. 20). Family hardiness serves as a buffer by mediating the effects of stresses and demands.

Social support (BBB) can include several dimensions: (1) emotional support that leads family members to believe they are cared for, (2) esteem support that conveys to family members that they are respected and valued, and (3) network support that leads family members to believe they belong to a network that can offer mutual support and understanding. Cultural context influences the social support process.

Family problem solving and coping (PSC) strategies can help by addressing the specific stressor, obtaining additional resources, managing the reduction of the family tension, and/or changing the meaning of the life event. Coping can further be identified in terms of specific coping behaviors (e.g., talk about ways to reduce family expenses and reduce eating out when facing a salary reduction) and general family patterns (e.g., communicate in a problem-solving manner about family problems and take actions based on the family discussion). These behaviors and patterns can be contrasted with another family in which the patterns are to hide problems and take risks to address them (do not discuss the cut in salary with others and purchase a number of lottery tickets in hopes of a big payoff to solve the problem). As part of the ongoing coping process, families need to find ways by which these new patterns become a natural part of the family lifestyle.

In the adaptation process, new family patterns may need to be established in one or more critical areas of family functioning: rules, routines and traditions, coalitions in the family unit; patterns of communication; and relationships to the broader community (p. 18). As a result, a family whose original rules established gender patterns by which the mother stayed home with the children while the father worked outside of the home may need to adjust these rules when the plant in which the father worked moves away from the area while employment possibilities for the mother exist in the community. Families in which the typical communication was through the mother will have to change these patterns when the mother has a stroke and can no longer serve as the "family switchboard," thus requiring the father to assume an important role of family communicator. Families who were able to cope without asking for help from the community might need to reassess the situation so that they can turn for the appropriate type of community support.

Family adaptation process, bonadaptation, and maladaptation, and crisis (XX) family adaptation can thus include changing the appraisal of the situation in ways that promote coping and support needed changes, addressing the specific stressor, and making needed changes within the family functioning. If families do not adapt satisfactorily (maladaptation) they return to a crisis situation and must find other ways to adapt. (p. 33).

The following two family situations represent ways in which families respond to crisis events in ways that reflect their appraisals of the event and their coping strategies. Their appraisals and coping strategies are influenced by culture, context, and family patterns. While these families come from different cultural backgrounds and are facing different problems, both illustrate the sense of "we" that can influence both the nature of the stressors as well as the resources available. This motif also helps guide appropriate responses to the family in ways that support resiliency.

> The Lo family came to the United States as refugees from the Communist government in Vietnam. They had lived previously in a small community in South Vietnam before fleeing the country and living in a refugee camp in Thailand for some time. They were currently living in a small community in rural Iowa where they were one of several such families in the area. The traditional authority role of the father in the family had been somewhat jeopardized because he had hurt his back and was unable to find work that did not require heavy lifting. His poor English language skills limited his employment possibilities to manual labor. Several of the older children were now grown and had moved to neighboring communities but remained in close contact with the family.
>
> The social worker from the local mental health center was called by the hospital staff and the church sponsor of the family because their high school daughter Song became severely ill at school caused by an overdose of pills. Song then had to be hospitalized. Such an event would represent a crisis in any family but the situation was even more layered with meaning for the Lo family. The parents knew that Song had taken the pills but had panicked because they were afraid that the whole family would be deported back to the refugee camp and, even worse, perhaps back to Vietnam where they would be imprisoned by the Communist government for their cooperation with the

United States government. As they appraised the situation, the action of the daughter placed the entire family in grave danger. Feeling desperate and not knowing what else to do, they tried to cover up the event by insisting that the older brother bring her to school and that neither of the young people reveal what had happened. The parents' fear also prevented them from seeking help from the church sponsor who had been an important resource in many other areas of life.

Fortunately, when the social worker met with the entire family (including the grown children), she was able to learn about the family's frightening interpretation of the situation and thus to correct their misunderstanding of the risk involved. She assured the family that the daughter's action would not cause them to be deported and that the important thing was to make sure that Song received the help that she needed. Song's attempt at suicide was defined in the context of teenage suicide being a serious problem in the United States and that Song's action would be understood in this way by the school and the church sponsor.

Song's behavior had been in response to her feeling caught between two contradictory alternatives that related to her obligations to a friend and her family. These alternatives and the situation reflected the influence of the two diverse cultures on her and the family as well as developmental issues. Song was a close friend with another teenager from a Vietnamese family living in a neighboring community. During their previous life in Vietnam, the family and community ties were very close and the behavior of the young people was closely regulated by shared family and community codes. In the United States these families were scattered throughout the area and were isolated both from their previous communities in Vietnam and the support of their fellow families. The families were struggling with a new problem—an increasing number of young girls becoming pregnant as young teenagers. Song felt torn because her parents had told her that she should tell them if her friend was going to do something that could cause the friend to become pregnant. Her friend had made her promise that she would not tell her parents. Caught between these set of contradictory demands created by parents and her friend, Song did not know what to do when she learned that her friend was going to run away with her boy friend. In the context of this dilemma she overdosed on the pills. Given the cultural context of the family, she had betrayed her family in several ways. In addition to creating the fear of deportation, she had also violated cultural codes of family honor and name because both the important institutions of the school and the sponsoring church became involved in the situation and the family felt a great sense of shame. These organizations represented the support system for the family and the family feared loss of support from them. The social worker thus helped Song apologize to her family for bringing shame to the family as well as communicate to her family the stress that she was experiencing due to this situation and some other circumstances reflective of the cultural transition of the family. The family members were able to listen to Song and to enlist the social worker as a cultural interpreter and ongoing counselor for their daughter and sister. The older siblings were supported in their ongoing role of support system for their parents and Song.

As a result, the family crisis was redefined both in terms of the consequences and potential resources in a way that enabled Song and her family members to problem solve and cope in a more effective manner.

The following situation indicates the complex role that family appraisals (in terms of the family as a whole and individual members) can play because valuing family and family members created both distress and the resources that led to healing.

Mrs. Roberts called a neighboring mental health clinic because their fifteen-year-old daughter, Joan, was suffering from bulimia. She also added that her husband was suffering from severe depression and perhaps suicidal thoughts but that he would not seek help for himself. She also indicated that the family was experiencing serious financial difficulties that were contributing to his depression. The Roberts family is the family mentioned previously in terms of the junior high boy explaining why they have come for help. As indicated previously, when the young people were asked why they had come the boy said that they were having problems as a family and had come to find ways they could work on them. The parents described the financial problems they were having with the family farm and said that they thought that these problems were bothering their teenage daughter but not their son. At this the son chimed in that they were bothering him because he felt that he was to blame for them. This comment astonished his parents, who thought that they had explained things to the children. The boy said that the parents had bought him a used moped that had cost $250 and this money had helped cause their problems. With this comment, the daughter interrupted to say that she was the one who was really to blame because in addition to her moped, her parents had also paid for her and her friend to go to the movies. Although the parents thought that they had communicated the nature of the problem to their children, clearly the children did not understand the complexities of a situation involving devaluation of land and changes in prices due to market conditions. The first step thus was to help the parents explain the situation in ways that were understandable to the children and reduced their sense of guilt.

When the social worker met separately with the parents, both expressed the burdens that they were experiencing. The father described his sense of despair and failure because he was putting his family through such a difficult time. The mother told of her sense of failure because she had not been able to help all the family members be happy. When the social worker met individually with the daughter, Joan, she forcefully expressed her anger that her father was being treated so unfairly by life. She described her father as a person who worked long hours for his family and was a wonderful man and father. Joan said she wanted to tell her father what a wonderful father he was and how much she loved him and how proud she was of him but did not know how to do so. After the social worker said she would help her, they returned to the family as a whole. With little prompting, Joan began to tell her father how much he meant to her, what a good father he was, and how much she loved him. Father and daughter then spoke of their love for each other.

When the family was seen the next week, the mood within the family had improved remarkably. The father indicated that although their family financial situation had not changed at all, he felt like a ton had been lifted off his shoulders now that he knew that the children did not feel that he was a failure. He was no longer feeling depressed. The children in turn also felt relieved of a great burden. Family members' love toward each other and sense of cohesion as a family were no longer burdens but had become resources that enabled the family to mobilize to cope with an external problem. The family members felt energized to address the problems without the burdens of guilt created such distress.

The preceding examples illustrate ways in which cultural and social contexts influence how families perceive the meaning of situations and legitimate coping strategies. Chapter 2 discusses issues related to culture in specific cultural groups.

Families also experience a variety of challenges. Some of these relate to changes in the family structure (e.g., divorce, loss of members, remarriage) and others to negative circumstances (e.g., illness, economic hardship). Sometimes these challenges are reflected in the problems experienced by children in the family.

## SUMMARY

Based on the literature on the resiliency of individuals, family strengths, and family crisis, certain themes emerge about the things that promote resiliency. These themes reflect the ways in which family members appraise their own competencies and the nature of life events, organizational and process aspects of families, and the support system available to family members. Such themes provide guidelines in terms of the assessing families and developing prevention and intervention strategies. Combining an assessment for risk and vulnerability with strengths and areas in which resiliency can be promoted can help family members address the variety of issues that they are currently facing as well as future life challenges.

Self-appraisals that encourage family members to view themselves as capable of dealing with a problem and the family unit as a resource for change promote resiliency. Paradigms and schemas that contain messages that permit family members to draw upon appropriate problem solving skills are important. Also needed are family organizational patterns that incorporate effective leadership, are adaptable, and provide members with a sense of belonging and stability through cohesion and dependable routines. Clear family communication enables people to support each other and problem solve effectively. Climates of trust and mutual respect support family members. Families need the skills that enable them to solve a wide variety of life problem. Social networks within the community that can offer appropriate types of social support are also invaluable. The presence of educational and economic opportunities within the community promotes resiliency and the absence of this represents a risk factor. Cultural issues help shape how events are experienced and the coping strategies that are appropriate.

The literature on resiliency offers guidelines in terms of social work practice with families. Understanding what contributes to resiliency offers a guide in assessing families and in developing prevention and intervention strategies that support the resiliency of families. Such an approach recognizes the reality of the risk factors and the stressors facing families while it searches for protective factors and ways to enhance resiliency. In view of the many interactive features that contribute to resiliency within families, it is useful to be able to draw upon a variety of models of assessing and working with families to strengthen families facing a variety of vulnerabilities and situations. Some important models include those that address ways in which family members interpret and create their stories of life events, that promote linkages between family members and the social network and community resources, that help family members learn and practice new problem-solving skills, that promote effective communication patterns within family members, that support family efforts to have effective leadership patterns within the family, and that promote trust and mutual respect within family members. While the emphasis has been upon the processes that promote resiliency within the family, clearly families do not live in isolation. The community plays a role in terms of vulnerability factors and support systems. Since community plays a role in family vulnerability and support, interventions that address the community context, for example, the promotion of safe neighborhoods, the provision of adequate and affordable housing, the implementation of wage scales that can realistically support families, are also crucial.

# 2

# *Cultural Issues and Family Resiliency*

Cultural issues profoundly shape many critical aspects of family resiliency by influencing the risk factors facing families and their path to resiliency. Cultural messages shape the meaning systems (the paradigms and schema that affect how family members perceive life events and potential solutions), the organizational patterns of families, the ways in which family members communicate, the characteristics of the social support system (the nature of the extended family and other external resources that are available), the nature of appropriate problem-solving and coping strategies, and the type of situations facing families. Furthermore, membership in certain cultural groups can place some families at greater risk for vulnerability caused by poverty or discrimination and injustice that represent important risk factors (Conger et al., 2002; Fraser, Kirby, & Smokiwski, 2004).

## CULTURE, RACE, AND ETHNICITY

Because social workers are engaged with individuals representing a wide variety of cultural backgrounds and racial and ethnic groups, it is valuable to understand some of the aspects that strengthen resiliency for specific groups as well as the challenges that their group members face. In any such discussion, it is critical to remember that within each cultural group there is wide variation among families depending on levels of acculturation, individual family life experiences, economic status, and subgroup membership. Within broad categories there are many subgroups that influence both risk and protective factors and the meanings attached to life events. Any broad strokes about cultural groups must be grounded in the individual experiences of families. Therefore, social workers must always be open to learn from family members what is appropriate for the specific family rather than to make assumptions based on general statements regarding the group in question. Culture can be linked to race and ethnicity as well as to vocation, social economic levels, and geographic area of residence. While gay and lesbian individuals come from all racial and ethnic groups, gay and lesbian families have some unique characteristics that are important to understand.

34

### Relational Perspective

Before discussing specific groups, it is useful to include McCubbin, Futrell, Thompson, and Thompson's (1998) discussion of a relational perspective on family resilience alluded to in chapter 1 because this perspective characterizes many of the groups encountered by social workers and other counselors. A relational perspective is characterized by an emphasis on harmony and the interdependence of relationships that include mind, body, and spirit. The resiliency model within this context "emphasizes the family's relational process of adaptation and the family's appraisal processes involving ethnicity and culture that facilitate the family's ability to institute new patterns of functioning and achieve harmony while promoting the well-being and development of its members" (McCubbin, McCubbin, Thompson, & Thompson, 1998, p. 5). The goals of harmony and balance influence the family's relationships with members and others in the community, the family's organization structure and means of functioning, their relationships with nature, the developmental process, the sense of well-being, spirituality, the family's dimensions of interpersonal relationships, community relationships and relationships with nature, the family's development, well-being and spirituality, as well as the family's structure and functioning (McCubbin et al., 1998, p. 37). The relationship processes influence how the family appraises life events, the ways in which the family uses family and external resources, and how the family attempts to problem solve. Drawing on a relational perspective, strong family bonds, including extended family members have been identified as moderators of risk for minority youth. Recognizing the strengths derived from cultural aspects of appraisal and coping, ethnic and racial socialization has emerged as an important resource. It helps to promote pride in one's group that can facilitate biculturalism, to enable youth to cope with racism and other forms of discrimination, and to help promote one's internalization of culturally prescribed values (Gonzales & Kim, 1997).

## RISK AND PROTECTIVE FACTORS

The following discussion identifies the risk and protective factors for members of specific racial, ethnic, and cultural groups. It is impossible to include all possible groups and those selected represent racial, ethnic, vocational, and regional patterns. While this discussion is organized in terms of specific groups, the themes that emerge echo those described in the resiliency literature in general.

### African American Families

A number of scholars have explored the source of resiliency among African American families, despite the challenge faced by many families due to a long history of oppression. Several excellent resources for understanding resiliency in African American families include the Resiliency in Families Series edited by McCubbin and colleagues who have studied a wide range of families and the Center for Family Research Institute that has focused on rural African American families.

According to Genero (1998), the crucial role played by a relational rather than an individualistic mode of adaptation is a key to resiliency. "Mutual participation in relationships facilitates and gives meaning to the adaptive processes that arise in response to environmental demands and challenges over time" (p. 35). In a context of "negative realities and social inequalities" families must find ways to judge when it is safe and appropriate to trust others and to engage in mutual relationship. (p. 36) "Meaning derived from mutual relationships is a critical source of validation" (p. 37). With the risks of external devaluation, the family serves as a critical source of validation.

Racism and poverty have been identified as key risk factors for serious childhood social problems generally (Fraser, Kirby, & Smowkiski, 2004) and have been a dual set of risk factors faced by many African American families (Hill, 1999). The following discussion recognizes that there is wide economic variation among African American families and their community context— from mansions within gated communities to desperate poverty—and that all comments must recognize these differences. For those struggling with economic problems, living in neighborhoods characterized by poverty has contributed to family stress and conflict and maternal depression (Conger et al., 2002; Murry, Bynum, Brody, Willert, & Stephens, 2001). In Robert Hill's (1999) synthesis of the research regarding the strengths of African American families, he identified the following potential risk factors facing these families. Economic problems as reflected in high unemployment rates and low family income have been critical in increasing family instability. Other risk factors include high rates of adolescent out-of-wedlock births, rise of drugs, AIDS, and community violence. Societal forces include individual and institutionalized racism, sexism that has subordinated women, a shortage of marriageable men, decline in employment opportunities, immigration, loss of housing, decline of support for affirmative action, reduction of appropriate services, and media images. Such risk factors have contributed to high levels of poverty, family instability, family violence, drug abuse, and health problems (Hill, 1999).

In this context, the concept of resiliency takes on new meaning. Given the great difficulties facing some families, Genero (1998) suggests the need to recognize that the ability to be ordinary under these circumstances represents extraordinary achievement (p. 32). Thornton (1998) stresses the importance of looking at the day-to-day activities, the mundane struggles of life that demonstrate the survival resources of families (p. 50).

In terms of protective factors, McAdoo (1998) identifies the following patterns that have promoted resiliency for families within the African American community: supportive social networks, flexible relationships within the family unit, a strong sense of religiosity, extensive use of extended family helping arrangements, the adoption of fictive kin who become "as if" family, and strong identification with their racial group (p. 22). Hill echoes these themes and also emphasizes the strong achievement and work orientations. These values have been inculcated by parents and are supported by high self-esteem, a sense of racial group identity, and internal personal control (Hill, 1999). The long history of the church and religion within the African American community serves as a source of affirmation of worth and dignity, spiritual strength, and mutual aid within this community. Currently, many churches in the African American community sponsor a range of programs that serve as healing forces within the community (Bagley & Carroll, 1998; Boyd-Franklin, 2003; Hill, 1999). In a study of African American married couples, qualities for the success of their marriage were described in terms of characteristics identified previously in the resiliency literature: communication and understanding, friendship and trust, commitment, and religion (Conner, 1998).

From the perspective of social support, extended family relationships and friendships can represent both protective and risk factors. The extended family, especially grandparents, in single-parent families offers potential emotional and instrumental support as well as mentoring for the mother and the presence of an effective caretaker for the children. These relationships can also contribute to family conflict and confusion regarding family roles. Grandparents can potentially lower the self-efficacy of parents (Murry et al., 2001). While support by friends can be extremely helpful for African American single parents and their families (Murry et al., 2001), reciprocity within these essential support systems is also important. Individuals can become so burdened down with obligations that the support system beomes a source of distress (Boyd-Franklin, 2003).

In terms of community protective factors, a study set in both rural Iowa and Georgia supported the value of collective socialization for deterring conduct problems among young adolescents. Collective socialization refers to communities in which its members "take responsibility for monitoring and correcting the children living in the area" (Simons, Simons, Conger, & Brody, 2004, p. 287). Such communities reflect the often-quoted phrase, "It takes a village to raise a child." It is possible that such a community approach may also foster positive developmental outcomes in terms of academic achievement and self-esteem (Simons et al., 2004).

In looking at the crucial kinship and social network that are essential sources of resiliency for African American families, Thornton (1998) emphasizes the need to look at the specific choices and actions taken by family members in this regard. The term "agency" is used to refer to the fact that people are not "passive bystanders in their lives" but make choices and act to change their world (p. 51). African Americans have played active roles within their communities and their families in the process of drawing together viable helping networks and preparing children to cope effectively with the world around them (Thornton, 1998).

Parents play critical roles in supporting resiliency of youth. The Center for Family Research identified important parenting patterns that enhance resiliency. A pattern of "firm control exercised within affectively positive parent-child relationships predicts positive outcomes such as self-regulation, social competence, good emotional health, and school success among African American children" (Murry et al., 2001, p. 139). Parenting styles that include vigilant parenting (monitoring the activities of youth), effective communication (the ability to discuss important issues in a collaborative manner) and warmth have been associated with resiliency among African American youth (Brody, Kim, Murry & Brown, 2004; Murry et al., 2001; Gibbons, Gerrard, Cleveland, Wills, Brody, 2004).

The nature of effective parenting is also influenced in part by the nature of the community context, for example, higher levels of monitoring are especially important for children living in high-risk areas in order to protect them from involvement in problematic behavior. More moderate levels of control can be effective in community contexts in which peers are less likely to engage in problematic behavior (Murry et al., 2001).

Economic stress creates a risk factor in part due to its impact on parenting style. Parent-child relationships are compromised by such stress in both African American families and those from European backgrounds by causing conflict between parents that in turn reduces positive parenting and creates problems for youth (Conger et al., 2002).

Studies of African American families living in impoverished rural areas of the South identified a circular process that promoted and maintained resiliency in youth. Effective parenting styles as described previously promoted competence in children that in turn supported self-efficacy on the part of parents regarding their ability to parent and reduced their risk for depression. This cycle in turn promoted the social and emotional competence of younger siblings (Brody, Kim, Murry & Brown, 2004).

Family relationship issues also play a role in promoting engagement in the educational system by African American youth from both economically impoverished and middle class families. Such engagement serves as an important protective factor because it provides opportunities for positive social relationships and increases the likelihood youth will gain needed coping skills and develop self-esteem. Lack of such commitment to education is associated with increased risk for behavioral problems (Caspi et al., 1987; Simmons, Simmons, Conger, & Brody, 2004). In a study of African American adolescents living in middle class families, positive parent-child relationships that include a sense of trust and caring and collaborative decision making about important issues emerged as important in encouraging the adolescents' school performance (Sirin & Rogers-Sirin, 2004). In rural single-parent

African American families, "structure, routinized home environments, positive mother-child relationships, high levels of control, and maternal school involvement fostered self-regulatory behaviors, such as self-discipline, planfulness, and persistence in children. In turn, these behaviors predicted high academic performance, good social skills, and few behavioral and emotional problems" (Murry et al., 2001, p. 142).

In terms of contextual factors and schooling, a classroom experience that is viewed as positive by the child supports the child's competence and resiliency (Brody, Dorsey, Freehand & Armistead, 2002). On the other hand, discrimination and oppression represent risk factors for lack of educational achievement and investment in education. Perceptions of discrimination and oppression combined with employment limitations, accompanied by a youth culture that discourages African American youth from succeeding in school, further contribute to lower academic achievement and lack of investment in education by these youth. While parents might be committed to education, when they communicate verbally and through the reality of their own lives that in spite their education black youth will probably not do as well economically as white youth, young people may become less invested in their own education (Sirin & Rogers-Siein, 2004).

In the important areas of substance abuse and other high-risk behavior, perceived discrimination (either of the youth or their parents) produced distress that in turn led adolescents to greater use of alcohol and related substances and to engage in thoughts that were supportive of risk behavior. On the protective side, effective parenting as described previously reduced this risk (Gibbon et al., 2004). Specific protective factors in terms of substance abuse include: "frequent church attendance, frequent parent-child communication, positive role modeling, negative parental attitudes toward deviance, parents' insistence upon school attendance, and parents' efforts to maintain healthy relationships with their children" (p. 143.) Low parental substance use is the most important protective factor against drug use (Murry et al., 2001) perhaps reflecting the power of family models and family culture.

## Native American Families

Native American families belong to a large number of nations with important and distinct cultural heritages. Thus any discussion must be set within this context. The following section identifies some themes that transcend national boundaries as well as those identified with specific national groups.

The relational model is important for understanding resiliency for Native American families from various traditions and nations. The relational model emphasizes balance so that interventions are organized in terms of establishing or restoring balance. Cross (1998) describes a model that includes the four domains of mind, body, spirit, and context (family, culture, work, community, history, environment). From a relational perspective families can draw upon resources within these four domains. The mind includes cognitive processes and emotions. The body includes all of the physical aspects. The spirit includes "the positive and negative learned teaching and practices as well as positive and negative metaphysical or innate forces" (p. 147). Given this holistic perspective, resiliency can be supported in a number of ways. Some of these methods are designed to protect family members against the risk factors associated with oppression. Contextual resources can include education of children about survival skills to deal with oppression, appreciation of the richness of the history of the people, the presence of extended family history based on interdependence among members, church and social organizations, and the roles of elders and natural helpers. In the area of the mind, family resiliency is supported by the nature of self-talk and the stories that are told within the family circle. The role of the father as a contributing member to the family system is an important resource. Cultural and family rituals and activities also contribute. In terms of spiritual influences, positive practices include faith, prayer, meditation, healing ceremonies, and positive thinking that are used to counter negative practices and promote healing and group solidarity. Folk teachings are important in this area. Harmony between these aspects of life is especially important and thus interventions that contribute to resiliency by supporting balance (Cross, 1998).

Lakota elders describe risk factors in terms of poverty, lack of culturally appropriate health and other services, low self-respect based in a sense of not being useful, unemployment, and poor housing (Bowen, 1995). Yellow Horse Brave Heart (2001) describes the long shadows of historical trauma that have affected Native Americans due to the many years of suffering and cultural degradation that were imposed on the people. Such trauma contributes to ongoing problems in the lives of family members. Extended family ties can protect by offering support or contribute to risk through enmeshment into dysfunctional patterns. Traditional spirituality and indigenous cultural practices can further positive coping efforts.

In terms of the Lakota people the concept of *mitakuye oya'in* represents a cornerstone of their beliefs and further reflects the relational view of the world described earlier. According to *mitakuye oya'in* "everything that has ever been, or ever will be created—every person, every animal, every plant, every stone, all the waters, Father Sky, Mother Earth herself—are related" (Bowen, 1995, p. 126). Strength within this concept means not only physical strength but also strength of character, self-sufficiency, and the bond of relationships. The concept of *tiospaye* (the collection of related families who are bound by blood or the traditional adoption ceremony of *Hunka* that creates ties more sacred than biological kinship) (Yellow-Horse Brave Heart, 2001) represents another important aspect of the relational nature of the Lakota culture. While oppression has created ongoing trauma and risk factors for members of the nation, these concepts provide important clues for resiliency.

A study of youth from the Odawa and Ojibway nations reveals risk and protective factors as reflected in alcohol and drug abuse. Enculturation (identification with one's culture) interacted with self-esteem in terms of drug abuse. Youth with high levels of self-esteem and enculturation reported the lowest levels of alcohol and substance abuse. However, youth with low levels of self-esteem and high levels of cultural identity reported the highest levels of drug abuse. Among the aspects of enculturation, the element of cultural affinity that reflects pride in one's background was positively associated with self-esteem (Zimmerman, Ramirez, Washienko, Walter, & Dyer, 1998).

Members of the Navajo nation share the holistic traditional views described earlier. The strong family system serves as an important source of resiliency for Navajo families. The extended family network is part of a larger network which is expected to actively support other members. Family groups are further clustered into clans that provide a strong sense of identity and govern acceptable relationships. As family members become acculturated into Western ways of thinking and behaving, tension can occur within family groups. Navajo families face some of the same risk factors described. As with other groups, such risk factors can contribute to problems with alcoholism and family breakdown (McWhirter & Ryan, 1991).

Several successful programs have been built on identified risk and resiliency factors within the Alaskan Native community and families. These programs reflect the holistic, relational, and contextual nature of resiliency identified in the earlier discussion. Simmons, Franks, Peters, & Burham (2003) describe a community-based approach for enhancing resiliency. Major signs of family and individual dysfunction (especially substance abuse and child abuse) were present among the Native Alaskan families in the small communities in Northern Alaska. Based on the assessment that the community as a whole was depressed and demoralized, it was important to find ways to promote a sense of self-worth and morale within the community. With this assessment and an understanding of the culture, the mental health program worked to recreate a sense of community and cultural reawakening among the people. Mental health staff members developed a holistic approach that drew upon traditional strengths within the community. They encouraged community members to engage in traditional activities and ceremonies and to celebrate life cycle events (e.g., birthdays). Such efforts at the community level had a profound positive impact on individual families and their members (Simmons et al., 2003).

The Village Service Program established in Alaska to address substance abuse problems also reflects the importance of recognizing the community context and supporting traditional cultural practices. Elders with knowledge of the cultural traditions play important roles in the healing process and are acknowledged as such in community efforts. Counselors have made help accessible by participating with clients in traditional activities. The act of providing services in the context of traditional activities has helped to build the clients' confidence in themselves and their community. The program allows community members to "be exposed to the strength and healing of their traditional culture" (Capers, 2003, p. 10).

## Latino Families

The many groups that comprise the Latino population represent the largest racial/ethnic group within the United States and are becoming larger. While there is a wide range of circumstances facing Latino families who represent the range from great wealth to poverty, unfortunately, many Latinos contend with poverty, discrimination, and reduced access to health and other services as a result of historical or community factors (Bushy, A., 2002). Because of important differences between Latino groups it is important to understand the historical context of the groups as well as the individual families in understanding specific families (Vega, 1995). While Latino groups differ on many dimensions, important values that are sources of resiliency within these Latino groups include *personalismo,* respect, familism that involves the extended family, and spirituality (Bernal & Shapiro, 1996; Falicov, 1996; Garcia-Preto, 1996a, b; Perez-Koenig, 2000).

A qualitative study of Dominican youth (a group traditionally with low levels of academic and economic success) who are succeeding academically revealed the individual nature of both risk and protective factors. For these youth resiliency was a process. The first step was the ability of the youth to identify their personal risk factors. This was followed by the action of the youth to seek out protective factors that would mitigate the risk factor. The cycle then proceeded with the youth and the protective factors working in concert. While one protective factor might have been more important than others and be instrumental in beginning the process with a specific individual, each of the youth required a combination of protective factors. The combination of internal processes (the recognition and awareness by the youth) combined with the presence of potential protective factors in their life space was critical (Morales, 2000).

Although Mexican youth have been identified as particularly high risk, some youth have demonstrated their ability to overcome these odds and have exemplified important resources within Latino families, for example, Cesar Chavez, the farm worker who successfully organized other farm workers to advocate for their rights. Cesar Chavez grew up in the context of multiple risk factors (growing up in an impoverished family, being homeless at times as a child, living in impoverished dilapidated neighborhoods, working as a migrant farm worker, and belonging to a disadvantaged minority group, Mexican). Countering these negatives were the important protective factors in his life: a supportive relationship with his mother and grandmother, his connection to the church, and his overall positive self-concept (Gonzales, 2003).

In a study with urban Latino youth, academic self-efficacy emerged as a critical source of resiliency for Latino youth. In examining the differences between children who succeeded academically (the resilient children) com-pared with those who did not, resilient children were more likely to have confidence in their academic abilities (Gordon, 1996). Educational programs that have sought to draw upon the strengths within the community and the family, to foster caring relationships and pride in and cope in a more so-cially adaptive manner have shown promise with Mexican immigrant youth (Chavkin & Gonzalez, 2000).

A study of low-income Latino families with young children revealed a diverse pattern in terms of important supports for the family. Members of the extended family and the church were very important for many of the families and seemed to serve as the front line of support for families. In families that lacked this strong informal support system, formal support services such as mental health and social service programs emerged as more important (San Miguel, Morrison, & Weissglass, 1998).

### *Native Hawaiian Families*

In the context of the great natural beauty surrounding them, the Native Hawaiian people have suffered greatly due to their economic, cultural, and social status losses. Their suffering is reflected in the high rates of physical illness, mental health and social problems, and poverty. Native Hawaiians have the worst health profile of any group in the United States and have limited access to health and other services (Bushy, 2002; Marsella, Oliveira, Plummer, & Crabbe, 1998). Many of these problems are viewed as a reflec-tion of their sense of demoralization and powerlessness within their own land (Marsella et al., 1998).

Unity of the person, family, nature, and spiritual world is essential as a basis of resiliency for Native Hawaiian families. The Native Hawaiian experi-ences one's self as united with the larger social, natural, and spiritual forces of the world. Harmony within this system is important and the breakdown of it is reflected in illness or misfortune. Harmony and health can be restored by acting with "kindness, caring, and responsibility toward the family, na-ture, and society" (Marsella et al., 1998, p. 105). The combination of social responsibility and reciprocity maintains the community context important for families.

Family pressures due to a pileup of life events and changes affecting the family emerged as the primary predictor of family distress for both single-parent and two-parent families although the nature of these stres-sors was somewhat different. Single-parent families were especially likely to experience distress due to absence of the father or husband and residual issues from this relationship, economic distress, and the experience of racial discrimination. Their minority status as single-parent families (within a cul-tural context that values two-parent households) seemed to combine with racial issues to contribute to their distress. Both family types experienced distress related to incendiary communication although two-parent families were more likely to stress the important of resolving conflict (Thompson, McCubbin, Thompson, Elver, 1998).

Social support is important for both single- and two-parent families. Families who view "themselves as integrated into the community, and feel that the community can provide emotional, esteem, and network support to the family unit and its members, appear to be less vulnerable and less distressed" (Thompson, McCubbin, Thompson, & Elver, 1998, p. 129). Although social support is an important buffer, the hardships represented by a pileup of stressful events experienced by families continue to pose serious difficulties.

## Asian Families

Asian families represent a wide variety of individual national and cultural groups with different histories and religions. Counselors working with members of different cultural groups need to be aware of the importance of both understanding and acknowledging these differences, especially in view of historical events that have caused tensions among different groups. Despite popular images of Asian Americans as the model minority, in reality members of this heterogeneous grouping represent great extremes—from people with high incomes and educational levels to those with very limited incomes and educational levels and major problems as indicated by a variety of health indices (Bushy, 2002; Lee, 1996). Understanding the process of immigration in terms of the nature of the generation involved in the process, the reason for the immigration, and their experience in their home countries and in the United States is important in assessing and working with families. Some family members have experienced major trauma due to war. Family situations can also be complicated as family members vary widely in terms of their adherence to traditional values and ways of life. (Goldenberg & Goldenberg, 1998; Bushy, 2002; Lee, 1996).

Recognizing the many differences present, certain characteristics of Asian and Pacific Island cultures influence and support how families cope. Reflecting the relational perspective described earlier, the family unit—immediate and extended—is central. Family extends back in time to include ancestors as well as the current family. Family members are expected to contribute to the family unit as a whole. Loyalty and respect for the family are very important and family members are expected to uphold the honor of the family and to avoid bringing shame to the family. This honor can be earned through good school performance or other behaviors that reflect favorably upon the name of the family (Goldenberg & Goldenberg, 1998; Lee, 1996; Lau & Takeuchi, 2001). When Chinese families experience shame due to the behavior of their children, for example, they are less likely to access help from professionals and other formal systems outside of the family (Lau & Takeuchi, 2001).

A series of studies examining how families deal with elderly members reveal patterns of protective factors among Asian families as well as ways in which contextual factors alter coping and resiliency patterns. The first study included older adults and caretakers of refugee families from Cambodia and Vietnam. These families typically "left their countries for reasons beyond their control, survived daunting circumstances involving hardship and human suffering, and have virtually no hope of return. Suddenly and traumatically, family and friends, personal identity, possessions, and a family world were lost" (Strumpf, Glicksman, Goldberg-Glen, Fox, & Logue, 2001, p. 234). Given the trauma that these individuals had experienced, they are described as fitting the prototype of "resilience despite major losses and stressors." Families revealed a powerful sense of filial obligation to care for their elders along with limited knowledge of or use of community services. Both Cambodian and Vietnamese caregivers indicated a strong sense of love and obligation to care for their elderly parents. Cultural ties with the previous world and life were also very important for the older adults. It was important for the older members of the family to see themselves in the role of preserving and transmitting their culture to the younger generation (Strumpf et al., 2001).

As families remain in America, however, such strong filial expectations in terms of caring for older members can shift. In a small study involving older Chinese individuals, one of the fastest growing groups in the country, they indicated the increasing role of friends alongside of children and grandchildren. Although older adults were willing to ask help of their children, they also recognized that their children were busy with their own responsibilities and many reported asking them for help only when necessary (Pang, Jordan-Marsh, Silverstein, & Cody, 2003).

A study conducted in Japan with caregivers of family members who had suffered strokes supports the protective role of sense of mastery identified in the resiliency literature in general. Caregivers who viewed themselves as high in self self-mastery, with useful problem solving skills, were less likely to feel depressed and to experience high levels of stress even though they were caring for people as disabled as those being cared by individuals with lower levels of self-mastery (Schreiner & Morimota, 2003).

## Rural Families

Rural families are characterized by great diversity in terms of their racial and ethnic identities, areas of residence, and economic situation. Rural communities vary in terms of their primary economic base (e.g., farming, fishing, mining, logging, tourism, manufacturing). Rural communities have also experienced an influx of families from different racial and ethnic groups as a result of refugee resettlements and migration of new families into the community to meet the labor needs. Some of the earlier studies that address resiliency among rural African American families were discussed in the section about African Americans. Many rural families from different geographic regions of the country and representing different aspects of the rural economy have experienced economic stress. Families caught up in the vortex of these economic problems have experienced a pileup of stressors within a context in which they have had limited control over the important social and economic factors that have created the problems. Studies have sought to identify sources of resiliency for families facing problems that potentially threaten a way of life for the family and the community. The following section discusses risk and resiliency factors in two very different contexts—rural Midwestern farming and New England and Canadian fishing.

### Midwestern Farm Families

Many rural Midwestern farm families have experienced financial hardships created by problems in the rural economy since the 1980s. Farming has not only represented a source of income but also a multigenerational way of life for family members accompanied by a sense of purpose and meaning. Family efforts to maintain the viability of the farm are challenged by a wide variety of social and economic circumstances beyond their control. Churches and schools represent key social institutions in these rural communities.

A major study conducted with Iowa families living on farms and rural communities identified several key elements associated with resiliency among their young people. Resiliency in this study was defined in terms of "better than expected outcomes" while vulnerability was defined in terms of "worse than expected outcomes" (Elder & Conger, 2000). Protective factors included strong relationships with the father, productive roles in terms of work and school that enabled youth to feel that they were contributing and gave them a sense of mastery, mentors within the community, and religious involvement. Academic success emerged as the most important factor in terms of avoidance of problem behavior. Such success was part of an interactive process. Young people who succeeded developed a greater sense of mastery and self-confidence. They also had greater access to other opportunities and mentoring relationships within the community. Experiences that promote resiliency and sense of mastery include participation in social activities within the school and community, relationships with caring adults within the family (especially the father, supported by mothers and grandparents) and the community, academic success, and participation in religious activities (Conger & Elder, 2000).

Another study of rural midwestern families facing economic crisis was based on the perspective of the adolescents and their parents rather than on objective measures of resiliency. When asked what helped their family cope with these difficult times, respondents' comments reflected the role of family cohesion (family members pulled together) and flexibility (family gender roles became more androgynous). Echoing the previous study, for teenagers, being able to contribute to the solution in various ways was important to them (Van Hook, 1990a).

Economic problems represented risk factors. They negatively impacted on youth by way of the distress experienced by parents that in turn affected the marital relationship and strained the parent-child relationship (Elder & Conger, 2000).

### New England and Canadian Fishing Families

Commercial fishing represents another way of life for families and communities under threat. These have families have developed paradigms and organizational patterns to cope with the demands of this way of life. Commercial fishing families have adapted to the typical lengthy absence of men from the home by clearly delineating the roles of men (dominating the work life) and women (dominating the home life) with these lengthy absences as part of the normal family life. Studies set in New England and Canada of families facing the threat of their loss of livelihood and way of life revealed risk and protective factors. Mederer (1999) illustrates the preceding adaptive patterns, as one husband described:

> *You have to understand when you are running a fishing boat, you're Jesus Christ himself. And I had my boat, and she had the house. When I gave up fishing, I gave my boat to someone else, and she still had her house. . . . So I lost my sense of identity coming back. . . . I hated it and it took us a long time to get used to being together with one another" (p. 215).*

The husband was described in the role of a periodic guest in terms of the family (Binkley, 1996; Mederer, 1999). With the onset of economic problems, the men began to be home longer but were also making less of a financial contribution. This combination constituted a family stressor due to the combination of the presence of the man that did not fit the normal family pattern, the severe economic strain on the family and the perceived failure by the man to carry out his role in the family. These fishermen typically valued their independence and grieved the loss of it when they had to give up this way of life (Mederer, 1999).

In terms of the meaning of life events, blame of family members did not play a role because the economic problems were clearly related to external events. The issue of mastery emerged as a protective factor. In the context of dealing with a situation beyond their control, some families sought to gain some sense of control by adapting a proactive stance—trying to obtain information and influence policies related to fishing. Learning alternative skills and ways to succeed economically also helped them. Careful financial planning was an important coping strategy (Mederer, 1999).

In terms of family patterns, flexibility regarding family roles contributed to resiliency. Unfortunately for many families, family beliefs supported strong gender role division and thus hampered flexibility in terms of family roles (Mederer, 1999).

Social support was complicated because fishermen who were still successful tended to distance themselves from those who were hurting financially in order to protect themselves from facing their own potential vulnerability. Women were able to turn to others for support but men tended to keep their concerns to themselves (Mederer, 1999).

### *Military Families*

Although members of the military belong to a wide range of ethnic and racial groups, the military has a culture that influences the members of the military community, poses specific demands on families, and has codes that influence the type of help that is viewed as acceptable (Drummet, Coleman, & Cable, 2003). Stress can be particularly related to several phases of life in the military: relocation, deployment, and reunification because of the disruption in family life that they create (Drummet et al., 2003). Current military families are also challenged by the increasingly involved role of women, including mothers, who are being deployed and away from home for long periods of time (Drummet et al., 2003; Pittman, Kerpelman, & McFadyen, 2004). Stress becomes particularly intense when family members are in combat situations. Separation from parents can be especially difficult for children (Drummet et al., 2003). Deployment can be especially problematic for single parents and families in which both parents are deployed (Drummet et al., 2003).

In military families, like other occupations in which families must adapt to the men's being gone for long periods of time, wives tend to cope by becoming increasingly independent, developing supportive networks, and realigning family responsibilities that allow for extended absences of the men (McCubbin, Dahl, & Hunter, 1976). With wives now being deployed, these family alignments also reflect this change. During the absence of the family member, the remaining partner must assume leadership roles and make important family decisions. When family members are reunited after a long period of deployment, families struggle because relationships within the family need to be renegotiated (Drummet et al., 2003). This reunification can be particularly stressful if life-altering physical or psychological injuries have occurred to the family member in the military that will entail major role changes within the family (Drummet et al., 2003).

Family strengths enable single fathers and mothers to contend with the demands of military life without the support of the other parent. These strengths echo those in other studies regarding family resiliency—families whose members were able to work together in a cooperative manner, who were able to maintain an optimistic mindset (hope) and a sense of mastery (self-efficacy). The family's experience with success in the military context helped them develop sense of family strength. Family flexibility in terms of roles is also protective.

Social support through services that enable families to meet both the pressing demands of work and family (e.g., help with housing, child care, emergency financial assistance), friends, relatives, and other community members help make it possible for families to have such experiences of success that in turn forge family strength. The role of the unit culture that encouraged support and was reflected in the commander's concern for families was especially important for families and their satisfaction with the situation in the military (Bowen & Orthner, 1993; Drummet et al., 2003; McCubbin, Dahl, & Hunter, 1976; Pittman, Kerpelman, & McFadyen, 2004).

African American military families, who are disproportionately represented in the military, can experience some unique stresses that reflect a pile up of stresses. Such families may have to deal with racism in some base locations. The importance of the extended family (both blood and fictive kin) can make relocation and deployment away from the family particularly stressful. Family time is important for African American families and this can be problematic in the military (Drummet et al., 2003). Family members were able to cope by means of the family strengths, social support from others, and a sense of coherence (McCubbin, 1998).

One of the very difficult circumstances military families have to face is to have a loved one missing in action. In addition to loss, there is the ongoing ambiguity that contributes to complicated grief. Boss (2006) describes the pain experienced by families facing ambiguous loss because there is no official recognition of the reality of the loss that permits some type of closure. A study of adult children of fathers missing in action during the Vietnam War revealed that family members still continued to experience ongoing pain, loss, and anger as well as the sources of resiliency in dealing with their painful situation. Drawing upon the resiliency model of family stress, adjustment, and adaptation described earlier, higher levels of family hardiness as reflected in sense of control over life and commitment to the family was associated with lower levels of distress. The mother's leadership role of enabling the family to cope was also important (Campbell & Demi, 2000).

Based on her extensive work with families who have experienced ambiguous loss in terms of the military and other tragedies, Boss (2006) emphasizes the need to acknowledge with these hurting families the ambiguity of their loss and the inherent extreme difficulty on this situation. As in other traumatic situations facing families, exploring the family's sense of meaning regarding this event is crucial. Some approaches that can be helpful include spirituality, rituals, some positive aspect of the event (e.g., the person missing was engaged in a heroic or self-sacrificing action), something that can engender hope. Boss also describes the burden that a strong sense of mastery can impose on families and the consequent need to temper this sense of mastery and to learn lessons of acceptance. Such a view can help reduce the sense of self-blame that families can experience during times of painful loss. Acceptance in this context represents an active coping strategy, not passivity. Families also need to establish a new sense of identity that recognizes the ambiguous nature of their current situation.

## Gay and Lesbian Families

Any discussion of gay and lesbian families must recognize that gay and lesbian families are very diverse. Family members have a multilayered identity because they also belong to racial, ethnic, and socioeconomic groups as well as live in specific communities that play a role in defining who they are and the relevant risk and protective factors. While studies of gay and lesbian families have identified risk and protective factors that can influence family resiliency, any broad statement must always be paired with an individualized assessment in working with families.

Social context plays a critical role with gay and lesbian families. Gay and lesbian families share a risk factor that is quite different from most other family groups. Unlike families in general where the social context supports the legitimacy of families, gay and lesbian families frequently live in social contexts that deny this legitimacy and stigmatize them. While efforts have been made to provide legal support to gay and lesbian families, their success has been very limited and has paired with conservative social movements that have sought to discourage such family unions through legal means. Lack of legal legitimacy has important repercussions for families who have to struggle with a context that in effect seeks to threaten the stability of the family relationships. Gay and lesbian parents, for example, have been threatened with loss of custody of children. Parents have been unable to be legally viewed as coparents. Members of gay and lesbian couples have been excluded from the medical decision-making process for their parents. Family members have been unable to provide medical insurance for others through employee benefit plans (Ariel & McPherson, 2000; Bigner, 1996; Bos, van Balen, & van den Boom, 2005; Grandvold & Martin, 1999; Hartman, 1999; Lott-Whitehead & Tully, 1999; Nichols & Schwartz, 1998). HIV/AIDS has also taken a tremendous toll on many gay and lesbian families, both in terms of their members and their circle of friends (Grandvold & Martin, 1999). Social stigma has led to violence against some gay and lesbian individuals with the consequent burden of family members (Grandvold & Martin, 1999).

The social support systems for gay and lesbian families can represent a mixture of risk and protective factors. The coming out process with other family members can be problematic and leave ongoing tensions with extended family while others have experienced support and affirmation. When an individual was married previously in a heterosexual relationship, the process of developing a family based on one's identity as a gay or lesbian individual has the added stress of dealing with the frequently very painful process of coming out with one's previous partner and sometimes children (Bigner, 1996). In terms of protection, families can create social groups that serve as families (Grandvold & Martin, 1999; Muzio, 1999). Children living in lesbian families indicated that their close friends were positive to the information that they had two mothers but that this was hard for some peers to understand (Bos, van Balen, & van den Boom, 2005). Gay and lesbian families can be reluctant to seek help from health and service organizations because they fear discrimination or not being understood.

In terms of the family interactions and structure, gay and lesbian families tend to be more flexible in their family roles. While this represents a protective factor for many families, it can create confusion and uncertainty in others. Lack of appropriate role models based on family background can be problematic (Grandvold & Martin, 1999). Studies of lesbian families indicate that the nonbiological parent tended to be more involved with the children than was typical of fathers in heterosexual families (Bos et al., 2005). Apart from the social context of stigma, many studies suggest that gay and lesbian families are more similar to heterosexual families than they are different (Bos et al., 2005).

## SUMMARY

Cultural contexts influence the nature of the extended family and the appropriate social network. Family members draw upon these relationships to gain a sense of meaning and strength to address life problems as well as instrumental help. While the specifics of the cultural contexts of the preceding groups may differ, the theme of the importance of relationships in promoting resiliency—within the family circle and between family members and the social network of the community—is a consistent one for many groups. Flexibility within the family, affectionate ties, and appropriate communication help establish effective family patterns. The strength derived from these relationships helps families develop a sense of confidence in their ability to cope. At the same time, perceptions regarding the event can deter family efforts to seek help from those inside and outside the family circle. Efforts to enhance family resiliency thus transcend the specific family unit to include the nature of the community and the relationship systems within the community that can support families. Community context influences both the nature of the problem facing families, the presence of risk factors, as well as the type of resources that are available to promote resiliency. As with all group memberships, any broad strokes regarding the group must be balanced against information gained from individual members in terms of what fits for the members.

# 3

# *Setting the Stage for Work with Families: Development of the Therapeutic Alliance*

The family counselor serves as a catalyst for change. The role of the social worker or other family counselor is to help create change within the family system and its relationship with the wider context. The terms social worker, family therapist, and counselor will be used interchangeably in the following discussion when referring to the role of the social worker as a family counselor or family therapist. The social worker works through a therapeutic alliance to become a partner with the family in order to meet their goals. Defining the counselor in this way recognizes that the role of the family therapist is always quite limited and the family occupies center stage no matter how long the counseling effort. This is even more accurate in the current world of managed care and pressures for brief treatment. Given the context of the life of the family, the few hours spent with the counselor pale in comparison to the time family members spend with each other and with other important people in their lives. As a result, taking a resiliency-based approach to engaging with family members serves as a way of enhancing the strengths that family members bring to the counseling effort as well as recognizing the risk factors that they face. The family and its support system take center stage while the counselor plays a supporting role.

There are two crucial steps in creating an effective working relationship with families. First, it is important to develop a therapeutic alliance—engaging or joining with family members and the family as a whole. Two systems join forces in family counseling—the family and its extended members and the social worker within the agency setting. If family members are going to entrust their family's pain, hopes, fears, troubles, and dreams to the counseling endeavor represented by this social worker/agency system, they need to trust the counselor's competence, ability to understand, and concern for the welfare of their family. The situation is further complicated for many families who are referred to social workers because they have been sent by others who view the family as having a problem.

The second step is to create the climate and structure for the counseling process. Family members frequently come to counseling with limited understanding of what is to take place or perhaps with misunderstandings based on the media, comments from others, or previous experiences with other organizations. In order for an alliance to be effective, there needs to be clarity and understanding regarding the respective roles and guidelines for how these roles are to be carried out by the parties involved. Adequate structure in these sessions is important in the success of this process. Families can come to counseling sessions with misunderstanding based on information provided by the individuals who made the referral.

## ENGAGEMENT PROCESS

The term "joining" as used in family therapy refers to the actions taken by the counselor in the engagement process. The concept of joining recognizes that creating a therapeutic alliance requires actions on the part of the counselor and that building trust is a process. Joining requires sensitivity to the nature of the family. "To join a family system, the therapist must accept the family's organization and style and blend with them. He must experience the family's transactional patterns and the strength of these patterns. That is, he should feel a family member's pain at being excluded, or scapegoated, and his pleasure at being loved, depended on, or otherwise confirmed within the family" (Minuchin, 1974, p. 123).

In joining, it is crucial to remember that the interview process is a two-way one. While social workers are assessing the family and its members, the members are also interviewing and assessing the counselor. When dealing with families, there are multiple interviews occurring because every member of the family is conducting his or her own interview of the counselor. Kantor and Kupferman (1985) describe key questions that clients ask in their interview of the counselor to determine if they can entrust their family concerns to the counselor:

- Is the therapist strong enough, gentle enough, honest enough for me to risk investing my fuller, deeper self?
- What is her experience with families (Married? Children? Divorced?)
- Does his experience prepare him for knowing what it is like to be a (man, woman, child) in this family?
- Is his caring and interest purely professional or will I become known on my own terms?
- Will she respect our differences?
- Will I be able to influence him or is it all one-directional?
- Does she know how to listen?

- Does he understand the unique culture of my experience (class, ethnicity, gender)?

- How does she know how to approach us? Me? How quickly to pace her moves, how close to get?

- Is his idea of a family (what marriage is, how to raise kids, how to make decisions, how to die) at odds with mine, others?

- What is the fit between the counselor and us as members of the family? (p. 231)

Several themes emerge from these questions—what is the fit between our family and the social worker; is the counselor competent enough as a person and a professional to be entrusted with our family; and how much will the counselor truly understand what it is to be us? The answers to these questions will help determine whether or not the family views the social worker as an appropriate person to partner with in order to address their family's concerns.

Both the family and the social worker bring to the encounter uniqueness in terms of gender, age, sexual orientation, and racial and ethnic background, as well as personal experiences that will influence the joining process. While the family members and the social worker do not have to be similar in these aspects, the social worker must be able to appreciate and understand the family's paradigms and how these fit with those of the counselor and be able to communicate this to the family. Unique life experiences of the family and cultural codes play important roles in how these characteristics will influence the joining process. Cultural codes regarding gender, age, and ethnicity all play a role here. As a result, the nature of this engagement will inevitably be unique to the specific family and counselor (Minuchin & Fishman, 1981).

Worden (2003) describes three important operations to joining.

1. Maintenance. The therapist confirms or supports a family's position (p. 42). The counselor can support a family dealing with major change by indicating the stress that such an event might create within a family.

2. Tracking. The therapist uses a series of clarifying questions to track or follow a sequence of events in the family and the interactions of family members (p. 42).

3. Mimesis. The therapist adopts the family's style and tempo of communication (p. 42). If the family describes events through understatement, the counselor follows suit in the initial process.

While all effective counseling requires a therapeutic alliance, joining with families represents an additional challenge from that of individual counseling because one needs to join both with the family as a whole and with the individual members of the family. Unlike individual counseling where there is typically only one agenda represented by the client, many family members have their own agendas and these may be competing or in conflict. When the family counselor is seeking to engage the family around the typical issue of the purpose of the family's coming for counseling and what the family hopes to accomplish, the counselor quickly discovers multiple and conflicting goals. Parents might be trying to enlist the social worker to make their teenager behave while their teenager wants the worker to get the parents to back off. Some family members want the tension in the family to be reduced, which frequently translates into someone else in the family changing. Families can also be motivated to get the school or the Department of Social Services to leave them alone. While this goal unites the family, members' views of how this is to be done and who has to change vary. The family counselor faces the important task of working with the family to identify a goal that can be shared by the family and thereby helping unify the family's efforts rather than having the family members work at cross-purposes.

Part of joining the family entails joining as a partner in the family dance. Family members have reoccurring behavior patterns similar to a dance step. Because of these patterns, everyone in the family knows what other people are likely to do in a situation. Everyone in the family is expert in knowing the buttons to push to create reactions in other family members. Children know the exact tone of voice used by their parents that signals the parents are about to become very angry or to cave in to their whining. When the parent says, "I mean it" in a certain tone of voice, children know they have pushed one of these buttons. It is these patterns that help make family life predictable to family members. Counselors quickly feel that they have been drawn into the extended family system as individual family members seek to enlist the counselor as their partner in the family dance. It is important for counselors to be aware of this process in order to do so freely rather than to have their behavior dictated in ways that perpetuates problems in the family patterns. Counselors can subsequently realize that they have been inducted into the family dance by ignoring the family isolate, by speaking primarily to the family spokesperson, by becoming annoyed with the family scapegoat, or by helping the helpless family member (Minuchin & Fishman, 1981).

Joining with the family requires that the counselor pass the family's test of fitness, work with the family to identify a purpose for the counseling that is meaningful for the family members, and be purposeful in the way in which the counselor joins in the family's typical ways of interacting—the family dance. The unique nature of the alliance will vary depending on the nature of the family and the counselor and the selected goals.

## *Greeting*

The first stage in joining is to make family members feel at ease in what is inevitably a situation with a degree of anxiety and uncertainty. Hospitality is the theme as family members are ushered into the family interview room and encouraged to choose their seats. The counselor then tries to help family members feel at ease through brief conversation that serves as a hospitable bridge, for example, How was traffic? Was is hard to find our office?

### Engagement with Members

The second stage in joining is to engage with each of the family members. This process can begin by asking members of the leadership structure (typically the parents or grandparents depending on the family situation) to introduce the members of the family. The counselor engages in a conversation with each of the family members through questions and interaction designed to get to know the individuals. Depending on the nature of the presenting problem, children, for example, can be asked about their school, what they like to do after school, their special interests (e.g., favorite teams, music groups). Such conversations also set the stage for recognizing that people in the family are more than the problems that brought them into counseling. These conversations also provide opportunities to identify some appropriate commonalties between the counselor and family members—for example, a shared interest in a hobby—that can help in the alliance process.

Carl Whitaker (1989) described in a workshop how he engaged effectively with a family who brought a baby to the session. He played with the baby and in other ways showed the family his admiration for its baby. By this time, he was thoroughly trusted and accepted by the parents and grandparents of the child.

## STRUCTURE OF THE COUNSELING PROCESS

One of the structuring tasks of the first session is to set the stage for the counseling process. Families need information regarding how the family counselor and the family will be working together. Part of this involves setting the ground rules for the session. This is a task that requires both tact and clarity. It is important that family members realize that all of the family members will be asked for their input regarding what they hope to accomplish and their views on what is happening within the family. Family members will be asked to speak one at a time so the counselor can hear each person because the perspective of everyone in the family is important in identifying the goals and the way to reach these goals. Family members will be asked about their concerns for the family and their ideas on how to solve these problems because they are the experts on the family.

The counselor also needs to clarify what the confidentiality ground rules will be. The issue of confidentiality may relate to your role as a mandatory reporter, information that needs to be shared with the insurance company or other referrals sources. It also refers to information that will be shared with other family members if the counselor should meet with family members on an individual basis.

Setting the stage also involves explaining the counselor's model of working together. While all counseling models encourage family input regarding ways to solve family problems, counseling using a resiliency model is explicitly a partnership arrangement. This means that the professional competence of the counselor is paired with the expertise of the family members regarding their life experiences and potential ways to address the problems they are facing. Family members need to be informed that their input will be solicited and valued. The family will make the important decisions in terms of identifying its goals, how to reach them, and how to evaluate the progress that is being made. Because the first session represents a sample of the way in which the counseling process will occur, it is especially important to demonstrate this manner of working during the engagement process.

The family counselor also discusses timetable issues—the nature of insurance, and the expectations of family members. Counselors can explain the process in terms of a time of learning about the family and its situation, developing with the family a plan for addressing it, working out a timetable for the counseling activities with the family, and mutually evaluating how helpful the counseling efforts are in reaching the family goals.

## *Identification of Goals*

The next step is to identify what the family hopes to accomplish and to link the counseling effort with goals that are meaningful for the family.

"What prompted you to come? What does the family hope to accomplish?" These two questions are paired. One seeks to identify the nature of the problems and the context of the process of seeking help and the other the goals of the family. The question of what one hopes to accomplish also sets in motion the process of solving issues. It is future oriented. This set of questions quickly elicits the agendas of family members. As indicated, family members frequently identify different reasons for coming for counseling: parents—make my teenager behave; teenager—get my parents off my back.

Families can also come to counseling because they have been forced to do so by a community agency with power over the family. Understanding what this referring organization expects you to accomplish, the family's understanding of this process, as well as the family's own agenda is important here.

At this stage, it is important to ask all of the family members why they came. There are several ways to go about doing this. The counselor can throw out the question to the family in general and wait to see who answers it. Typically this is the family spokesperson (not necessarily the family leader) and frequently the person who made the contact. It is important to recognize when cultural codes or family situations dictate who should be shown the respect of being asked first. Asian American and Latino cultural codes have hierarchal patterns in the family that indicate the value of supporting such by soliciting information from the parents initially. A quick assessment of the situation, perhaps based on the early telephone call, referral source, or initial appraisal can also clue the counselor into recognizing that the leadership structure of the family (parents or parent surrogates) are under siege and need support. As a result, it is important for the counselor to demonstrate support through the respect of asking the parents' view first. When in doubt, the safest approach is to begin with adults who are responsible for the family.

The counselor uses a respectful questioning style described in greater detail in chapter 4. These questions are designed to elicit a family view on both the problems and risk factors and the protective factors for families. Families tend to view family events in linear fashion—Bob's (aged 15 years) behavior is causing the parents to become distrustful of him and to place greater restrictions on him. During the engagement and assessment process, the family counselor also seeks to create a more realistic circular and systemic view of the family dance. Careful tracking of the sequence of events might reveal that the more the parents voice their distrust of Bob and place severe restrictions on him, the more he loses hope that he can ever gain his parents' trust, gives up even trying, and shows his anger by rebelling. The vicious circle winds tighter and tighter. A related circle is the praise that the parents give the older sister (aged 17 years). Words meant to motivate Bob ("You could be like your sister if you tried.") to improve his behavior might only fuel his anger, hopelessness, and acting out behavior. The relationship between Bob and his sister that might be a source of support for Bob becomes even more strained and distant. The counselor thus seeks to expand the family vision of the situation to reflect a more comprehensive and circular picture of the problem and the type of solutions that reflect this expanded view.

An important task in identification of goals is to help the family move beyond the agenda of specific individuals to a goal that involves the family and one that members can agree on. Family members frequently come with a specific issue and attempt to enlist the counselor to side with one the coalitions within the family. Rather than being caught up in the ongoing family arguments, the family counselor can help the family move up to another level that represents process, for example, helping the family members discuss issues in such a way that they can resolve them. In this way, the issue is not "getting Bob to behave" or "getting Mom and Dad to stop nagging me" but "How the parents and Bob can work together more effectively to resolve the issue at hand."

In working with families toward change, it is important to recognize that families have two pressures placed on them. The first relates to stability needs—morphostasis, the pressure for people to stay in their old roles. It is this pressure that causes old family roles and patterns to play out during family gatherings. The second is the need for change—morphogenesis, the pressure for change to meet new situations. People and families must adapt as life cycle and external events create new circumstances. The challenge of the family is thus to respond adequately to change imposed by life cycle and external events while maintaining adequate stability (Worden, 2003). Stability supports a family's sense of coherence. Yet families also need flexibility in terms of roles and the capacity to learn and implement new coping strategies. As a result, the role of the social worker in terms of the family dance is to promote new patterns that enable families to be flexible while at the same time retaining a sense of stability.

Recent brief therapy models raise the important question whether we have a problem focus or a solution focus in our working relationship with families. The problem focus is organized in terms of what is the nature of the problem, what has caused it, and how do we address it. While strengths are required to address it, sometimes there is a danger of emphasizing the problems and who is contributing to these problems. The solution focus directs the attention to what are the potential solutions and what inputs and individuals can be used in the solution process.

## *Selection of Participants*

In the engagement process, the decision to use problem focus or solution focus can influence the answer to the question, Whom do we need to engage in order to promote change? From a problem focus, the question becomes, Who is contributing to the problem? The solution focus raises the question, Who can contribute to the solution? This in turn raises the question, Who can contribute to healing in this family? The last question is particularly relevant to resiliency-based treatment given the role of support systems and positive organizational patterns within the family.

The decision to use problem focus or solution focus also influences the basis on which people are asked to be part of the process. Are parents enlisted because there is an implicit blame for having created the problem or are they enlisted as resources—the people who know their children best and can be of help? Are there other family members who are invested in the family situation and are willing to help in this process? Family members naturally make these decisions but the counselor frequently needs to set the context and raise these issues by asking a question such as "Are there other people in your family or circle who are concerned about your family and could be of help?"

Additional family members can be enlisted early in the engagement process or later as issues arise. Reflecting cultural as well as individual family patterns, when the Lo family was seen following the overdose of pills by the their high-school-age daughter, all of the grown children from neighboring states came to be part of the first family interview. Their presence was very supportive to the frightened parents and their endorsement of the ongoing counseling situation was very helpful.

### Seeking for Strengths

As discussed in chapter 4, the social worker needs to take seriously the problems that brought the family for help while also to seek evidence of what the family is doing right and the protective factors within the life space of the family. As family members describe the pain and tension within the family, maintenance operations can include giving credit for recognizing the problem and seeking help for it, for being willing to face and trying to address these difficulties. One can explore times in which the family members managed to handle the situation in a less painful way. By engaging family members in terms of both the problems and favorable outcomes, one can also help inject the important elements of self-efficacy and hope into the counseling relationship and process.

## BARRIERS IN THE ENGAGEMENT PROCESS

During the engagement process, many issues can contribute to the family members' reluctance to create a partnership and to participate in the ongoing process of change with the counselor. The source of these barriers can come from both the family and the counselor as well other organizations within the community. As a result, counselors need to examine how their own behaviors can be contributing to this process. Reluctance can be protective and must be assessed accordingly.

### Ambivalence About Change

Families and individuals are sometimes ambivalent about change. Although they are seeking something different, there are many reasons for being uncomfortable about change. Family members are accustomed to their long-standing dance and are frequently uncertain and sometimes even fearful about what will replace it. While the current situation brings pain to family members, it also represents stability within the family and the unknown can be a source of fear and anxiety.

Family members might fear what could be the alternatives. Parents might be distressed by the defiant behavior of their teenager but are also afraid about what a change in their behavior might produce—will taking a stronger stance create an irrevocable breach or cause the teenager to act in a way that would be dangerous to himself/herself or others? Earlier life experiences within the family or others that they know might contribute to these fears. Perhaps a nephew felt pushed from his home and ended up in a serious accident. While problems bring stress, they can also be viewed in other ways as helpful to the family. The problem in this situation has become a solution to yet another issue. The difficult teenager can represent a project that helps keep parents together rather than having to address the tensions in their relationship. The young adult who continually rebels against his parents might really be afraid to grow up. Rather than deal with employers and landlords, he continues to bait his parents in a familiar family dance. Parents in turn might doubt the competence of their son or daughter and continue the circle. While family members might want to change, they can doubt their ability to do so because they have lacked role models and have not developed the needed skills.

### *Contribution of the Counselor*

Family counselors can contribute to these barriers by not being sensitive to the individual family and related cultural issues. As Minuchin (1974) asserts, family members need to sense that the counselor can truly understand what it is to be a member of this family. In this sense the family's reluctance to engage serves as a protective function. Counselors can create inappropriate expectations of family members. Based on their own view of healthy family behavior, counselors can encourage children to speak up about their concerns regarding the family without recognizing that such behavior in this family with their cultural background means bringing unacceptable shame to the family in the presence of outsiders. For example, asking children from an Asian American or Hispanic family to do so would be especially problematic. Counselors can hold different views regarding family gender roles than are supported by the culture of the family. Counselors can move too quickly before family members trust the counselor or are ready to discuss certain issues. Family counselors can also allow themselves to be pulled into the family dance in ways that are viewed as problematic to other family members.

The important role of the counselor requires counselors to be self-reflective in terms of their own biases and life experiences. Bias is always a potential danger—whether the counselor is similar to or different from the family in question. Even the best-intentioned counselor can discover that specific family circumstances evoke thoughts and feelings that are problematic. Sometimes this is triggered by cultural differences or the unique life experiences of the parties involved. Problematic responses can take the form of being judgmental or distant from the families or overly identifying with the family and thus losing objectivity.

### Previous Negative Experiences

Family members might have had previous negative experiences that make them reluctant to engage with their current counselor. They might have met earlier with counselors who did not show respect or violated cultural patterns. This can be particularly true of families with multiple problems, families from cultural groups that are different from the counselors, and members of groups that face potential stigma. As a result, these families protect themselves by being wary and testing the counselor in a variety of ways. It can take time before the family realizes that this counselor will respect them and their cultural values and can be trusted.

### Other Organizations or Community Members

Family members can also bring to the counseling situation negative experiences with other organizations that make them distrust the current counselor. Referral sources can be imposing changes that are viewed as unwelcome and anxiety producing to family members. It is thus important to identify how the family views these interaction and expectations. It may also be necessary to interpret to the referring source what are appropriate expectations. A family was once referred to the author by a pastor to "make" their child forgive the grandfather who sexually abused her. It was thus important to explain to the referring source the unrealistic nature of this expectation and to clarify this with the family.

## STAGES IN THE CHANGE PROCESS

Studies of the change process in therapy and individuals struggling with various addictions have identified some important steps in the change process that can be useful in engaging with the family to work toward its goals in a variety of areas. Prochaska, DiClemente, and Norcross (1992) have identified the following stages: precontemplation, contemplation, action, and maintenance.

### Precontemplation

Individuals do not recognize that they have a problem and are not interested in changing. While others (staff of the school, judicial or child welfare system) view the family as having problems, the family does not share this view. As soon as the external pressure is off, the family or members of the family return to their former ways. Solution-focused therapists view such families as visitors. Unless such families can come to recognize that they have problems and that it is to their advantage to address them, these families are not truly invested in the change process. The task of the social worker is to try to find some way to help family members realize that addressing this problem represents a step that is in the interest of the family.

## *Contemplation*

Individuals recognize that they have a problem and are considering changing but have not yet made a commitment to actually take this action. Individuals in this stage are continuing the weigh the pros and cons of change. As indicated in the previous discussion, recognizing and addressing ambivalence toward change is important in creating an effective working alliance. The therapist can help family members identify some of the potential advantages of making the changes that would help meet the family's stated goals and also promote the self-efficacy of family members in terms of their ability to take these steps. Family members can be helped to identify other situations in which they were able to take such steps or the positive effects for the family when they made similar changes in the past.

## *Action*

Individuals are in the action stage if they have actually modified their behavior to address their goals. This stage represents considerable time and energy to create such change. Parents who had relied on physical force with their children can be actively taking the steps to use alternative strategies such as time-outs and natural consequences. Couples who had turned discussions in to shouting matches that left everyone hurt and angry can be practicing their new skills of problem solving and conflict resolution. The family counselor needs to recognize with the family the big step that they have taken and the effort involved in doing so.

## *Maintenance*

Individuals are seeking to maintain and stabilize the change that they have made. Such a stage recognizes that the process of change requires ongoing commitment and effort in order not to slip back into old patterns. Parents that have developed more effective parenting skills can find themselves slipping back under the pressure of other demands on the family (e.g., loss of a job, illness of family member) or transition to a new developmental stage in the family (e.g., child becomes a teenager). Families can thus seek help because they fear relapsing into their old patterns and are looking for help in maintaining positive changes. The social worker validates the difficult challenge of maintaining change and works with families to identify what are the challenges to their maintaining the positive changes and what offers them needed support.

# SUMMARY

The engagement process is in important ways a sample of the way in which the counselor and the family will work together. Family counseling from a resiliency perspective involves a partnership between the counselor and the family. The family-counselor alliance is collaboration. How the counselor engages the family represents whether or not the family is viewed as a contributing partner to this endeavor. Recognizing possible signs of reluctance and identifying the issues involved in the change process can aid in the engagement. Families can also be in different stages in the change process with accompanying implications regarding the response to the social worker.

# 4

# *Assessment of Families*

Assessment of risk and protective factors and their interaction is a key step in using a resiliency-based approach to counseling families. The counselor and the family are partners on a collaborative venture to understand the life space of the family, the distress experienced by family members, the potential resources and sources of resiliency for the family, and the barriers that might prevent the family from accessing these resources. The assessment process also sets the tone for the working partnership between the family and the counselor. As Walsh (1998) indicates, "a common approach regarding family resiliency is the conviction that there are strong advantages to working with family members in a collaborative manner and finding solutions to shared problems. Family therapy is most effective when it identifies key processes for resiliency and encourages a family's own best efforts for recovery and growth. Such an approach is empowering and enables families not only to address the current problem but helps to prepare them to address the challenges of the future" (p. 16). The assessment process is a critical step in guiding decisions regarding the appropriate intervention strategies.

## *RESILIENCY-BASED APPROACH TO ASSESSMENT*

Families are often discouraged and demoralized when they come for help. Before seeking help from a social worker or other professional counselor they have typically tried their usual coping strategies and turned to their informal support systems within their extended family, friends, and other sources of help without success. They might have been sent for counseling by organizations with authority in the community with a message that they need help because they were unable to handle the problem. These are clearly not the descriptions of families who feel empowered. This potential demoralization of families is important. It is not only painful for the individuals involved but also depletes the sense of coherence and self-efficacy that support resiliency. Rather than being strengthened by viewing themselves as successful in and capable of addressing life situations, families can become even less able to handle already difficult situations. Their family stories risk becoming problem saturated.

Assessment from a resiliency-based perspective thus seeks to support the resiliency of families by explicitly identifying sources of resiliency within the family in ways that can engender hope to family members. The social worker searches for signs of strength within the family and protective factors within the life space of the family. Evidences of strength and tools for resiliency are not merely noted in charts but acknowledged as such with family members throughout the process. In so doing, the family's sense of self-efficacy and mastery is enhanced and the family becomes a more effective partner.

Assessment also identifies areas of family functioning that need to be strengthened or addressed as well as stressors within the environment. Problematic communication patterns, unresolved family conflicts, lack of effective parenting skills, and isolation from potential sources of community support represent several areas that can need strengthening. Community violence, lack of educational opportunities, and high levels of unemployment represent community stressors.

While a theoretical framework guides assessment and treatment decisions set within the resiliency framework, use of this framework does not limit the family counselor to a single treatment theoretical model. Based on the results of the assessment of the risk and protective factors at the individual, family, and contextual levels, a variety of treatment approaches might be appropriate depending on the areas of risk factors and sources of strength identified. As illustrations, the assessment process with the Anderson family might identify a family with good communication among family members but isolation from needed community supports due to their recent arrival in the community. An assessment of the Bowen family might reveal love of parents toward their children but ineffective parenting because the parents are overreacting to the abusive treatment they received from their own parents. The Cutler family might be struggling with health problems of a parent that have caused severe financial problems. They also have the potential strength of an extended family that might be willing to help if asked. The Dodge family has a teenage son who has begun to skip school and abuse substances despite concerned parents' frightened threats to punish him severely. The Eduardo family might be homeless because the house they had lived in for many years was destroyed in the recent hurricane. These abbreviated assessments identify specific risk and protective factors that require different intervention strategies. Based on the assessment, the counselor in partnership with the family identifies the appropriate and effective ways to help the family members cope with the current sources of distress and strengthen protective factors for the present and, hopefully, ones that will also serve them for the future. Use of a resiliency approach in this manner can facilitate clinical judgment regarding the selection of appropriate intervention strategies. Discussion of assessment and selection of intervention approaches must recognize that this is an ongoing process subject to revision based on new information and developments within the life space of the family.

Chapter 1 describes family and contextual characteristics that support resiliency (see table 1). Family characteristics include belief systems that engender hope, a sense of mastery and self-efficacy; a sense of purpose and meaning; family organizational patterns that promote effective communication, a balance of flexibility and cohesion, and adequate leadership; positive interactions and trust; humor; problem-solving and coping skills to address the problem at hand; and appropriate support systems in the wider community. Risk factors can be contextual: poverty, community disorganization and violence, and lack of economic and educational opportunities. They can also reflect family patterns that lead to conflict, lack of leadership, poor coping skills, rigidity, or chaotic family patterns. Families can also be isolated from potential support systems or appropriate resources can be absent from the community.

## ASSESSMENT PROCESS

The assessment process can use a variety of strategies, including formal assessment tools, visual devices, an interview format, observation, information obtained from others, and the social worker's general knowledge of the community context. Regardless of the tools used, assessment from a resiliency-based framework is organized around the following questions that reflect a risk and protective factors perspective as appraised by the family members.

What are the sources of distress in the lives of family members? (risk factors)

How do family members view these issues? (appraisal)

What aspects within the family and their extended world contribute to these sources of distress? (risk factors)

Are there additional factors that contribute to this distress? (additive factors)

What are the resources for coping and support possessed by family members, the family as an organization, and their external world? (protective factors)

How can family members use these resources? (access to resources)

How can these resources be enhanced? (strengthening of resources)

What barriers are preventing family members from using these resources? (barriers to resources)

The information used to answer these questions will come from information obtained from the family, other relevant sources (e.g., school, referring agency), and the counselor's understanding of the community and the broader context.

While assessment occurs at the beginning of work with families, it can take place throughout the entire process. New information can emerge as the social worker gains the trust of the family members. Life circumstances of families change due to circumstances within the family extended circle as well as the larger community context. As a result, social workers need to be responsive to these changes and reflect these changes in their professional judgment regarding the appropriate intervention strategies.

Based on the recommendation of Fraser and Galinsky (2004) and Chazin, Kaplin, and Terio (2000), the following skills and principles are important in using a resiliency model in the assessment process.

1. Assess the risk and protective factors present within the family, the community, and the larger social context.

2. Demonstrate respect for the clients as possessing strengths and potential resources—listen for their survival strategies.

3. Help clients recognize their strengths.

4. Engage the family members as partners in the assessment process.

5. Identify the risk and protective factors that can be changed.

6. Engage the family in the selection of the interventions.

7. Be knowledgeable about practice interventions that can address the risk factors and support their protective factors.

Fraser and Galinsky (2004) stress the importance of practitioners identifying keystone risk factors—the family and social conditions that are important causal factors and can be changed through an intervention. Identifying the factors that are both causal and subject to change enables the social worker and the family to address the problem in an effective manner. Families bring to counseling sessions a variety of problems. One important task is to help family members identify where we can begin. What are the areas that are amenable to change and if changed would have an important impact on the family (and frequently on some of the other problems as well)? The concept of keystone risk factors can be helpful in answering this question. Efforts directed toward these factors can help create additional positive change because positive changes reverberate throughout the family system and thus encourage families to believe that they can make a difference.

## Assessment Tools

Assessment tools have been developed to help understand the current functioning of the family unit. Several of these are relatively narrow in focus like the behavior of the children or the nature of conflict within the family, while others provide a wider picture of the functioning within the family.

### Measurement Instruments

Some of these measures look at the wide range of family functioning and others target more specific aspects of the family. The following list of instruments designed to look at a wide range of family functioning followed by those that target more specific areas.

The following three measures evaluate a wide range of family functioning.

> The Self-Report Family Inventory (SFI) developed by Beavers & Hampson (1990) measures family functioning. It has been used with families from a wide range of socioeconomic groups (Thomlison, 2004).

> The Multi-Problem Screening Inventory (MPSI) (Hudson & McMurtry, 1997) assesses family relationship problems, marital satisfaction, partner abuse, personal stress, and partner or child problems (Hudson & McMurtry, 1997).

> The McMaster Family Assessment Devise (FAD) (Epstein, Baldwin, & Bishop, 1983) measures six areas of family functioning including problem solving, communication (verbal communication in terms of instrumental, affective, clear or masked, direct or indirect), roles, affective responsiveness, affective involvement, and behavior control. These dimensions are relevant to a resiliency perspective. The information obtained from this instrument can be used to identify transactional patterns within the family. Whether or not specific patterns are dysfunctional or adaptive is determined by the larger context of what emerges as helpful for the individual family in this setting (Miller, Ryan, Keitner, Bishop, & Epstein, 1999: Miller, Kabacoff, Bishop, Epstein, & Keitner, 1994).

The following two measures evaluate specific dimensions. McCubbin and colleagues have developed instruments designed to assess dimensions of families. These scales are based on their theoretical work on family coping discussed in chapter 2.

> The Family Crisis Oriented Personal Evaluation Scale, developed by Hamilton McCubbin, David Olson, and Andrea Larsen, looks at family problem-solving strategies. It includes thirty items of different problem-solving strategies. There are also French and Hebrew versions of the scale (McCubbin, Thompson, & McCubbin, 1996).

> The Family Coping Index, developed by Hamilton McCubbin, Ann Thompson, and Kelly Elver, examines how families cope with difficult life circumstances. It includes twenty-four possible coping strategies (McCubbin et al., 1996).

### Visual Devices

The ecogram and genogram are two visual tools used widely in assessment with families. They are useful in identifying patterns within the families and the family's relationships to the larger environment. These tools provide mechanisms by which the family counselor and the family can collaborate to identify sources of strain and distress and important resources for the family.

The eco map is a visual representation of the family's transactions with the wider environment. These transactions include those of individual family members as well as the family as a unit. Families can be asked to map out their relationships with important aspects of their external world. Some of the important dimensions that are typically included are schools (for families with school age children), extended family members, employment, health systems, and other social services that are part of the family life. Families can be encouraged to identify other entities that are relevant to their family life, for example, the church, and local recreation program. Arrows and lines are then used to describe the flow of energy from family members to aspects of the environment. Arrows describe direction and the width of the line indicates the degree of energy involved. Conflictual transactions can be delineated by cross hatching. This set of lines thus conveys to the family sources of support as well as possible exhaustion and tensions.

The eco map has the advantage of making visible the sources of support (external resources) and strains within the family in terms of its transaction with the wider world. While people often experience distress or feel nourished by other interactions, seeing such patterns on paper can be quite powerful in identifying the nature of them in their lives. Creation of the eco map sets the stage for discussion about what might possibly be done to reduce the stresses and to enhance the resources in ways that can promote the resiliency of the family.

> The Kastor family consists of Mr. and Mrs. Kastor, their seven-year-old son Jack, and five-year-old son Chad. The family receives support from a grandparent who helps take care of the children when they are ill and cannot attend day care. One of the children has been having difficulty in school and the parents dread calls from the teacher. The parents have been pillars of their church for many years. They feel valued in this setting and experience their relationships with fellow church members as their main support system. Mr. Kastor is concerned about the stability of his job because there have been layoffs and people are worried about who will be next. As a result, there is pressure on everyone to work extra hours to prove their worth to the company so that they can escape the next round of layoffs. Mrs. Kastor is feeling satisfied with her employment situation. One of the children has some serious health problems and the parents have had problems in getting clear answers regarding the nature of these problems and possible effective remedies. The family's current health insurance is linked to the threatened employment situation of Mr. Kastor.

See figure 1, Kastor family eco map.

The genogram is a visual map of the family over time (McGolderick & Gerson, 1985). Families can use the genogram to describe the family story as

**FIGURE 1.** Kastor Family Eco Map

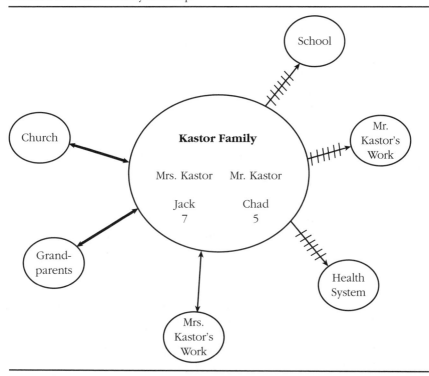

it emerges across several generations. Use of the genogram is based on recognition that family messages, loyalties, expectations, or tensions are communicated from one generation to the next. As one student said after doing a genogram of her family, "I realized I either had to marry a Lutheran pastor or become one." The genogram includes available information about the parties involved—names, brief personal descriptions, employment, health, and other relevant information. A history of substance abuse can represent a multigenerational risk factor. Several generations of substance abuse followed by lack of such problems in the current generation can be used to identify sources of strength and resiliency within the family. The genogram can reveal a history of physical problems, for example, early death caused by heart problems, which represent a legitimate health concern within the family or prompt unrealistic worry. The genogram can represent expectations in terms of education, religion, employment, and other areas. Names from one generation to the next can convey important messages.

The genogram can also describe relationships among people. Circles are used to describe close ties among groups of people, broad lines to indicate strong relationships, and jagged lines to describe conflict between people. Lines can also be drawn to identify cutoffs that have occurred within the family.

The genogram enables family members to place family events within a cultural or historical context. The family might have emigrated to another country or lost family members due to war. Historical events also help explain why families made the choices that they did. People may discover the limited options that family members had due to war, political oppression, and community poverty when they made decisions that might appear puzzling or hurtful without this context. A social work student had felt abandoned by her parents who had placed her as a young child with relatives. Although she came from a Mexican family in which such relative placements are acceptable, she always felt hurt by the parents' actions. When she created her family genogram and placed the historical context in the background, she realized the terrible economic hardship to the point of the danger of starvation that was facing her family during these times. The visual image of the genogram helped her understand for the first time the social context of her parent's decision and to recognize that it was made to protect her rather than because her parents did not care enough for her.

> The Loden family came to the session because Ted Loden feels that Sue Loden is too overprotective of their twelve-year-old son, Mark. Mark is resentful of his mother's overprotective ways, and the father and son have created a close alliance from which the mother feels excluded. As the family creates a genogram, a family pattern emerges that helps put some of her anxiety into perspective and enables the family to problem solve alternative solutions. The Lodens have one child because Sue had several miscarriages both prior to and following Mark's birth. Mark has been a healthy child but has seen more than his share of doctors' offices due to Sue's anxiety about his health. A genogram revealed a history of health problems on the maternal side of the family. Although the family was aware of some of this history, they had not fully recognized the extent and impact. Sue has a sister, Carol, who has been healthy, but her brother, Jim, died when he was eighteen. He had been playing basketball with a friend when he died suddenly of a previously undetected heart problem. Her father, Mark Matthews, died of a heart attack when he was in his forties leaving her mother, who has always been very healthy, to financially support and in other ways raise the family. Her uncle Peter had successful heart surgery for a birth defect when he was a child and has been able to live a relatively normal life. Another uncle, John, died in his fifties from heart disease. The genogram of the paternal side revealed no pattern of significant health problems for the Lodens, and the men in this family were described as very physically active.

Although Matthews family members were aware of health problems within the family, the genogram gave a vivid reality to the health problems facing the male members of Sue's family and the fear that had been deeply embedded into her. While it helped other family members appreciate her worry, it also helped her begin to recognize the need to distinguish her son from other family members and to recognize their son's potential strengths from his father. Creation of the genogram contributed to a better understanding within the family of the situation facing the family currently and enabled family members to dialogue more effectively about ways to address it. See figure 2, Loden family genogram.

Creation of the genogram is a process that involves members of the family and the family counselor. Relationships among family members and between the family and the counselor can be critical in this process. As a result, one should not expect that a final genogram is accomplished during the first visit with a family or that it is always advisable to begin the process of a genogram during the first visit. Families frequently have secrets that they are protecting due to codes of family loyalty or a sense of shame. As families learn to trust, they may be more willing to include these aspects in the genogram and to incorporate them in ways that can promote healing within the family. Sometimes family members have kept secrets from each other and are reluctant to reveal them. An adult friend of mine who was involved in family genealogy was excited because he discovered some colorful characters in which had otherwise been a rather staid family background. When he shared his excitement with his mother, she was horrified at his discovery and responded that this was a family secret that he wasn't to learn about. As the genogram is created, the social worker and family members can explore themes that illumine the current situation.

Family legacies take many forms within families. Some of these legacies support people's ability to survive hardships while others contribute to vulnerability. A family in the Orlando, Florida, area was featured in the local paper as a result of their legacy that family members are still carrying out. Family members are caring for people with severe handicaps in their homes. Now adults, family members describe their home as a place in which their mother regularly cared for people with severe handicaps as members of the family. The children in this family grew up with the assumption that the presence of such individuals within the family circle was a normal way of life. After the death of their mother, the children have continued this tradition of caring for individuals with these severe handicaps as a way of honoring their mother and her legacy (Roen, 2004).

## *Interview*

The interview is an essential assessment strategy for the family counselor. The assessment interview within the resiliency-based framework is guided by a search for risk and protective factors that provide the context for understanding the distress of the family and potential sources of healing. This search is carried out by asking key questions, requesting family members to enact family events, and by observing the family members in action. The

**FIGURE 2.** Loden Family Genogram

interview process thus includes both a directed conversation and observations of nonverbal behavior. The moving drama of the family is played out during the family interview and reveals much about the life of the family.

The social worker has access to a wealth of information conveyed by the interaction of family members in addition to the facts family members offer in response to the counselor's questions and comments. Everyone who has ever lived in a family knows the power of the verbal and nonverbal gestures of other family members during a conversation. When a family member rolls his or her eyes to the ceiling or leans forward attentively when another family member is expressing a concern, these gestures convey powerful messages. Silence can communicate volumes of multifaceted meanings within families. It is important for social workers and family counselors to inquire whether or not their interpretations of these silences fit with the meaning intended and experienced by the family members. For example, when one member of a family brings up an issue and there is marked and tense silence by the other members, the family counselor can ask "I am getting the impression that this is a topic that people find difficult to talk about—am I reading this situation right?" On the other hand, if people feel comfortable with the silence, the counselor could comment, "I am getting the impression that the rest of you feel comfortable with the way that (dad, mom) has described this issue—am I reading you right?" Comments such as these not only help the counselor understand the family accurately but also convey the message that the assessment process is a partnership endeavor. Observation of the family patterns gives access to the metamessages of communication within the family. Family members understand the subtext of comments made. Their verbal and nonverbal reactions in turn provide additional information to the social worker in the assessment process. Family members interact during the interview by adding their comments to statements made by other members or becoming obviously silent.

### Thematic Dimensions

In addition to verbal and nonverbal messages, two major thematic dimensions relate to content and process and to linear and circular understandings of family interactions.

*Content and Process.* Content refers to the specific topic or events being discussed. Family members can be talking about a curfew for their adolescent daughter, financial struggles, decisions regarding employment, and a host of other specific topics. Process refers to the ways in which the family interacts in terms of communication, family roles, and issues related to family organization. While family members typically talk in terms of content, understanding process is critical in identifying the repetitive patterns that occur within families. Family members might be arguing about curfew, but this topic reveals the ways in which parents attempt to exert control over their growing children, how parents deal with their own relationship, how parents and children communicate their differences. These process themes are likely to transcend specific topics in the family situation and reflect family system characteristics.

The family dance of process takes place as the family members deal with a variety of content issues. If the assessment and subsequent interventions are limited to content, important family patterns that maintain problematic interactions can remain unidentified, untouched and unchallenged. The struggle for growing independence by an adolescent family member, for example, can occur in the context of curfew, participation in family activities, use of money, and appearance. When the focus in on content, the family counselor can quickly become overwhelmed with the multitude of issues and begin to lose a focus with the family.

*Linear and Circular Questioning.* The assessment process is a good time to introduce the concepts of circularity rather than a merely linear perspective on what is occurring within the family. Families frequently come to the session with the mindset that A causes B. They do not consider the various circular loops that are occurring.

The family can view the tension in the family as due solely to thirteen-year-old Jim's problem behavior and, therefore, that this is the only change needed. Of course, from Jim's perspective the problem is that his parents are being too strict with him. Each party in this family is hoping that the social worker will accept his or her linear perspective of which of these themes is responsible for the family tension and the circle of blaming within the family that serves to increase the tension. A careful tracking of the sequence through questions such as, Who steps in first when there is tension? What has been happening with other family members? How have the parents changed in their reactions? How do other siblings react to what is going on? might reveal a more complex and circular pattern within the family. It might uncover tension between the parents regarding how to discipline Jimmy, or increase worry within the family because Jimmy's older brother has developed a substance-abuse problem and the frightened parents have created a very strict code for Jimmy because they are frightened that he will get in the same trouble. It might also reveal a boy who has not found ways to earn the praise of his parents for his academic or sports performance and has discovered a way to get his worried parents involved in this life. It might reveal a boy who is worried because he has overheard his parents talking about possible layoffs at his father's job. These concerns on the part of the parents have made them less attentive to the children and more impatient of the behavior of the children who in turn have reacted by adopting more difficult behavior. Such circular patterns of behavior frequently are a more realistic reflection of events within the family. Inclusion of these circular patterns in the assessment process also offers additional opportunities for addressing problems within families.

### Information From Other Family Members

Eliciting information from various family members gives a broader and more systemic picture of the family story and relationship issues. Recognizing that individuals always come to situations with their own agendas and perceptual frameworks, differences in the family story that emerge can subsequently be explored as appropriate. Aside from personal differences within family members, there are several factors that contribute to these differing scripts.

*Life cycle issues* can be important contributors to these differences. Children and adults typically view life events from very different developmental perspectives. Teenagers and their parents, for example, frequently disagree on many issues. Young children can be limited in their understanding of complex situations and create a sense of meanings based on life as they see it. The following example illustrates how developmental issues influence perceptions in as they relate to the counseling process.

> Five-year-old Anne was referred for counseling because she had become very frightened of bugs. She had also become very good but this change had not prompted the referral. Her family included her mother who had been recently widowed leaving her with the responsibility of the two teenage boys from her husband's previous marriage. Anne revealed that she felt that she had to be very good or her mother would kill herself. Apparently when her mother was feeling upset, she would say, "You boys will be the death of me yet." From the literal perspective of a five-year-old, Anne interpreted these words to mean that her mother would kill herself if she did not help by being good. Naturally the mother was astonished as her daughter explained what these words meant to her. Anne's mother quickly clarified that she was not going to kill herself and that these words were just an expression of her frustration. Anne's fear of bugs and her excessively good behavior went away almost immediately.

> Sarah, another five-year-old, was referred for counseling because of her serious behavior problems in school combined with excessive fears. She had been adopted at birth and had had no contact with her birth mother. When she was two her adoptive mother developed bone cancer and died within six months. Because of her mother's severe health problems, Sarah's aunt cared for her. Sarah was cared for by her aunt until her father remarried. In order to help the child bond with her stepmother and because her own health was problematic, the aunt then dropped out of the picture. During the counseling process, the child revealed that she believed two of her mothers had already died and she was thus afraid that her third mother would also die. From her perspective, the odds were against her stepmother living. Although her parents had never told her that her birth mother had died, the young child assumed that if she had been adopted, her mother must have died. While giving her the correct information did not affect the immediate change evident in the earlier situation, it represented a crucial step toward reducing her fears.

*Communication patterns* within the family can contribute to differences in perspectives because information might be shared selectively within the family. Generational boundaries are frequently marked by the information that is shared. My husband was motivated to learn some Dutch because information that the children were not supposed to understand was spoken in Dutch when he was a child. When I interviewed youth in rural families that were experiencing financial problems, many described a pattern of generational boundaries that contributed to their anxiety. The parents would talk about the family's financial problems between themselves but would not discuss them openly with the children. The children of the family would join forces to elicit or overhear whatever information they could in order to piece together what was happening in their family. As one can imagine, such a situation is ripe for multiple interpretations and misunderstandings of a situation.

Problems in clear communication in the family can contribute to differences in perspective. People can communicate in oblique, ambivalent, or contradictory patterns. Even when parents believe that they have communicated with their children, the example of the Roberts family in which the children believed that their mopeds had caused the family's financial problems demonstrates that people can still not understand the larger picture. Sometimes situations are complex and parents assume that children understand this complexity or do not think that it is important to give detailed information.

Jim, a teenage boy, was referred to me because he had been stealing gas from the neighbors. He was frightened that the family would need to live on his mother's Avon earnings because the family was going into bankruptcy. What he did not understand was that the father was declaring Chapter 11 bankruptcy for the family business. His parents had not realized the importance of explaining to Jim the different types of bankruptcies and the implications of Chapter 11 for the family.

*Family alliances* based on gender, generations, or unique family circumstances can also influence communication patterns within families. Family members who are part of a specific family alliance are likely to communicate more with each other and perhaps exclude others. They can also share a similar perspective on family issues. Eliciting information about the situation and potential resources from different family members can help identify some of these issues. The patterns reflected in these differences can potentially reveal problematic communication patterns, family alliances, or other issues that potentially need to be addressed in the counseling situation.

### Social Worker's Reaction

The social worker can also use her or his own reaction to the family as part of the assessment process. Since families enlist their counselor into the family dance, the social worker also begins to experience the family patterns. One can begin to experience the pressure to blame or ignore a specific family member or to avoid certain topics because family members dodge around them. I have caught myself turning toward family members who engage me and in the process ignoring others until I realized that I was mirroring long-standing family patterns that tended to marginalize certain family members. Without intending to do so, I was reinforcing patterns that isolated family members. The family dance can be a very powerful one.

## COPING PROCESS

In assessing the ability of family members to cope, it is important to recognize that coping does not occur within a vacuum. It is influenced by the nature of the challenge facing the family. Community and cultural expectations also create varying scripts regarding appropriate ways to cope. These scripts help family members learn coping skills as well as offer support or censure for differing behaviors.

The following represent key areas identified in the resiliency literature that influence how families are able to cope. As is evident from the discussion regarding family coping, these items form a circle as events are appraised and addressed. This circle sets in play yet a second circle in response and interacts with other ongoing patterns within the family and the community.

### *The Current Stressor*

This stressor is frequently the presenting problem. Questions such as, "What brought you here?" "Why did you contact our agency?" "What type of help are you looking for?" "How can we help you?" and "What changes do you wish to occur?" can be useful in eliciting this information. Given the complexities of family life such stressors can represent one of a wide variety of life circumstances. The current stressor may be a referral from the school because the thirteen-year-old son or daughter is skipping school or a major conflict between the parents on how to spend their limited money. It can be the discovery by parents that one of their teenagers has been abusing alcohol or other drugs, the sudden illness of the grandmother who had been the emotional mainstay of the family, the family's eviction from their apartment, or pressure from the court due to neglect of a child. While this list contains only single items, families frequently seek help because several related problems are creating distress. This issue will be discussed subsequently in terms of additive sources of stress. The nature of this stressor can begin to shape the picture of the needs to addressed in the counseling process.

### *Onset of Stressor*

It is valuable to identify the issues related to the onset of this stressor. Is the problem at hand a recent one with a sudden onset (an acute problem) or a long-term problem that has in some way become more serious, or intolerable due to other life circumstances that make it difficult for the family to cope with it, or has now caused community members to insist that the family seek help? The exploration of these differences can help identify the context of the current stressor, the presence of additive stressful events, the meaning of this event in the life of the family (appraisal), and potential resources.

The following families are seeking help for housing with quite a different combination of onsets and accompanying situations. The Andrews family comes for help with housing because they were recently evicted from their apartment for nonpayment of rent. They have a long history of being evicted from apartments for failure to pay their rent. The employment pattern of both parents is sporadic. The Bowen family is also seeking housing help in response to eviction but their situation is quite different. One parent recently lost a steady job that had been held for several years due to downsizing at the plant. Loss of income combined with family health problems by the other parent resulted in the family being unable to pay their rent. The Conner family is also seeking housing because a major hurricane devastated their home. They returned from the shelter to discover that the storm had blown off their roof and a large tree had fallen on it and made the house unsafe for habitation. They had lived in this home for the last ten years following a move to the community after they retired. Their home was part of a neighborhood that had been devastated by the storm. While they had insurance, it was not adequate to cover their costs and they needed additional financial aid.

Based on this information, the Andrews family reveals a risk pattern of long-term financial instability and poor management coping strategies with possible problematic employment skills. While further information is needed before making a final assessment, it is likely that the situation will not be solved merely by referrals for a new low-rent housing option or job placement. On the protective side, family members have stayed together as a family despite all of these problems that might have driven them apart. This suggests a level of cohesion and sense of identity as a family. They have not become demoralized from their ongoing problem. The Bowen family demonstrates the coping strategies needed for long-term employment and generally adequate financial management coping abilities. Their family members also have retained a sense of family despite their current crisis. The Conner family was caught in the vortex of a natural disaster. Its ability to turn to neighbors is limited because they too were caught up in the storm but have been together as a couple for some time. Fortunately, the Connor family will be eligible for federal assistance because their community was declared a disaster area. Further exploration might reveal that the Andrews family appraises their current situation as part of their usual pattern of life while for the Bowen family it represents a major disruption in their pattern and family identity. The Conner family members are feeling the shock of their long-term home and mementoes being destroyed and the destruction of their neighborhood but are grateful that they survived it together because others were killed in the storm.

### Impact on Family

What has been the impact on the family of this stressor? Typically people do not seek help unless some event has either created distress for members of the family or on the part of people who have some power or influence over the family. The impact of the stressor of the family is a reflection of the potential disruption, the family appraisals of the problem and resources, and the family coping strategies and resources. The impact of life events of family members can vary widely depending on the appraisal of the situation and potential individual, family, and contextual resources. Assessment must include positive as well as negative changes. Some useful questions that elicit information regarding the impact of the event on the family include

> How has this affected you as a family (as well as individual family members)?
>
> How has this been difficult for you?
>
> What was there about this event that led you to contact our agency?
>
> What have been your concerns?
>
> How has this changed your family and your way of thinking?
>
> What do you think might help?
>
> In what ways has this affected your relationships with people outside of your family?

The nature of this impact is influenced by various risk and resiliency factors. Exploration regarding the impact often opens the door to these issues. The impact of events on families is affected by additive factors, appraisals, coping strategies, as well as the risk and protective factors identified earlier and discussed in greater detail in this chapter.

### Additive Factors

Resiliency research indicates that a series of difficult events is more stressful for families than even the summation of the individual situations. The question here relates to what are some of the other issues in the life of the family that are increasing the distress the family experiences. Such additive factors may be related to the following issues.

*Life cycle issues* within the family. Families go through a variety of changes during the ongoing life cycle and people enter and leave the family circle and change their roles within the family and the wider context. A child who had been the intermediary between the parents goes off to college. A parent or grandparent dies. A much-awaited new baby creates time and energy demands on the couple who are now parents. A marriage brings together two very different families. Retirement changes roles within the family and the family's relationship within the wider community. A child moves into adolescence.

*Additional circumstances.* Families are frequently experiencing several difficult life circumstances at the same time. Family members can lose jobs, experience legal problems, or have substance abuse issues or other health problems. They can live in violent neighborhoods that impact in various ways in the family. These circumstances can interact in complex ways that increase the stress experienced by families.

*Unresolved issues* activated by current stressors. Family members can re-experience difficult times in their lives that are activated by current stressors. Divorce can reactivate the feelings of being rejected by parents. Absence of a partner who has been called to active duty can evoke feelings of being vulnerable due to an earlier experience with rape or fears of abandonment. Loss of a job can reactivate feelings of worthlessness. A child's difficulties in school can activate parental feelings of failure due to the parent's own educational problems in school.

*Contextual issues.* Community poverty with the attendant lack of opportunities can increase the pain of job loss. Discrimination can be experienced as oppressive and reducing hope for new opportunities. Violence and crime within the community can create realistic fears of safety or worries about the role models available to youth.

Additive factors can be explored in many ways. The following are useful questions or prompts for eliciting the family's perspective on additive factors that can increase the stress.

- Have you had your hands full with any other problems or difficulties?
- Has anything happened in your family that has made this more difficult to cope with?
- Are you having to contend with any other problems/or changes?
- Has anything been happening in your own family life or your community that has made this worse?
- Has this problem prompted any other difficulty in your life?
- Are there other worries you have that are making this problem worse?
- Has anything else been happening in your family that has influenced how you have been able to handle this?

Mr. Warren illustrates the power of several of these additive factors as well as the resiliency present within the family system.

> Mr. Warren (a man in his late fifties) contacted the local mental health center at the urging of his wife due to his deepening depression. He was experiencing serious financial problems with his farm and was depressed and discouraged

about the future. He was also feeling that he had failed his family. As a boy he had grown up in the Netherlands during World War II. As the older brother, he felt that it was his responsibility to take care and protect his younger brother. But a ten-year-old boy was no match for the bombs, devastation, and near starvation experienced by the people in the community. Appraising this situation within the cognitive framework of a child, he believed that he was a failure. He was committed to protecting his family in the future. As an adult, Mr. Warren was true to his word. He worked hard, supported his family well, and provided his children with college educations. Now caught up in the economic major depression of the agriculture sector, his careful arrangement of care for his family was falling down around him. The depressed economic situation in his community had decreased other employment opportunities. He was worried that his age would also jeopardize these opportunities. As a result, additive factors due to life cycle, previously unresolved life issues, and contextual issues all interacted with the initial stressor to set in motion and intensify his depression. Fortunately for Mr. Warren, powerful resources were also present. His wife was a caring person who loved him deeply. When she learned of his feelings of guilt and sense of failure, she took steps to alter them with other sources of information. She contacted the adult children who in turn were quick to reach out to their father with words of thanks and appreciation for all that he had given him. The family mounted a campaign to change his view of himself from that of a failure to a hero who had created a viable business out of very little and had launched his children into successful adulthood through his efforts. They also indicated that they were now at a stage of life where they could and should help out their parents if the need should arise.

While the message of additive life events relates to the presence of increased risk factors, this part of the assessment process can also be used to highlight family resources. As family members describe the presence of multiple stressors that the family is experiencing, the social worker can highlight some of the signs of resources that have also emerged in this context. That the family has somehow or other managed to stay together as a family, or ensured that children continue to go to school, that no serious abuse has occurred, or that family members have not succumbed to the temptation of substance abuse or have been able to stop abusing drugs to escape the tension, are all signs of strength within the family. The counselor can comment that other families might have long ago given up and thrown in the towel, while they are still staying together trying as a family. This information provides the opportunity later to explore with the family what have been some of their sources of resiliency—how did they manage to cope, what gave them the strength to go on, what kept them from giving up, what enabled them to pick themselves up during these difficult times.

## *FAMILY APPRAISALS OF THE SITUATION*

As described in the family strengths and family crisis literature, how family members interpret life events is critical in influencing how they will experience and respond to stressors. These appraisals are influenced by the family's own unique paradigms as well as the schemes that are part of the cultural framework. The family therapy technique reframing in which events are placed within a new meaning system is based on recognition of the importance of the meaning that is attributed to an event. Mr. Warren interpreted his business financial problems as evidence that he had failed his family members yet again. His wife and children fortunately did not share his interpretation. The Lo family feared that their daughter's attempted suicide would cause the family to be deported. In the Roberts family, both the young people in the family felt guilty because they felt responsible for the family's problems. The family resiliency literature indicates that resilient families are able to recognize complex causes of situations instead of blaming and scapegoating family members. Understanding events within a developmental perspective can also be helpful because it permits family members to recognize the role that development plays and that change is possible.

Appraisals can include attributions of responsibility, views on what is the likely impact of the event, and ways to address it. As family members describe their current and past stressors, questions that evoke attributions of responsibility and meanings of events can be useful. This information can be elicited as part of the ongoing conversation with the family about the event. Patterns of blaming and scapegoating within the family can emerge.

Attributions can be powerfully influenced by cultural views of what is important or appropriate behavior. Families can also be influenced by the way in which community members view issues. HIV/AIDS is associated with stigma in many societies. This community definition can be a powerful influence on the nature of resources available to the family. Community appraisals that have been internalized by the family members will be reflected in the appraisals given by family members. The process of exploring other resources within the community often reveals other community perspectives on the issue. Questions such as the following can help prompt information in the areas of attribution and impact.

- What did you make of . . . ?
- What do you think helped make this happen?
- What have you told yourself about this event in your family?
- What has been your interpretation of this event?
- Have you ever asked why this happened?

Appraisals of how to address the problem are important in understanding the family's view of the nature of appropriate resources and ways to access them. Questions related to this issue are helpful in identifying information regarding several critical areas including the family's expectation of the counseling situation, the family's paradigms regarding how to address problems of this nature, the nature of the family's support system within the larger community, and the family's previous attempts to address this problem. Some useful questions and probes in this realm include

- What have been your thoughts on ways to help this situation?
- Has anything been useful so far that would be valuable in trying to address this problem?
- What do you think would be helpful?
- What do you hope to get out of coming here?

## IDENTIFYING APPROPRIATE RESOURCES

### Coping Efforts

A repertoire of coping efforts is an important source of resiliency. While the nature of effective coping efforts varies depending on the situation, the ability of the family to pull together to address family issues is a consistent important family resource. Eliciting information about what the family has already done to try to solve this problem and the results can be valuable in assessing family coping as well as the nature of the resources available to family members.

- How have you tried to solve this problem and with what results?
- What have you already done to try to make this situation better (and with what results)?
- Have there been people in your family or community that you have turned to address this problem (with what results)? If not, what has kept you from seeking help from others about this problem?

These questions can be effective in identifying possible resources within the extended family and community as well as barriers in this process and views of the community regarding the stressor. One can elicit feelings of support as well as those of shame, alienation, and isolation.

### Belief Systems

Exploring coping efforts gives valuable information about the belief systems of families.

#### Self-Efficacy, Mastery, Hope

In terms of beliefs of self-efficacy, mastery, and hope, families quickly reveal their sense of feeling defeated in their coping efforts or feeling that they can address the problem given a little extra help. These families seem hopeful that their problem can be solved. When families are demoralized about their coping efforts, it is common for them to use words to convey that they are discouraged because they have tried everything and feel that nothing has helped. They project a sense of hopelessness about their situation.

The family's definition of appropriate and available resources and ways to access these resources are important. Cultural background, community definitions, the nature of the problem, and unique family circumstances all help shape these definitions. Questions that relate to whom they can turn for help and in what way are useful in eliciting this information. As discussed earlier, while one family in a community might view a resource as available and acceptable, this same potential resource can be reviewed as unavailable and unacceptable by others.

From a resiliency perspective, the social worker needs to be constantly surveying the situation for possible sources of resiliency. As a result, it can be valuable to extend the focus of the conversation beyond the immediate problem and situation. What evidence is there in the family history or current context that might have some parallels to the current situation that can be used to enhance the family's sense of self-efficacy and hopefulness regarding their ability to address this problem or to identify supports within their family or community?

> Have you ever experienced a situation at all similar to the one that you are going through now? If so, how did you handle this?
>
> What did you do as a family to try to make it better? (identification of coping strategies)
>
> Were you able to turn to others to try to make it better? (with what effect)

A family can become so overwhelmed by its current situation that it loses sight of possible strengths within its family or support system. Information regarding effective coping with similar current or past events can be used to highlight the ability of the family to cope. Similarly, information about help received from others can be used to highlight possible resources.

### *Family Trust, Loyalty, and Affection*

Family trust, loyalty, and affection are important sources of family resiliency. The counselor needs to be attentive to verbal and nonverbal signs of such traits within the family as they play out the family drama in the session. Beyond specific comments by family members that reveal concern and unity versus anger and mistrust, gestures such as posture and seating positions can be revealing. Tones of voice that express caring or protection in contrast to anger or disdain are important clues. Sometimes hurt can be an indirect sign that people in the family are important to each other—the people who are important to us have the power to hurt us. If family members are embroiled in a current situation and are unable to access feelings of affection and caring, the social workers can probe for evidence that such feelings were present during the past. Explorations regarding potential sources of help within the extended family can elicit information about possible sources of affection and caring within this wider circle.

Once the family counselor has identified important supports within the family circle, the question arises as to how one can most effectively tap these sources of resiliency. On the principle that one wants to bring together the people who can help solve the problem, the assessment process will influence the nature of the cast of the family members invited to future sessions. Perhaps there are members of the extended family or other support systems that would be appropriate to include in the sessions and it can be useful to discuss this possibility with the family members.

### Patterns of Spirituality or Faith

Spirituality and faith can emerge as resources in several ways. In describing the impact of life events on families, members can describe the meaning that events have had in terms of their growth in sense of meaning or purpose, or perhaps their deepening of faith in others or their religious life. Family members can describe coping efforts that involve turning to members of their religious community for emotional or instrumental health. Relationships with the divine (as viewed by the family and their spiritual tradition) can be important sources of support. While these represent positive responses that support resiliency, families can also feel alienated from their traditional faith or from members of their religious community. Individuals within the family can vary widely in terms in their experiences in the area of spirituality and religion and thus the assessment must incorporate these differences.

## Organizational Patterns

### Family Cohesion

A related and essential source of family resiliency is cohesion, the family's ability to band together as a group to address the problems of life. As described in the chapter regarding cultural issues, cultures vary in terms of what this means regarding codes of relatedness compared to individualism within families. Regardless of the continuum involved here, the ability of the family to view itself as a unit (we), for members to care about what happens to other family members and the family unit, to band together to address the problems facing the family is an essential aspect of family resiliency. Family patterns of cohesions can be identified by the family's descriptions of how they appraise the nature of the problem (especially, their concern for its impact on the family as a whole) and views of potential ways to address the problem or their history of coping efforts.

### Family Leadership

Resilient families have an effective leadership structure within the family that can direct family efforts and ensure that family member needs are met within the resource constraints of the family. Ineffective leadership patterns can range from those in which leaders abuse their power in a dominating manner or where there is no sense of order within the family. Leadership patterns can be identified as family members describe how they have responded previously to the presenting situation or other events within the family. Communication patterns within the session can also reveal leadership patterns within the family. Do children evidence appropriate respect for the parents who are speaking or are there constant interruptions or disparaging comments made? On the other hand, is leadership by one of more of the parents so overbearing that other family members are reluctant to speak?

As described earlier, it can be useful to expand the discussion beyond the problem at hand to other situations currently or in the past to identify leadership patterns. There may be evidence that effective leadership was present in the past but some event or circumstances, for example, the demoralization of loss of a job, the onset of depression or illness, has diminished the ability of the parents to exercise leadership. Such circumstances suggest that the skills for leadership are potentially present and can be reactivated with appropriate help. Perhaps one of the parents had assumed the leadership role within the family and now this parent is no longer able to carryout this role due to separation or death. Families might have had leadership styles that were effective when the children were young but are no longer effective now that the children are adolescents and are challenging the previous leadership style. Cultural disjuncture can also play a role. Family members who have emigrated to other countries can sometimes have difficulties in establishing leadership styles that fit with the new culture and the change in roles in terms of the new community.

If gaps are identified, what are the possibilities for skill development or support for currently dormant leadership abilities? Identifying these aspects helps guide the treatment process.

### Family Communication

Family communication patterns are important in terms of resiliency because effective communication is essential for problem solving and can contribute to the sense of trust within the family. Some of the issues of communication were identified in the earlier discussion regarding different perspectives of family issues.

The counselor can observe family communication patterns within the family interview. Are family members able to talk about difficult things? When sensitive topics arise, do they veer off, change the subject, and become overly angry at one another? Who are the people who appear to influence what is talked about and by whom in the family? Can family members listen to each other? Are the comments of some family members valued while others are discounted? What patterns emerge as family members discuss the situation?

Social workers can also ask family members to enact in the family session some typical communication interaction patterns. When family members describe an ongoing disagreement or successful resolution, the family counselor can ask them to demonstrate in the session what occurs at home. This enactment permits the counselor to check with the family if the communication pattern present in the session reflects what occurs at home.

The social worker can use this information to identify effective and ineffective communication patterns to problems that need to be addressed in the counseling process. Assessment of family communication must, of course, consider cultural differences in communication. A social work student who had grown up in an urban community described her confusion in working with rural families who used terms such as "small problem" to refer to major events such an impending eviction or serious health problems. A counselor accustomed to direct communication can be puzzled while working with a family from cultural groups that value indirection or understatement. What is critical here, of course, is how this family communication patterns work for the family members involved and their support systems.

### Flexibility of Family Roles

Family resiliency is enhanced by the ability of family members to assume different responsibilities and roles within the family. As family members are called up to military duty, become ill, or lose jobs, other family members must be able and willing to carry out the roles of family members who are missing or are no longer able to meet the needs of the family in the previous manner.

Family flexibility can be assessed by using the information provided by family members regarding how they have attempted to cope with the current stressor and other issues within the family. Families can give evidence of parents who return to work, adolescent children who help out more with household tasks or grandparents who become more active in helping with the care of the children. On the other hand, they can reveal patterns that indicate that family members are locked into rigid family roles. A variety of these factors can contribute to this rigidity. Understanding the nature of these factors can be useful to identifying ways to increase flexibility within the family. Family members may be reluctant to take on new responsibilities because they lack these alternative coping skills or the needed self-confidence in their ability to take on new home or employment roles. Family and related community appraisal issues (strong family, community, or cultural prescriptions regarding family roles) may also deter flexibility.

When my son was going to be a father for the first time, his in-laws held a shower for them in which many of older members of the church were invited. When they received a set of diapers, the older men joked about how they had never touched these in a way that assumed that my son might try to change a diaper once but would leave changing diapers to his wife. Reflecting the generational shift of family roles, my son was quite insulted because he planned to parent equally in this area. He and his wife belong to a generation in which diapers, cooking, and employment are expected to be shared responsibilities by both parents and negotiated on an ongoing basis depending on needs and schedules.

### *Humor*

Humor can be an essential family resource in dealing with some of the very tough circumstances of life. Humor might not emerge initially as family members are absorbed in their situation and pain. As family members become more relaxed with the family counselor and have had the opportunity share their pain, the family's gift of humor may begin to emerge.

## *Community Context*

Cultural and community codes provide for a context for learning and reinforcing specific coping efforts. Families in transition can face a disjuncture between the coping strategies that they have learned and the current context in terms of the coping strategies that are viewed as appropriate. The following illustration highlights how cultural codes influence the appropriate ways to access potential resources.

Our family faced such a cultural juncture in an anxiety-producing manner several years ago when we visited our daughter in her village while she was serving in the Peace Corps in Chad. This experience has helped me appreciate the stress created by these situations and the need to recognize the influence of context. When we arrived in her village, our daughter informed us that while she had managed to get a ride for us into the village (a distance of a few hours), she had not yet found a ride out to catch our plane a week later (and planes only left twice a week). This was in a context in which there was absolutely no public transportation available. As Americans used to asking people in relatively direct ways we were operating in a cultural context in which it was viewed as inappropriate to do so and all conversations began with an hour asking about the health of immediate and extended family members. Culture mandated that one could tell others of one's situation but could not ask people if they could help you. Furthermore these conversations were taking place in French (a language we possessed only limited understanding). Our skills to cope with this situation were woefully ill-matched to our needs. As a result, we would visit the handful of families who owned a vehicle and after an hour my husband anxiously asked our daughter if she had obtained a ride yet. She would whisper that she was still asking about the health of the uncle. After another hour, we would leave without an offer for a ride. Finally, someone was going to the city where the airport was located and came to our rescue.

The community context plays a vital role in terms of both risk and protective factors. Information regarding this context emerges in the interview as well as the eco map. Individuals can feel stressed as they handle two jobs as well as a family in order to meet ends meet or can have friends and family in the community to whom they can turn for help. The social worker also draws upon her or his knowledge of the community to identify potential and risk and resiliency factors. Understanding if the family lives in an area of the community noted for high crime and violence or is protected from these problems is valuable information. Some schools have strong financial and other types of volunteer support from educated parents while others seek to educate children whose parents are frequently too overwhelmed by their own struggles of life to contribute to their children's education. Some families live in areas of the community noted for their youth orchestras while others are on the news for the latest in gang violence.

Based on the resiliency perspective that there are potential resources within each environment, the social worker goes beyond these general descriptions to try to identify whatever resources might be available in the community. It might be a dedicated teacher; a youth leader at the church, mosque, temple, or synagogue; a concerned neighbor; or a community program for youth or adults.

The social worker collaborates with the family to use the information obtained through these various means to identify key aspects related to the nature of the distress experienced by the family, the relevant risk factors, the strengths, protective factors, and sources or resiliency that are either part of the family system or that can be accessed as resources. Such a complex picture helps the worker identify appropriate strategies for helping the family to address problems in ways that contribute to healing and empower them to cope in more effective ways.

## Levels of Family Functioning

Kilpatrick (2003) organizes the risk and protective factors of families in terms of levels. These levels indicate the risk and protective factors that are in place in this context of family needs and strengths. She uses the metaphor of a house in which the different levels represent aspects of the building.

Level I represents the foundation (basic survival needs of the family in terms of food, shelter, protection, medical care, minimal nurturance). These families tend to move from crisis to crisis and become overwhelmed with the number of risk factors and problematic events facing them. There are typically a number of contextual risk factors in the areas of housing, safe neighborhoods, access to health care, interpersonal support systems, steady employment along with problematic coping skills to address family needs. Family leadership is ineffective in meeting family needs (Kilpatrick, 2003).

Level II families represent the framing and the roof (structure and organization). These families have the protective factors that enable the family to meet the basic needs of members. There are risk factors in the area of effective family leadership along with difficulties in communication and coping skills needed to provide adequate family leadership (Kilpatrick, 2003).

Level III families represent the placement of the walls and doors (space and boundaries). They have the protective factors to enable them to meet the basic needs of the family and to offer leadership within the family that can insure the safety and basic organization within the family. Risk factors here relate to family organizational patterns that prevent families from being appropriately flexible, creating appropriate boundaries within the family, and family members from developing close and supportive relationships that also permit family members from creating their own sense of identity (Kilpatrick, 2003).

Level IV families represent the furnishing and the decorations (elements of richness and quality). They have the protective factors that enable them to meet to meet the basic needs of survival as well as adequate leadership and organizational patterns that permit flexibility and appropriate family boundaries. Families have the communication and coping skills to meet these important family needs. At this level, families are looking for greater sense of intimacy and meaning within the family. Issues of meaning in current relationships and those over time assume greater importance (Kilpatrick, 2003).

The combination of risk and protective factors within this context offers guidelines for selection of the appropriate intervention strategies. The more families are contending with a number of basic risk factors, the greater their need for an explicitly strengths-based focus (Kilpatrick, 2003).

## ASSESSMENT AND TREATMENT PLANNING

The concept of key factors discussed earlier is valuable at this point in identifying a sense of direction for the counseling process. What is amenable to change and can make a difference? What are the relevant risk factors that can be addressed in this regard? What supports do family members need? Do the family members lack specific coping skills (perhaps parenting or other family relationships, adjustment to a new culture)? How do the appraisals of the family influence how they are experiencing the problem and potential solutions? Is the problem one of a weak support system or problematic interpretations (that a teenage suicide attempt would cause a family to be deported)? Does the family lack crucial resources (homes damaged by a storm, lack of income, major health problems without access to care) or some combination of these factors? What are the protective factors that can be supported or need to be enhanced? The answer to these questions can help formulate the goals and intervention strategies.

In this process, the counselor must never forget what Worden (2003) describes as the key rule of thumb with families: "Do not get ahead of the family. Address the members' chief concerns first" (p. 129). The assessment process within this framework permits the counselor and the family to develop the appropriate intervention plans. The social worker can also maintain a focus on patterns and look at possible circularity in the process. The family counselor brings to this partnership knowledge of different interventions along with an understanding of the evidence of their effectiveness in addressing the present situation. The social worker also has information about potential community resources and ways to access them or at least ways to find out about such resources. The social worker's information is shared with the family in a collaborative manner so that important decisions can be made in terms of the selection of intervention strategies.

From the perspective of resiliency theory, if families can be helped to address some of the issues facing them more effectively, they will also strengthen their sense of self-efficacy to address problems in the future. This process will strengthen their protective factors that can serve as tools for future concerns.

The following family vignettes illustrate several patterns of risk and resiliency factors and implications for treatment approaches. These illustrations are selective and do not do justice to the entire range of risk and resiliency patterns and potential intervention strategies. They do suggest ways in which the assessment process can influence the professional judgment process in terms of the nature of the interventions that are appropriate for specific families addressing their current life circumstances. Subsequent chapters will describe specific treatment approaches and their applications with families.

## *Basic Needs*

The family contacted the crisis center for help to find housing after it had been evicted from their apartment for nonpayment of rent. The family consists of Mr. Alvarez (aged twenty-four), who does unskilled labor when he is able to get employment, and his partner Miss Colon (aged twenty-three), who does housekeeping at a local motel. They have a son, Jose, eighteen months old. Due to problems in the economy, Miss Colon's work hours have periodically been reduced. When she does not work full time the family lacks medical insurance but they do have insurance for their son through the state insurance plan. The couple met when both moved to the area to find work. They have lived together on and off for three years but have been together steadily for the past year. Neither Mr. Alvarez nor Miss Colon graduated from high school.

Their relatively poor reading skills have posed employment problems for them but they work hard when they are able to find employment. One of their current problems now relates to their car that needs frequent repairs. Because they do not live near a bus line, they have problems getting to work when their car does not work. As a result, Mr. Alvarez lost his last job and the salary of Miss Colon was not enough to pay the rent. Their extended family members live out of the area and lack the financial resources to help out more than with occasional funds. They have some friends in the area but these friends are also struggling financially. Mr. Alvarez has been taking care of Jose while the mother works. Miss Colon has been worried about Mr. Alvarez's temper when he gets frustrated with situations like their present one. While he has never hit her or hurt Jose, she is afraid that his increasingly short fuse will cause him to hurt the boy. She is also worried that he will begin drinking again—a problem that he had earlier in their relationship. She has been afraid to say anything to Mr. Alvarez about it. While she is nervous about this situation, she is also worried that if she says too much that he will leave as he used to do in earlier times before Jose was born. As a result, she has been very tense and finds herself shouting at Jose when he makes too much noise. Despite the family's financial problems Jose is dressed very nicely in clothes that Miss Colon has found at garage sales. He is a friendly little boy who seems especially attached to his mother but appears to be comfortable with his father. He is beginning to use words and developmentally seems to be on track. In terms of the community, there are few housing options for families with low incomes or limited economic resources.

This family and its members demonstrate some key resiliency resources along with risk factors. In terms of resources, both parents have a good work ethic when they are able to find work that matches their skills. Despite recent pressures Mr. Alvarez has not relapsed in terms of drinking and has been able to handle life events without turning to alcohol. The parents have demonstrated some effective parenting skills as demonstrated in the way in which their son relates to people and is dressed. The family roles are flexible enough so that either parent can take care of Jose depending on their job commitments. Although Mr. Alvarez shouts when he is angry, he has not resorted to hitting either Jose or Miss Colon and Jose does not seem afraid of his father. Miss Colon is resourceful in terms of finding clothing at garage sales. Although the couple had an unstable relationship in the past, they have been together in recent months since the birth of their son. Jose demonstrates qualities of resilience in terms of a friendly personality, age-appropriate development, and good relationships with his parents, especially his mother. They have family members and friends who are interested in their well-being even if they cannot help financially.

The family is also struggling with contextual, organizational, and personal risk factors. At the community level, recent economic problems have limited their employment options and there is little in the way of low-income housing. Transportation is also a problem. This combination caused them to be evicted and is making it difficult for the couple to get back on their feet and provide an adequate living and stable housing for the family. Their support system cannot be of any consistent help financially. Although the parents have a good work ethic, they lack some essential employment skills (especially in the area of reading) and have not graduated from high school. There is a history of instability in the relationship. There are also relationship and communication problems as reflected in Miss Colon's reluctance to express her concerns out of fear that Mr. Alvarez will leave. Mr. Alvarez has a history of substance abuse and tends to lose his temper when under pressure. Miss Colon has begun to shout at Jose as a result of her frustration. In addition to the specific problems cited, the combination of issues facing this family creates a situation of additive risk factors.

The family illustrates the need for a multisystems approach useful with families in a state of crisis and with complex needs. The family is in a crisis situation that needs to be addressed (safe housing). Family members would also benefit from some longer term efforts to strengthen their ability to meet the needs of family member and to reduce the likelihood of similar future crises. Recognizing the need to do a risk assessment process to ensure the safety of Jose in these circumstances, Grigsby (2003) emphasizes the need to take a strengths-based perspective with families like Mr. Alvarez and Miss Colon who are already overwhelmed with difficult circumstances. As described earlier in the summary of resources, this family does have some important resources that can be identified with the family. Family members can sometimes lose sight of these strengths because they risk being over-shadowed by the difficulties facing them. As part of this strengths-based approach, it is important to create a situation in which family members identify the issues that are important to them. In this context Grigsby also discusses the need to provide emotional support to deal with the stresses involved as well as advocacy to identify and connect families to these needed resources. Such families can also need help in dealing with conflict and communicating in such a way to help resolve conflicts. Case management models (Greene & Knopf, 2003) can also be useful in helping these families connect with resources to address the immediate crisis and strengthen family coping.

This family could benefit from an improvement in their life skills. Addressing the needs of this family might involve linkages with community resources as well as counseling. Housing is clearly a pressing key issue here so that help in this area is critical. Employment issues are also important. The low reading levels of Mr. Alvarez and Miss Colon will continue to make this family economically vulnerable. Using a case management approach, they might be linked to community programs in which volunteers tutor people in their reading skills. Although their extended family members and friends are not in a position to offer any substantial financial help, they might be able provide some needed emotional support for the parents. The couple might be helped by some counseling focused on improving their communication skills to help provide needed support for each other and to strengthen their relationship. The parents might also benefit from some help in stress management as they are coping with a realistically difficult situation. This help can reduce some of the strains in their relationship and between the parents and Jose. The counselor can identify ways in which Mr. Alvarez has managed to cope without drinking as support for his maintaining sobriety. With the pressure facing this family, such an assessment might identify further resources within the family that can be tapped. While this assessment identifies a variety of possible approaches, an essential part of the assessment process will involve the family in identifying their priorities.

### *Structure and Rewards System*

Mr. and Mrs. King have been married for two years. Both were married before. Mrs. King has three children, aged eight, eleven, and fourteen, from her first marriage. She and her first husband were divorced five years ago. Mrs. King's first husband left the family for another woman. She was hesitant to become involved again but once Mr. King helped her overcome her doubts, she became committed to making this relationship work. She does not want to put the children or herself through yet another painful divorce. Mr. King has two children, aged seven and ten, from his first marriage that ended when his wife died four years ago. The couple met through their church group for single parents. Fortunately the family has adequate financial resources because Mr. King earns a good salary and there was life insurance money from his first wife. Mrs. King's first husband also helps pay some of the bills for the children. The maternal and paternal grandparents are supportive of this new family but do not live in the same geographic area. Mrs. King stays at home and has primary responsibility for the house. Mr. and Mrs. King have, however, been unable to work out an agreement regarding how to discipline the children. Mrs. King is relatively firm in her standards for the children and believes that children need structure and discipline. Mr. King believes that his children were traumatized by the death of their mother from cancer and is hesitant to exercise discipline. Prior to his marriage to Mrs. King the household was organized around the wishes of the children and the word "no" was seldom heard in the family. When Mrs. King seeks to discipline Mr. King's children they are quick to complain to their father about how unfairly they are being treated. Mr. King then caves in to their pleas. Mrs. King becomes angry because the children do not listen to her and she fears that her own children will also stop doing so. In fact, they are beginning to also turn to Mr. King as an ally during these times. Mr. and Mrs. King love each other and want a good family life for everyone but tension is rising between them as well as between Mrs. King and the children.

From a risk and resiliency perspective, the King family has a number of resources. Unlike Mr. Alvarez and Miss Colon, they have adequate financial resources that provide important stability in their lives. They are committed to each other (family cohesion) and to making their marriage work. They have a strong support base through their church. The grandparents are supportive of this family. Aside from the problem at hand, both parents are able to function effectively in their lives and have a sense of mastery in other areas.

The risk factors here relate to conflict between the parents regarding how to raise the children and problems in communication regarding this issue. This is a situation in which both parties brought to their marriage their own paradigms of child rearing shaped by a variety of factors. As a result, the children are being given mixed message from the parents in terms of appropriate behavior and the parental substructure is being weakened and pulled apart by this issue. The children are becoming quite adept at the "divide and conquer" strategy for getting their way.

Drawing upon a resiliency framework, the social worker can readily point out the strengths of this family in terms of sense of commitment to the family unit and concern for the welfare of the children. The counselor can recognize the good organizational skills of the parents as evidenced in the work setting and other aspects of the family.

Several counseling approaches can be used to help this family. From a social learning perspective, parents can be helped to understand how the children are receiving mixed messages from the two parents and the impact of this on the children. They can be helped to understand that the mixed messages create a different set of reinforcements from the two parents so that parental leadership has become compromised. They can be helped to recognize how their differing paradigms influence how they parenting the children. Recognizing the important role of belief systems in terms of behavior, parents can begin to examine their respective beliefs systems in terms of their appropriateness for the current situation. Parents can be helped to gain the needed communication skills required in blending their two different paradigms regarding parenting and in understanding how each party's approach was shaped by life experiences. Structural interventions can also be used to create more effective boundaries around the parental subsystem so that the parents can be united in their parenting efforts.

### Communication Patterns

The Roberts family was discussed in chapter 1. In this family, the teenaged daughter was struggling with bulimia and the father was feeling very depressed. The setting for this family was the severe financial problem facing the family. Everyone in the family was experiencing the burden of these financial problems in their own way. In this situation, communication was a key to helping family members understand the situation and in supporting each other. Communication required the ability to explain complex factual phenomena as well as emotional affirmation. Communication was especially effective because information created new meaning systems within the family. The children were helped to understand that they were not to blame for the family's plight. The father was helped to recognize that his children loved him and were proud of him. Family members realized that they could contribute to the healing process within the family even if their financial situation could not be readily resolved.

## Interpersonal Relationship Issues

Mr. and Mrs. Norris have been married for twenty-three years. Currently they are spending more and more time arguing. They argue about their teenage son who is not doing as well in school as they expect him to. They also argue about the maternal grandfather who needs more support from Mrs. Norris. His wife died a few months ago and he is having difficulty coping by himself. They have begun to view their relationship as marked by conflicts rather than appreciation for each other. They are committed to their marriage but are becoming discouraged about what their future will be like. They both work full time and have an adequate financial basis. Mrs. Norris has been under pressure at work because she has had to take time off to help her father. Mr. Norris thinks that she should be more willing to ask her siblings for help.

This family has important resources that support resiliency. They have a commitment to each other (cohesion) and their family. They demonstrate responsibility at work and in their family and have an adequate financial base.

At the same time, they are struggling with increased tension due to problems regarding their son and the Mrs. Nolan's father. These tensions have created discouragement within the couple that has diminished any previous sense of mastery regarding their family and relationship.

Several approaches might be appropriate for this set of risks and resiliency factors. Solution-focused treatment might address some of the risk factors and mobilize their strengths. The discouragement of Mr. and Mrs. Norris who have begun to view their family relationships as marked by tension and disagreements could suggest the value of a solution-focused approach. The couple has some realistic problems to address but have become discouraged by their disagreements. Their view of the situation has hindered their ability to problem solve effectively. Helping them to recognize the presence of exceptions and enabling them to identify the small steps they can make to improve their situation can reduce their discouragement and encourage them to enlist their resources to begin to make a positive difference.

## Meaning Systems

Mrs. James sought counseling for her two children because they had been previously abused by their stepfather. She had been frightened when she learned from the children what was happening and confronted her husband with this information. She then decided to leave her husband. She had been supportive of the children during this time although it presented some major financial hardship when she had to leave the family and lose her employment. She worked cooperatively with the local child protection team. Currently the daughter is in high school and the son is in junior high. Mrs. James continues to worry that the scars of the past will make it difficult for her children to become healthy individuals and feels guilty that she brought Mr. James into the family life. Both of the children are doing reasonably well in school but their personalities in other areas are quite different. The daughter, Marie (aged sixteen) is an outgoing sociable girl who is engaged in a variety of school activities. This pattern matches the mother's view of a well-adjusted child. The son, John (aged thirteen) is quiet and likes to spend time in his room listening to his music or playing computer games. While he will go out when friends call, he typically does not take the initiative. The teacher does not report any concerns about his behavior in school. Mrs. James worries that his behavior is a sign of the scars of the past because it does not fit with her view of how a well-adjusted child behaves. Mrs. James continues to pressure John to lead a more active social life. It has reached the point that John is beginning to feel that he is letting his mother down and that she does not accept him as he is. The family dance is a circular one. The more Mrs. James pressures him the more insecure he feels which in turn diminishes his confidence in the social realm. To make matters worse, his mother will ask him why he can't be more like his sister. Marie is usually too busy with her own life to say anything but will occasionally try to reassure her mother that John is going through a difficult time and her mother should stop worrying so much. Her mother does not really hear these words and continues to pressure John.

This family also has some key risk and resiliency elements. The family unit has successfully coped with a very difficult time. While the larger family unit separated, Mrs. James and her two children remained together and have developed into a very close unit. Mrs. James clearly loves her children dearly and wishes to protect them. There is evident family cohesion in the relationship between the mother and her two children. The two children are doing well in school. Maria demonstrates considerable social competence and has tried to reassure her mother about John. John will join his friends socially. Both of the children have received the support of counseling to help them deal with the abuse.

In terms of risk factors, both Marie and John were abused by their stepfather when they were younger. Mrs. James experienced the pain of having to deal with this difficult life event. Mrs. James is feeling guilty because she did not protect her children from being abused and is frightened that they might still be bearing scars as a result. As a result, she is pressuring John to act in a certain manner that will reassure her that he does not carry deep scars. Her actions only make John more insecure and he too feels that he is letting his mother down. The communication between the mother and John has become a circle by which the more the mother pressures John to be sociable, the more he retreats from her into his room which in turn only makes his mother more anxious and thus pressures him more. At thirteen, John is developmentally at a difficult age between childhood and adolescence.

From a resiliency perspective, addressing the meanings of these events can help this family. The mother has become so overwhelmed by her own sense of fear and guilt so that she can only see signs of pathology in John (and thus in herself as a parent) rather than the abundant evidence that John has coped quite well. This in turn creates the vicious circle described earlier. Family counseling approaches that enable the mother to reduce her fear and to see signs of appropriate coping by John can be valuable. These signs can represent evidence of her own adequate care of the children and enable her to reduce the pressure that in turn is increasing behavior that intensifies her anxiety.

Solution-focused and narrative family interventions represent approaches that could help this family identify signs of coping and strength within the family. Both approaches help family members identify exceptions to the stated problem and ways in which family members can increase these positive outcomes. Narrative approaches stress reframing life events in terms of strengths. In helping to alter their family story from a problem saturated one to a more positive one, the James family can be helped to claim their identity in terms of survivors.

## SUMMARY

Families bring to the counseling endeavor a variety of risk and protective factors that influence how they are able to cope with their current life circumstances. Using a partnership approach, the counselor helps the family identify their current sources of distress as well as the other factors that are contributing to the risk facing the family. The counselor also searches for protective factors in such a way to identify potential healing resources. Along with structured instruments and visual tools, the interview with the family provides a wealth of information regarding the family. The assessment process is also used to help the family members claim their resources in order to increase the sense of self-efficacy and hope experienced by family members. Based on the assessment process, the counselor identifies intervention models and specific intervention strategies that are appropriate to the family goals and the risk and protective factors facing the family. The assessment process is an ongoing one as new information about the family and their situation emerges or changes occur. The social worker and family members use this new information in the ongoing process of designing and implementing intervention strategies.

# Part II

# Approaches to Social Work Practice with Families

Box 1. Intervention Models

## *SOCIAL LEARNING/COGNITIVE APPROACH TO FAMILY COUNSELING*

*Basic emphasis:* Learning new skills, Performing behavior, Modifying beliefs

*Major tenets:*

Behavior is learned. Individuals learn from their social context how people behave and how others are likely to respond to them.

Behaviors that individuals demonstrate are the product of their learning context.

Belief systems influence the learning and the performance of behavior.

Individuals behave in such a way as to maximize rewards.

Consistent and immediate reinforcement is effective in influencing behavior.

Inconsistent reinforcement is effective in maintaining behavior.

Educating clients about the process of learning and performance and the role of belief systems is valuable.

*Role of the social worker:* Coaches, educates, encourages, helps modify belief systems

## *STRUCTURAL FAMILY THERAPY*

*Basic emphasis:* Creating a more effective family organization

*Major tenets:*

Families are organizations with structural patterns that are important to the lives of the family members.

Symptoms within families are signs of a family under stress.

Assessment and treatment are organized to address the organizational pattern of the family.

Structural dimensions include boundaries, alignment, and power.

The interaction pattern demonstrated by the family in the family session is a critical source of information.

Change occurs through active involvement of family members in alternative behaviors.

The family session is used to enact new behaviors and family change.

*Role of the therapist:* Activist, stage manager—Arranges for families to act out current and potential new scripts to create more effective family structures.

## SOLUTION-FOCUSED FAMILY THERAPY

*Basic Emphasis:* Developing new solutions to problems or activating current possibilities

*Major tenets:*

The emphasis is on the future.

Solutions are unrelated to how problems began, history does not provide the key.

People tend to be locked into negative and pessimistic views of problem and themselves.

People want to change.

People are suggestible.

*Role of the counselor.* Using a not-knowing stance helps family members identify and implement solutions (family is the expert on the problem and the solutions).

## NARRATIVE FAMILY THERAPY

*Basic emphasis:* Transform problem-saturated stories into stories of hope and possibility—"victim to survivor"

*Major tenets:*

Language shapes life experience.

People construct stories that shape life events and how we experience life.

Stories shape what we see and remember.

Social context influences life stories.

The emphasis in treatment is on the stories people create.

It is important to expand life stories—new possibilities for growth and healing.

Families contend with problems—families are not the problem.

*Role of the therapist:* Coedits the family story with the family to help replace their problem-saturated stories with those that offer possibilities for healing and growth.

## *PSYCHOEDUCATIONAL APPROACHES TO FAMILY COUNSELING*

*Basic emphasis:* Enable family members to cope more effectively with illness and other problems facing family members.

*Major tenets:*

Families are the major support system for members with mental health and other types of illnesses.

Family members are partners with the professionals.

Families need the appropriate tools (information about the illness and the skills to deal with it).

Family members need support in dealing with such a difficult life event in the family.

In terms of mental illness, family members are not responsible for causing the illness. Tensions within the family can exacerbate symptoms but the family does not cause the illness. Some of the disruption in the family is in response to the distress created by caring for an ill family member.

Family context and interpersonal relationships have an impact on the illness as well as are influenced by the illness.

Family members can help identify potential signs of response and thus be helpful in preventing serious relapse.

Culture helps define how illness is experienced and the nature of the response of family members.

*Role of the counselor:* Educates and provides support for family dealing with difficult situation.

# MULTISYSTEMS APPROACH TO FAMILY THERAPY

*Basic emphasis:* Enable families to deal with multiple problems by linking with wider support systems and helping families cope more effectively.

*Major tenets:*

Families live in complex multisystems environments that need to be incorporated into the assessment and treatment process.

Family counselors need to use a variety of intervention skills to address families' multiple needs.

Families need to be treated with respect and given decision-making power; they tend to be distrusting of counselor based on prior experience.

This model focuses on the strengths of these already overwhelmed families.

*Role of the family counselor:* Assumes many roles in a flexible manner to create linkages with the external support system and enable family members to cope more effectively.

# OBJECT RELATIONS FAMILY THERAPY

*Basic emphasis:* Address interpersonal relationships issues with roots in earlier life experiences.

*Major tenets:*

Family members bring to their current family the object relations system that was developed during their earlier life experiences.

Individuals project their conscious and unconscious internal object relationships upon the spouse or other family member who in turn can fit and identify with this projection.

Problems in the family occur when family members are unable to separate from these projections and both members of the family are unable to grow as individuals.

The task of the family therapist is to enable the family members to cope with their anxiety and begin to recognize and respond to people in a more open and healthy manner.

Transference and countertransference are important tools in the therapeutic process.

*Role of the family counselor:* Enables family members to cope with anxiety through positive relationship and understanding regarding links between past and current relationships.

# SPIRITUALITY

*Basic emphasis:* Addresses sense of meaning, values, and relationship with transcendence that can be part of many aspects of life.

*Major tenets:*

Not a specific model of treatment but can be incorporated into various treatment models.

Demonstrates respect for the dignity and value of family.

Healing can occur at many levels even if events cannot be changed—issues of meaning and purpose can play important roles.

Client is the expert in their spiritual journey, not the counselor.

Counselor needs self-awareness.

*Role of the counselor:* Opens doors to possible spiritual dimensions. Acts as a partner, not an expert on the client's spiritual journey.

# 5

## *Social Learning/Cognitive Family Counseling*

James Grant had to assume the roles of mother and father for three children (aged seven, eleven, and thirteen) when his wife died in a car accident. Prior to her death his responsibilities had been primarily on weekends because he worked long hours and his wife had the major responsibility for raising the children. The family was not only dealing with the grief of the loss of a wife and mother, but Mr. Grant was floundering in his role as a parent. He vacillated from feeling sorry for the children and thus imposing no limits on them and becoming overly strict when he felt that the situation was getting out of control. The children were further confused by his inconsistency and dealt with this by testing limits further. Discouraged in his role as a parent, he found excuses not to spend time with the children and volunteered to take on extra responsibilities at work. This was a world in which he felt competent. The children responded to his increasingly unavailability by testing him further and seeking attention by negative behaviors. When the thirteen-year-old began to have behavior difficulties at school, the school social worker identified the presence of family problems and referred the family for further counseling. Mr. Grant was both defensive at the implications of failure on his part and relieved that some help might be at hand.

Sarah became a mother at aged fifteen. Her boyfriend ended their relationship when he learned she was pregnant. Although there had been conflict with her parents, she continued to live with them while going to school and taking care of her child. She is now caught between the two worlds of an adolescent mother—trying to establish her separate identity from her parents and trying to learn how to be a parent herself. When her parents try to give her advice or other types of help, she interprets their actions as indicating they think she is still a child and resents their help. As a result, she finds it difficult to accept the help they offer. Her peer group of high school friends is no help in her new role as a parent and do not understand the pressures that she experiences. Sarah has become very discouraged about her ability to take care of her baby and feels overwhelmed by her responsibilities. She confided in the school social worker that while she loves her baby, she wonders if she had made the right decision to keep her baby and fears that she might hurt her child sometime when she becomes frustrated.

Jennifer and Martin's marriage was dissolving in ongoing tension. While they loved each other, they found themselves hurting each other as they tried to talk about the issues in their marriage. Both of them had grown up in conflictual family situations. Each of their parents had argued bitterly for years before finally getting divorced. While Jennifer and Martin desperately wanted something different for themselves, they found themselves repeating the patterns of the parents. Jennifer would withdraw from Martin who in turn would shout at her. The more she withdrew, the more threatened Martin would become and the louder he would shout. Jennifer would then think that Martin did not love her and would withdraw further. Martin in turn interpreted her withdrawal as lack of interest in him and felt further threatened. When they finally sought counseling help for their marriage, they were extremely discouraged about their ability to save their relationship. They feared that they were about to repeat the pattern of their parents and doubted both themselves and their partner's ability to change.

Members of these families are struggling with troubling relationships and difficulties in carrying out their family responsibilities. While motivated to make things different, they find themselves repeating problematic patterns and unable to create effective new patterns. The vicious circle becomes more intense as they become discouraged about their ability to make things better and their efforts fail to make positive changes. In terms of the context of resiliency, these families lack critical coping skills to deal with the situation at hand and interpret their family situations in ways that intensify the problems. Although the family members are motivated to improve their relationships, lack of these skills has intensified the nature of the problems that they are facing and has destroyed their sense of mastery and self-efficacy. Skills and beliefs systems go hand in hand. Family members are also burdened by beliefs that are creating problems within the family. Family members lack a sense of self-efficacy regarding their ability to carry out important tasks and roles within their families and have become discouraged about their ability to do so. They also interpret the behavioral response of others in ways that create further fears and difficulty. These belief systems represent a further burden in the relationship and make it difficult for them to use some of the skills that they currently have. In terms of protective factors, these families have adequate housing and the economic resources to meet their other essential basic needs. They are also motivated to improve their situations. Using a resiliency assessment of these families, a social learning/cognitive approach could be a valuable approach to helping them gain new skills and address their belief systems. It can help them develop a critical sense of mastery and self-efficacy and begin to replace their current dysfunctional belief systems with those that can be more productive within the family.

The social learning approach is essentially an optimistic and strengths-based approach that assumes people are able to learn. The current patterns that one sees in families can be understood in terms of the family members' past and present learning opportunities. The central approach within a social learning perspective is to provide effective learning opportunities that enable family members to learn and implement new coping skills. Family members might need skills, for example, in communicating, in parenting, in dealing with other community members, in addressing employment issues. While social learning approaches have some patterns that are general to the approach, the nature of the appropriate coping skills and reinforcement systems are tailored to the individual family in terms of their culture, the developmental stages of family members, and the many unique characteristics of the family. As a result, the approach can be adapted to people from a wide range of cultural backgrounds and contexts.

Belief systems can constrain people from learning new skills and using the skills they possess. Parents who believe that their children will not pay attention to them are not likely to try to exert their repertoire or discipline skills. Parents who believe that good parents must always have harmonious relationships with their children or fear the loss of their child's love can find it difficult to set appropriate limits. Children quickly learn the art of emotional blackmail of their parents. Partners who believe that if their partner loves them he/she should understand what they are feeling without being told. They might not use their existing communication skills and instead feel hurt and rejected when they are not understood by their partner.

The preceding families demonstrate this interaction of skills and belief systems. James Grant needs to learn more effective parenting skills now that he is a single parent and cannot rely on his wife to assume the major role of raising their children. He also feels so sorry for his grieving children that he is uncomfortable setting limits on his children. He feels defeated in his ability to effectively parent his children as the children push him to become more engaged through negative behavior. He misinterprets their actions and withdraws further. Sarah needs to learn the skills of parenting a young child as well as balancing her responsibilities as parent and student. She interprets her parents' offers of help in this realistically difficult situation as a message that they view her as still a child. As a result, she rebuffs what might be valuable help and feels even more alone in her situation. Jennifer and Martin need to learn the skills of communicating and facilitating a mutual relationship. Each interprets the actions of the partner as lack of love and responds in ways that only compound the misunderstandings and hurt.

## *THEORETICAL BACKGROUND*

Social learning approaches developed from behavioral traditions that emphasized the role of contingencies in maintaining behavior. From the perspective of operant conditioning, voluntary behavior is shaped by the consequences of this behavior. Change is organized in terms of changing the nature of responses to behavior. Reinforcement increases behavior; punishment or extinction (not responding) tends to decrease behavior.

In terms of family counseling, the social worker conducts a *functional analysis* of the behavior to identify the immediate antecedents (what occurs prior to) and the consequences (what occurs as a result of) the problem behavior. Parents might be asked to identify what was taking place when their child started sulking and what consequences followed this behavior. The consequences frequently become *reinforcers* that serve to maintain the behavior. In this process, parents could identify that they were perhaps inconsistent or in some way gave in to the child in ways that only perpetuated the behavior. They might be going to great lengths to find something that would make the child happy again and stop sulking and thus be inadvertently encouraging (*positive reinforcement*) the very behavior that they were trying to eliminate. Parents often engage in *intermittent reinforcement*—sometimes giving in and other times remaining firm. Behavior that has been reinforced in this manner is the most difficult to change. Using the results of this behavioral analysis, parents might be encouraged to alter their reinforcement system to reduce the nature of the difficult behavior. This model of working with families has been an important element in parental education programs as well as work with individual families.

The behavioral model identifies a set of responses that influence the frequency of behavior. As indicated above, positive reinforcements are responses that encourage behavior to occur more frequently. *Negative reinforcements* also increase behavior when a specific behavior results in the termination of something aversive. These two types of response are frequently paired. The common situation of parents and children at the checkout counter represents this duet. When parents finally give in to the child's whining and buy candy, they are positively reinforcing the child's whining behavior. The child in turn negatively reinforces the parents by stopping the whining when the parents hand over the candy. Both parties are reinforcing the other for their part in the duet. Responses that decrease behavior are called *punishment*.

Behavior is influenced most quickly if the response occurs shortly after the behavior and is consistent. It is most difficult to change behavior if the reinforcement system is intermittent. People continue to put coins in to the slot machine in hopes that the next coin will produce a larger payoff.

*Extinction* occurs when there is no reinforcement for the behavior. Since the individual involved frequently escalates the intensity of the behavior at first in hopes of gaining the desired goal, extinction does not result in an immediate decrease in behavior (Jordan, Cobb, & Franklin, 1999). If parents finally give in to these louder demands, they inadvertently set in motion an intermittent reinforcement system.

The nature of these reinforcers is also idiosyncratic to the individuals and context involved. Over the years my children and I have frequently had very different sets of reinforcements in terms of music. While music by Bach might be a positive reinforcement for one person, heavy metal music might work for another.

Stuart transferred this nature of behavioral reciprocity to work with couples using contingency contracting (Goldenberg & Goldenberg, 2000; Nichols & Schwartz, 2001). Stuart focused on developing and enhancing positive behaviors by applying a "reciprocity reinforcement paradigm" (Nichols & Schwartz, 2001, p. 267). Within this arrangement, couples would identify a positive behavior that they would like to occur, record the frequency of the behavior, and identify and exchange positive responses.

## *Social Learning Paradigms*

Bandura and colleagues identify how current behavior is not only shaped by the actual reinforcers but also by social context and cognitions, especially the person's expectations for such responses (Bandura, 1977, 1978). They also describe how complex behaviors are learned through the process of *modeling.* Individuals learn new behavior from others who demonstrate (model) this behavior. Models are especially likely to be emulated if these models are perceived as successful and their behavior is followed by positive consequences. If models are also viewed as similar they serve as especially effective models (Bandura, 1977). Younger siblings mimicking older brothers and sisters is an example of this pattern.

As a result of this broadened perspective, social learning focuses on the triad of learning *opportunities,* the *reinforcement systems* at work, and the *thoughts* of individuals that influence the nature of the behavior that is learned and the actual practice of adaptive or maladaptive behavior patterns. Cultural and unique individual life experiences shape relevant beliefs, learning opportunities, and anticipated rewards. Expectations regarding the impact of behavior are critical in the actual performance of behavior. If people believe that they are able to carry out a specific behavior (self-efficacy) and will be positively rewarded for this behavior, they are more likely to act in this manner. As described in the above situations, the thoughts and consequent interpretations of the family members in the previously described family situations play critical roles in the behaviors of family members. Mr. Grant does not feel confident in his parenting and withdraws from his children. His beliefs about the impact of the death of his wife and their mother further make it difficult for him to discipline the children. Sarah's interpretation of her parents' actions in the context of her own developmental journey causes her to rebuffs her parents' often well-meant and potentially helpful advice. Mr. and Mrs. W's relationship is caught in a vicious circle of withdrawal and pressure that leads both of them to become discouraged about their relationship and thus to further withdraw and pressure.

The family context provides a critical learning environment. Children learn the myriad of behaviors that are necessary for their life as children as well as for adult responsibilities. They emulate their parents and their siblings as well as relevant extended family members. They watch how parents deal with older siblings and thus they learn how to deal with conflict and to communicate their wishes in effective ways. They learn patterns of violence or verbal negotiation. They learn to expect certain responses from others for their behaviors. They learn what is valued in their family context. As children become older, their models become part of their wider context of peers, neighborhood, school, and the media. As a result, family members who come for help represent a wide array of learning opportunities in their current and past relationships and belief systems that are relevant to their situation.

As people begin to believe that they can carry out various tasks effectively, they develop a sense of self-efficacy in this area. Parents who experience success in helping a child learn a new skill develop a sense of self-efficacy in the area of teaching their children. Parents who do not experience children as being responsive to their efforts to enforce limits begin to doubt their self-efficacy as parents in this area. *Reciprocal determinism*—the concept that individuals both influence their environment and are in turn influenced by it—represents another important concept relevant to family life (Jordan, Cobb, & Franklin, 1999).

### *Cognitive Therapy Paradigm*

Cognitive therapists have traditionally looked at the patterns of belief systems of family members as well as specific responses to individual situations. As described in the work of Hill in chapter 1, McCubbin and McCubbin (1996), and Beck (1976), these underlying belief systems (variously called paradigms, schemas, core beliefs) influence how family members view the world, themselves, and the family and thus shape the families' thoughts and behaviors in individual situations. These beliefs are shaped by the family origin as well as ongoing events within the life of the family. Cultural patterns profoundly influence these schemas. These schemas in turn influence the types of help that are valued or viewed as demeaning. Families with core beliefs that "You cannot trust anyone who is not family" would have great difficulty seeking supports beyond the family circle and would be very guarded if referred for counseling. Beliefs about what is appropriate behavior for men or women influence family options and probably played a role in the current problem facing James Grant. Life cycle development also shapes beliefs and makes it especially difficult for Sarah to accept help from her parents. Helping family members identify these core beliefs, how they are affecting what is occurring currently, and examining their validity in the current situation can enable family members to adopt more effective ways of interpreting the world and behaving accordingly.

## SOCIAL LEARNING/COGNITIVE THEORY MAJOR TENETS

From a family perspective, a social learning/cognitive approach has several key tenets that guide the assessment and intervention process. These tenets address both the process by which behavior is learned and the motivation system that influences which behaviors will be demonstrated in a specific setting. They include both cognitions and behaviors.

1. Behavior is learned. Individuals learn from their social context how people behave and how others are likely to respond to them.

2. The behaviors that people demonstrate are the product of their learning context.

3. Belief systems influence the learning and the performance of behavior.

4. Individuals behave in such a way as to maximize rewards. As a result, they anticipate that the behaviors they demonstrate will accomplish this for them (based on their experience either personally or in terms of the models in their life setting—vicarious reinforcement). As a result, behavior is logical within the context of this learning experience and the current cognitions of the individuals.

5. Consistent and immediate reinforcement is effective in influencing behavior. Inconsistent reinforcement is effective in maintaining behavior.

6. Educating clients about the process of learning and performance and the role of belief systems is valuable.

These tenets shape the social learning/cognitive assessment and treatment approach with families. If individuals can learn one set of behaviors, they can learn others that are more effective in addressing their current situation. If people act in such a way as to maximize pleasure, then it is important to understand the context and their expectations. If people continue to act in ways that would appear to have a negative impact on their lives, is it because they lack more positive ways to behave? Do they fail to anticipate the negative impact due to earlier learning experiences or are seemingly negative responses in reality positive for the person involved? What role are expectations and other cognitions playing in behavior that might otherwise seem self-defeating or having negative consequences? Children, for example, have been known to prod parents into yelling at them because being yelled at may be better than being ignored. People sometimes continue in abusive relationships because they fear the alternatives.

## GOALS OF TREATMENT

The goals of the social learning/cognitive model are to enable families to meet the needs of members and to cope more effectively. Based on a paradigm that includes skills and motivation, the model seeks to promote family functioning by helping family members learn appropriate skills, promoting a motivation system that encourages family members to perform behaviors that meet the needs of family members, and addressing the belief systems that foster effective behaviors by family members. While the model includes interventions with negative behaviors and belief systems, the focus is on promoting positive changes.

## ROLE OF THE FAMILY COUNSELOR

In the social learning approach the role of the family counselor can be viewed as that of a coach. An effective coach helps individuals learn new behavior through modeling and other forms of instruction, provides opportunities for practice, offers feedback regarding the nature of the performance, and motivates individuals to learn and persist in the process of improving their performance through encouragement or other ways to promote positive cognitions. Since family members frequently do not understand the process by which behavior is learned and performed and the role of their belief systems, the social worker as coach helps educate family members about these important aspects.

Horne and Sayger (2000) stress the critical role played by the counselor's attitudes toward the family members on the therapeutic relationship. It is important that the counselor hold to the belief that each member of the family is "doing the best he or she can given the circumstances of that person and given the previous learning experiences that person encountered" (p. 472).

Viewed through the lens of resiliency, the family counselor provides a model of the new skills required and helps family members carry out these new skills. The counselor might serve as the model personally or identify other models in the life space of the family members. The counselor arranges for family members to have the opportunity to practice these skills in the counseling session and uses these occasions to give corrective feedback to ensure success. The counselor helps the family members identify ways that they can practice these skills in other settings to facilitate the process of generalization. The counselor encourages family members in terms of their ability to learn and the progress that they making. The family counselor helps family members identify and alter cognitions in ways that promote the family functioning. In the process the family members develop the critical skills needed to address their family situation and gain an appropriate sense of self-efficacy. For James Grant this means learning ways to parent his three children without vacillating between setting no limits and being overly strict. It means addressing some of his cognitions that prevent him from being an effective parent. It means gaining increased confidence in his ability to parent his children so that he does not have to retreat from parenting to the world of work where he views himself as successful. For Sarah it means learning how to parent her baby while balancing her own needs as a teenager. It also might mean learning ways to communicate more effectively with her parents. In the process Sarah can begin to accept the help her parents could give her and to view this help in rewarding rather than in negative terms. It might also mean working with the parents to help them understand Sarah's perspective and to offer their help in ways that might be more acceptable to her. For Jennifer and Martin it means learning new ways to communicate in their marriage so they do not continue to destroy their love for each other by their learned patterns of retreat and attack. It means beginning to learn to trust each other and their relationship.

### *Assessment*

The assessment process from a social learning/cognitive perspective includes identifying issues in the following areas: skills, motivation system, signaling system, and belief system. Difficulties can arise in any of these areas and the nature of the intervention differs depending on this assessment.

*Skills.* Family members or the family unit can lack the essential skills needed to address family issues within their current context and stage of development. These issues might include how to parent a toddler or a teenager, how to manage money, how to communicate with a partner, how to negotiate with extended family members, how to deal with a new culture, and how to adjust to changes in family roles due to illness or other major shifts, as well as various other family issues. Sarah and James Grant both struggle with lack of skills to parent their respective children. Jennifer and Martin's pain arises from their lack of skills in communicating with their partners.

As described previously, family members have typically learned their skills from past experiences; however, they might have had role models that were not appropriate for their current circumstances. What did they learn that could help in raising teenagers in the current world, in coping with circumstances in which the wife is the major wage earner, in dealing with the give and take of marriage, in caring for children as a single parent, in communicating between parents? While their previous models might have demonstrated coping skills that were effective within this context, families can be facing a disjuncture between these previous contexts and their current life. This can be especially critical for families that have moved from one culture to another (families in cultural transitions). In the rapidly changing world in which people move from community to community and the wider social context changes, such a disjuncture can be experienced by many families.

*Motivation system.* There can be a problem in the motivation system for the family or members of the family. Cognitions play an important role here because motivation is related to the perceived reward system within the family and the larger context. In terms of the parent-child relationship world, a child might know what to do but lacks the motivation to do it because the child gets more attention for misbehavior than for listening (a parent's version of punishment might thus be a positive reinforcement for the child). A parent might be reinforced by the child to just let things slide because the fight to get the child to listen is just not worth the effort given the other demands on one's time and energy. A parent might be stymied by a child's emotional blackmail "I hate you; my friend's parents are nice and you are mean." Another parent might give up on setting limits because the child tests extinction by pushing the limits harder. Parents might be setting opposite reinforcements in place—what the mother praises the father devalues and vice versa. Lack of self-efficacy can contribute to a person's difficulty in acting in an effective manner.

Cultural context is important in this reinforcement system. Family members who come from cultures in which extended family or relational issues are valued more than individual accomplishments might make choices that seem lacking in responsibility or ambition from the perspective of a more individualistic counselor. Another issue relates to the nature of the reinforcements within the current cultural setting. People in cultural transition situations frequently live with cultural messages of what one should do (for example, care for older family members) but without the supports that enable one to carry these behaviors out in their current cultural context. Couples can experience tension if they come from different cultural contexts and expect behavior to be rewarded accordingly. Parents also must contend with powerful cultural messages from the media and the community that contradict family values. While parents might, for example, value academic achievement, the peer group of a teenager might place its value of athletic prowess.

*Signaling system.* There can be ambiguity in the current signaling system. People not only need to be able to carry out a certain behavior and be motivated to do so, they also need to be aware when such behavior is appropriate and required. Parents frequently stress this by saying words like "I mean it now" as a signal that the parent is serious about what he or she is saying. Parents and teenagers often end up in arguments because the parents and the teenager interpret words like "don't be late" in very different ways. Children who have done well in structured situations with clear behavior clues often slip back into old ways of acting without the presence of these structural clues. As a result, helping parents develop clearer signals can be an important intervention.

*Belief system.* There can the problems and distortions in the belief system (cognitive part of the system) that in turn impede proper responses. The interaction between beliefs and the behavioral interaction between family members is often a cyclical one. A parent whose self-talk is "It doesn't do any good to tell the children what to do because they won't do it anyway" is not likely to assert one's self in an effective manner with the children. The

children's disregard in turn only reinforces this belief system and further discourages the parent from acting in an effective manner. The individual who
thinks that it doesn't do any good to tell the partner something because he
or she wouldn't listen or care is not likely to communicate these wishes to
the partner. Again, this individual is not likely to respond in an effective way
and the partner's anticipated lack of response becomes a perceived reality.

The assessment process is a joint one with the social worker and the
family members. Family members are encouraged to identify patterns to
help them understand what is taking place. Tracking sequences of behavior
can give important new insights. Parents, for example, can chart the patterns
of what is occurring prior (A = antecedent) to a child's specific behavior
(B = behavior) and the nature of the consequences (C = consequences).
These categories can include belief systems as well as actions. They might
discover that the child's whining occurs when the child is hungry or tired,
or perhaps when the parents are busy with another child or other family responsibilities. They might learn ways in which they have been inadvertently
reinforcing the behavior by redirecting their attention from the other children
to this child in response to the whining and ignoring the child when he or
she is behaving appropriately. Family members can recognize that their beliefs are triggering issues or maintaining certain behaviors. In counseling
families, it is common for family members to be surprised at the thoughts
evoked in each of the family members and how these belief systems are
pushing them farther apart. Understanding these behavioral and cognitive
patterns gives clues to the solution. Family members need to be involved
in the development of these tracking systems with an emphasis on trying to
make them as simple as possible. If they are too complex and difficult for
the family to carry it out, family members can become discouraged by the
process and be viewed by their family counselor as resistant to change.

Including the family members as partners in the assessment process
serves several purposes. First, they are in a unique position to identify what
is taking place within the family context. Second, they are learning an important skill of identifying family patterns that can stand them in good stead
in addressing future problems. Third, the experience of identifying patterns
helps them in developing a sense of mastery that encourages family members in the process of change. Family members are helped to gain a sense
of ownership over the nature of the problem and possible solutions.

## TREATMENT PROCESS

The following represent important steps and principles in the intervention
process.

**Build intervention efforts on the identified nature of the problem.**
If the social worker addresses motivation, for example, but family members
lack the necessary skills, the result will only be frustration for all concerned.

**Identify positive changes.** Families typically come for help because they want to change something wrong with their family or its members or because some outside party wants them to make these changes. As a result, the emphasis is upon something negative to eliminate. Families can easily spend the entire session complaining about what the other family members are doing wrong. One of the first steps in the counseling process is to help family members begin to think in terms of what are the positive changes that they want. Goals and the steps to reach them must be positive and clear in their direction. This step can be difficult for some families at first because they have become locked into their negative patterns and have not been able to envision other approaches.

Positive changes can give a meaningful direction to the efforts of family members. Parents, for example, can shift from "He has to get rid of that attitude" to "I want him to show a sense of responsibility by helping with the dishes without complaining." Sarah can identify ways that her parents can help her without making her feel that they are putting her down. Jennifer and Martin can identify something positive that they would like from the other one. As family members are helped to identify some positive actions, the counselor can help assess what further skills are needed to accomplish these changes and what reinforcement systems the family might put in place to encourage these positive steps.

**Strategize for success.** Family members usually come for counseling feeling defeated in their efforts for change. As a result, it is important for the counselor to help the family members identify changes that are realistic and can really be carried out. The counselor can problem solve with family members about what small behavior would be realistic as a beginning step, ways to identify if it has taken place, and how to reinforce this positive change. By breaking down changes into understandable and manageable steps, the family is more likely to experience success and to gain important self-efficacy. Such an experience of success helps motivate the family members to persist and believe in the possibility of change.

Success is more likely if the identified behavioral steps are specific. "Doing better in school" is open to a multitude of interpretations by parents and their children with the potential for misunderstandings and consequent mistrust. "Raising the grade from a D to a C on the next science test" or "helping by loading the dishwasher after the evening meal" are specific and clearly understood by everyone. In the partnership context, "Showing that you care" is another ambiguous request. Helping partners identify what actions might reflect this, leads to specifics such as "Ask me how it went at work/or with the kids today when you come home," "Read the children a bedtime story so I can get a break," "Sit with me to watch X TV show in the evening," that are understandable to the individuals involved. To be effective, steps must be realistic for the parties involved and the counselor can discuss this issue in the session with family members.

**Educate the family about the learning process.** A knowledgeable partner is a more effective one. Helping family members learn about ways in which behavior is learned and reinforced can give family members the tools to understand their family and to make additional positive changes in other areas and in the future. If parents understand that the first response of children to the process of extinction is to raise the volume of their whining, they will be able to interpret such behavior as a beginning sign of progress rather than the failure of their efforts. This knowledge can help parents persist rather than give in and create an even more entrenched pattern by their intermittent reinforcement.

**Help family members develop needed new skills.** Family members might lack the skills to carry out this positive change. As a result, they will need help in learning and carrying out these new behaviors. The family counselor can use the family session to model the new behaviors and to enable family members to practice them. Jennifer and Martin, for example, have few skills in communicating with each other about troubling issues without their pattern of withdrawal and shouting. The counselor can model beginning steps of stating their views. The counselor then encourages the couple to practice these skills in the session in areas that are manageable for the couple. These practice sessions permit the counselor to give feedback about ways to improve their skills. Without this critical step, Jennifer and Martin are likely to go home and repeat the old troubling patterns and dig the hole of distrust and lack of self-efficacy deeper.

**Build in ways to generalize use of new skills and response patterns.** Homework is a key element in helping people begin to generalize changes from the office setting to the daily life of the family. The social worker can problem solve with the family members ways to practice these new skills in their daily life. James can be helped to begin to make change in his behavior with his children or he and the children can identify steps that each of them will begin making. Sarah can be helped to identify a way she can handle a troubling situation with her baby more effectively. Jennifer and Martin can practice a specific new way of discussing an issue in their marriage.

**Recognize that learning is a process.** People have learned and practiced their current behaviors for many years so that these behavior patterns are well entrenched. Use of these old behavioral patterns is automatic, especially when people are under stress. It also takes time to generalize new behaviors from one setting to another. Family members can become discouraged by their responses or angry with other family members who slip back into old ways of behaving. The social worker can encourage family members to realize that learning and change is a process and thus that relapse into old ways is a normal part of change. They can also be encouraged to see signs of progress—the blowups occurred only three times instead of five times last week or the time of conflict lasted for only half an hour rather than an hour.

Sessions can be used to problem solve with family members the nature of some of the challenges in responding in new ways. These challenges might be in several areas: An individual might still lack some of the skills needed. Motivation might be a factor, perhaps lack of confidence that the new behavior will really work—worry how the other family members will respond (Will the children really listen if I do not threaten to hit them? Will my partner really listen?). Lack of clarity in the signaling system leads to confusion about what behavior is expected. It also takes time to generalize behavior from one setting to another—from the counseling office to the home, and from one aspect of life to another. Jennifer and Martin might find it difficult to transfer their new communication skills to another topic of concern for them. James Grant might find it difficult to transfer his changes in response to the thirteen-year-old to the seven-year-old due to the differences in developmental needs. Based on this assessment, the counselor can both encourage family members that learning and change takes time and identify some of the specific issues facing this family that can be addressed in the counseling setting.

**Help families reinforce positive behavior meaningful for individuals involved.** Family members need to find ways to encourage behavior that is identified as positive in order to help individuals maintain this behavior. If people do not believe (expectancies) that their positive changes will be favorably recognized (positive reinforcement), they will be less likely to continue these behaviors and to make them part of the life of the family. Frequently, troubled families have developed a pattern of negative comments about problematic behavior while positive behavior is ignored. Sometimes family members have grown up in families in which words of praise or other forms of positive recognition were uncommon. There are thus several aspects to altering the reinforcement system depending on the specific family situation. If family members lack role models who have given affirmation, the counselor can serve as a role model for such behavior as well as educate family members about the valuable role of these responses. The counselor can problem solve with family members about the reinforcements that would be meaningful and feasible within this family context and the ways to implement them in the life of the family. This new skill can be practiced within the session as well as in homework opportunities.

**Help family members identify and counter destructive cognitions.** Our belief systems influence whether we expect (expectancies) that it will be worthwhile to act in a certain way. As discussed previously, sometimes our cognitions prevent positive changes from occurring and trap us into self-defeating patterns. Recognizing and addressing some of these cognitions can help people begin to carry out new behaviors. For example, in terms of the discouraged parent who interprets the child's testing behavior as a sign that the child does not care about the parents, this cognition can be recognized and then reframed within a more benign developmental context: "You might be right that your child does not care what you want, or perhaps your child is like all other children that age, they try to test you because in their hearts they want limits. Being a parent at these times can be difficult." This cognition might reflect a more pervasive schema of not feeling valued by others generally. Generalizing the intervention to this larger schema may be useful. When partners begin to make changes, one partner can dismiss this change with a comment that "He/she is just doing this because I asked for it." Sadly neither of the partners experience positive validation through this interchange. Helping people recognize that "doing something because the other person asked for it can be a sign of caring" might be another way of interpreting this new behavior that furthers the healing process. The family can also help in creating these changes. Sarah's parents might be encouraged to phrase their help in ways that can be less threatening to Sarah. Sharing with her their own uncertainty and fears when they were new parents might reduce her thoughts that she is being criticized. They can also comment favorably on things that she is doing in her care of the baby.

Brock and Barnard (1999) describe three keys to success in teaching new behaviors within the context of family counseling. First, The counselor discusses the skill and presents a rationale for learning the skill to the clients. Second, The counselor demonstrates the skill. Third, the clients have the opportunity to practice and receive feedback while performing the skill. (p. 84).

The family therapist needs to explain the nature of the skill, its importance, and how it will benefit family members. Encouraging further discussion between the family members and the counselor regarding the rationale is helpful in obtaining commitment to learning this skill. In the second stage of demonstration, the family therapist must ensure that the modeling gives an accurate picture of what is being taught and the context in which it will be used. Asking clients to explain what they saw you doing and discussing what occurred helps clarify any misunderstandings. The next crucial step is to have family members practice the new skill within the session. This can be difficult for family members not only because it is a new skill but also because the topics involved or the situation can be a highly emotionally charged one.

Brock and Barnard (1999) indicate the importance of having clients begin with situations in which the tension and threat is relatively low and gradually move to more emotionally charged ones. Encouraging feedback is important. The therapist needs to let clients know that they are doing well. When there are problems in the performance, it is useful to stop and determine if there is need for further clarification of the skill that might require another demonstration or if the topic at hand is too emotionally charged to be appropriate at this time.

# APPLICATION

## *Parent-Child Relationship*

Parent-child relationships play important roles in supporting resiliency. As discussed in the earlier chapters, unfortunately external stressors on the family as well as the previous learning experiences of family members can jeopardize these relationships. Issues related to parenting play critical roles in terms of risk and resiliency factors regarding child maltreatment and positive child development. Protective factors include parental competencies in parental roles and related satisfaction in the parenting roles while risk factors involve poor problem solving skills and harsh, inconsistent discipline, and low nurturing skills (Thomlison, 2004).

Horne and Sayger (2003) describe the situation facing many Level II parents as "relying on spanking, lecturing, or grounding to punish children for their behavior. These punishments are typically ineffective, particularly if the parent's authority is not secure or respected" (p. 125). Social learning approaches offer family members opportunities to learn new parenting techniques and strategies to implement them in ways that restore parental authority and respect.

There are several alternative strategies that parents can use to help shape the behavior of their children. These include timeouts, the Premack Principle, natural and logical consequences, assigning extra chores, and loss of privileges.

*Timeouts* involve sending a child to a nonreinforcing environment for an appropriate length of time to gain self-control. This technique provides a way for both the parent and the child to detach from an escalating situation. The length of the timeout is dependent on the age of the child because too long a length of timeouts for very young children quickly loses their sense of meaning. Parents also need to be aware of the potential reinforments present in a setting. Sending a child to a room full of toys or computer games may represent a reward rather than a timeout.

*The Premack Principle* requires children to complete an activity they are less likely to choose before they can do something that they are more likely to choose to do. A child might be required to complete homework or a household chore before playing a video game. Naturally the parent has to ensure that the child has not rushed through homework or the chore at the expense of quality in order to get to the video game.

*Natural and logical consequences* is a means of teaching children that behavior has consequences through experiencing the results of their behavior. The child who impulsively spends his or her allowance on the first day will need to experience waiting until the next week before getting more money. A child who rushes through a task by doing a poor job will have to spend the extra time redoing it and missing out on some desired activity. A teenager who drives recklessly can be denied permission to drive the family car for a period of time.

*Assigning extra chores* involves giving additional task for older children who have violated important rules.

*Loss of privileges* involves taking away privileges that are important for a child (response cost) when the child has violated a family rule. These might involve use of the telephone, the car, or a weekend at a friend's house. As with all parenting techniques, it is important to respond in ways that match the loss of privileges to the severity of the behavior and the developmental stage of the child. If parents impose too severe of punishment, they might later feel the need to recall the punishment (thus undermining their future effectiveness) or generate serious resentment on the part of the child.

*Contingency contracts* is a useful technique for use between parents and older children. "A contract is negotiated wherein each participant specifies who is to do what for whom, under what circumstances, times, and places" (Goldenberg & Goldenberg, 2000, p. 285). The terms of the contract are clear and precise. Description of a contract between an adolescent and parents illustrates this clarity. The contract specifies that if the adolescent earns "a C or better on her weekly quiz," the parents in turn "will give $10.00 toward the purchase of her clothes for that week" (p. 285). As discussed, both sets of statements must be realistic for the parties involved. The contract opens the door to the opportunity for success in this specific interaction and helps build new ways of relating between the parties involved. Each of the parties reinforces the other to carry out their part in the contract. Hopefully the good results of this process generalize to other aspects of the family and thus help the family problem solve and resolve conflicts generally.

Working with families requires more than educating parents about the nature and possibility of these alternative-parenting strategies. Several important interventions can also be necessary. Addressing the belief systems of parents can be crucial. Parents who have grown up with physical punishment as the norm and have relied upon it as their primary means of discipline might be reluctant to try what they view as softer techniques. They might fear losing control of their children, perhaps based on a core belief they will lose control of their children and their children will get into serious trouble if they do not impose such punishments. The social worker may need to address their reservations by explaining the value of these new strategies. It also means helping parents in the actual implementation of these new strategies. Since these are new techniques for parents, it will also be important to discuss ways to implement them given the developmental age of the child and the nature of the infringement. Ineffective implementations of these alternative strategies can reduce their effectiveness and fail to create the important parental authority and respect. A fifteen-minute timeout for a two-year-old can seem like an eternity and quickly loses its meaning. Upset parents can fall into the trap of creating overly harsh responses, for example, a loss of privileges for a month. After the parents have cooled off, they might rethink their actions. They are then caught between being inconsistent and or unrealistic. Parents can frantically try a series of responses ("We have tried everything") without being consistent in their application. As a result, helping parents create realistic arrangements and ways to implement them consistently are important parts of the skill development with parents. Parents can also be helped to understand that the emphasis needs to be on positively reinforcing what the child is doing right rather than merely deterring negative behavior. Parents who might fear losing the love of their children or at least alienating them might be reluctant to set limits that cause the child to become angry and say hurtful comments. Children quickly learn the power of words like "I hate you, you're not my friend" as well as the silent treatment. Parents need encouragement and positive recognition from the counselor for their own efforts to implement alternative parenting techniques. The family counselor needs to recognize small steps toward this goal. It is also important to look at the support systems available to parents and other family members as they seek to implement new ways of behaving. James Grant, for example, might find a grief support group of other single parents who are facing some of the same issues that he is. Parents who find themselves being blackmailed by their children might be able to benefit from a parent support group to receive support from other parents and to realize that others parents are also facing this challenge.

### *Communication Skills*

Communication skills are important in supporting family resiliency as ways to problem solve and create emotionally affirming relationships within the family. Many of the families who seek help have experienced a breakdown in communication between family members. Family members often report that they are not listened to or are misunderstood. The situation escalates and erodes the sense of trust within the family. As Jennifer and Martin illustrate, frequently family members misinterpret what is said or not said in ways that increases hurt. As a result, helping family members identify and develop valuable communication skills can be an important step in restoring family relationships and promoting resiliency. Again, this process requires assessing the current skill levels of family members as well as their expectancies. If family members do not believe that other family members want to hear from them, they are unlikely to invest themselves in these efforts and addressing these belief systems is important. The counseling session is an important venue for teaching family members about communication strategies, identifying problems in the communication sequence, and giving useful feedback. By asking family members to carry out these activities in the session, the counselor can identify verbal and nonverbal messages and problems that impede the communication process. For example, while a family member might ask in the session why his partner does not believe that he is listening, observing him turning his eyes up the ceiling while she talks gives an important clue to her reaction. The counselor might also discover that a parent states an expectation of children in such a tentative and hesitant way that it is very clear why the children do not follow these instructions and the parent feels devalued. As described earlier, such behavior reflects skills as well as belief systems.

Horne and Sayger (2003) describe the following steps in the communication process.

1.  Speak your piece. Individuals must express their own thoughts rather than expecting others to understand their thoughts.

2.  Find out what others are thinking. Family members are encouraged to ask others what they are thinking rather than making assumptions. Frequently in counseling situations, partners are surprised to learn what the other person was really thinking because it was far different from what they had assumed.

3.  Show others that they are being heard. Demonstrate through words, eye contact, or other culturally appropriate behaviors that one is listening and hearing what is being said.

4.  Ask questions when confused. Ask for clarification when family members are uncertain rather than making assumptions.

5.  Stop and let others know when communication is breaking down. When the discussion begins to escalate with the danger of hurt statements, it is important to ask to stop the interaction and wait for a calmer moment. (pp. 125–126)

The social worker can model these behaviors and then problem solve with the parties involved ways to implement them regarding a specific topic. Family members can be praised for changes that they are making as well as helped to identify behaviors that continue to disrupt communication. The social worker and the family members can also problem solve ways to implement these changes within the home context and possible challenges in doing so. Using the principle of strategizing for success and beginning with small realistic steps, they can identify issues that are realistic to communicate about using these new techniques and other issues that might be too explosive to tackle without the presence of the counselor at this point in time.

Anger control can play an important role in family communication, especially if angry comments have escalated and created major conflicts. Jordan, Cobb, and Franklin (1999) describe a sequence of steps to help families learn to reduce these negative interaction. The first step in this process is to educate family members about the nature of anger and ways in which anger can escalate through the family system through the interaction among the family members. The next step is to engage family members in agreeing upon another way to deal with handling these angry interactions. Family members must be willing to recognize when the situation is escalating. When this occurs, family members agree to give each other a sign agreeable to all that indicates "I am getting too angry to continue this discussion and I need a break and cool off" (p. 81). The discussion then stops for a period of time but resumes again later enabling the family to resolve the issue. The request for the timeout occurs again if needed while the family works on the issue at hand. Family members learn new skills of handling conflict with the accompanying sense of being able to control anger within the family (Jordan, Cobb, & Franklin, 1999).

## *Problem Solving*

The ability to problem solve is a critical aspect of resiliency. Problem solving requires family members to assess the problem facing them and to identify possible steps that can help resolve it. Gaps in the problem-solving process can create further difficulties within the family and relationships with the external world. Within the social learning approach, the social worker can help family members problem solve more effectively by modeling more effective problem-solving skills or helping family members carry out these steps in addressing a specific problem facing the family.

Family members might lack skills in problem solving generally or demonstrate this ability in some contexts, but lack specific skills pertinent to the family situation. James Grant demonstrated effective problem-solving skills at work but lacked critical ones in the area of parenting. Sarah might have good problem-solving skills in terms of dealing with her girl friends, but feels lost in her parent role. A further assessment of Jennifer and Martin might have revealed problem-solving skills in other areas of life that were not being tapped in their marital relationship. Using a strengths-based perspective, the social worker can help family members identify ways they are solving problems effectively in other areas of life and possible ways that they can transfer these skills to the family arena. This approach helps build an important sense of self-efficacy as well as improving family problem-solving skills.

Horne and Sayger (2003) identify four key questions to help families guide their problem-solving efforts.

1. What is your goal? What would you like to see happen?
2. What are you doing to achieve this goal?
3. Is what you are doing helping you achieve this goal?
4. If not, what are you going to do differently? (p. 127).

These questions can help family members identify the steps in generating and evaluating possible alternatives to reaching family goals. It also helps translates problems (negative) into goals (positive).

## EVALUATION

The social learning/cognitive approach represents opportunities that enable family members to develop more effective coping strategies and relate to each other in more positive ways. Jordan, Cobb, and Franklin (1999) reviewed the literature on family counseling derived from behavioral learning principles and found them to be effective in addressing parent-child and marital issues. Increasing communication skills has been one of the most effective aspects of couple therapy (Nichols & Schwartz, 2001). Parent-child issues have also responded well to programs combining cognitive and behavior components (Jordan, Cobb, & Franklin, 1999, p. 91). Parental education has emerged as helpful for the targeted behavior but as having less impact on other behaviors, thus suggesting limitations in generalizability (Nichols & Schwartz, 2001). While parental education has demonstrated effectiveness in addressing conduct disorders with children, families with many risk factors show less improvement than do families with fewer risk factors. Length of treatment (especially more than ten sessions) and the therapist's knowledge of social learning principles and skills were also associated with increased effectiveness of this approach (Sexton, Robbins, Hollimon, Mease, & Mayorga, 2003).

## SUMMARY

The social learning/cognitive approach to counseling with families can be effective in helping families learn and practice new skills and alter belief systems that contribute to dysfunctional patterns within families. The approach is strength-based in that it assumes that people are able to learn more productive patterns of behavior. The counselor acts in the role of a coach helping families learn and practice behaviors that are adaptive and identifying and altering belief systems. The implementation of the model is tailored to the unique circumstances and cultural context of the families involved.

# 6

## Structural Family Therapy

Alicia and Matt were discouraged with their family life. They felt beaten down in their role as parents. Their three boys, aged five, eight, and twelve, had clearly gained the upper hand in the house. The family was in turmoil. When Alicia and Matt would shout at the boys to try to get them to behave, the boys typically would not listen to them. Alicia and Matt would throw up their hands in despair and walk away or turn on the TV louder to drown out the sound of the boys' fighting. When things got too bad, they would order the boys to their rooms but would quickly give in when the boys began to cry or shout at them. Alicia and Matt would argue about which parent was to blame for what had gone wrong. Matt had grown up in a family in which his father was clearly in charge, almost to an abusive manner and Matt wanted his children to feel closer to him rather to fear him as he had feared his father. Alicia's father had left when she was a small child and she had grown up very close to her mother. She had felt responsible for taking care of her mother and had never really challenged her own mother. She feels overwhelmed by her boys who are constantly testing their parents. Out of their frustration, Matt and Alicia are constantly criticizing each other in their handling of the boys. They are especially frustrated with their twelve-year-old son who they feel is modeling defiant behavior that the younger boys are imitating. They are not sure how to regain their parental leadership and end up blaming each other for not making this possible. When the family finally contacted the local center for help, the parents indicated that they no longer felt in control of the family and were trying to find some way to restore their parental leadership.

From a resiliency perspective, this family has important protective factors including an adequate financial basis, a safe home, and a sense of commitment to the family. The parents are motivated to maintain their family but their lack of effective leadership skills have left them overwhelmed in trying to establish their sense authority in this family. Their earlier life models did not provide them with the opportunities to learn parenting skills that would be effective in their current situation. The parents almost abdicated their authority to the children who in turn continue to push their parents by testing whatever limits the parents still attempt to set. The situation escalates as the children's efforts to search out and test the limits create further turmoil while the parents' inability to establish leadership contributes to the boys' difficult behavior.

Valerie is a single parent of three children, a girl aged five, a boy seven, and a boy thirteen. She seeks help because she is feeling overwhelmed by the boys, especially her thirteen-year-old son, who has started to increasingly ignore her instructions. She fears that he will also start getting in more difficulty in school if the problem gets worse. Valerie and the boys' father were never married and he left the family three years ago. He has no contact with the family and only pays child support when forced do so by the court. Valerie works as a health aid at the local hospital. Her income is adequate to meet the basic needs of the family but not enough for any extras. She has several sisters and brothers in the community and spends time with them on a regular basis. They also have school-age children. Valerie attends her local church when she can (her work requires her to work some Sundays). During the session, the social worker notices that Valerie's tone of voice varies from angry to resigned when her older son speaks in a defiant manner to her or ignores what she is saying to him. She speaks with greater confidence with the two younger children, especially the daughter. She describes many effective parenting tools that she has learned and used in the past. In an exhausted manner, she indicates that she is very tired from her long hours at work and feels so discouraged with her son that she finds herself often not trying and just letting things slide. She fears that the other children will soon start following in his path.

Valerie loves her children but finds it difficult to be an effective leader in this family. While Valerie has a knowledge of effective parenting skills and is able to use them more consistently with the youngest child, she has become so tired and discouraged that she is no longer able to assert herself as an effective family leader with her oldest child. The family is experiencing a vicious cycle because the more Valerie becomes resigned to this situation, the more her son disregards her authority, and thus the more Valerie becomes discouraged about the family situation and her ability to create order. This pattern is also beginning with the middle child. In addition to Valerie's knowledge of parenting skills, this family also has other important resources. Valerie is a capable worker who earns at least an adequate salary. The father could potentially be required to pay additional child support. The family has an extended family that lives nearby and plays a regular part in their lives that offers them emotional and social support. The family members attend church when they are able to do so and thus have spiritual support and the potential support of the church members.

Structural family therapy can be a viable option for families like Alicia and Matt and Valerie and their children where an effective leadership structure is currently lacking. Discussed earlier, effective family leadership represents an important factor that contributes to resiliency and lack of such leadership is a risk factor. Effective leadership enables family members to meet the myriad needs of family members occasioned by external circumstances and family development stages. Helping families develop appropriate leadership skills can be extremely important for families in which the leadership structure is ineffective and needs strengthening.

Structural family therapy is an important model of family therapy that looks at the family as an organizational structure with the goal of helping the family create a structure that can more effectively meet the needs of family members. The emphasis in structural family therapy is on the organization of the family, the reccuring behavioral patterns that reflect the organizational structure of the family. Symptoms in families are a reflection of the stress and strain experienced by the family. The role of the family therapist is to help the family experience and establish more effective organizational structures by means of a series of active interventions. The family therapist focuses on the healing capacities of the family to transform its organizational structure and view of the family reality (Minuchin & Fishman, 1981).

## THEORETICAL BACKGROUND

Structural family therapy began with Salvador Minuchin and his work with the boys at Wiltwyck School and their families who came primarily from poor areas. These families were typically headed by single mothers who were overwhelmed by their lives. The role of fathers in the lives of the boys was frequently minimal. "The youngsters themselves did not have a clear sense of family rules, hierarchy of authority, or whom to depend on within the family for help with life. The model sought to bring effective organization to the family so that its members could find better solutions to their problems" (Aponte, 2003, p. 104). Based on his experience with these families, Minuchin developed a treatment strategy that was action oriented and relied heavily on engagement (enlisting families to bring their family behavioral sequences into the therapy session). The focus was on using the active role of the therapist in this setting to alter the structure and related interaction patterns of family members (Aponte, 2003; Minuchin & Fishman, 1981; Minuchin & Nichols, 1993).

Minuchin was joined by colleagues who helped to develop the clinical strategies and organizations in which structural family was developed and implemented. From its origin in the 1970s, it has developed into a widely used and highly regarded form of family therapy whose value has been recognized as applying to families facing an array of problems. Given the context of the early families treated, structural family therapy has also looked at the social environments of families. Recognizing that spirituality can be a resource for demoralized families, Aponte (2003) recently expanded the model to incorporate ideas of values and spirituality.

## MAJOR TENETS

Structural family therapy is based on six tenets.

1.  Families are organizations with structural patterns that are important to the lives of the family members.

2. Symptoms within families are signs of a family under stress (Minuchin & Fishman, 1981).

3. Understanding the organizational patterns of families as they relate to the problem at hand is essential to the assessment and treatment process. Families include subsystems. The three basic structural dimensions of families include (Aponte, 2003):

   Boundaries. Who is in or out of a family relationship vis-à-vis the focal issue, as well as what their roles are in this interaction

   Alignment. Who is with or against the others in the transactions generating the problem

   Power. What is the relative influence of the participants in the interactions that create the problem

   Triangulation can be a destructive form of alignment within families when family members with greater power compete for the alignment of a family member with lesser power. The family member with less power is really not in a position to refuse to play a role in this part of the family dance. Parents who are in conflict can seek to align one of the children on their side so the child is forced to choose between one of the parents and does not feel that he can opt out of this arrangement (Minuchin, 1974).

4. The interaction pattern demonstrated by the family in the family session is a critical source of information and more reliable than a family member's self-reports.

5. Change occurs through active involvement of family members in alternative behaviors.

6. The family session is used to enact new behaviors and family change

## GOALS OF TREATMENT

The goal of structural family therapy is to change the structure of the family in order to enable family members to "free the symptom bearer of symptoms, to reduce conflict and stress for the entire family, and to learn new ways of coping" (Minuchin & Fishman, 1981, p. 29). In order to respond to internal or external demands on the family, these changes can include developing a more effective leadership subsystem, reducing overly enmeshed family patterns, or encouraging closer relationships among family members. By using an active approach, structural family therapy also seeks to change the family's view of reality regarding its members and context and thus create opportunities for new behavior and family structures.

# ROLE OF THE THERAPIST

With the goal of changing the structure of the family, the family therapist plays a very active role in joining with family members and enabling family members to experience new patterns of behavior. The therapist's active involvement in the family serves as the basis for the assessment process as well as for the interventions. The therapist joins the family dance (interaction patterns) but creates new patterns in this process. The therapist sets in motion new patterns of behavior by family members through active use of the therapist's self. The family therapist in many ways acts as stage manager with the family—arranging for family members to act out their current and potential new roles. This role is critical because active engagement of family members in their changed behavior in the therapy session is a key element in structural family therapy.

To be effective, the family therapist must first join with the entire family so that the family members will trust that the therapist is "working with and for them" (Minuchin & Fishman, 1981, p. 32). In order to join the family in an effective manner, the therapist needs to be sensitive to the culture of the family (Minuchin, 1981). Culture here refers to the unique patterns of this family as well as to membership in a specific cultural group. Is this a family that tends to understate, or to express thoughts in a dramatic manner, or to rely on silence? The therapist in turn adapts one's manner to this manner of communication. The therapist imitates the family in some key ways to solidify the therapeutic alliance. The therapist activates parts of the self that facilitate the joining process. This can occur through sharing aspects of the therapist's life that link with the family (e.g., a shared enthusiasm for soccer or music) or assuming behavioral patterns that reflect the family. The therapist also identifies strengths within the family and uses confirming statements regarding members of the family. The therapist enables family members to feel that the therapist understands them and looks for strengths within the family. While joining the family system, the therapist also remains an outsider and thus has the freedom to respond in different ways that challenge the family's typical interaction patterns.

## Assessment Process

Assessment and joining of the family are intricately linked in structural family therapy. The therapist observes the family's organizational pattern during the sessions. As a participant in the system, the family therapist experiences the family and uses this information in the assessment process of the family's functioning. The family therapist attempts to create a map of the family that identifies the positions that family members take in terms of other family members. "This map reveals coalitions, affiliations, explicit and implicit conflicts, and the way family members group themselves in conflict resolution. It identifies family members who operate as detourers of conflict and family members who function as switchboards. The map charts the nurturers, healers, and scapegoats" (Minuchin & Fishman, 1981, p. 69).

In this process, the family therapist identifies possible areas of strength or dysfunction in the family. For example, as the social worker joins with Alicia and Matt and their boys, the worker sees how the parents view themselves as unable to exert control over their boys. The social worker can also observe how the boys have mastered the divide and conquer strategy so that they Alicia and Matt end up undermining the efforts of the other parent rather than supporting each other as fellow parents. As the parents begin to criticize each other for what they are doing wrong or not doing, the children are left free to disregard their parents' authority. The social worker is also able to observe both how Valerie is able to be effective with her youngest child and her sense of defeat and resignation with the older son that undermines her leadership.

Dysfunction can typically involve either overaffiliation (too much closeness) or underaffiliation (lack of adequate closeness). In families in which there are inadequate boundaries between individuals and overaffiliation are present members of the family often speak for others in the family session. Lack of adequate closeness can be revealed through bodily posture, nonverbal gestures, seating arrangements, lack of knowledge regarding the other family members, or other signs that indicate the separate nature of the lives people in this family lead.

The therapist also assesses the family in terms of areas of flexibility and rigidity. As evident in family resiliency research, families need a degree of flexibility to address changes in life as well as stability to give members a sense of security and coherence. More information about these issues emerges as the counselor engages with the family in the change process. As the family is encouraged in the session to assume new patterns, areas of flexibility and rigidity become clearer as the family responds by their ability or willingness to make changes (Minuchin, 1994; Minuchin & Fishman, 1981). This information is thus used by the therapist in planning for future intervention needs.

## TREATMENT PROCESS

### Treatment Strategies

Minuchin describes three main strategies of structural family therapy. These strategies relate to actions of the therapist in terms of the family dance:

**Challenge the symptoms.** Families typically come to the session with one person identified as the problem. From the perspective of the therapist the problem lies in the interaction patterns rather than in the client. The family therapist seeks to help the family reframe the problem in terms of the family structure (Minuchin & Fishman, 1981; Nichols & Schwartz, 2001). While Alicia and Matt might blame the other parent for being ineffective or blame one of the boys whose behavior had been the most difficult to control, the family therapist looks at the organization patterns that play a role in creating and maintaining the problems. The task of the therapist is to "challenge the family's definition of the problem and the nature of their response" (Minuchin & Fishman, 1981, p. 68). The goal is to "reframe the family's view of the problem, pushing its members to search for alternative behavioral, cognitive, and affective responses" (p. 68). Instead of Alicia and Matt dealing with the problem by blaming each other in ways that only serve to undermine the parental coalition, they can be helped to begin to support each other in setting limits on the children. This change thus counters their original view of their reality that the parents cannot exercise leadership, or that one of the parents is to blame, or that they have a set of impossible to control children. Valerie can be encouraged to assert herself more forcefully with her older son rather than speaking in a manner that is already resigned to being ignored or defied. By doing so she can begin to create change within the family and thus challenge the original view of the family.

Useful techniques to help reframe the family's view of the situation include enactment, focusing, and achieving intensity (Minuchin & Fishman, 1981). Enactment occurs as the family therapist sets the stage for the family to reenact the family patterns within the counseling session. The therapist can ask the family to discuss a specific matter of concern within the session (Aponte, 1992; Minuchin & Fishman, 1981) The therapist can also use spontaneous interaction in the family session to identify and transform patterns. The therapist changes the meaning of these events and "suggests alternative ways of acting that become actualized in the therapeutic system" (Minuchin & Fishman, 1981, p. 77). When Alicia and Matt describe their situation as impossible because the children are not able to listen to them, the therapist can challenge this interpretation in terms of their children are doing what comes naturally to children, testing out their parents to see if they will actually follow through on what they say. The symptom is challenged as family members try these alternatives and experience their family members and the family in different ways.

As the family therapist suggests alternative ways to view and experience the interactions, he can present this information in such a way that it heightens the intensity of the experience. The family therapist can intensify the family's response by insisting that they persist in reaching a goal rather than giving up or by exaggerating the expected behaviors. For example, when the children do not listen to Alicia and Matt—as is typical and the parents follow their usual pattern of throwing up their hands and giving up on making difference—the therapist can encourage the parents to come together in the session and to persist until they have evidence that the children are listening to them. Valerie is encouraged to speak in a firmer tone with her children and to insist that her son listen to her when she is talking to him. The family's response to this intervention reflects the flexibility of the family patterns. The therapist's pressure to persist rather than giving up as they do at home raises the intensity of the situation. Change in the behavioral patterns within the family are also used to change the meaning that family members have given to this situation. The use of enactments can address some of the core dynamics in families (Fellenberg, 2004).

The family therapist uses focus to organize the data around the theme. The therapist selects a specific pattern of interaction and focuses the session on this aspect. The therapist tracks with the family the sequence of behavior related to these themes as part of the assessment and treatment process. By changing the outcome of the pattern of interaction during the therapy session, the therapist has begun to challenge the previous reality and replace it with a more effective one (Minuchin & Fishman, 1981). As Alicia and Matt and Valerie are able to be more effective with their children in the sessions, they can begin to challenge their previous hopeless view of reality and re-place it with a view of themselves as more effective parents.

**Challenge the family structure.** Family life is organized along long-standing patterns. The longstanding nature of these is often reflected in comments made by family members (She has always been that way; He never listens to me; That's the way it has been with us; She has always been a stubborn kid). Dysfunctional patterns can involve the range of overaffiliation (over involvement) or underaffiliation (lack of appropriate closeness). The social worker uses both her role in the family system and her relative freedom to challenge the structure and support the development of other structures. The family therapist can challenge the parents' view that they are powerless by supporting the parents' joining forces to insist on setting limits on the children during the session. The therapist can help Valerie identify some consequences that are in her control in asserting her leadership and to potential sources of support within her extended family members. The therapist can insist on talking with the family isolate whom the other family members ignore and thus potentially alter the role of this person within the family structure.

The therapist uses a strengths-based perspective to highlight and re-inforce positive areas of functioning within the family interaction. The thera-pist can comment on even small examples in which Alicia and Matt are join-ing together and thus punctuate the interaction cycle in a positive manner. Valerie's therapist can comment on the way in which she demonstrates her authority with the younger children. The therapist seeks such opportunities within the session and stops the current action to highlight such a positive family dance step. Such strengths-based approaches help alter family pat-terns and negative views of reality about the family.

The family therapist tries to avoid doing for the family what the family members can do for themselves. When the therapist takes over for the family members, the inadvertent message can be that the family members are incompetent. Thus instead of the therapist "helping the parents" by setting limits on the children in the session (which translated into the message that the parents are incompetent to do so), the therapist sets the stage so that the parents begin to take these steps and are confirmed by the therapist for their actions (Goldenberg & Goldenberg, 2000). As a result, instead of the therapist's setting limits on Alicia and Matt's children, the therapist would continue to find ways to encourage and support the efforts of Alicia and Matt and highlight what they are able to accomplish.

Minuchin & Fishman (1981) describe the techniques of boundary making, unbalancing, and teaching complementarity. Boundary making helps family members create meaningful subsystems that enable the family to function more effectively. Unbalancing refers to "altering the hierarchical relationship of the members of a subsystem (Minuchin & Fishman, 1981, p. 161). The counselor temporarily takes sides to change the family interaction or broadens the focus of the situation.

Alicia and Matt have had difficulty creating an effective parental subsystem. Not only have they been overwhelmed by the children, but they have been quick to criticize each other rather than to work as a team. Like all intelligent children, their children have long learned the route of divide and conquer to prevent the parent from creating a firm stance. The social worker helps the two join forces (boundary making) despite the efforts of the children to continue the older patterns. As the children, led by the oldest son, try to distract the parents and interrupt the parents' discussion, the social worker acts to keep them focused on their discussion rather than being distracted. This intervention helps to establish boundaries around the parental subsystem. As the children continue to try their well-tested divide and conquer maneuvers in the family session, the worker uses her influence to support the alliance between the parents and their right to set limits on the boys (unbalancing). In this process the parents begin to give each other increased support and begin to exert more effective leadership with the children. As the parents do so, the social worker also highlights this interaction to help the family perceive itself in a more positive manner and the parents to view themselves as a more effective team.

In another family system, the social worker might observe that one of the family members is consistently absent from the family conversation or perhaps his comments are disqualified by other family members. In this situation, the worker might alter the family structure by engaging this isolate in conversation or carefully attending to the words of this person.

Teaching complementarity refers to understanding that problems within the family result from family patterns "to see their behaviors as part of the larger whole" (Minchin & Fishman, 1981, p. 194) rather than residing within one member of the family. Rather than simply defining the children as "uncooperative" or defining Alicia or Matt or Valerie as an "ineffective parent" family members can begin to experience the ongoing reciprocity of the pattern that occurs within the family with consequent possibility for change.

Repetition plays an important role in structural family therapy because long-standing patterns become habitual and do not change immediately. The family therapist identifies other areas in which similar patterns occur and seeks to change the family interaction pattern in these settings also. Through such repetition change in the family structure emerges. Alicia and Matt might unite initially around one issue with the older son. The therapist would then help them practice similar strategies with the other boys as they relate to other issues and find ways to solidify their own relationship. Valerie might begin by not letting her son interrupt her so that she can finish her sentences. She can then be helped to practice her leadership skills by insisting that he listen to what she is saying or by placing consequences on his making derogatory comments about her. The therapist's focus on this interactional pattern and the structure that it supports thus gains increased power through repetition.

**Challenge the family's reality.** As family members change their structure and patterns of behaving, they also begin to experience their family and context differently and cognitive changes occur within family members in terms of the family. Such an experience is part of altering the family's view of reality. Alicia and Matt can begin to shift from viewing their children as impossible to control and each other as ineffective parents. Their therapist highlights these new views of reality by emphasizing the evidences of strength. Valerie can begin to view herself as a parent who can assert some control over her children. As indicated earlier, the family therapist actively seeks out constructive patterns as well as attempts to encourage them in order to replace the family's negative reality with more constructive conceptions of the family. Symbols and metaphors can be used to capture this new view of reality (Minuchin & Fishman, 1981).

## *Treatment Principles*

Aponte (2003) describes basic principles of intervention that provide the foundation for structural family therapy. These principles can help families develop and strengthen the effective leadership that contributes to resilience in families.

**Focus on concrete issues.** The counselor should direct the therapy to that which the family views as urgent and important to the needs of family members. "Structural therapists look for concrete issues rooted in current life experiences which carry the deepest investment and motivation for change in the life of clients" (p. 108). Because this issue affects the family in this manner, it also helps mobilize the family's efforts to try to address it. Change can be difficult for families with hard choices and changes to make. Addressing important problems helps provide adequate motivation to mobilize people to make these changes. Motivation is also supported by moral and spiritual beliefs of family members.

**Locate in the present.** Past is embedded in the present of family relationships and is thus amenable to change through the present. Selecting issues that are meaningful in the present carries these messages from the past. As a result, by working through current issues, the counselor can address the deeper structural and dynamic forces.

**Mediate interventions through the client's experience in the session.** "The principle field of intervention for the SFT is the family's enactment of their issues in the session" (p. 108). Enacting family issues within the session activates both the intellectual and emotional aspects of the family members. The therapist either takes advantage of spontaneous situations that arise in the session or creates such opportunities within the family session. As family members enact new behaviors in the session, they experience new aspects of themselves and their family relations and thus potentially begin to revise the structure of the family and their view of the family.

**Reorganize the structure of relationships.** "Structural therapists intervene to resolve conflict, repair brokenness, and build new strengths in the underlying structure of issues that clients present" (p. 109). Therapeutic interventions are designed to realign family structures that create family distress and to replace them with structures that are more effective in meeting the needs of family members.

**Build on client strengths.** (p. 109). Structural therapists search for strengths within family members and seek to build on the power of change within the family to create more effective family patterns. They seek to tap whatever strengths are involved within family members, the immediate and extended family system, the support system, and the community to enable families to create and maintain these patterns. The social worker can highlight family strengths by punctuating the interaction after family members have demonstrated an effective interaction. The family therapist acknowledges the power of the family members to make critical decisions for the family.

**Aim at palpable outcomes.** "The family therapist enters the family's struggle through the enactment, the actual reliving of the family drama in the session" (p. 110). The therapist seeks to create within the family session opportunities for family members to interact with each other in new ways that offer more promising alternatives and outcomes that contribute to positive change within the family.

Homework is used to supplement the actions that are taking place within the session. People have further opportunities to experience these new interaction patterns. "When people experience a change in a new, palpable experience, it reaches deep, taking root more profoundly in the heart of the psyche and the relationship" (pp. 110–111). Alicia and Matt are given home-work that includes activities that they view will strengthen their relationship as a couple as man and wife and also as parents. Valerie is given homework on specific ways that she can continue asserting her authority at home. If she feels in need to support from another adult, she can be given the homework of seeking out support from one of the members of the extended family to help strengthen her role as a parent.

**Intervene through the active involvement of the practitioner with the family.** (p. 111). The family therapist engages the family in new ways of relating and relates with the family in ways that promote these new be-haviors. The therapist begins this process through joining with the family in order to create trust and to enable the counselor to begin to make changes within the family structure. Counselors use themselves in a creative and ac-tive manner to challenge old patterns, unbalance rigid structures, encourage more adaptive patterns. Such active use of the self requires a careful knowl-edge of the self by the counselors.

Aponte (2003) also describes the important role of spirituality in terms of family strengths. Spirituality gives some family members valuable re-sources in term of a sense of meaning as well potentially faith communities and a relationship with God (p. 110).

Nichols and Fellenberg (2000) identify elements of implementing enact-ments that seem to be associated with a positive shift in the family interac-tion process. Unsuccessful interactions are those in which there is no evi-dence that change has occurred. The strategies of the therapist are examined in terms of initiating, facilitating, and closing the enactments.

**Initiate the enactment.** Successful enactments were more likely to oc-cur if the therapist took a directive stance in terms of getting the individuals to talk with each other and specifying the topic of the conversation, and at the same time removing the worker's own chair away from the interaction. Unsuccessful enactments included not positioning people to talk with each other, not specifying the topic or the way to talk with each other, and not moving the counselor's chair away.

**Facilitate the enactment.** Once the family members began with the enactment, the following actions by the family therapist were associated with a productive enactments. Positive actions of the therapist included not inter-rupting family members once they began talking with each other, engaging family members to continue speaking to each other rather than the thera-pist. When enactments began to bog down, two kinds of interaction seemed helpful: "pushing family members to keep talking or to explain themselves more fully or digging beneath the surface of defenses, for example, probing deeper into clients' feelings or points of view, encouraging family members to try harder to understand what each other was feeling" (Nichols & Fallen-burg, 2000, p. 146) and offering encouragement to family members. On the other hand, problematic interventions included the counselor's interrupting family members prematurely or interjecting oneself before clients had a chance to communicate with each other.

**Close the enactment.** In line with efforts to help family members challenge their current reality, it is helpful to close the enactment by the therapist's helping the family to recognize the meaning of this event for their understanding of their family life. Thus family members are able to recognize the meaning that this interaction has for the future possible interactions between family members. For example, following an enactment in which Alicia and Matt were helped to stop blaming each other and instead to join forces and insist that the children listen to them, the therapist could point out the problematic dynamics that occurred when they would blame each other and the positive changes that occurred when they joined forces. The therapist could praise them for their efforts and emphasize the need for future efforts in this regard. In contrast, closing the enactment without commentary is not helpful (Nichols & Fallenburg, 2000).

Nichols and Fellenberg (2000) suggest three major lessons: (1) Family therapists must guard against interjecting themselves too quickly. "The important thing is that family members test their resources, get past the point where they are tempted to give up, and feel the pressure to speak up and to listen until they get somewhere" (p. 152). Family therapists need to help families keep the dialogue going rather than intervene too quickly. (2) When family members seem to bog down in unproductive blaming or bickering, it can be effective for the counselor to probe deeper into the feelings—frequently to get to the hurt behind the anger. Once family members open up with these feelings, the therapist again backs away to encourage the family members to continue their conversation. (3) The process of family members' improving their ability to communicate was more important than whether or not they agreed with each other. Interventions that enabled family members to learn something about themselves and clear guidelines for continued improved communication were important in enactments.

## CULTURAL ADAPTATIONS

Families seeking help come from a wide variety of cultural backgrounds that influence family patterns. The Spanish Family Guidance Center in Miami was established to offer services to the local Hispanic community and subsequently broadened its services to families from other cultural backgrounds. In the process, the center adapted the structural family model to be responsive to families from different cultures. The counselors recognized that family structures were also impacted by social systems external to the family (e.g., school, neighborhood) and thus that the intervention needed to include the interactive patterns between families and these systems as well as patterns within the immediate family. The treatment approach thus began to incorporate a multisystem approach as well as a structural approach within the family itself. This broadened approach is called Structural Ecosystems Theory. Similar to structural therapy described earlier in this chapter, this model includes the concept of the need to look at repetitive patterns of interactions between parts of the system with the goal of identifying and changing maladaptive patterns of interactions that keep the family from reaching its goals (Kurtines & Szapocznik, 1996). Following is a discussion of some of the cultural adaptations involved in using the structural family therapy model with families from different cultural groups.

Cultural context and norms are important considerations in the assessment process. Cultures that value the extended family and kinship networks might have different patterns of the executive system than from families that emphasize the nuclear family. Such patterns can occur and be very adaptive, for example, within Hispanic, Asian, and African American families. The grandmother/mother subsystem in which a single mother lives with her mother can represent the executive subsystem. Within Asian American families, the husband's mother can play an important role in shaping the behavior of her daughter-in-law in a culturally sanctioned manner. The important question is—what arrangement is functional given this cultural context? What do cultural norms support as adaptive? (Kurtines & Szapocznik, 1996).

Joining with the family is also influenced by the culture of the family. In the process of joining, the counselor must respect the culturally influenced nature of the family. For example, in families from Hispanic and Asian communities in which respect for those with power in the family hierarchy (especially the parents and grandparents) is important, Grant stresses the need for the therapist leadership role not to usurp their power (1999). The therapist must also respect the family's definition of who are family members in terms of those who participate in the session.

The amount of closeness between family members varies depending on the cultural context. Hispanic family members, for example, tend to be closer than are members of Anglo families. When family members interrupt and speak for each other, while it might be signs of problematic enmeshment it could also reflect cultural patterns that value closeness. Whether or not it is problematic depends on its function within the specific family (Kurtines & Szapocznik, 1996).

Developmental issues that influence family roles and structure also vary depending on culture. These differences also vary within cultural groups depending on subgroup membership. Kurtines & Szapocznik (1996) describe intracultural differences, for example, "in a Hispanic migrant family, it might be expected that an 8-year-old girl miss school to work with the family in the fields. Yet, in an urban context in some Latin American cities, a 16-year-old girl may not be allowed to date unchaperoned" (p. 678). Cultures also differ in terms of the extent to which children are expected to provide support for parents and extended family members.

Conflict resolution styles also reflect cultural differences (Kurtines & Szapocznik, 1996). Hispanic families, for example, frequently use conflict diffusion rather than conflict emergence with resolution.

Reframing, one of the key strategies in restructuring families, is also influenced by culture. The meaning of events varies between cultures and thus what is considered as admirable within one culture might be given a different meaning in others. A graduate student belonging to one of the Native American nations indicated to his Anglo professor that he was going to take a break in writing his dissertation because he needed to be home to take care of his ill father. From the perspective of his culture, caring for family members was an essential priority. The student described his hurt and anger when his faculty advisor accused him of not taking his studies seriously.

Working with boundaries and alliances is another key strategy in structural family therapy. Again, culture influences the nature of adaptive boundaries and appropriate alliances. In working with single parent families within, for example, the Hispanic and African American cultures, the counselor might be able to take advantage of opportunities within the extended family to support the mother (Kurtines & Szapocznik, 1996). As indicated in chapter on culture this depends on the assessment whether or not extended family supports or undermines the mother in her authority role.

## EVALUATION

Structural family approaches have been useful in working with families presenting with a variety of problems. Jordan and Franklin describe it as demonstrating more effectiveness with families that are enmeshed rather than disengaged (1999). There has been extensive support for the value of structural family therapy with families dealing with anorexia, various psychosomatic problems, (Minuchin, Rosman, & Baker, 1978) and drug addiction (Aponte, 2003). Structural family therapy has been an effective approach with Latino families (Grant, 1999; Romeo, 2000) and African American families (Grant, 1999). Early versions of structural family therapy have been criticized as being too rigid in terms of gender roles, especially in terms of supporting a patriarchal view of family hierarchy that disadvantaged women (Jordan & Franklin, 1999).

## SUMMARY

Structural family therapy can be a useful family therapy approach because it helps develop and support the leadership structures within families that are needed for meeting the needs of family members. Efforts to create appropriate leadership systems can enhance the organizational patterns of families that contribute to family resiliency while lack of such leadership represents an important risk factor. These efforts also alter the family's view of the situation. An understanding of cultural patterns is important because they influence the nature of these organizational patterns and thus the approaches that are appropriate. Structural family therapy sessions emphasize the active role of the therapist along with the present life of the family and change that occurs within the sessions themselves.

# 7

## *Solution-Focused Family Therapy*

As discussed in chapter 4, Mr. and Mrs. Norris have begun to define their relationship in terms of the difficulties and tensions that are present and have lost sight of other possibilities in their family relations. The solution-focused treatment model could be appropriate for this set of risks and resiliency factors. Mr. and Mrs. Norris are discouraged and have begun to view their family relationships as marked by tension and disagreements. This family situation suggests the need to create hope for the possibility of change. The couple has some realistic problems to address but have become discouraged by their disagreements and have come to define themselves and their family in these terms. Their negative and discouraged view of the situation has hindered their ability to envision and create new alternatives and thus to address their problems in an effective manner. Helping them recognize the presence of exceptions and enabling them to identify steps that will help solve their family problems can be important for this family. Such steps can help change their definition of the reality of family and thus enable them to use their creativity to begin to solve family problems.

> Martha Martin and Joyce Kimble have been living together for the past year and a half. Martha has an eight-year-old daughter, Megan, from her marriage to George Martin. About four years ago she began to feel that her marriage to George did not fit her increasing identity as a lesbian. The process of revealing this to George was a difficult one and there is ongoing tension between the two. Her parents were distressed at the time but gradually came to support her decision. George's parents have remained distant from her although they continue to send cards and gifts to their granddaughter. George initially threatened that he would deny Martha custody of their daughter but came to terms with the situation and the two now share custody. In the meantime George has remarried and his second wife is pregnant. Both families live in the same community. Martha and George share the parental roles in important ways, including support when discipline was required. Martha works as a computer programmer. George is a teacher and contributes financially to the care

of Megan. Joyce has a twelve-year-old daughter, Stephanie. She and her first husband have been divorced for over ten years and he subsequently died of cancer. She has ongoing contact with her extended family who initially found her lesbian identity difficult but after a few years became reconciled and have recently been supportive of her. Her husband's family has stayed distant. Joyce is an office manager of a medical office. The two met through mutual friends and were friends for about a year before living together. They are members of a support group of lesbian mothers in their community.

Martha and Joyce contact the office because they are having difficulty creating an effective family group. While the two women care deeply for each other and their children, they have had difficulty in working out their parenting styles with the girls. Joyce and her daughter have been extremely close during these years. In many ways, the two became the chief support for the each other and Joyce found it difficult to set limits on her daughter. While extremely organized and able to deal with difficult people at work, as a parent she assumed more a best friend rather than parental role. Martha and Megan moved into Joyce's house because it is larger and each girl is able to have her own bedroom.

Stephanie has found it very difficult to accept her mother's new relationship with Martha and Megan. She shows her resentment toward both of them in many ways. She vocalizes her unhappiness about having to share the house with them. She refuses to accept any of the limits that Martha sets for her and is openly critical of Martha. Faced with this situation, Megan withdraws or tries to avoid spending time home and turns more to her father. She has started asking her mother if they can return to their old home. While Martha and Joyce want their new relationship to succeed, this tension is causing them to question if this arrangement is a good one. The two have begun arguing increasingly about how to co-parent. They turned for help to their support group who have been sympathetic and encouraged them to seek professional help.

This family has some important risk and protective factors. In terms of protective factors, Martha and Joyce have a strong commitment to each other and to their daughters. They have employment that gives them an adequate economic base. Their work performance demonstrates their intelligence and ability to relate effectively with others. They have a support group of friends as well as extended family members. Risk factors include their socially marginalized status as a lesbian family. While they receive support from friends, there is no legal support for their relationship and thus separation remains more of an option. They are struggling with the skills of co-parenting with each other, especially because their parenting styles are quite different. Stephanie is fearful of the loss of her close relationship with her mother at the same time she is entering into the developmentally insecure world of preadolescence. They have become demoralized and discouraged about their ability to cope with the current situation.

Solution-focused therapy offers them an opportunity to regain a sense of hope that their relationship can survive by identifying times in which things are going better. It mobilizes their energy to focus on potential solutions to their situation. It further looks at the small steps that can make this possible.

Solution-focused family therapy is an important school of treatment within the brief family treatment model. It is part of the brief treatment movement that emphasizes the family's strengths and sources of resiliency to promote positive change. The focus on solutions and the value of small changes has enabled solution-focused therapy to be viewed as brief therapy model. With a focus on the future, treatment is organized around successfully achieving the identified goals rather than understanding the origin of the problem. Families are helped to draw upon their coping strategies and to expand their repertoire to meet their goals. With the belief that people and families are constantly changing, the emphasis is on helping families envision and create positive changes within the family. The therapist engenders hope by identifying signs of previous successful functioning as evidence of the potential for future progress (Berg & Dolan, 2001; Homrich & Horne, 2000; O'Connell, 1998). Berg and Dolan (2001) summarize the philosophy of solution focused as "the pragmatics of hope and respect" (p. 1).

The solution-focused approach enables family members to focus on the solutions that have been or might be helpful in creating new realities for the family. From this perspective, family members are doing the best that they can. They may lack the skills, or more likely, lack the awareness that they have the skills to engage in solving the problem and thus feel stuck (Homrich & Horne, 2000; Koob, 2003).

Recognizing that families frequently come to treatment with a reduced self of self-mastery about their ability to address their situation and are concentrating almost exclusively on the problems that they are facing, solution-focused therapy places the spotlight on family actions that can solve these problems. It expands the family's vision of reality to incorporate the possibilities that can enable them to reach their desired goals. Such efforts can enhance hope. The emphasis is on creating solutions (emphasis on future possibilities) rather than solving problems (emphasis on problems) (Berg & Dolan, 2001; Butler & Powers, 1996; Koob, 2003; Nichols & Schwartz, 2003). The approach has grown extremely popular in a world in which brief treatment is valued by managed care as well as by family members.

## THEORETICAL BACKGROUND

The founders of solution-focused treatment began their work at the Brief Family Therapy Center in Milwaukee. I remember attending early workshops with one of the leaders, Steve de Shazer, whose theme in these presentations was "find out what is working with the family and help the family do more of this." Important contributors to the development of the clinical aspects of solution-focused treatment include Insook Kim Berg, Eve Lipcheck, Michele Weiner-Davis; Scott Miller, Peter DeJonge, John Walter & Jane Peller, and Bill O'Hanlon (Nichols & Schwartz, 2001).

## *Major tenets*

Solution-focused therapy is based on seven tenets.

1. Solution-focused therapy places its emphasis on the future—what in the future will be different or what can be different. The emphasis is on the future because it is in the future (rather than the past or the present) that problems will be solved. As a result, envisioning the future is an important first step.

2. The solution to a problem can be unrelated to how the problem began. As a result, one does not need history as a necessary guide to solve the problem. Understanding the past does not necessarily provide the key to changing the future. Problems can develop a life of their own unrelated to their origin.

3. People are hindered in their efforts to solve problems because they are locked into negative and pessimistic views of the problem and feel unable to solve the problem. They have focused so much on problematic events and aspects of the family that they have forgotten times in which problems did not occur or result. They have so become trapped into the negative meaning systems that they cannot look at the positive alternatives or new ways to attempt to solve their problems. Instead of trying new approaches, they continue using their old methods. When these do not work, they redouble their efforts to try to make things improve.

4. People really do want to change. Solution-focused therapists do not view the family as ambivalent or resistant to change. When family members do not cooperate, it is their way to guide the therapist into more appropriate ways to be helpful. Problems are not viewed as serving some hidden purpose within the family.

5. People are suggestible. People can thus be highly influenced by the theoretical orientation of the counselor. As a result, the interpretations that occur in the sessions between the therapist and the family tend to be influenced by the orientation of the therapist. To avoid this situation, the solution-focused therapist comes to the therapy session with a perspective of not knowing and seeks to identify how the client perceives the nature of the problems and the possibilities for solving them.

   An example of how easy it is to view one's own theoretical formulation as the answer occurred when I taught solution-focused therapy to my graduate social work students. Many of them expressed initial frustration with the counselor on the video because she was not addressing the problems that the students were sure were important. Instead the counselor was asking questions of the family members in terms of what was important for them and following up on these issues. These students became further frustrated when the family members did not identify the solution that their (the students) theoretical formulation indicated should be the solution. As the session continued the power of allowing family members formulate their own views of the key problems and means to solving them emerged. The students then began to realize how the solution-focused approach had empowered individuals to create viable and relevant solutions predicated upon the family's interpretation of key problems and helpful solutions.

6. Language is powerful in shaping reality. Solution-focused therapy is influenced by the constructionist tradition that believes that language shapes reality (deShazer, 1994). As a result, the important task of the therapist is to change the way people talk about their problems. People who have suffered a great deal can thus be described as either victims or survivors. Rather than encouraging clients to continue to talk in terms of their problems, the therapist seeks to have them talk about potential solutions (from problem talk to solution talk).

7. People judge what is important and thus select their own goals. Solution-focused therapy does not prescribe a specific way of living one's life. It recognizes that families choose different ways of life and thus what is appropriate and acceptable for one family may not be so for other families (O'Hanlon & Weiner-Davis 1989; Nichols & Schwartz, 2005).

## GOALS OF TREATMENT

Solution-focused therapy seeks to help families reach the goals that they define. Solution-focused therapists have faith that the family can define the appropriate goals and have the skills in order to work toward this goal. Problems occur when people are unable to use their skills because they have lost sight that they have these skills or have become overwhelmed by the problem at hand. Helping families focus on what they are doing right and expanding their own ability to use these skills can be very effective. Such an approach expands the family's vision of their possibilities. Families can also find it difficult to use the skills that they have used in the past because for various reasons these skills are not longer part of their current behavior pattern. As a result, the therapist needs to find ways to help the family members begin to restore these skills and use them to address their problem.

Goals in solution-focused therapy represent the presence of something positive, rather than the absence of something negative. Goals are also most effective if they are phrased in concrete behavioral terms (what someone will be doing differently) that are measurable. While clients often begin talking about what others will do differently, the therapist can gradually expand this set of questions to include what the involved family members will also be doing differently (DeJong & Berg, 1998, p. 74).

The family therapist uses questions to help family members identify their goals. The following represent some possible questions: "What do you think the problem is now?" "How will you know when the problem is solved?" "How will you know when you don't have to come here any more? What will the signs be?" (Nichols & Schwartz, 2005, p. 238).

A related process goal is to help family members shift from talking about problems to talking about solutions. Families who can make this shift can begin to build on the solutions that emerge from these new conversations.

Solution-focused therapy is organized around accomplishing modest goals. The very step of helping individuals set goals that are clear and achievable represents an important intervention. It is part of the solution-focused approach to help individuals think about their future and how they want it to be different. The assumption is that such an effort sets in motion the possibility for ongoing positive change in the family. These small changes can alter the direction of the change that is ongoing within the family in a positive manner. These changes also influence the way in which the family envisions itself and the future (Walter & Peller, 1996).

## ROLE OF THE THERAPIST

The therapist assumes a not-knowing stance with family members as the experts regarding the family and their solutions. The stance of the therapist is one who asks questions to elicit the family's view of potential solutions and behavior patterns that exemplify exceptions to the problem stance.

The therapist also acts as an encourager for the family. The therapist comments in an affirming manner about any evidence that family members can change in a positive manner and are able to solve their problematic issues (DeJong & Berg, 1998).

The twin major roles of the therapist are to provide acknowledgement and possibility (Butler & Powers, 1996; O'Hanlon, 1993). Acknowledgement refers to the therapist's being with the family in their life circumstances. The therapist makes comments that convey to the family members that the therapist understands and empathizes with their current situation. Possibility refers to therapist's orientation to the future when the current problems are resolved. The therapist brings a stance of curiosity to learn how the family will solve their problems. Possibility also conveys to the family the therapist's view that such positive change is possible in the life in the family.

## TREATMENT PROCESS

Treatment is organized around the goals, resources, and exceptions to the problem. "The task of solution therapy is to help clients amplify exceptions to their problems" (Nicholes & Schwartz, 2001, p. 375). The family therapist seeks to identify solutions that are already part of the repertoire of the family members and to expand upon these. Exceptions are evidence that the family can address their problems in more effective ways.

The process of expanding on solutions is a collaborative effort on the part of the therapist and the family members. The solution-focused therapist is willing to work with the members of the family who are willing to come.

In addition to the general emphasis upon looking for interactions that represent an exception to the problem and a focus on the family's view of potential solutions, several key techniques have emerged in solution-focused treatment. These techniques take the form of questions, with the family as the expert on the family.

**What do you want to continue?** (Formula one): Following the first session, family members are asked to observe their family during the next week (or until the next session) to identify what happens in their family they would like to continue. This homework assignment places the family members in the role of looking for exceptions to the problem and positive aspects about the family (DeJong & Berg, 1998; Nichols & Schwartz, 2001).

**The miracle question.** The therapist formulates the miracle question to help family members begin to develop their solutions (Nichols & Schwartz, 2001, p. 376). "Suppose one night you were asleep, there was a miracle and this problem was solved. How would you know? What would be different?" This question is designed to help family members look beyond the immediate problem and to visualize what it is that they want. The emphasis then becomes on helping family members construct the steps that they view would enable them to make these changes possible. The counselor asks a series of questions designed to identify what small and manageable step would indicate that things were different. As people are able to take more steps that move in the direction of the desired goal, the problem itself becomes less of an issue.

DeJong and Berg (1998) remind therapists that asking the client to imagine how life will be changed when the problem is solved can be difficult. Use of the miracle question represents a major shift in the client's thinking. They suggest several techniques that can be helpful to make this transition in using the miracle question with families. The first involves the therapist's use of the voice. Speaking slowly and softly helps the client make the shift from the problem to a solution focus. Introducing the miracle as something unusual or strange marks it as a new approach. Using future-directed words helps the client think in terms of the future—"What would be different? What will be signs of the miracle?" (p. 78). Repeating a phrase during the follow-up questions, such as "a miracle happens when the problem that you brought here is solved" (p. 78) helps to reinforce the transition to solution talk. Refocusing the client's attention to what will be different when the miracle occurs can be helpful when the client returns to problem talk (1998).

**The exception question.** This question is designed to elicit from the family members the times in which the problem did not exist or occurred to a lesser degree. In the case of Mr. and Mrs. Norris, exceptions would occur when were they able to agree on their son, to support each other in dealing with a problem, to come together on ways to help Mrs. Norris' father. For Martha and Joyce it might represent a meal in which the four were able to talk about what happened that day without it turning into a verbal battle or Stephanie walking away from the table in anger. For another family the questions might revolve around when they could discuss finances without a fight (or a lesser degree of conflict) or show the other party that they appreciated them. Exploring these times opens the door to examining how these exceptions occurred. This information enables family members to begin expanding these times. As family members are able to expand their exceptions, they are able to develop a greater self of self-efficacy and mastery in dealing with the problems (DeJong & Berg, 1998; Nichols & Schwartz, 2001).

**Scaling questions.** Scaling questions can be helpful in enabling individuals to identify more clearly what they want, to move them beyond all-or-nothing thinking, and to think in terms of small steps. Family members are helped to identify what small changes can make a difference in the life of their family and ways to accomplish these changes. Scaling questions can relate to family member's perceptions of the seriousness of the program and of their confidence that they can make changes. Family members can be asked these types of scaling questions.

First, family members are asked to indicate on a scale from 1 to 10 how serious they view the problem. One can be described in terms of just terrible and no hope while 10 can represent the lack of any problem. If family members describe themselves at 4, they can be asked what might make is possible for them to see their family situation at 5. This question sets the stage for engaging family members in strategizing what steps or actions would make it possible for this change to occur.

A second scaling question relates to the issue of motivation: How motivated are you? How hard are you willing to work to help solve this problem? Family members can be asked what could help increase their motivation. This information can be used to identify sources of motivation and ways to enhance it.

A third scaling question relates to the issue of confidence: How confident are you that you can do what has been identified? Answers to this question can identify what might be blocking one's being able to change or issues that can facilitate it. Family members can be encouraged to identify small steps that might help address these issues to support confidence (De Jong & Berg, 1998).

The family therapist takes a hopeful and encouraging approach to families. This hopeful approach supports the possibility side of the solution-focused approach. The family therapist acknowledges evidence of small positive changes, successes, and efforts to respond in new ways. The therapist continually seeks evidence of exceptions and elicits information about how the family members make this possible. During the session and in the end-of-session-feedback the emphasis is upon the competences of the family.

Solution-focused therapy distinguishes between customers and complainants. In this context customers are concerned about the problem and are willing to change to make things better. Complainants are concerned about the problem but are not yet willing to change to improve the situation. One of the challenges of the solution-focused-therapist is to move complainants into customers. A useful strategy is to help individuals identify the advantage to them of this change. For example, an adolescent might see the advantage of gaining the trust of his parents because he would have more freedom. A family might view less intense supervision from the Department of Children and Families as worth the effort. Visitors are individuals who are neither concerned about the problem nor willing to change (De Jong & Berg, 1998).

### *Application*

The following describes a prototypical two-session therapy scenario using solution-focused therapy (Koob, 2003).

**Session 1.** The family therapist seeks to identify who in the family are customers because these individuals will help ensure that change will occur. This may be evidenced by the family member who speaks first or who made the contact to this the agency. A useful technique is to ask the family "Who is most concerned about resolving this problem? Who is second? Who is third?" (p. 136).

As described earlier in chapter 4, the therapist joins with the family by listening in an emphatic manner to their concerns, identifying the nature of the problems cited, and asking family members how they have managed to cope. This combination serves to help the family members feel that they been heard and understood as well as places the focus on the potential strengths of the family. The conversation regarding how the family members have coped also helps them identify positive exceptions in the current life of the family.

If family members are able to engage in solution-focused conversation, the therapist can ask the miracle question described earlier in this chapter. The therapist can then pursue the answers given by family members to identify clearly what are the specific changes and actions that would represent the desired change and the solution.

Family members are then asked to rank by scaling questions how close they are to reaching this miracle. The therapist can comment favorably if they indicate that they are at least halfway there. The therapist can comment on any step beyond one—How despite all the many problems you describe have you managed to keep up some hope for things becoming better? Since solution-focused treatment is based on encouraging the family to at least make small changes, the therapist asks family members what would have to happen for them to move ahead from 5 to 6 or a fraction of a number if this seems too great a change. This latter part helps move the family members into a solution-focused conversation. Family members can also be asked how motivated and how confident they are about being able to do so. Answers here can be used to identify what would help family members become more motivated or confident as well as what enables them to be as motivated and confident as they are now.

The therapist then takes a break to consider the issue and to consult with a team located behind the one-way mirror (if such resources exist). The therapist returns with a message that includes the following components: compliments for the family, normalizations, reframes (positive). The therapist then prescribes the strength-based Formula One perspective: This homework assignment requires observation on the part of family members. "When people enter therapy, they begin to change. There are things in your life, however, that you do not want to change because they are positive. So between now and the next time we meet, pay attention to those positive things in your life, and we will discuss it next week" (p. 137).

**Session 2.** The therapist follows up on the first session by exploring what the family has identified that they want to keep in the family. The therapist also explores positive changes that are described in terms of whether or not this is a new behavior, what made it possible, and how can it be encouraged in the future. If family members do not identify anything positive, the therapist explores in detail to discover any evidence of small signs of positive changes. The family is again asked to scale their situation. Positive changes are marked by asking what made this possible and how can it be kept going. When situations are either the same or worse, the therapist can ask what the family did to prevent things from getting even worse.

The therapist also uses presuppositional questions. These questions involve asking the family members to identify circumstances that occur either before or after the exceptions that might enhance such exceptions. (Blumenthal & Green, 2003). These questions have a strengths-based focus. They emphasize what family members did to make the difference that helped the family members reach its goals. This emphasis highlights the actions of the family members that contribute to the solutions. What did your husband (wife) do that made you feel that you could work together as parents? What did your parents do that helped you feel that they understood how difficult school is for you right now?

Solution-focused therapists can use several other techniques to help family members reach their goals. These are behavioral tasks organized around types of actions by the family members. Such tasks are particularly appropriate if the family members have identified clearly defined goals. The specific nature of the tasks involved depends on the goals identified and information about previous behaviors that have been identified as helpful (De Jong & Berg, 1998). The following represent several behavioral tasks.

- Do more of what works. This task draws on already identified effective coping strategies within the family. When family members describe something that has helped, family members are encouraged to do more of these actions; for example, "If you are able to talk better when you both take a ten-minute break to cool off, do this when you are getting angry trying to solve this problem in your family."

- Do something different. When families report their failed attempt to address a problem, the therapist can encourage them to experiment and think of some other approach. This task encourages families to discover their own solutions. It also helps family members break out of rigid and ineffective patterns.

- Go slowly. In order to help families overcome any fear of change, solution-focused therapist can encourage family members to change slowly. The therapist can ask the family, "Could there be any advantages to things staying the way they are?"

- Do the opposite. If family members report that their current solutions are not working, they can be encouraged to try the opposite. This technique is based on the idea that current solutions can be maintaining problems. A parent who has been using scolding to correct the behavior of a child can be encouraged to try praise for good behavior.

- Prediction task. The therapist instructs the family members "each night before you go to bed, predict whether or not things will be better. At the end of the day, examine if your prediction was correct. 'Account for any differences between your prediction and the way the day went and keep track of your observations so that you can come back and tell me about them'" (DeJong & Berg, 1998, p. 124). This task can help people gain a sense of patterns that are associated with improvement and increase their expectation for change.

### Application: The Norris Family

As described earlier, Mr. and Mrs. Norris's relationship has become organized around disagreements regarding their son and his disappointing academic achievement and ways to provide help for Mrs. Norris's father. Mr. and Mrs. Norris have begun to define their relationship in terms of these two concerns and points of disagreement.

**Session One.** Mr. and Mrs. Norris arrive for the first session somewhat nervous about whether or not therapy can really help their difficult problems. Since Mrs. Norris in her role as mother and daughter has felt the burden of the problems on her shoulders more than Mr. Norris, she made the call and speaks up first in the session. The social worker asks both Mr. and Mrs. Norris how the therapy session can be of help to them—how will they know if therapy has been helpful to them (O'Connell, 1998). Framing the question in this way permits the family to express their concerns regarding their family but sets the stage for a forward stance in terms of the therapy effort. Mrs. Norris begins to describe their worry about their son as well as the burden she is feeling in terms of her father. The social worker is careful to ensure that Mr. Norris also has the opportunity to express his concerns.

The social worker listens empathically to the concerns of both parties— their worries about their son, their frustration about being unable to talk about and reach any agreement on how to handle the situation, the tension about Mrs. Norris's father and how to handle this trouble. Mrs. Norris describes their concern about their son Jason who is not doing well in college. They are afraid that he will drop out of school. She describes how she and her husband have become angry with each other because they are so frustrated and do not know what to do. As a result, they end up blaming each other and accusing the other partner of contributing to the problem because of the way that they have treated the son. Mr. and Mrs. Norris then begin to start blaming each other because of an incident last night. Mrs. Norris goes on to say that she also feels under pressure due to her father and does not feel supported by Mr. Norris because he thinks that she could help solve the problem by taking his advice. This then prompts a brief sharp interchange between the couple. Mrs. Norris accuses Mr. Norris of not understanding and Mr. Norris accuses Mrs. Norris of talking about problems but never wanting to hear any advice. The social worker listens empathically to this exchange but recognizes that the session could easily be consumed by this couple's well-rehearsed negative exchanges. The worker delineates the concerns expressed by Mr. and Mrs. Norris about the son in terms of their shared concern that their son not waste his talents and do well in school and the difficulties in knowing what to do to help an elderly parent.

The social worker also explores and underscores what they hope the therapy session will contribute and what would make them think that their time here was worthwhile. The couple indicates that while they are concerned about both their son and Mrs. Norris's father, their primary source of contention and worry now is their son and they would like to concentrate on this. Respecting the family's choice of the priority issues, the therapist not only explores further about the nature of the problem but also probes for exceptions—times in which the parents see eye-to-eye about their son. While the parents have limited control over the actions of their son, they are able to control how they view each other as parents and their ability to act as a united front. These questions can also explore times in which they were able to relate to each other as husband and wife rather than anxious parents. The therapist can also explore with the parents any possible times in which their son shows some signs of more responsible behavior.

Recognizing how difficult these situations are for concerned parents, the therapist uses acknowledgement to affirm their role as concerned parents and asked how they have managed to cope as parents with this situation. When Mr. and Mrs. Norris seem puzzled, the therapist explores further how they have managed sometimes to find a way to agree on how to handle their son or at least have handled their differences without the other party's feeling being put down.

After further listening to the concerns of the family and identifying them so that the family members realize that their concerns have been heard and that they have been acknowledged, the therapist asks the couple if they would be willing to try something different and introduces the miracle question. After some thought, Mrs. Norris states, "I would know that something was different because my husband would listen to my concerns without minimizing them. When he minimizes my concerns, I feel he doesn't respect me and I in turn press the issue further. I find myself then criticizing how he handles our son." Mr. Norris states, "I would know the miracle occurred when my wife would acknowledge that at least I am trying." The therapist asks both to describe exactly what they mean so that everyone can have a clear picture. When asked to describe their view of the seriousness of the problem on a scale from 1 to 10, Mrs. Norris describes it as 5 and Mr. Norris as 6. The therapist then asks each of the parties what it would take on everyone's part to move their view up one step. Mr. and Mrs. Norris are then asked to identify some small step that would make this difference and what would be different if this small step occurred. The emphasis here is on a small step that might be realistic for each of the individuals to accomplish. After the couple is asked to identify how confident they are that they would be able to carry out this step, the therapist explores with them what would help them to be able to do so and what might prevent them from doing so. This provides the basis for further discussion on possible solutions to these barriers. They are also asked how motivated they are to make these changes and both express a high degree of motivation (steps 6 and 7).

The therapist then explores any possible times recently in which Mrs. Norris feels that Mr. Norris shows an appreciation for her concerns and that Mr. Norris has felt that his wife gives evidence that she thinks that he is trying. Small and fleeting examples are noted and then explored in terms of what the couple thinks helps make them possible. The social worker asks further questions to amplify information about what occurred prior to these times and the impact that this had upon their relationship. These examples are discussed with the family in terms of evidence of coping strategies that the family already possesses and has been able to use.

Toward the end of the session, the therapist indicates the need for a break to consider what would be the recommendation. The therapist comes back and compliments Mr. and Mrs. Norris for their love and concern for their son and their commitment to their family. The therapist then normalizes the situation by indicating that it can be painful and frustrating when grown children appear to be going in directions that cause concern and it can be difficult to handle this new stage of parenting when children become young adults. The therapist also recognizes their stress as being part of a sandwich generation with responsibilities for two generations in addition to their own. The therapist comments on the frustration experienced by both of them as a sign of their commitment to their son (reframing). The therapist then gives a version of the Formula One session task that is to focus on the things within the family that people do not want to change. "When people enter therapy, they begin to change. There are things in your life, however, that you do not want to change because they are positive. Between now and the next time we meet, pay attention to those positive things in your life, and we will discuss them next week" (Koob, 2003, p. 137).

Mr. and Mrs. Norris both indicate a positive thing that they want to keep is their investment in their son despite the pain that it sometimes gives them. Mr. Norris states, "I appreciate her caring manner in general even though sometimes it creates tension in the family." Mrs. Norris states, "I appreciate his hard work on the job that has helped us meet our financial obligations, especially since my own family often struggled to make ends meet." The therapist then asks them to scale their current situation. Both rate the situation as slightly better. The therapist then explores individually with Mr. and Mrs. Norris what happened during this past week that helped make this difference. Mrs. Norris: "My husband was able to listen to me without pressuring me to stop worrying too much." Mr. Norris: "My wife was able to talk to me about our son without implying that I was in some way at fault for his actions and had even gone further and commented positively on something that I had said to him last week." They reported that while these changes had not yet made their son become more responsible, they felt that the problem was not pulling them apart as much as it had been. "We are starting to feel like we are a team again instead of arguing with each other all the time. This is important to us because we used to be able to talk about things. This used to be an important part of our marriage that has been lost."

### Application: Martha and Daughter Megan, and Joyce and Daughter Stephanie

Several possible treatment models might be appropriate for this family. There are structural issues in terms of the two parents finding it difficult to create a parental coalition. As a result, a structural approach might be useful. A solution-focused approach can help the family claim and enhance some of the positive aspects of the family relationships that have become buried in the tensions of the present and the transitional process of this family. The following discussion relates to the use of a solution-focused approach with this family.

As with the Norris family, this family has become organized around a set of defeatist beliefs and family interactions. As the problems intensify,

Martha and Joyce have begun to question the wisdom of their new family situation. Their relationship has started being defined in these terms so that they are considering separation. While encouraged by their friends to seek help, they have become discouraged and demoralized.

**Session 1.** The therapist begins the session by asking the family how the counseling session can be of help to them and how they will know if counseling has been helpful. The therapist is careful to listen to all the family members as they tell their story—Martha and Joyce's wishes to be a family, their current tensions, their fear that this new family will not work out; Stephanie's comments that she would like to have her mother back like old times; Megan's complaints that Stephanie hasn't given her and her mother a chance and her wish to have things peaceful again.

The therapist listens to their accounts of the situation while aware that the session also needs to highlight some of their hopes and goals for positive change. The therapist delineates the concerns raised by all the members—their hopes for having a family together, their fears that it will not work, the unhappiness of Stephanie with the current situation and wish to return to the old times, and Megan's wish that Stephanie would give them a chance or if she cannot do so, that she and her mother have peace again.

The therapist acknowledges with the family that creating a new family from two separate families is a difficult thing to do because every family has its own ways of things and what is important for them. The therapist also comments favorably on their willingness to come to work on their family situation.

While listening to these problem-oriented accounts, the therapist also explores for exceptions—times in which the family managed to overcome this very difficult task of blending two families together (times in which all the family members were able to get along, times in which Stephanie still felt that she was special for her mother, times in which Martha and Joyce were able to relate to each other as a couple rather than as frazzled parents, times in which the parents were able to agree on how to handle the children, times in which Megan found home a peaceful place to be). The therapist uses this information to affirm the efforts and ability of family members to handle this realistically difficult situation.

After listening to the concerns of the family members and identifying them so that all the family members recognize that their concerns have been heard and have been acknowledged, the therapist asks them if they would be willing to try something different and introduces the miracle question. After some thought the family members say what this would mean to them. Martha states, "I would know that something was different because when I come home from work Stephanie would say something nice to me rather than making me feel like I was unwelcome in her house." Joyce says, "I would know that something was different because Martha and I would be able to enjoy being together rather than spending our time talking about the problems we were having with our daughters." Stephanie jumps in with a comment that if they just moved out they would not have this problem. Her mother indicates that they are here to work things out, not to just move out. Stephanie first said, "I would know a miracle had happened because my mother would tell me that we were moving out." When her mother says that this is not the plan and asked her to come up with a miracle that does not include moving out, Stephanie quietly states, "I would know a miracle happened because my mother would ask me to go to a movie with her like we used to do—just the two of us." Megan says "I would know a miracle had happened because people would be sitting in the family room together watching TV rather than arguing." Each of the family members is asked to clarify what they mean by these statements so that the other family members understand what they are trying to say.

The social worker then asks the family members to mark on a scale of 1 to 10 how serious the problem is. Martha indicates 7 and Joyce 8. Stephanie indicates 2 and Megan 4. The therapist comments on the relatively favorable perspectives of Martha and Joyce. The social worker then asks each of the family members to think of something that would help move their view of the situation just one step up and what would be different if this small step occurred. The emphasis was upon a small step that would be realistic for each to accomplish. Martha indicates that she would know that a small step occurred if Stephanie would at least stay in the room for a couple minutes when she entered rather than walking right out. Joyce says, "I would feel a small step has occurred if Martha and I could talk about something other than the problem with our children for a few minutes during the evening when we are together like we used to do before we moved into together." Stephanie says, "I would know that a small step occurred if my mother would ask me what I would like for supper the next day like she used to do when we were together." Megan says, "I would know that a small step occurred if we could at least watch part of one TV program together one night during the week." After ensuring that all of the family members had heard the comments of the others, the therapist asks them if they would rank from 1 to 10 how confident they were that they and the other family members could carry out this step. After obtaining this information, the family discuss what would help them be able to do these things and what would prevent them from doing so. They are also asked how motivated they are to make these changes. In this discussion, both parents indicate a strong motivation (8), Stephanie a relatively low motivation (3), and Megan a 5. The therapist comments on the commitment of Martha and Joyce to improve their own relationship and that of their family as a whole and their children.

The therapist explores times in which the family currently have been able to act in ways that at least approximate these steps. Even small and fleeting examples are noted and family members are asked to think about what has made these possible. The therapist asks further questions that amplify information about what occurs prior to these times and the impact that this has had on their relationship. These examples are discussed in terms of evidence that the family already has some coping strategies and ways in which they can be amplified.

Toward the end of the session the therapist indicates the need to take a break to consider what would be an appropriate recommendation. After returning, the therapist compliments the family members for coming to deal with what is a very difficult situation. The mothers are complimented on their commitment to their children and to each other. Stephanie is complimented on her concern for her mother and her wish to maintain a close relationship with her mother (positive reframing of her needs). Megan is commended for her wish to have a peaceful family.

The therapist then gives a version of the Formula One session that helps individuals focus on the things within the family that they do not want to change. "When people enter therapy, they begin to change. There are things in life, however, that you do not want to change because they are positive. Between now and the next time we meet, pay attention to these positive things in your life, and we will discuss them next week."

**Session 2.** Family members are asked to identify positive things in their family that they do not want to change, why these are important, and how can they be encouraged. Martha indicates that she is able to spend time with Joyce, someone who is very important to her. Joyce indicates that she has felt quite alone with her daughter before and now has another adult to share her parenting concerns. Stephanie is reluctant to mention anything that she would like to continue but finally adds that her mother does not seem quite so worried about money now that she can share expenses with another family. Megan said that she had wanted a sister and hopes that Stephanie will someday want to be a sister to her. Family members are then asked to scale their current situation. If it improved, they are asked to indicate what helped it improve. When asked to rate their current situation compared with last week, all the family members rated as slightly higher except for Stephanie. Family members were encouraged to identify what had happened that made them rate is somewhat higher. In terms of Stephanie, the therapist explored what helped prevent things from getting worse. Her mother also jumped in to remind Stephanie that she had done what Stephanie had asked earlier—get her input regarding the menu for dinner one might and that she had tried to fix her favorite food. Stephanie grudgingly admitted that this has helped make her feel better that day.

The therapist acknowledges with the family the important efforts that they have been making. Recognizing the tension between responding to the wishes of some family members for rapid change and the reluctance and fear of others (especially Stephanie) the therapist encourages the family to remember that addressing an important issue like theirs cannot be done overnight. It is important to move at the speed people feel comfortable. Family members can also be asked if there are any advantages for things staying the way that they are to elicit some of the ambivalence.

Another possible intervention with this family is that of prediction. Members can be asked to predict the night before if the next day will be better. This information can be then used to explore what are the patterns related to improvement.

These sessions set the stage for building on the strengths of the family members in the context of what is important for the individuals involved. Family members are encouraged to identify ways in which the family can gradually bring their miracle to life through small steps.

## Applications for Specific Problems

The following section describes some basic elements of using solution-focused therapy for specific problems. The basic theoretical approach described also applies to these applications and is not repeated in detail. The readings cited give further description of the assessment and treatment process.

### Substance Abuse

Solution-focused therapy addresses the problem of substance abuse by focusing on what is right—the strengths and resources of the individuals and the family. This translates into a search for and focus on times in which family members are able to not drink or abuse other substances and ways to increase these times. The emphasis is thus on the possible resources within the client, the family, and context that support not drinking to excess or abusing substances. The role of the family therapist is to elicit from family members "those strengths, resources, and healthy attributes that are needed to solve the presenting problem" (Berg & Miller, 1992, p. 5). The therapist thus guides the therapeutic conversation to identify the family's potential solutions to addressing the problem. Solution-focused therapy does not take a particular theoretical framework toward a substance-abuse problem. Instead it accepts the family's way of explaining and defining the problem and the solutions related to this explanation. This approach helps build a therapeutic relationship based on genuine cooperation (Berg & Miller, 1992).

As in other problematic issues, the therapeutic-client relationship can involve a customer (recognizes the problem and willing to work on it), a complainant (recognizes the problem and not willing to personally work on it), or a visitor (no agreed-upon problem). Understanding the nature of this relationship is important for success because these relationships require different approaches. In terms of people who are complainants or visitors, the therapist needs to identify goals that are relevant to the person involved. In terms of substance abuse, while individuals might not be a customer for their drinking problems, they might be willing to be one for other issues in life (Berg & Miller, 1992), for example, to keep their driver's license, their job, their family. Motivation to make a difference in these life issues can enlist the individual as a customer.

As with solution-focused therapy in general, establishing goals and criteria for success is another important step. The very process of identifying goals can be therapeutic. Effective goals are organized around the following characteristics: importance to the family members, small and manageable goals, realistic and achievable, concrete and specific goals, and positive goals. Creating goals that are important to all the family members can be complicated because family members can have different goals and the family therapist has the challenge of identifying goals that family members share. Such characteristics enable family members to have a clear picture of the steps involved. They also encourage people because progress is realistic.

It is also important to help families recognize that the importance of the goals that represent steps along the way in moving toward the final goal. Specifying what are the first steps toward accomplishing this final goal helps create manageable action steps and reduces people's fear that they are being asked to do the impossible. Being able to meet these steps along the way promotes a sense of mastery and hope rather than discouragement because the final goal seems too far away. As a result, the family can concentrate on helping the family member deal with their strategy for the office party next week (two beers with food rather than five mixed drinks) instead of feeling that they need to cope with the years of sobriety ahead.

The family therapist also acknowledges the reality of the hard work involved in creating change. Such an acknowledgement reflects the realistic nature of the difficulty in making such changes and thus also promotes the dignity and respect of the individuals involved (Berg & Miller, 1992).

The miracle question is used with family members to identify potential future goals and the small steps to begin the journey toward accomplishing them. Recognizing that the challenge in treating individuals with substance-abuse problems is to help them maintain progress and prevent relapse—solution-focused therapy emphasizes the times and circumstances during which the client is not demonstrating this problematic behavior. The therapist searches for small steps of progress and seeks to identify how family members managed to accomplish it. The therapist is very supportive and affirming of these efforts and steps of progress and the hard work involved. When relapse does occur, the therapist maintains the focus on seeing prior success and encouraging the client to return to the current goal as soon as possible rather than letting the family become bogged down with feelings of failure and shame (Berg & Miller, 1992). Such an approach is compatible with helping individuals deal effectively with relapse when individuals become so discouraged by a slip back into their old patterns that they give up their efforts to change.

### Grief and Loss

Butler and Powers (1996) describe the value of using a solution-focused approach in helping families cope with grief. The role of acknowledgement that validates the client's experience of the problem plays a critical role. When clients feel validated regarding their feeling of grief and loss, they are also able to begin to think of about possibilities and recovery from loss. Once family members feel understood and acknowledged, the miracle question can be a helpful tool in enabling them to think in terms of the possibility of emotional healing. Questions related to coping can be useful in identifying exceptions—times in which either the problem is not present, is less intense, or handled in a way that the individual feels better. When the family members are asked how they coped, it adds focus to the possibilities that they might be able to use in their current situation.

The scaling questions also provide a way to explore with family members ways that they are able to move in positive directions toward their goal. Since the approach is set within the coping resources and strategies of the family members, it enables family members to identify resources within their own framework. Butler and Powers (1996) have discovered that families will often identify spiritual resources.

Tasks represent a further healing strategy. The family therapist assesses whether action-oriented, thinking, or observational tasks would be most appropriate for the clients. "Whatever the task, the message is designed around the basic acknowledgement-possibility paradigm" (Butler & Powers, 1996, p. 240). While pacing is always important in working with families, this is a particularly critical issue in therapy with families dealing with grief. Therapists need to be attentive to the messages that families are giving them in this regard (Butler & Powers, 1996).

## EVALUATION

As in all models of family therapy, therapists must always tailor interventions to the individuals involved and to the matter of timing. As in other therapy models, this can mean ensuring that family members feel understood in terms of the reality of their situation. Clients might need to express their pain and fears and feel that their therapist understands this aspect of their lives before they are able to take the next step to look at the future and solutions. Failure to do so can make these potentially effective techniques appear mechanical. I taught for a brief time in a community in which solution-focused treatment was very prominent. Students reported that their clients would sometimes say, "Oh no, not another miracle question." While I could not interview these individuals, I wondered if their comments reflected their sense that the technique had been and was being applied in a rather mechanistic way without giving them the opportunity to feel understood and validated.

Butler and Powers (1996) describe the importance of validating hurtful and painful aspects of the client's feelings through an example of working with a woman with a long history of depression. When counseling a woman who was suffering from depression in response to recent losses, the therapist listened in an emphatic manner rather than asking about the future. During the second interview, the woman again told of her long history of depression and loss. This time the therapist recognized with the client her many losses and used this to introduce a solution-focused question: "When I look over this long list of losses and consider what you've been through, I can't but wonder how you keep it from getting worse" (p. 230). Waiting to introduce the solution approach in this manner helped the woman feel understood and ready to listen to a strength-based approach.

Gingerich and Eisengart (2000) reviewed a number of studies evaluating the effectiveness of solution-focused treatment. Outcomes in terms of individuals experiencing problems including depression, antisocial behavior, and orthopedic health problems indicated that solution-focused therapy was helpful. A study of parents indicated improvement of parenting skills for participants in solution-focused treatment. Other studies using client's perceptions of progress revealed that about 75 percent of the clients had made substantial progress in meeting their goals and that this progress was maintained for at least the eighteen months of the follow up period (O'Connell, 1998).

In follow-up studies with couples that had received solution-focused therapy, family members and therapist reported somewhat different versions of what was helpful. While the therapist focused primarily on the techniques that they used, the family members were more likely to attribute this to their relationship with the therapist (Nichols & Schwartz, 2005).

Some have raised the question whether or not solution-focused therapy is genuinely collaborative or directive in the positive approach (Nichols & Schwartz, 2005). As discussed earlier, therapists can err in being too insistent in emphasizing the positive aspects of the lives of families. Critics have raised the question whether families have genuinely moved into a more positive mode or have stopped raising these concerns given the strong positive message from the therapist and disregard for anything negative (Nichols & Schwartz, 2005).

In seeking to create a balance between theoretically based techniques and the reality of working with families, Nichols and Schwartz (2005) quote Michele Weiner-Davis's confession that she doesn't always practice what she preaches. "My clients cry and express pain, anger, disappointment and fears just as they might in any other therapist's office. And I respond with compassion. . . . My therapy story [what she presents in workshops] is not the total picture of how I do therapy" (p. 157). Her comments reveal the essential need to join and acknowledge as part of the process of eliciting solutions and future possibilities from family members.

# SUMMARY

Solution-focused therapy has emerged as an important brief family therapy model that helps families focus on their strengths and on ways to solve problems more effectively. Family members are viewed as the experts regarding their goals and ways to accomplish them. By using a future orientation, it enables family members envision possibilities and to identify the small steps that they can take to create these changes. By searching for exceptions to the problems, it helps family members identify potential skills in problem solving and enhances the self-efficacy of family members.

# 8

# *Narrative Family Therapy*

As discussed in chapter 4, Mrs. James and her children, Marie and John, come to the counseling center with the family still dealing with the scars created by the children's sexual abuse by their stepfather. Mrs. James has taken a courageous stance to leave her husband and support her children during this difficult time as well as arrange for the children to receive the help that they need. In important ways the James family can be characterized as a problem-saturated family—the problem has become the dominant story of the family and healthy aspects of the family are not incorporated into this family narrative. Mrs. James has great difficult seeing the positive signs in John and in her as a parent. Instead of Marie's outgoing adaptation reassuring her mother, it only serves to confirm the mother's worries about John in their current family narrative. Encouraging words from the teacher have also not found a place in this problem-saturated story.

Narrative family therapy builds on the assumption that family problems and solutions rest in large measure on the meanings that people attribute to life events. Human beings are by nature meaning-making creatures. Families create stories that help make sense of past and current events as well as influence their expectations for the future. No family gathering is ever complete without family members telling stories about family events. Families maintain their sense of continuity and identity through the stories that are told. The stories that families create and tell are strongly influenced by their social and cultural context as well as specific life events. Narrative therapy uses a strengths-based approach to reconstruct family stories.

From the perspective of narrative family therapy, families become stuck due to problem-saturated stories. "When a problem-saturated story predominates, individuals are repeatedly invited into disappointment and misery. It becomes increasingly difficult to liberate themselves from habitually performing in the same old problematic way" (Green, 2003, p. 195). Families seek help when their life story does not meet the current needs of the family (White & Epston, 1990). The central theme of narrative therapy is to empower families to create stories that liberate them from these problem-saturated versions and in the process to recreate new and more empowering meanings. These alternative stories are strength based and highlight the resources of family members. From a resiliency theory perspective, the meanings that families attribute to life events are critical in terms of both risk and protective factors. Meanings influence how life events are interpreted and experienced and the coping strategies that are deemed appropriate. These interpretations promote self-efficacy or a sense of powerlessness within family members. As a result, helping families create meaning systems that enable them to cope and to meet the needs of family members represents an important therapeutic effort that supports family resiliency. From the perspective of narrative therapy, "the question for the narrative therapist isn't one of truth but of which points are useful and lead to preferred effects for clients. Problems aren't in persons . . . or relationships. . . . Problems are embedded in points of view about individuals and their situations" (Nichols & Schwartz, 2001, p. 316). Since problems are embedded in points of view reflected in the language of story, the narrative therapist seeks to help the family reexamine and alter the family story to become a more empowering one. Changing the story enables individuals to change their behavior and family relationships.

Narrative therapy provides a means for the James family to claim its identity as survivors rather than as "damaged goods" and to thus envision the strengths that are present in the family. With this altered view of the family reality, the actions of family members and their responses to each other will also be shaped and altered in accord with their new story. For example, when Mrs. James is able to view John as a healthy boy with a more introverted temperament than Marie's and to recognize that some of the behaviors that she sees can be attributed to the development stresses of being thirteen years old, she will be able to hear the affirming words of the teacher and Marie about John. She will also be more able to relinquish her burden of guilt and sense of failure. She will be able to more accepting of John as he is and reduce the pressure on John to be more extroverted. As John begins to feel that he not a disappointment to his mother, he will regain some of his self-confidence in the social realm. He will also not have such a need to escape into his own room and will be able to more sociable with his family. As Marie is no longer used as a standard for John to meet in order to feel accepted, the strain in their relationship can decrease and the two siblings can be a stronger support system for each other.

## *THEORETICAL BACKGROUND*

Narrative therapy grew out of the social constructionist movement that argued that social interaction rather than objective descriptions of reality plays a powerful role in generating meaning for people (Hoffman, 1993). Cultural beliefs and patterns strongly influence how people view their world. It is thus important for therapists to understand their own social context and that of the families they serve. Language emerges as an important vehicle for change because it is the means by which people share their view of reality. Cultural group membership as well and family and individual life experiences shape the language that gives meaning to life events. Social constructionists also assert that therapy should be collaborative in nature because "no one party has a corner on the truth and new realities emerge in the process of the dialogue" (Nichols & Schwartz, 2001, p. 316).

Michael White, Cheryl White, and David Epston were the original developers of the narrative movement in family therapy (Nichols & Schwartz, 2001). They developed narrative metaphors and techniques to help families recreate their stories in order to move from problem-saturated stories that burden families to ones that empower and free families from this burden (White & Epston, 1990). Nichols & Schwartz (2001) provide an excellent discussion of the theoretical journey of the founders of narrative family therapy. Other early contributors include Jeffrey Zimmerman, Gene Combs, and Vicki Dickerson (see Dickerson & Zimmerman, 1992; Freedman & Combs, 1996; Zimmerman & Dickerson, 1996). Currently narrative therapy represents a major model of treatment within therapy.

## *MAJOR TENETS*

Narrative therapy is based on the seven tenets of the theoretical model.

1.  Experience is shaped by the language we use. Language helps us create the meaning of life events and thus is an important avenue for change.

2.  We construct stories that shape our life events. How we experience life events is inherently shaped by the stories that we construct.

3.  Our stories shape what we see and remember. As we live our lives, what we see and how we remember it are shaped by our stories. These stories in turn are further influenced by perceptions of subsequent life events. My husband and I joke that we take separate vacations because the stories that we tell and the memories that we share following trips are so different. Family therapists discover that family members sincerely give very different accounts of what happened the previous evening.

4.  Social context has a profound influence on the stories that shape life events. Culture shapes values, social roles, gender relationships, concepts of justice, and many other aspects of life. Therapists need to understand ways in which cultural narratives trap people into stories that create problems in their lives and to promote alternate stories that can be strength affirming.

5.  Stories don't mirror life, they shape it. Our stories do not represent reality, they shape how we experience life. The emphasis is on stories rather than a search for facts. As a result of the way in which family stories shape life, incidents and meanings that do not contribute to this problem view of the individual or the family are lost and do not actively counter the problem focus. People continue to react to this problem-focused view of life, their family, and family members. Strengths and positive

ways of viewing life are lost in this process. Parents who are worried about one of their children may focus on the reports of teachers who describe problems in the classroom and give less credence to the reports of teachers who give positive reports.

6.  It is important to expand our life stories. Current life stories can be too narrow and fail to include possibilities for growth and healing. Problems can occur when we accept cultural or familial views that are narrow. These views thus limit alternative interpretations or alternative ways of responding. Problem-saturated stories begin to represent the family reality (Nichols & Schwartz, 2001).

7.  Families are not the problem, families experience problems. Instead of viewing problems as within the family structure or system or members of the family, it is important to view the family as contending with a problem rather than being a problem. This view offers the possibility of uniting family members to address the problem facing the family (Nichols & Schwartz, 2001; White & Epston, 1990; Zimmerman & Dickson, 1994).

## GOAL OF TREATMENT

The goal of narrative therapy is to alter the family's interpretation of themselves and their situation. As family members are able to change the meaning of life events, they are also able to change their responses. Nichols and Schwartz (2001) describe the goal as transforming "clients' identities from flawed to heroic" (p. 397).

Therapy seeks to reconstruct problem-saturated stories by helping families deconstruct them and replace them with alternatives that enable family members to identify and claim their strengths and resources. The family therapist seeks to create these alternatives through several specific strategies. The first is described as externalizing the problem. By separating the family from the problem (the family has a problem but is not the problem) the therapist can help unite the family to fight this common enemy. The second approach is to search through the "family's history to find unique outcomes or sparking events—times in which they resisted the problem or behaved in ways that contracted the problem story" (Nichols & Schwartz, 2001, p. 397).

## ROLE OF THE THERAPIST

The family therapist plays the role as a coeditor of the family's stories rather than an outside expert who manipulates people to make specific changes. The therapist helps the family deconstruct their problem-saturated stories and reconstruct more empowering stories. The therapist assumes a collaborative relationship with family members. The therapist takes a nonknowing stance with the family and thus embarks upon a series of questions with the family as the expert. The task of the therapist is to engage the family in ways that give room to new meanings (the role of the coeditor). The therapist seeks to help the family develop healing narratives.

The family is treated with great respect in this process and the counselor remains optimistic regarding the family's potential resources. Guided by these principles, the therapist asks the family members a series of questions to help identify exceptions and examples of resourcefulness. These examples help to separate the family from the current problem-saturated narratives that have dominated the family's view of reality and the family.

The therapist also engages the clients in externalizing conversations to separate them from the current negative narratives. The therapist can help conceptualize the problems facing the family as an externalized entity (e.g., "damaged goods" for the James family). Given the impact of social forces on family narratives, the therapist also explores with the family ways in which cultural themes can be limiting (e.g., cultural messages regarding gender) in order to create possible alternative realities. The therapist must be aware of her or his own cultural or personal narratives because they could influence viable alternatives for the family. The therapist must also be aware of her professional authority and its potential to shape client's stories.

## TREATMENT PROCESS

Narrative therapy consists of a series of questions designed to edit the stories of families in order to free families from the hold of problem-saturated stories and to reconstruct more empowering stories.

**Listen to the family tell their problem.** The therapist begins by a respectful eliciting from each of the family members a picture of the current family life through a series of questions. In addition to a description of the problem and situation that prompted the family to come for help, the therapist seeks a broader picture of the life of family members. Such a conversation not only helps establish rapport so that family members feel understood, but also enables the therapist to begin to identify some of the resources and accomplishments of the family. This information helps expand the view of the family beyond the problem-saturated story. The initial conversation also helps establish a collaborative relationship with the family members.

**Externalize the problem.** Based on the assumption that the problem does not reside within the family but within the family's narrative account, the narrative therapist seeks to help the family members detach themselves from the problem by externalizing it (White & Epston, 1990). The family contends with the problem but the problem is not equated with the family, rather portrayed as an "unwelcome invader that tries to dominate family members' lives" (Nichols & Schwartz, 2001, p. 401). For example, the James family can be helped to externalize their problem in terms of damaged goods. The children in this family experienced the pain of abuse by their stepfather and this family has been contending with both the direct effect of this series of events and the fears of what this effect might be. White describes a family that has become dominated by their child's smearing his pants. This problem becomes externalized as "sneaky poo" (White & Epston, 1990). If a family has many angry shouting arguments that tear the family members apart, the problem could be externalized as "the storm cloud." The process of externalizing taps the creativity of the counselor and the family. The therapist suggests this term to the family and it is offered for their input rather than being imposed as a label by an expert. Externalizing the problem takes the burden of blame off the family member and helps unite the family to address the problem.

**Map the influence of the problems and of the persons** (relative influence questions). Once the problem is identified and the beginning process of externalizing has begun, the counselor asks each family member to discuss the effect of the problem on the family members. The important message here is that the problem is not equated with the individual or the family. Family members can be asked both how the problem influences them (influence of the problem) and how they have influenced the problem (influence of the individual). Family members can be asked a series of questions that explore these two dimensions: how has problem made them do things they might not ordinarily have done; how did they fight back against the problem; how has the problem tried to sneak up on them; how has it affected them as a parent/spouse/daughter; how have they held out against the power of the problem? Related questions can be asked to indicate the type of relationships that exist with the problem and that underline the difference between the problem and the family members themselves (White & Epston, 1990).

These relative influence questions map out the interplay between the family and the problem. Mrs. James can be helped to identify the impact her belief that the family members are damaged goods has on her relationship with Marie and John. She can be asked to discuss when she has been able to push back that thought and take pride in her accomplishments for the family. John can be asked to talk about his response when he is pressed because of the fear of damaged goods. He can describe how he turns up the radio louder and hides out more in his room. He can also describe how he also enjoys doing things with his friends and feels a part of the group when asked to join them. Marie can be asked how it affects her and might indicate how she spends more time with her friends where she does not have to deal with it. She can also describe how she sometimes encourages her mother to view John as a normal thirteen-year-old boy going through what is frequently a difficult time in life.

The following strategies are important ways of mapping the impact of the problem on the family and the family's ability to fight back against the problem.

*Search for a unique outcome.* Using a strengths-based approach the therapist seeks to identify with family members times in which they have managed to win against the problems or at least were able to be less controlled by it. Family members can thus be helped to identify times in which they, not the problem, took charge over what happened. Since family members have been dominated by the problem-saturated narrative, family members have frequently overlooked these times. The therapist seeks to identify and validate these times in order to help the family begin to construct a new story (White & Epston, 1990). As in all counseling efforts, the therapist must be sensitive to timing because people need to feel heard and understood and will resist moving forward until they feel understood.

The therapist can help Mrs. James recognize times in which she did not let her fears win and has been able to accept John's more introverted personality without becoming alarmed. John can describe times in which he went out with his friends or watched TV with his mother. He can also report how his recent report card was good. Marie can describe times in which she enjoyed spending time with her mother and brother.

*Ask spectator questions.* These questions explore how family members speculate how others people might experience them. This technique is designed to gain a wider perspective on the narrative account (Williams & Kurtz, 2003). Mrs. James might be asked how her other family members or friends would have explained how she found the strength and courage to leave her husband and make a new life for her children. She might also be asked what information the children's teachers have used as the basis for the good reports that they have given them.

*Collapse time.* Family members can be asked to explore the issue over time. This exploration includes both the past and the future (Williams & Kurtz, 2003). Mrs. James and her children might be asked if damaged goods is a greater problem for them now than it was last year. Perhaps the children would agree that their mother is gradually fighting back more effectively (or less so as the case may be). Family members could then be asked what would be happening in the family in the next six months if they continued to push it back, or let it get the best of them.

*Predict setbacks.* The therapist can help family members prepare for setbacks in ways that will not demoralize the family. This technique recognizes that the process of reconstructing a narrative and changing life circumstances is an ongoing process with inevitable ups and downs. As a result, the family finds a way to incorporate setbacks in the family story without becoming overly discouraged and feeling defined by these problems. The James family members might be asked how they will fight back if damaged goods manages to strike back and makes their mother worried again, or makes John want to avoid others in the family by staying in his room, or encourages

Marie to stay away from her family by spending all of her time with her friends. The family can be helped to identify such events as part of the ongoing life story and help them find ways to fight back against the problem.

*Reauthorize the story in terms of the family members* (significance questions). The therapist now uses the exceptions that have been identified as evidence to change the views held by family members about themselves, others in the family, and the family as a group. If a family member has been able to withstand the pressure to cave in or to refuse to become defeated by the problem, what does it say about the person? The therapist asks family members questions that make them reflect on what it says about themselves that they were able to withstand the pressure of the problem. The answers to these questions help people reclaim the strengths evident in their actions and to define themselves in terms of strengths rather than the problem-saturated stories. Questions can also be asked in terms of the family as a unit in terms of identified exceptions. "What does it say about you, Mrs. James, that you were able to conquer your fears and hear good reports from the teacher?" "What does it say about John and Marie that they are able to be such good students?" "What does it say about your family that you can have these good times together?" (a specific example described by family members).

*Identify cultural messages that support problem-saturated stories.* Since family stories are influenced by the cultural context, it can be important to help family members identify the cultural messages that shape these narratives. Some of these messages might relate to gender prescriptions or family power roles. What is the impact on the family when young women are valued in terms of their sexual appeal to men, when boys are supposed to be athletic, when mothers are supposed to feel responsible for everything related to their children, when men are supposed to be strong and not express their fears? Are these messages that have had an impact on the family story, are these messages that the family has accepted or has something managed to resist? How do these messages help the family meet the needs of family members or have created burdens for the family members?

If Mrs. James comes from a cultural background that views women as needing to keep a family together despite the odds or one in which women are expected to be submissive to their husbands, this cultural message could have made it difficult for Mrs. James to leave her husband. It could also have influenced the nature of the supports that were available to her during this difficult time. Cultural messages that suggest that John's more introverted personality does not fit with a masculine identity could make it more difficult for Mrs. James to accept John's personality as normal rather than a sign of damaged goods. The therapist can thus help to help the family look at ways in which cultural messages have shaped the alternatives available to the family and the family's interpretation of life events. For Mrs. James, such an understanding could be used to emphasize the courage that she demonstrated in the face of these cultural constraints. Broadening of the cultural message regarding John could help decrease the problematic interpretation of the current situation.

**Create ways to reinforce the new narrative.** The therapist can help family members identify others within the community or extended family members who can support the family and their reconstructed narrative. Are there other women, friends, or extended family members that Mrs. James can turn to for support when she is fighting back her fears and guilt? Can Mrs. James ask for another visit with the teacher to learn more about John's current school performance that could be supportive of this more strength-based narrative?

**Communicate with the family by letters from the therapist.** Letters from the therapist can be used to support the reconstructed narrative. Summary letters following a session can be used to reinforce the issues raised in the session, especially as they relate to the possible alternatives to the problem-saturated story. These letters are available for the family to read on an ongoing basis. The therapist could write the following letter to the James children following an early session.

> Dear Mrs. James, Marie, and John,
>
> I have been thinking about our session today and our conversation. Please let me know if I missed some important things or need to understand anything more accurately.
>
> You described how you escaped from an abusive family situation to create a new family group without your husband and stepfather. Mrs. James, I understand that this took a great deal of courage on your part because you had to find a way to support the family and risked the anger of your husband. I understand that you helped Marie and John receive counseling to deal with being abused by their stepfather. Marie and John, I realize that you both took advantage of this opportunity as shown by how well you have been doing in school. I realize from our meeting that the three of you have a great deal of love for each other and have been doing the best that you can to make a new life for your family.
>
> I also learned that you have been struggling with the problem of "damaged goods." This has affected all of you in different ways. Mrs. James, you have been afraid that you failed Marie and John by letting them be abused by their stepfather and by not protecting them enough. You worry that both Marie and John, and especially John, are still carrying serious scars from it. I learned that "damaged goods" becomes especially strong when John spends time in his room rather than going out with his friends or being with his mother and sister. John, I understand that when your mother worries about you, you feel that you are not living up to your mother's expectations. You then spend even more time in your room, watching TV or playing video games. When your mother compares you with Marie, you begin to doubt yourself and "damaged goods" gains more power. Marie, I understand that your mother is not as worried about you because you go out frequently with your friends.

I also learned about times when your family is able to put "damaged goods" in the background. Mrs. James, there are times when you are able to relax and hear good news from the teacher. There are also times when you are able to feel that you have given both John and Marie the help that they need. Marie and John, there are times when you are able to have a good time together—quite an accomplishment for a thirteen-year-old brother and a sixteen-year-old sister.

I wonder how you have been able to be such a strong family and show such care for each other. I wonder how you managed to push back the power of "damaged goods" when you did? Where did you find this strength?

I know I will have more questions next week when I learn more about ways that you are continuing to push back "damaged goods." I will be glad to discuss this with you further as I remain your partner in your important efforts.

**Use a reflecting team.** The reflecting team as developed by Anderson (1991) consists of several other therapists who listen to the family session and are invited to give their input to the therapist and the family. For narrative therapists, reflecting teams join with the family to help the process of developing new narratives—both deconstructing the problem-saturated descriptions and helping shape more positive and strength-affirming alternatives (Freedman & Combs, 1996). In contrast to the Milan approach in which the team behind the one-way mirror remained unknown to the family and spoke only to the therapist, as befitting the egalitarian and strength-based approach of narrative therapy, the reflecting team speaks openly to both the family and the therapist (Goldenberg & Goldenberg, 2000). The precise way in which the process is organized varies from therapist to therapist. In general the members of the reflecting team speculate about the nature of the problem and the family's response to it. They seek to identify further exceptions. The team uses language that reflects the context—the presence of the family members. The team members are respectful and strength affirming in their comments.

I wonder how the family managed to stick together despite all of their long history of difficulties.

I am impressed by the way the family has managed to fight back against the problem of distrust that might have torn another family apart.

Family members are encouraged to ask questions of and dialogue with members of the team. The team also raises questions about possible alternatives.

What did the family expect to happen by choosing this path?

Are there other routes that your family could take?

Have you thought about any of these other possibilities?

How might you talk about some of these other paths?

The questions and comment of the team members can encourage family members to consider new possibilities (Goldenberg & Goldenberg, 2000).

Transparency is another aspect of the narrative model. The reflecting team members reveal aspects of themselves that can offer healing to the family members. I remember Anne Hartman at a National Association of Social Workers conference describing her experience serving as a member of a reflecting team while working with Michael White. The mother in this family had struggled hard to keep her children together. Anne had been hospitalized with polio as a child and had experienced the fears and sense of aloneness of being hospitalized for a long period of time as a young child. She was encouraged to use this personal experience to further support the value of the mother's struggles in this family. She described how sharing this information with the mother had served to validate the mother and her efforts in a powerful manner.

The reflecting team could join the James family and the therapist after learning about the situation facing the family. They could ask questions: How did Mrs. James find the strength and courage to leave her husband when she learned about what was happening to the children? She did not have a steady source of income and her extended family did not approve of her taking this action. This took a great deal of strength and it would be helpful to learn more about how she went about seeking support to make this move.

How have the children been able to do so well in school?

How does a family with two teenagers do things together as a family? I wonder how they manage to do so (refer to specific events).

What would happen if Mrs. James could feel more relaxed about John spending time in his room when the thought of damaged goods sneaks up on her?

**Using certificates and celebrations.** The counselor can mark victories or the creation of new meanings through celebrations or certificates. White and Epston (1990) describe ways in which certificates can be used to validate progress. The certificates designed by White include the new individuals or family narrative combined with a dash of humor.

The social worker can create a certificate for the James family that would acknowledge their success in creating a health affirming family narrative. There could be a celebration of their growing success in defeating "damaged goods" and replacing it with "doing fine."

## *EVALUATION*

There is limited outcome data related to narrative therapy, especially studies using objective outcome measures. Most of the outcome information is impressionistic. Part of this limitation relates to the social constructionist nature of the therapy that resides in the subjective perceptions of families. In a study using ethnography to identify the experience of eight families regarding narrative therapy, the clients found narrative therapy to be helpful. They reported that the presenting problem was reduced. The clients also appreciated the respectful approach of the therapists, the recognition they received from the team members to overcome their problem, and the reflecting team's helpful comments (O'Connor, Meakes, Pickering, & Schuman, 1997). Another small (six families) single-subject evaluation of narrative therapy used to improve parent-child conflict revealed significant improvement (88–98%) in conflict in five of the families (Besa, 1994). Another small study revealed more mixed results. Four clients indicated that they were able to see the problem in a more helpful way and another four indicated that they were not able to so (Coulehan, Friedlander, & Heatherington, 1998).

A recent study evaluated narrative family therapy from the perspective of the therapists who were conducting therapy using this model of treatment. Based on ethnographic observations and interviews with eight therapists, the following themes emerged. All eight of the therapists indicated that the narrative approach was helpful to their clients. They attributed this success to three reasons. First, narrative therapy promoted "personal agency" in clients. Second, the therapist demonstrated respect to the clients and did not pathologize clients or place them in categories. The third reason was a weaker one—clients became more able to deal with their problems. They viewed narrative therapy as unburdening the therapist and the family and opening up new pathways for growth. Therapists also expressed the limitations due to the requirement for specialized training, the time- and resource-consuming nature of the model. The last was especially an issue when the reflecting team was used. While the reflecting team was viewed as helpful in terms of opening new possibilities, it could also be overwhelming to both the family and the therapist (O'Connor et al., 2004). On the other hand, findings from several other studies suggest that the reflecting team helped the family make positive changes and that the multiple perspectives were viewed as helpful (Biever, Gardner, & Bobele, 1999).

Reservations have been voiced about the fit of narrative therapy for some families. There are families where the members might not be able to be successfully encouraged to join together to fight the problem by means of the techniques of this model. Nichols and Schwartz (2001) raise the question whether externalizing and searching for unique outcomes necessarily mean that the family will be able to join forces in this way.

The relativism of the social constructivist basis of narrative therapy also poses questions and potential problems. There is the dilemma that occurs when the issues at hand are difficult to place in relative terms. Violence within the family has been raised as particularly problematic in this context (Laird, 2000; O'Connor et al., 2004). The latter also reflects the controversy within narrative therapy about how to deal with cultural patterns that could be viewed as oppression in the family. According to Laird (2000), some narrative therapists consider "bringing culture into the therapy room in a way that challenges dominate ethnic practices or cultural discourses as an imposition of personal politics" (p. 352). Others, including Laird (2000), "argue that clients need to be helped to deconstruct not only their self-narratives, but the dominant cultural narratives and discursive practices that constitute their lives" (p. 352). According to Laird (2000), "Deconstruction means to explore how these dominating discourses are shaped, whose interests they serve and whose they may subjugate, to explore the marginalized possibilities" (p. 352). She also raises the issues of how the presence of both dominated and subjugated narratives influences the stories that are available to clients in their situation. The therapist does deal with this issue by delivering his or her own views as truths but by being aware of the voices that are silenced due to lack of power and by helping these voices find a way to emerge (Laird, 2000).

Nichols and Schwartz (2001) in their critique of narrative family therapy ask if the therapist is not more directive than the model purports to be. Although the therapist engages in the family in a series of questions rather than giving answers, these questions are targeted to leading people in certain directions.

Laird (2000) describes narrative therapy as well-suited to culturally sensitive practice. "The therapeutic stance—a stance that is highly respective, collaborative, and nonhierarchical—is one that encourages the expression of multiple ideas and possibilities. It avoids blame or pathologizing; searches for strengths, rather than defects; is grounded in a value stance; and fosters transparency by the therapist" (p. 350). Such an approach requires the therapist to be self-reflective regarding his or her own narrative.

## SUMMARY

Narrative therapy has emerged as a major school of family therapy arising from the social constructionist perspective. Narrative therapy seeks to make changes within the family by helping families replace their problem-saturated stories with alternative ones that include examples of strengths and success over problems. Such a model of therapy can be especially helpful for families for whom the meaning that they have attributed to life events has become problematic for the family.

# 9

# *Psychoeducational Family Counseling*

Gregg (aged nineteen) became ill during sophomore year in college. He began to experience voices telling him that his roommate and others on his residence hall floor were trying to hurt him and that he should avoid them as much as possible. He found it difficult to concentrate on his studies as a result of the voices and his fears of what might happen to him. He gradually stopped going to classes because he found it too difficult to concentrate and could sometimes be found pacing about one of the quieter spots on campus. During the night he would fight sleep by walking the hallways because he feared what would happen while he was sleeping. His residence hall counselor became concerned and insisted that Gregg see someone at the student health center. This visit led to a meeting with staff members of the counseling center where Gregg was diagnosed with schizophrenia. Because he felt so threatened by the college situation, he left school and returned home to his parents where he began receiving help from the local mental health center. Gregg's parents' were bewildered and frightened about what had happened to their son. They were unsure about the nature of the illness and how they should respond in ways that would be helpful.

Lillian (aged seventy-eight) was the matriarch of the family. Her married children lived in the area with their children. The family gathered at her home on a weekly basis and this gathering was the centerpiece of the family ties. Lillian was free with her advice for her children and they respected her suggestions. She had been widowed for the last ten years and supported herself through Social Security and her own and her husband's pensions. Suddenly everything in this family changed. Lillian had a serious stroke. She could speak with difficulty and needed help in taking care of herself. Her emotions changed rapidly and this once proud and independent woman would find herself crying even in the presence of her family. Her adult children found this change troubling and puzzling.

Bradley (aged thirty) rode his motorcycle to work and joined his friends on weekend rides. One day coming home from a ride with his friends, he skidded at a turn and his bike turned over and he hit his head. Unfortunately, he was not wearing his helmet. While Bradley survived the accident, he suffered a severe closed head injury that left him with major cognitive and emotional disabilities. His wife and parents were relieved that he had survived the accident but were now distressed about the changes that they were seeing and uncertain about how they should react to Bradley.

All these families share a major change in terms of one of the family members. The above individuals and their families are struggling to cope with a difficult health situation of a family member. Family members are uncertain about the consequences of the illness or disability, what they can expect, what effective treatments are, and how they should respond in ways that are helpful. The health problem of one family member represents a source of distress for the entire family.

Psychoeducational approaches are designed to help family members cope with these and other difficult circumstances. While the specific nature of the programs vary in terms of content and format, psychoeducational models share the following components: education involving information about the nature of the illness or specific problem, symptoms and signs of relapse, and treatment options; ways that the family members can cope and help the person with the problem and about the potential impact on the family members; skills to cope more effectively and emotional and social support for the family members. Families can also be empowered to take on an advocacy role as appropriate for the family. Psychoeducational treatment of families can occur with individual families or in multifamily groups. This chapter includes a discussion of the basic assumptions and elements of psychoeducational treatment models, the role of the counselor, cultural implications for psychoeducational approaches, and a description of some examples of approaches in dealing with specific problems. The term "psychoeducational" is used in the broad sense as an approach that contains the above elements rather than referring to specific treatment models related to families with mentally ill members. The concept of a combination of education regarding knowledge and skills and support for family members has a wide applicability with families.

## *THEORETICAL BACKGROUND*

Psychoeducational models in the field of mental health, specifically schizophrenia, grew out of an understanding that some of the problems evident in families in which a family member had a mental illness were in response to the distress created by the disruptions of living with an ill family member rather than the cause of the illness. While these patterns did not cause the illness, they could create stress with the potential to increase the risk of relapse. Psychoeducational models were also created in the context of a growing appreciation of the crucial role the family plays in caring for individuals with illness. As Simon, McNeil, Franklin, and Cooperman (1991) describe in their classic article regarding psychoeducational approaches, this trend was accentuated by the deinstitutionalization in mental health. The very short term stays in hospitals for all illnesses generally place family members center stage in caring for their members. As important as the mental health and general health care systems are in providing care, it is the family typically that assumes the ongoing responsibility for the person.

Despite the important role of the family, in various studies family members reported that they had not received any information about the nature of the illness and ways to cope. In addition to being burdened down by worry and lack of knowledge, family members with a member with schizophrenia felt blamed by the professionals and stigmatized by the illness (Simon, McNeil, Franklin, & Cooperman, 1991; Solomon, 1998). As a result, ignorance and blame increased their already difficult caretaking burden. Rather than view the family as the cause of the illness of the family member, the new approach has conceptualized family members as potential resources who need information and skills in order to carry out their important responsibilities. Recognizing the cyclical nature of stress and distress, psychoeducational approaches seek to reduce the distress of family members and to help family members respond more effectively to the ill family member. These changes can in turn reduce the ill family member's experience of distress that can contribute to relapse or a worsening of symptoms. Psychoeducation with family members is now viewed as an evidenced practice model in adult psychiatry (Dixon et al., 2001).

Early models of psychoeducational approaches with families in the field of mental health were generally organized especially around the need to help families decrease their level of expressed emotion (high EE), referring particularly to critical and hostile comments and climate, and included a rather lengthy process of family counseling (Solomon, 1996). Solomon also describes family educational models based on a coping-adaptation model designed to offer family members information to enhance the self-efficacy of family members (Solomon, 1996). In many subsequent discussions in the literature, the term "psychoeducational" is used to describe a variety of specific interventions organized around the general themes of education regarding the nature and treatment of the illness, skills for coping, and support for the family in terms of dealing with a difficult situation. The model can be implemented with individual families or multifamily groups. Families can be seen both with and without the member with the problem. As indicated earlier, this chapter draws upon this broader concept of psychoeducational approaches.

Research in the area of chronic disease also supports the value of psychoeducational approaches. An ecological perspective has emerged as the most effective treatment model of chronic disease, whose care and management make up the largest single cost to the health care system (Fisher & Weihs, 2000). Rather than focusing on the patient, the intervention addresses the social setting in which disease management occurs. The social context generally is the family. This approach emphasizes the "relational context in which the disease takes place," includes the family environment, addresses the broad needs of the patient and family members, views the disease as ongoing process, and includes the patient and the family in the assessment of outcomes (Fisher & Weihs, 2000, p. 562). Fisher and Weihs describe examples involving a range of health issues including children with cystic fibrosis, type 1 diabetes, and older adults at risk for rehospitalization (2000).

The psychoeducational approach mirrors resiliency-based research in terms of how family members cope with difficult illness in the family as discussed in chapter 13. In studies of families coping with children with chronic illness (Kliewer, 1997; Patterson & McCubbin, 1983), with family members with HIV/AIDS (Thompson, 1999), and other health problems (Chesla, 1999), parents and family members did so by increasing their knowledge through seeking information about the illness from the medical system and by seeking social support.

The National Working Group on Family-Based Interventions in Chronic Disease identified potential mechanisms by which relationships within the family influence disease management and risk and protective factors (Fisher & Weihs, 2000). Research has identified two ways that relationships with the family influence chronic disease management outcomes. First, the emotional climate within the family influences the physiologic systems of the patient. Secure attachments among family members have positive effects while family hostility and criticism impact negatively on the "hormonal, immunologic, and other biological systems that are linked to the outcomes of chronic disease through the physiologic stress responses" (Fisher & Weihs, 2000, p. 562). Family relationships also influence the disease process through the patient's self-care behavior. Fisher & Weihs (2000) point out that many "chronic diseases require tedious, repetitive, and at times invasive management procedures that force major changes in family life style, allocation of power, personal autonomy, role functioning, and decision making" (p. 562). Family response can either lead to family members working together to encourage effective disease management or undermine it by their response and actions. Thus the family's response affects the disease process directly as well as the emotional lives of all the family members.

Linking research between family resiliency in general and protective family factors related to chronic disease, the following characteristics have been identified as playing a protective role in disease management: "family closeness and connectedness, problem-focused coping skills, clear family organization and decision making, and direct communication among family members related to the chronic diseases" (Fisher & Weihs, 2000, p. 562). Risk factors included "intrafamily hostility, criticism and blame, psychological trauma related to the initial diagnosis and treatment of the disease; lack of an extra familial support system; family perfectionism and rigidity; and presence of psychopathology with onset prior to the chronic disease" (Fisher & Weihs,

2000, p. 562). While improving protective factors is valuable, reducing family risk factors is especially important (Fisher & Weihs, 2000).

Family responses that include hostility and criticism (high EE) have been identified as particularly problematic in families with a member with schizophrenia (Simon, McNeil, Franklin, & Copperman, 1991). Solomon (1998) raises the question whether these reactions are contributory or a response to the distress related to the illness.

## MAJOR TENETS

1. Families are the major support system for members with mental health and other types of illnesses.
2. Family members are partners with professionals.
3. Families need the appropriate tools (information about the illness and the skills to deal with it).
4. Family members need support in dealing with such a difficult life event in the family.
5. In terms of mental illness, family members are not responsible for causing the illness. While tensions within the family can exacerbate symptoms, the family does not cause the illness. Some of the disruption in the family is in response to the distress created by caring for an ill family member.
6. Family context and interpersonal relationships have an impact on the illness as well as are influenced by the illness. Family relationships can serve as both risk and protective factors in terms of disease management.
7. Family members can help identify potential signs of relapse and thus be helpful in preventing serious relapse.
8. Culture helps define how illness is experienced and the nature of the response by family members.

## GOALS OF TREATMENT

Psychoeducational family therapy seeks to help family members provide effective care for a family member with special needs while at the same time ensuring that this effort does not sacrifice the welfare of the family as a whole and the other family members. The approach includes information and emotional support for family members.

## ROLE OF THE COUNSELOR

The family counselor creates a working alliance with family members as partners in addressing the special needs of the family member. The family counselor assumes the dual role of educator and provider of emotional support. The counselor insures that family members receive adequate information about the nature of the illness, appropriate types of treatment, available resources, and signs of relapse. The family counselor sometimes conveys this information personally or arranges for other professionals to communicate this information. The counselor also helps the family learn effective ways to respond to the individual with the illness. The counselor helps the family identify potential resources within the family and the external world. The counselor also helps the entire family recognize and attempt to meet the needs of the family as a whole and other family members. Families in these situations risk ignoring the needs of other family members in ways that are harmful to all concerned. The counselor helps family members to identify ways in which the situation is creating negative responses within the family and to cope in more effective ways for the entire family. The counselor provides social support for the family in meeting their relational and emotional needs and helps link the family with other sources of support.

## *TREATMENT PROCESS*

The following represent important steps in the treatment process.

**Create a working alliance with family members as partners.** Such an approach recognizes the critical role that family members play in providing essential care for their family members. The family counselor seeks to empower the family to carry out this role as effectively as possible.

**Assessment.** What are the issues that relate to stress within the family as well as the person with the health problem? In terms of the family, such stress can take various forms depending on the situation and the family, for example, the loss of Lillian's effective leadership within her large family, the grief that Gregg's parents feel as they see their son unable to cope with college and life, and the worry of Bradley's parents and wife as they realize that he will not be able to care adequately for himself, much less provide for his family. These stresses are paired with those experienced by the person with the problem. Gregg's illness has plunged him into a world of fear and anxiety, compounded by his inability to pursue education as he had planned and his fears for the future. Lillian's stroke has robbed her of a role that was central to her identity and has compromised her ability to control her emotions in ways that further diminish her family leadership. Bradley faces a period of major rehabilitation with a guarded prognosis about his ability to assume his prior life, compounded with the stress of ongoing problems in cognitively and emotionally processing life events.

What are the resources that the family brings to this situation? The assessment includes an exploration regarding how the family members are coping both with the current situation and how they have coped in the past. Sometimes the shock of a current stressor prevents families from accessing and demonstrating their potential resources. Identifying past evidence of coping can help identify these potential resources for the family. Such an exploration also helps identify patterns of coping of the family that can be used to address the issues at hand. Identifying present coping strategies serves as valuable information to support current coping efforts and to identify the appropriateness of these efforts given the immediate situation.

**Maximize the family coping resources.** Several elements help maximize the family coping resources to deal with a realistically difficult situation.

Families need accurate information in order to cope. Providing the family with information about the nature of the illness, the symptoms and the meaning of symptoms, treatment possibilities (medication, therapeutic modalities), and the signs and circumstances of relapse is an essential part of the model, and ways in which the family can cope more effectively. The specific information will depend on the nature of the situation. Social workers can arrange for an expert in the illness to provide this information or provide it personally—depending on their expertise and the resources involved. Written material that is culturally and educationally appropriate for family members is valuable so that family members can study it later at home and share it with pertinent others in their support system. Families are also seeking information in terms of what the future is likely to hold—the prognosis.

In terms of the family's coping efforts, the social worker can help Gregg's parents realize that he is having difficulty processing multiple stimuli and to reduce this in their conversations with him. Gregg's parents can be helped to identify how he can realistically function at this time and to adjust their expectations accordingly to reduce the context of criticism. Bradley's family can be helped to realize that his closed head injury makes it difficult for him to deal with abstract concepts and to identify more concrete forms of discussing issues with him. Lillian's family might be helped to understand that Lillian still treasures her importance to the family and her dignity but to reduce the numbers of people who are meeting with her in order to help her currently compromised language ability. They can be helped to realize that her emotional instability is probably part of the impact of the stroke and to find ways to prevent overwhelming her emotionally.

Important information can include the nature of the types of available treatment and how families can access this help. Families need information about the relevant health care or rehabilitative system, the related social services that can be helpful for the family, and ways in which the family can connect with these services for their family.

Families also need information about the impact of these changes on the other family members. A family systems perspective suggests that what happens to one family member has an impact on every member of the family. Helping family members identify the stresses that they are experiencing and ways to meet the needs of family members is an essential part of the psychoeducational approach. Family members can try to deal with the emotional stress in many ways. Some of these can be problematic, for example, by denying the seriousness of the illness, by submerging their own needs, by overly compensating for the ill family member, or by becoming angry with the ill family member or the health-care system. Caregivers can become overwhelmed and thus begin to experience their own stress and finally become ineffective in their caregiving role. Families can be helped to find ways to maintain a normal family life as much as possible under the circumstances rather than letting the entire family revolve around the illness of a family member. Counseling family members to cope in ways that reduce these negative responses can be helpful for both the family and the ill family member.

Family members need information about signs of potential relapse and the type of help that would be appropriate in these circumstances. This information can help reduce some of the damage that might occur due to this behavior and to recruit help as quickly as possible.

**Arrange for supportive help.** Family members are facing a difficult situation and ongoing support through groups, family meetings, and other formats can be essential in dealing with this. Meeting with other family members facing a similar problem can be extremely supportive emotionally as well as provide family members with potential coping strategies. Arranging for other members of the community to be part of an informed support system can also be useful.

## Cultural Issues

Because culture influences how families experience life events and family caretaking responsibilities, it is important to understand the cultural context of families when designing psychoeducational approaches. The medical explanatory model that has been supported by the traditional psychoeducational programs does not do justice to some of the varying cultural interpretations (Guarnaccia, 1998). Designing culturally appropriate psychoeducational approaches needs to consider how the relevant illness or life events are viewed within the culture, the nature of the family system, and the cast of influential individuals within the community that can be supportive of these efforts and the family. The following represent some of the modifications described as useful for families from several different cultural groups.

### Indochinese Families

Vandiver and Keopraseuth (1998) describe some of the cultural considerations in conducting psychoeducational efforts with Indochinese families (especially from Vietnam, Cambodia, and Laos) who are caring for a relative with mental illness. While there are differences among the groups representing the Indochinese people from South East Asia, there are also some similarities that influence the nature of treatment.

The extended family with an emphasis on "family obligations, filial piety, respect for one's parents and siblings, harmonious interpersonal re-lationships, interdependence, and collective responsibilities and decision making" (Vandiver & Keopraseuth, 1998, p. 77) is important. Children learn early that their behavior is a reflection on the entire family. The stigma of mental illness thus means that the illness of one person brings shame on the entire family. At the same time, the disruptions experienced by many members of these groups along with isolation from family and relatives have contributed to higher levels of depression and posttraumatic stress disorder (PTSD). Many of these families have experienced major losses both prior to and after their move from their homeland. The stigma associated with men-tal illness leads families to be reluctant to admit that a family member is ill. Given the shame attached to mental illness, these problems are frequently described and viewed in terms of somatic complaints. Traditional healers are important resources for family members. Families that have a member with mental illness frequently lack knowledge about the problem and feel isolated from sources of support (Vandiver & Keopraseuth, 1998).

Cultural patterns tend to make these families hierarchical with respect due to older members of the family. As a result, aspects of caring for older family members by younger members can be problematic because older in-dividuals might be unwilling to accept instructions from younger members about medication compliance and other issues (Jordan, Lewellen, & Van-diver, 1995).

Given the importance of the extended family setting, it can be important to engage the wider family circle in these psychoeducational efforts (Jordan et al., 1995). Recommendations in terms of the format for family sessions vary. Given the context of stigma, some families might be reluctant to partici-pate in a group setting. As a result, providing psychoeducational services to the family privately or in the context of their home would fit with their cul-tural preferences (Vandiver & Keopraseuth, 1998). In terms of Laotian fami-lies that have member with a mental illness, Jordan, Lewellen, and Vandiver (1995) describe the benefits of using a multifamily group model organized as a social event and the importance of involving people with credibility within the community and knowledge of the culture. Social workers thus need to explore with individual families what would be appropriate for them.

Direct comments about needed lifestyle changes of family members can also convey messages of family weakness and cause family members to lose face. Consequently, Vandiver and Keopraseuth (1998) suggest the value of using indirection or making suggestions regarding alternative behavior that the entire family can try. Coping efforts that involve the entire family and comments regarding how well the family is doing are supportive of the important role of the family.

Counselors also frequently need to serve as cultural brokers with the family. For some families, this might mean education about survival skills for functioning in their current society (Vandiver & Keopraseuth, 1998).

## African American Families

In describing considerations in implementing psychoeducational approaches with African American families, Jordan, Lewellen & Vandiver (1995) point out the need to recognize the vast diversity among such families, especially in terms of socioeconomic status. Some considerations in implementing psychoeducational models of treatment include the value of including the extended family network or the network of supportive families. As a result, arrangements in terms of hours need to be flexible in order to permit many family members to attend. Time-limited approaches that incorporate direct communication and convey respect for the family also fit with cultural codes.

## Hispanic Families

While the basic model including involvement of the family, education, and support to empower equip families to help their family member and to reduce feelings of shame fits with the Hispanic culture, Rivera (1988) and Guarnaccia (1998) suggest several adaptations in working with families with a member with mental illness. These include the use of counselors who are bilingual or bicultural who can be more effective in communicating with the family members. Families might also view illness in terms of spiritual factors and be seeking help from a spiritualist. Counselors are recommended to be accepting of these actions and to encourage families to continue to do so as a parallel path to the mental health system. Counselors also need to be careful not to misdiagnose some spiritual behaviors as psychosis and to recognize the close family ties within families rather than assessing them as problematic overinvolvement. On the other hand, mothers can become overly involved with their ill sons and sacrifice their well-being to the detriment of themselves and their sons. The counselor can help by indicating that good mothers also take times for themselves (Rivera, 1988).

Hispanic families frequently have high stimuli contexts in terms of people, music, and other activities. These high levels of stimuli can be overwhelming to a person with a chronic mental illness. Helping families to problem solve in different ways to reduce this stimuli can be useful.

Counselors need to be aware that the mutual help-giving that is part of the Hispanic culture means that people are ready to share their medications with other people and thus people might be taking additional medication than prescribed. As a result, care needs to be taken to support the family's intent but to educate family members about the need for proper medication and the potential problems in combined and shared medications (Rivera, 1988). In addition to placing families in groups with other families who share only the illness of a family member, the extensive family and social network of Hispanic families suggests the value of capitalizing on and enhancing these family and community resources by including these members in the psychoeducational efforts (Guarnaccia, 1998).

Given the importance of the extended family in Mexican American families, Jordan, Lewellen and Vandiver (1995) emphasize the need to include family members in the treatment process. In addition, folk healers, spiritual leaders, and other nonrelative helpers can be helpful in supporting treatment recommendations (Jordan et al., 1995).

### Native American Families

Based on their extensive work with members of many different nations, Johnson and Johnson (1998) describe family education as part of respectful treatment model for members of Native American nations. Counselors need to be aware of important cultural differences among the nations and educate themselves about pertinent cultural issues. In the context of these differences, generally family involvement in the treatment is considered to be a natural part of the treatment process. There are local affiliates of the National Alliance for the Mentally Ill (NAMI) that can provide information in a culturally appropriate manner. Families can be helped to identify ways in which the family member can feel safe and ways to reduce extra stimulation. Family members can be helped to identify a meaningful niche within the community that can enable the person to have a predictable routine that helps reduce stress.

## Chronic Illness

Studies of psychoeducational approaches for helping families cope with illness suggest the need to look at two basic types of chronic illnesses. The first type includes illnesses that begin with an acute or traumatic episode that can lead to remission or potential recurrence (e.g., heart disease, cancer). The second type includes illnesses that begin slowly but are ongoing and progressive and require routine management practices (e.g., Alzheimer's disease). The first type of illness typically involves crisis management, posttraumatic stress management, and invasive disease management. The second type involves "caregiving, disease management, and the risks of disease management taking over the lives of family members over time" (Fisher & Weihs, p. 2000). As a result, psychoeducational models need to look at the nature of the illness and the impact of its pattern on the family.

### Alzheimer's Disease

Alzheimer's disease is a devastating disease that creates distress for the family and the individual with the disease. Mittelman, Ferris, Shulman, Steinberg, and Levin (1996) conducted a psychoeducational approach with families with an elderly member with Alzheimer's disease. Family members included the spouse, adult children, and other involved family members. They attended a six-week session of meetings that provided members with information about the nature of the disease and its management. Family members learned skills to resolve family conflict, enhance family problem solving, and identify signs of emotional overload by caretakers. Families received follow up treatment for several years to help them deal with ongoing problems. Compared to a control group that did not receive this service, caregiver mental health was better and placement into nursing homes occurred later in the illness.

### Type 1 Diabetes

A brief educational intervention with adolescents and their parents during the regular visits for medical care proved useful in terms of the medical care of the adolescent with type 1 diabetes and reduced parent-child conflict (Anderson, Brackett, Ho, & Laffel, 1999). Parents and their adolescent children who participated in this program showed better disease management and less conflict than families who were not part of the program.

## Mental Health Issues

Dixon et al. (2001) identify the following fifteen principles for working with families of individuals with mental illness that address the treatment needs of the individual and equip the family to respond more effectively and to meet their own needs:

- Coordinate all elements of treatment and rehabilitation to ensure that everyone is working toward the same goals in collaborative, supportive relationships.
- Pay attention to both the social and the clinical needs of the individual.
- Provide optimum medication management.
- Listen to families' concerns and involve them as equal partners in the planning and delivery of treatment.
- Explore family members' expectations of the treatment program and expectations for the individual.
- Assess the strengths and limitations of the family's ability to support the individual.
- Address feelings of loss.
- Provide relevant information for the individual and his or her family at appropriate times.

- Provide an explicit crisis plan and professional response.
- Help improve communication among family members.
- Provide training for the family in structured problem-solving techniques.
- Encourage family members to expand their social support network (e.g., participate in family support organizations such as NAMI).
- Be flexible in meeting the needs of the family.
- Provide the family with easy access to another professional in the event that the current work with the family ceases. (p. 904)

Schizophrenia is a major mental illness. Many of the early psychoeducational models were designed to address the needs of individuals with this disorder and their families. Psychoeducational treatment models for families were developed with the goal of enabling family members to become better caretakers and reduce the risk of relapse of a person with the illness. Families played especially critical roles because of the central role of the family as caretakers. Individuals who returned to families in which there were high levels of expressed emotion (high EE) of a negative and critical manner were more likely to relapse. The details of specific models varied but all shared some basic themes. First, educate family members about the illness to reduce the family stress and improve the ability of the members to care for their ill family member. Second, reduce the stress of the family (especially as reflected in high EE). To reduce the family members' feelings of being overwhelmed, they were provided with information about the nature of the illness (including symptoms and signs of relapse), appropriate treatment, and strategies for dealing more effectively with the illness (Simon, McNeil, Franklin, & Cooperman, 1991). Family members were also helped to stop blaming themselves for the cause of the illness. In a review of the outcome literature regarding treatment, psychoeducational programs with a family context emerged as extremely effective, more so than medication alone (Friedlander, 1998).

Based on early studies of the model, the multiple family group format was demonstrated to be a very effective format (McFarlane, Link, Dushay, Marchal, & Crilly, 1995). Dixon et al. (2001) in their analysis of the impact of psychoeducational models indicate that these programs ideally should be relatively long term (at least nine months).

### Borderline Personality

Gunderson, Berkowitz & Ruiz-Sancho (1997) describe a psychoeducational program created for families with a member with a borderline personality disorder. Such programs were slower to develop than programs for families with a member with schizophrenia because these families were less likely to be viewed as partners in the care of the family member. The family situation related to a borderline disorder is frequently characterized by underinvolvement by the parents, sometimes to the point of neglect. There can also be a history of conflict with high levels of dysfunction within families.

The program was developed through a process of exploring with adults with a borderline disorder and their parents the nature of the burdens that they wish to have addressed. Both agreed that the major issues were communication, the problems of conflict and anger within the family. Parents were concerned about suicide by the adult children (Gunderson et al., 1997). Parents described their families as healthier than did their adult children. In this context, individuals with borderline personality disorders can have a pattern of characterizing others who have cared for them in negative terms. Unlike other mental health problems like schizophrenia where the theme has been on the etiology as a brain disease, the emphasis in these sessions is on how to cope with the problem rather than etiology.

The counselors first meet with the families individually to join in a nonthreatening manner and to provide them with relevant information. Families then join together in a larger group for a review of information about the illness followed by a discussion of ways to solve common problems. Sessions include a social time followed by a problem-solving period. The intent is to reduce the crisis orientation of the families and to replace this with more stable patterns and relationships not tied to threats and rages. Families are helped to listen to the anger of their adult children without retaliation while at the same time learning that they can limit the length of time that they are willing to permit this exchange to take place. The treatment approach is not designed to treat the borderline condition, but rather to reduce the stress within the family that might serve as a trigger for an outburst. This family approach is relatively lengthy (can take place for a year or longer) (Gunderson et al., 1997).

### Affective Disorders

*Children.* Families raising children with mental illness struggle with meeting the needs of the entire family and the special needs of these children. As discussed earlier, high EE that includes hostile and critical attitudes has been associated with increased problems among persons with mental health problems but can also be a reflection of the burden experienced by caretakers. This burden is accentuated by lack of appropriate information and support and the inability of obtain adequate help for their child. When parents feel that they are being blamed and also lack adequate information about the illness and treatment, they can become demoralized and feel hopeless (Goldberg-Arnold, Fristad, & Gavazzi, 1999).

Multifamily psychoeducational groups for parents of children with mood disorders are designed to give parents accurate information about the nature of the illness and treatment approaches, the skills they need to cope, and support. By including multiple families in these groups, family members can share wisdom and support each other. Goldberg-Arnold, Fristad, and Gavazzi (1999) developed a six-week psychoeducational group for parents. The nature of these sessions is similar to others in their basic outline: understanding mood disorders and their symptoms, treatment medication, interpersonal aspects of the illness on individuals and families, effective parenting techniques, communication strategies within the family and external organizations (e.g., schools), problem solving, and review of family issues. The specific problems and issues vary depending on the families involved in the group. A follow-up with parents revealed that information, coping skills, and support were important for families and remained important for months following the group. During this six-month period, parental attitudes toward their child and the illness became more positive. Goldberg-Arnold et al. (1999) hypothesize that as family members replace shame and stigma with empowered thinking they might be more active in seeking support and begin to think more positively of their child and the illness. Such programs thus reduce caregiver burden.

Another program was developed to help children with attention-deficit/hyperactivity disorder (ADHD) and depressive disorders (Lopez, Toprac, & Crismon, 2005). Children and their parents were given information materials about the nature of the problem and treatment. These materials were developed in both English and Spanish and designed to address different developmental levels and participants in care (e.g., parents, teachers).

*Adults.* Psychoeducational approaches have also been developed for families with adult members with affective disorders. Papalos (2002) describes a five-session psychoeducational approach that includes the individual with the affective disorder and other relevant family members. During these sessions, information is shared about how the family members have experienced the illness; the nature, symptoms, and course of treatment of the disorder; the effects of it on the relationships within the family; and strategies to respond more effectively. The approach is designed to help the individual with the disorder and family members to accept that a family member has an illness that could be recurrent and the nature of the symptoms. Family members are helped to understand the impact that this has had on the relationships within the family and ways to resolve these more effectively. Information is shared about signs of potential relapse and ways to monitor treatment and the course of the illness (Papalos, 2002). While this approach includes only five sessions, other studies indicate the value of longer programs (Dixon et al., 2001).

### Bipolar Disorders

Brennan (1995) describes a closed entry multifamily group program that included family members diagnosed with bipolar disorder and their family members. The program consisted of fourteen sessions in which some of the sessions included the individuals diagnosed with the illness and the other family members and other sessions were divided into groups of individuals with the illness and groups with other family members. He describes the value of having both the individual with the illness and other family members in most of the sessions to ensure that all parties are receiving the same information and to enhance the understanding of the impact of illness on all of the parties involved. Sessions topics included the nature of the illness, medications and treatment, the impact of the illness on the parties involved (individuals with the illness and the family members were in separate groups twice during these weeks), signs of relapse, the nature of the mental health system, guest psychiatrist, suicide, managing symptoms, guidelines for managing the illness, and topics of interest to the parties involved. Participants indicated that although they were apprehensive about the group at first, they found it very helpful. They were especially likely to describe content about the illness and ways to manage it as helpful as well as the awareness that they were not the only families facing this problem. The group facilitated communication among family members, including the person with the illness, about the illness and the family (Brennan, 1995).

### Parents with Major Depression

The goal of this approach is to help family members, especially the children, gain a better understanding of the nature of the illness experience as well improve the parents' behavior in terms of their children (Beardslee et al., 1993). This approach was based in part on previous research regarding resiliency of children whose parents had affective disorders. Resilient adolescents were able to be aware of their parents' illness, thought about their parents, and understood their parents' illness. They realized that they were not the cause of the illness and were able to see themselves separately from their parents. It was important to understand how family members, especially the children, had experienced the illness of their parents.

The format of the intervention consisted of six to ten sessions with individual meetings with the parents, meetings with each of the children, and several family meetings. Children were also given age-appropriate literature about depression and children of depression. Family members had access to a clinician as needed. Didactic information about depression, risks to children, and ways to support resiliency was presented to the family. This information was linked with the family's own experience of the illness. Parents were helped to understand the impact of depression on the children. A plan was developed with the family in terms of ways in which the family could cope and create a life separate from the illness of the parent. According to the authors, the following components are core to the intervention: factual information is presented in a way that links it to the experiences of the family, there is a focus on the resiliency of the children, and concrete plans for the future are developed (Beardslee et al., 1993).

Given the prevalence of affective disorders in adults and the impact on the children involved, a clinician-led intervention was compared with a lecture format. Both approaches included information about the nature of the illness, and risk and paths to resiliency of children, the general experience of a family in terms of the illness, and ways to cope. They also received written material. The clinician-led group also included establishment of a therapeutic alliance and discussion on the specific impact on the individual family and ways to address it.

While participants in both groups reported a decrease in upset following the intervention, those of the clinician-led group reported higher levels of helpfulness, an increased understanding of the illness, as well as behavioral changes in terms of greater communication within the family and more adaptive coping strategies. As in the previous model, linking the discussion to the specific family situation seemed to be useful here (Beardslee et al., 1993).

## EVALUATION

As indicated in the previous discussion, there is extensive evidence that psychoeducational approaches that combine education with support and problem-solving results can be an important adjunct to treatment for a variety of problems and can substantially decrease relapse. Family members are helped to become more effective partners in caring for the individual, develop greater self-efficacy in their ability to handle the situation, and experience reduced levels of distress.

## SUMMARY

Psychoeducational programs that provide family members with information and support can be valuable in helping family members cope with a variety of illnesses. Social workers can take an active role in arranging for family members to receive appropriate information, to cope more effectively, and to meet the needs of the entire family.

# 10

## Multisystems Family Therapy

As discussed in chapter 4, Mr. Alvarez and Miss Colon contact the crisis center for help to find housing after they had been evicted from their apartment for nonpayment of rent.

Miss Kenisha White contacts a crisis social service program. She and her children have been living with her mother for the last few months after she left her partner of five years who had been abusing her, especially when he was high on drugs. Miss White has three children, Tyrone, aged eighteen months, Anthony, four years, and Karmella, seven years. The two youngest are by her previous partner and the oldest is by another man who has lost contact with the family. Miss White's mother is not able to keep the family on a long-term basis because she has very limited room in her apartment and the addition of Miss White and her children puts her at risk for losing her apartment. Her mother also has Miss White's high-school-age brother and sister living in the apartment. While her mother used to work, serious health problems have forced her to stop working and apply for disability benefits. Her father died due to a work-related accident when she was in high school. Miss White's children have been frightened by the events of the past months and cling to her. Karmella has been reluctant to go to school—a situation complicated by a school change caused by the move to her mother's apartment. Miss White fears that Karmella might have to change schools again when they move. Miss White has applied for assistance with the local Department of Children and Families. Miss White has been staying at home taking care of the children because Tyrone has a chronic health problem. She fears that she will have to go to work to support the family and is worried what she will do about child care for Tyrone. She dropped out of high school when she became pregnant with Karmella and has held minimum-pay jobs in the intervening years. Her mother has been active with the local church but Miss White has drifted away from it.

Miss White tries to be a good mother to the children but sometimes gets very discouraged about her situation. At these times, she finds it hard to be patient with the children and will either snap at them verbally or withdraw from them. She has been able to turn to her mother and friends for support during these difficult times but it is important now for her to try to find a place for her own family to live.

Mr. Matt Cole seeks help for his family. He has been raising his two children, aged seven and ten years, since the death of his ex-wife three years ago in an accident. Prior to that time Mr. Cole had visited the children but had not been the caretaker because they were divorced and Mr. Cole had been hospitalized several times for severe depression. Mr. Cole is on disability but would like to begin working to provide a better living for his family. He has been receiving his medication through his family doctor but has not been taking his medication recently and has been feeling increasingly depressed. His seven-year-old daughter is doing reasonably well in school but his ten-year-old son has recently been having difficulty both academically and behaviorally. Mr. Cole has been reluctant to talk with staff members of the school because his own experiences with school as a child were difficult ones. He dropped out of school at the age of sixteen and has bad memories of the school experience. He had difficulties academically and took a job with a company. Mr. Cole is alienated from one of his siblings but does see another one on a regular basis. His parents are dead. He does not live near his ex-wife's parents who are still alive and interested in their grandchildren. The Cole family lives in a part of the community where many of the homes need major repairs and their home is no exception. Mr. Cole is feeling overwhelmed with his responsibilities as a father. He fears that he might become depressed again and will not be able to take care of the children. While he wants to help his son in terms of the school he feels intimidated by the school situation.

As illustrated by the preceding families, many families that seek help from social workers are experiencing multiple problems. These families either do not have some of the basic resources of life that other families take for granted or are at great risk for losing them. They lead lives that are frequently on the edge of survival and typically have experienced a series of crises. These are the families described by Kilpatrick as Level I families. The basic foundational needs of the family are in jeopardy and that in turn has an impact on the family's ability to meet the emotional needs of family members (Kilpatrick, 2003). Such families are at heightened risk for neglecting or abusing their children (Thomlison, 2004). Children in these situations face many risk factors for serious childhood social problems (Fraser, Kirby, & Smokowski, 2004). In looking at these vulnerable and overloaded families at high risk for future serious problems, Walsh (1998) urges counselors not to "view them as 'problem families' but families struggling with many problems which are largely beyond their control and often not of their own making. Crisis situations are often embedded in problems in the community and the larger society, which must be addressed. Crises may also be fueled by reactivation of past traumas, which need to be understood and integrated for greater resiliency" (p. 238). As a volunteer at a program for homeless families, I marvel at the strength shown by some of these families as they contend with such difficult life circumstances, and I wonder how I would cope.

Addressing only the issues within the family system fails to meet some of the essential needs and ignores some of the potential resources of these families. As illustrated by the three preceding families, these needs involve many aspects of the community and its wider support systems (e.g., housing, employment, the school system, childcare, transportation, health care, extended family and friends). Using a risk and resiliency perspective, these families face a variety of risks derived from their wider context. These environmental risk factors interact with potential risk factors related to the family (e.g., organizational instability, poor problem-solving skills, negative interpersonal interactions, and low self-efficacy of family members). From a resiliency perspective, the social worker seeks out potential resources (protective factors) within the family and the larger environment to strengthen the family and its ability to meet its needs and to enhance the resiliency of the family. The family counselor recognizes the overwhelmed nature of the family and tailors the intervention accordingly. The goal is to empower the family to be able to meet the needs of the family members more effectively on an ongoing basis.

In looking at the importance of using a larger community lens in understanding and addressing the needs of these families, Aponte (1994) uses the analogy of the "canary in the mine"—their suffering is a warning of the toxicity of our social environment. The situation of these poor families makes us recognize that we need to work to restore health not only to these families but also to the community and the larger society.

As a result, while the focus of this book is on working with families, it remains important to recognize that social and economic policies selectively advantage and disadvantage members of groups in ways that have important implications for the families that we serve. Policies that define what constitutes a legal family, who are eligible for employer-based health plans, what are the levels of benefits provided for people with disabilities, what types of support for health care or housing are present in the community all play critical roles in the lives of many people. Social codes that influence the nature of wages comparable to the cost of living in the community as well as laws regarding the minimum wage have a major influence on many families. As a result, family practice at the microlevel cannot be divorced from concern for social and economic policies and general efforts to create change in these areas (DiNitto & Gustavsson, 1999).

A multisystems model of treatment helps social workers address these complex family needs. In doing so, the worker assumes a variety of roles in terms of the family itself, the extended family, and wider community systems.

The multisystems approach is defined as "a problem-solving approach that helps families with multiple problems to focus and prioritize their issues and that allows clinicians to maximize the effectiveness of their interaction" (Boyd-Franklin, 2003, p. 4). This definition emphasizes the active role that families play in the decision-making process (prioritizing their issues) as well as the multifaceted aspect of the treatment model. Described by Boyd-Franklin in terms of African American families, the model is applicable to members of all ethnic groups living with multiple needs (Boyd-Franklin, 2003; Grigsby, 2003; Thomlison, 2004). The multisystems model recognizes that the organizational structure of the family and the internal processes of the family are profoundly shaped by the wider systems in which the family lives. Resolving family issues will probably require addressing issues within the wider system and enlisting members of wider systems to make a difference. Kilpatrick (2003) describes one of the jobs of the social worker with these families as to "marshal the troops" (p. 5). The following discussion draws extensively on the work of Boyd-Franklin (2003) with African American families, the work of Walsh (1998) with vulnerable multicrisis families, multisystemic treatment designed for antisocial behavior in children (Henggeler, Schoenwald, Bouduin, Rowland, & Cunningham, 1998), and the treatment discussions related to Level I families generally (Grigsby, 2003).

## *THEORETICAL BACKGROUND*

Multisystems models of treatment built on the earlier work of a variety of family therapists and theoreticians. Boyd Franklin (2003) describes its foundation in terms of the following three theoretical approaches that illumine the organization of the family and the ongoing interaction between the family and its environment.

First, the structural family system model (Minuchin, 1974). This model views the family from the perspective of an organizational structure. The approach is active and present-focused. The therapist joins with and thus enables the family to solve their problems more effectively.

Second, the ecological approach (Bronfenbrenner, 1979). This approach places human behavior in an ongoing interactional context between the person and the environment. Bronfenbrenner (1979) portrayed this process through a nesting of concentric circles leading from the individual through the family, the community, and the larger social contexts (microsystems, mesosystems, macrosystems, and ecosystems). Families are understood in terms of the interaction among three dimensions: life transitions, interpersonal processes, and environment (including both the physical and social) (Holland & Kilpatrick, 2003). Assessing and addressing the transactional process between families and these larger systems is critical. Hartman and Laird's work on family treatment within this ecological framework has been helpful (1983).

Third, the ecostructural approach (Aponte, 1994). Looking at the wider social structure in which people lead their lives, several elements are important in working with people who are struggling economically.

> Options and power—people need to feel control over their own lives rather than be treated as if they were powerless given their social context.
>
> Purpose and meaning in life—people need to reach for purpose and meaning in life that is rooted in psychology, family history, and cultural and spiritual origins.

The personal ecosystem's multilevel structural organization—communities are crippled through chronic economic deprivation and cultural supports, leading individuals to feel incompetent. (p. 10)

## MAJOR TENETS

1. Families live in complex multisystem worlds that need to be incorporated into the assessment and treatment process.

2. Family counselors need to use a variety of intervention skills to address these multiple needs. Family counselors must be flexible in their roles in working with these families.

3. Families need to be treated with respect and given decision-making power in the treatment process. While this assumption is true for all models of effective treatment, the counselor needs to recognize that many of the families with multiple problems have frequently experienced interactions with wider systems that have left them feeling disrespected and unable to make crucial decisions. As a result, families frequently anticipate such behavior from their current counselor.

4. This model focuses on the strengths of families. These families are already overwhelmed by their current life circumstances and are frequently in crisis. Searching for strengths within the family and the wider context provides clues for addressing the problems facing the family without further overwhelming them. As Walsh (1998) describes, "When treatment is overly problem-focused, it grimly replicates the joyless experience of family life, where problems seem all-pervasive. Interventions that enhance positive interactions, support coping efforts, and build extra familial resources are more effective in reducing stress, enhancing pride and competence, and promoting more effective functioning" (p. 241).

## GOALS OF TREATMENT

The goals of multisystems treatment are to enable families that are being overwhelmed by issues within the family and their relationship with their larger context to meet the needs of family members. The approach has a strong dual focus on the family and the wider context. The family counselor seeks to enhance the resources available to the family. Because families are already overwhelmed, the approach is strength based and action oriented.

## ROLE OF THE COUNSELOR

The family counselor needs to be flexible in the use of the self and assume a variety of roles within this multisystems framework. In terms of relationships between the family and the larger system, the counselor may be acting as an advocate for the family, as a broker between the family and the larger system, and as an educator with the community. Within the family the counselor may be acting as an encourager and as a role model. The family therapist typically uses an action-oriented approach rather than an emphasis upon reflection and insight.

The counselor takes a strength perspective, helping the family identify potential resources within the family and their context and seeking to help the family mobilize these resources. The location of counseling is flexible and may range from the office to the home or other relevant location.

## TREATMENT PROCESS

The multisystems model includes treatment organized around the family and the wider social context. Interventions can be office and home based. The following discussion draws on the work of Boyd Franklin (2003) with African American families, Level I families described by Grigsby (2003), families with major problems (Henggeler, Schoenwald, Borduin, Rowland, & Cunningham, 1998; Thomlison, 2004), case management (Greene & Kropf, 2003), and strength-based family-centered services (Walsh, 1998). Although the details of the implementation vary, these models all share a strength-based approach, a flexible holistic approach to treatment, attention to both the family and the wider context, and a collaborative approach with family members and others in the community. Working with the family requires the counselor to join and engage the family, to assess the needs and resources, and to help the family gain the needed problem-solving skills and organize the family in such a way that it can address the multiple issues facing it.

Treatment is organized around four steps: joining, initial assessment, problem solving, and restructuring the family.

**Joining.** While joining is always important with all families as discussed in chapter 4, it is especially critical with these families because of their past history and sense of being overwhelmed. The strength-based approach is valuable in this process for several reasons. Most of these families have had prior experience with the social service or related systems. It is not uncommon that these encounters were judgmental and deficit-based. As a result, family members are likely to expect this of their current encounter and will be wary that their present counselor will be yet another person in this negative chain. In addition, family members who are feeling overwhelmed by their situation are also likely to feel hopeless and defeated. Such an emotional state makes it even more difficult for family members to mobilize themselves to problem solve effectively and thus the negative cycle becomes even more intense. Listening to their past encounters with the social-service system, including their problematic experiences, can help reveal some of the reasons why they are wary and also offers the counselor opportunities to explain how he or she hopes to work with the family. This information suggests some of the reasons why the family is pessimistic about counseling and why the family members feel discouraged and defeated. The counselor can use this opportunity to identify potential strengths within the family that can facilitate the joining process as well as explaining how the worker seeks to work with this family.

Grigsby (2003) reminds us of the importance of the social work mantra, "Start where the client is" in this process. Asking the family members what is important to them indicates respect and gives a message that they are partners in the process. With the myriad of problems facing families, it also helps begin to prioritize the most important ones.

Treating family members with respect translates into the myriad of details that are involved in interactions with others. How the counselor conveys dignity and respect (or fails to do so) through the ways he or she addresses or dialogues with people is critical in this joining process. The counselor has the responsibility to build the bridge over the potential chasm created by differences in education, social class, and other life opportunities offered the worker and the family members. The following represent some examples.

Addressing adults with Mr., Mrs., Miss connote respect and dignity. Asking people what they would like to be called sends the message that they are respected partners who share in the decision-making process.

Using vocabulary that is meaningful and understandable to the people involved sets a collaborative tone in addition to facilitating communication. If people do not understand the counselor's vocabulary, they might be unwilling to ask for clarification and could feel demeaned in the process.

Behaving as an appreciative guest during home visits is strength affirming. Body language here is as powerful as words. Many years ago, our family was dealing with a realtor who taught me this lesson in a vivid way. At the time we had four young children and so she seemed to assume that every chair in the house would be dirty. Before she sat down on any of our chairs she would always turn around and carefully wipe off the chair. No matter how diligently I cleaned the house before she came, she always went through this same routine. I was offended and felt that she was nonverbally labeling me a dirty housekeeper. I felt demeaned by her actions. Certainly I never joined with her in a trusting manner. However, it gave me an understanding of the power of these nonverbal gestures and the messages they convey and a determination to find ways not to repeat this with others.

The counselor might also need to reach out to others within the broad family circle to recruit them into the counseling endeavor. Boyd-Franklin (2003) discusses the importance of reaching out to family members within

African American families because key family members might be unwilling to come in to the session. Negative past experiences with other helpers can contribute to this reluctance. It can be useful for the counselor to do so directly either through telephone, letters, or home visits rather than giving this task to other family members. These actions by the counselor can help set a new tone for this encounter. From my experience in working with families, the preceding comments also apply to families belonging to a wide range of cultural groups.

Boyd-Franklin (2003) also discusses the importance and challenges of reaching out to men within African American families. The history of discrimination experienced by many African American men generally with accompanying personal experiences of being slighted and negatively stereotyped can make these men even more reluctant to become involved with yet another member of a system that might be demeaning. Although the man might not be living in the home currently, he might have a potentially important relationship with the family or the child that can be a resource for the family. For example, Kenisha White's high-school-age brother might be a resource for her boys who have lost their father/stepfather under difficult circumstances. The counselor needs to send messages about his importance. Walsh (1998) reminds counselors that questions pertaining to the men who have been part of the lives of women and children are important in working with families generally. It might be the father of the child, an uncle, or a grandfather.

The counselor can also explore with the family others in their life space that might be valuable resources. Boyd-Franklin (2003) describes seeing a counselor "walk into a waiting room and invite the 'family' in for a session and leave the friend or neighbor they have brought along sitting outside" (p. 231). Rather than ignoring these individuals, their presence provides an opportunity to explore their place in the life of the family. It is possible that including these individuals in the session with the family's permission might reveal a gold mine of resources for the family.

**Initial Assessment.** The assessment process begins with the counselor's initial observation of the family and then proceeds to the communication that occurs between the family members and the counselor. While the assessment process identifies some of the pressing problems and risks facing the family, an emphasis on the strengths of the family, their coping abilities, and the potential resources available to the family is essential. The assessment process is also an ongoing one and influenced by new information. While the emphasis on strengths is important, it is also essential to assess the risk of abuse and neglect within such overwhelmed families in order to ensure that the appropriate help is offered to everyone involved (Thomlison, 2004).

As in other family models, verbal and nonverbal messages of families offer valuable clues to the family. Selection of seating patterns can reflect family alliances and boundaries. Certain individuals can emerge as family spokespersons. Family communication patterns reflect whether family members are able to listen to each other in ways that demonstrate mutual respect and caring or reflect scapegoating and hostility. Such behavioral patterns also reveal family leaders or isolates. Issues of power and leadership within the family emerge as family members defer to those with power or perhaps hesitate to make decisions without the presence of a family member who is not present in the session.

In addition to assessing the family, it is also important to assess the process of joining between the family and the counselor and the nature of this collaborative relationship. Boyd-Franklin (2003) identifies a series of valuable questions to organize this assessment. Again, while she frames these in terms of African American families, these questions can be important for other groups who have also experienced being marginalized or oppressed.

How is the family responding to the therapist?

Are key family members beginning to trust the therapist?

Should the issue or race (or class) be raised at this point?

Who referred the family? Has the therapist made a distinction between her or himself and the referral agency?

How does the family feel about being in therapy? How do other key family members (not represented at the meeting) feel?

Why does the family believe they are coming to therapy and what do *they* want from the process? (p. 232)

Walsh (1998) reminds us that "Assessing whether overwhelmed families are motivated poses the wrong question. Rather, we need to ask ourselves how we can help them keep their heads above water to take on efforts for change" (p. 253). This assessment also helps identify what the family can realistically take on at this time. Asking the family to take on responsibilities that are unrealistic for them will only result in a further sense of failure and reduced self-efficacy.

While problems such as poor housing, loss of jobs, and economic poverty are realistically important to families, Aponte (1994) urges family counselors to look beyond these concrete signs of poverty to signs of poverty of the spirit that robs people of a sense of meaning, purpose, and hope. Ongoing experiences of being denied opportunity and power by society can lead to a pervasive sense of injustice, helplessness, and anger. Such poverty of spirit represents a major risk factor in contrast to a sense of coherence and meaning that promotes resiliency. Assessment of this aspect of life is most effectively accomplished in the context of the trusting and respectful relationship described earlier.

Acknowledging how difficult the situation facing the family can be while at the same time looking for evidence of strengths can enhance relationship. "After just an hour of pandemonium in a session, or hearing about the myriad of problems they are facing, we can use our own overwhelmed reactions to identify with their predicament and applaud them for hanging in there all week" (Walsh, 1998, p. 253).

The counselor must be sensitive to timing in terms of the assessment process. Information is valuable to create a collaborative working relationship and solving problems. Families need to trust why the counselor needs this information and what he or she will do with it. While these words apply to all families, they have special meaning for members of the families we are discussing. In this context, it can be useful to explain to family members why you are asking about specific information and what you plan to do with this information. Boyd-Franklin (2003) discusses the importance of waiting until trust is established to use tools such as the genogram with African American families lest families view the counselor as "prying into their business" (p. 21). Families are likely to withhold important information and become more distrusting of the social worker. This caveat applies also to other families with negative prior experiences with counselors or those who are so overwhelmed with their current crisis that the genogram is not viewed as meeting the family needs.

When the family has gained trust in the counselor, genograms can be useful. Genograms can be created jointly with the family or developed by the counselor with information obtained. Questions such as "Who lives with you?" or "Who lives in your household?" are valuable and neutral in eliciting information about the immediate family context. "Who helps you out" can be useful in identifying important people in the extended family or nonblood relatives who are viewed as kin (Boyd-Franklin, 2003).

When family members are experiencing great turmoil, it can be valuable to identify times of peace and healing and individuals who have contributed to this period (Walsh, 1998). The counselor can explore some of these times in the course of creating the genogram. This information can help in several ways. It gives family members a sense that life can be better and can also suggest possibilities to restoring some of these in the life of the family currently. Such information can be used later in the counseling session to help the family in their problem-solving process.

When family members seek help because they are overwhelmed by problems, the counselor needs to use the assessment process to identify the strengths (protective factors) of families as well as the nature of problems facing them. The counselor seeks to frame a balanced picture of the family and their situation by seeking information about ways in which family members have coped in the past; ways in which they are still managing to cope; ways the family members can still enjoy each other; possible resources within the immediate, extended family, friends, and the wider community. The fact that the family is there to work on the problem is strength. Identification of such resources also provides clues for future work with the family and creates a foundation for a strength-based approach to families. Use of the risk and resiliency framework helps identify strengths as well as organize the potentially chaotic picture.

While tailoring one's questions to the social context is always important in the assessment process, it can be especially a sensitive issue with these families. Boyd-Franklin (2003) suggests asking people "Who lives with you or who lives in your household?" (p. 236) rather than the standard set of questions regarding what might be viewed as typical family structure. This question enables the family to tell its unique story without creating inappropriate categories of family relationships for this family. Other useful questions to learn more about the family and their context are, "Who helps you out?" "Who can you turn to?" (p. 236). Asking about grandparents and their relationship with the family can tap another potential resource.

**Problem Solving.** Families characterized by Level I functioning typically are overwhelmed by a series of problems—where to live, how to support the family, how to deal with a health problem, how to guide the children, how to deal with school problems, and the list can go on and on. The situation is further compounded because the executive function of the family is often compromised because the parents are overwhelmed or lack effective parenting skills.

Mr. Alvarez and Miss Colon and their family have at least the following set of problems to contend with: eviction from their home, loss of a job, lack of transportation, fear of potential abuse and return to substance abuse, lack of viable job skills. Miss White and her children are struggling with at a minimum with housing, health problems for the youngest child, school adjustment issues, the trauma of abuse, and economic stress. Mr. Cole and his children are contending with his problem of depression, limited job skills, lack of confidence as a parent, loss of the children's mother, and the son's poor performance in school. The list of these problems that is rather typical for many families would challenge any of us. Furthermore, beyond these concrete problems Aponte reminds us that families can also experience a sense of helplessness that destroys the spirit (1994).

It is important to engage the family in the process of prioritizing the problem that is especially important for them or the one that the solving of which would make an important difference for the family. Engaging the family in this decision-making process grants the family needed respect. Selecting and prioritizing a problem helps make the situation more manageable because no one can work on many problems at once. Working with the family to address the identified problem helps create a sense of teamwork and grants the counselor and the counseling process credibility. Mr. Alvarez and Miss Colon's family might identify housing as their critical priority issue. Mr. Cole might indicate either his own depression or perhaps the school situation with his son.

In terms of selecting and prioritizing, families also need to recognize what cannot be changed and to focus on "their capacity to right themselves and move forward" (Walsh, 1999, p. 259). This capacity enables families to master the art of the possible—an important element of resiliency. Miss White blamed herself for having become involved with her last partner: "I should have known he wasn't any good. He started being mean to me when I got pregnant with Anthony. My girlfriends told me to get rid of him. Look what this has done to my kids." Miss White cannot undo the past. She can look at what this means for her future and what she can now do for herself and her family.

In designing problem-solving strategies, "action-oriented, concrete problem-solving approaches work best with overloaded families" (Walsh, 1998, p. 258). It is especially useful to develop specific, concrete goals with realistic steps to reach them. Small steps help make success possible with the accompanying increase in confidence and self-efficacy to address other family problems.

It is useful to prepare families for setbacks as well as to help them identify ways in which they will cope if a setback occurs. Such an approach is consonant with the premise of resiliency that "failure is not falling down but staying down" (Walsh, 1998, p. 259). Mr. Alvarez, Miss Colon, and Miss White might not find housing in their first attempts. The counselor can empathize with their discouragement and praise them for their efforts. The counselor can problem solve with them how they will handle these setbacks if they occur so that they will be able to persist in their efforts and their discouragement will not damage other parts of their lives.

Collaboratively developing specific tasks to address the concrete goals the family established gives a sense of dignity to the parties involved. Being able to accomplish small steps successfully begins to address their sense of powerlessness and to feel that they are able to make a difference in their lives (a key aspect of family resiliency). Mr. Cole and his son might use the session to talk about ways in which they will deal with the school situation. The worker can encourage Mr. Cole to think of ways he can discuss the situation with the teacher that separates his role as parent from his earlier life experiences as a youth. The worker can use role play as a way to help Mr. Cole gain confidence in his ability to handle the situation. As Mr. Cole is able to take steps in this area, he begins to experience himself as a more effective parent.

Active involvement with family members through participation in the daily activities of the parents is useful. This approach provides needed nurturing for the parent and also serves as a role model for carrying out these activities. These in vivo demonstrations that occur within a trusting relationship can be very helpful for parents' nurturing (Grigsby, 2003). As discussed in terms of Mr. Cole, the steps of educating through role modeling can be helpful in learning and implementing new skills.

**Use of enactment, prescriptions, and tasks.** Encouraging the family members to interact with each other and to enact their family drama in the session serves to involve family members in the therapeutic process. It also helps create ties between talking about and acting to solve problems. If Mr. Alvarez and Miss Colon select housing as their priority issue, the counselor can encourage them to discuss how they are going to go about solving this within the session. The worker can use enactment to enable the couple to discuss this critical issue more effectively and to problem solve some very specific tasks that they can work on to address the problem. While Boyd-Franklin (2003) recommends using this treatment approach with African American families who frequently are new to the concept of therapy, this applies to many families from a range of racial and ethnic groups. It can also be important to give people a constructive experience if family sessions have been used in negative and demeaning ways in the past.

Boyd-Franklin (2003) stresses the importance of thinking in terms of empowering rather than helping. "When a process is initiated whereby the family does the work in the session and members speak directly to each other rather than through the therapist, the likelihood of generalization outside of the actual session is far greater" (pp. 234–235).

**Restructuring the Family.** Restructuring efforts with the immediate family and the support system represents an important treatment strategy. As indicated in the resiliency literature, families need an effective organizational pattern with leadership that helps family members meet their needs. Looking at the family's interaction in the session as well as at information obtained through other avenues suggests ways to strengthen the family structure. Family members who have leadership responsibilities might be overwhelmed. Others in the extended family might be able to serve as resources or might be undermining their leadership ability. The leadership coalition might be compromised due to conflict, or an inability to communicate. Members of Level I families may lack the skills of conflict resolution and thus minor conflicts are not resolved and can escalate into further problems (Grigsby, 2003). Active involvement of the family can be useful in helping people gain and practice these new skills. The following represent some ways that the leadership structure in these families could be strengthened.

Mr. Alvarez and Miss Colon have two critical important problems to solve—housing and employment. Difficulties in discussing family issues hinder their problem-solving efforts and their alliance as parents. Miss Colon is afraid to bring up issues because she fears that Mr. Alvarez might leave her or return to drinking, therefore she does not bring up her concerns. The counselor can use the family sessions as a way to help the couple communicate in a problem-solving manner about steps to address these important issues. This strategy not only helps the family in their problem-solving efforts but also strengthens the parental subsystem and the relationship of this couple. The experience of being able to do this successfully in the session can empower the couple to begin doing so at home.

Miss White is now separated from her partner and is responsible for her three children. She is feeling overwhelmed by the trauma and the difficult situation facing her. Although she wants to be a good mother, the stress of the circumstances is compromising her parenting ability. Although she cannot continue to live in her mother's apartment, the counselor can explore ways in which the mother and the siblings can be a stronger support system for her. Miss White and these other family members could join together in the session to discuss ways these family members can strengthen each other. There might also be friends who can serve in this role. Perhaps someone in the wider support network might have some leads for housing.

Mr. Cole is also feeling overwhelmed in his role as a parent, especially in dealing with the school system. He fears becoming depressed again and is not taking his medication. Perhaps his sister with whom he has a good relationship can be a support in his role as a single father. She might be able to encourage and problem solve with him in dealing with the school system and well as helping him resume his medication.

Home visits as well home-based counseling can be valuable in working with families (Boyd-Franklin, 2000; Boyd-Franklin & Bry, 2000). Such visits give a picture of the life of the family that hours of conversation in the office can never reveal. Some of the stresses faced by the family in the neighborhood and the physical condition of the home emerge as well as the inability of the family members to organize a household. Dirty laundry scattered about the house and dishes piled around the kitchen reveal a great deal about the family's current ability to organize family life. Family resources also emerge. In addition to major problems, I have discovered hidden creative talents by family members, good organizational skills, family warmth as well as other family strengths that had not emerged in the office visits. Sometimes the counselor can find signs of efforts by family members that can be used in later family sessions—a book for the child, pictures by children on the refrigerator, pictures of the children with a grandparent. Boyd-Franklin and Bry (2000) also describe the value of these visits in terms of engaging family members with power who have not come to the office-based sessions.

Boyd-Franklin and Bry (2000) give six important guidelines for home visits that have special relevance for families with multiple problems, although the guidelines can be helpful in general. First, counselors must recognize "how they would feel if a stranger came to their home asking painful, difficult, and sometimes intrusive questions" (p. 38). The situation is further complicated if the family has not been in control of this decision and they have had to comply with an outside authority. Since family members are likely to feel wary and uncomfortable, the counselor should be extremely gracious to help put people at ease. Counselors should also be aware of the risk of violating confidentiality in terms of their presence at the home of the family. Second, counselors must recognize they "are on the client's home turf" (p. 39). Families are likely to be engaged in a variety of family activities so the counselor needs to be able to "go with the flow" (p. 39) and take advantage of this opportunity to get to know the family better. Third, counselors need to spend time joining with the family in the ways that are culturally appropriate. Such activities can be important in bridging barriers between the family and the counselor. Failure to do so can create major problems in joining. If the family welcomes the counselor by asking her or him to join in eating something, the family may feel devalued if the counselor turns this down. Engaging with the children can be helpful. Fourth, counselors need to recognize the power of genuine praise. This can be especially important for people who are overwhelmed with problems and a sense of defeat and hopelessness. Fifth, counselors need to understand and be able to use themselves in an effective manner. Home visits can evoke powerful feelings from counselors that require self-knowledge. Sixth, "empowerment is the goal" (p. 42). The goal is not to fix or help things for the family but to enable the family to address their issues. Part of this process is to ensure that family members are given credit for the change that has taken place (Boyd-Franklin & Bry, 2000).

Social workers and family counselors need to ensure their personal safety in home visits. Representatives of the organization should know their plans. Cell phones can be important for protection. The worker does not want to dress in a way that makes him or her stand out in the community any more than is necessary. The family members should be expecting the worker. Family members can also give further guidance in terms of location and any potential risk factors (e.g., do not park in front of the blue house). Social workers need to have an understanding of the area where they are going, including the potential risks in the neighborhood. Agencies need to give permission not to enter the home or to leave if there are any hints of danger. The mantra "Be aware of your surroundings" is an essential one in making home visits.

### Multisystems Levels

The counselor takes an ecological systems approach to identify the potential resources and strains in the wider context of the family. Family members might come to counseling already connected with wider levels. Sometimes these connections are supportive, other times people might be working at cross purposes, or these connections are only adding burdens to families. The White and Cole families have important issues related to their connections with the school system. Working with families in terms of this wider system requires the counselor to assume a variety of roles.

Boyd-Franklin (2003) describes eight multisystems levels influenced by Bronfenbrenner (1979), Falicov (1998), and Aponte (1994).

Level I: Individuals

Level II: Family subsystems

Level III: Family household

Level IV: Extended family

Level V: Nonblood kin and friends

Level VI: Church and community resources

Level VII: Social service agencies and other outside systems.

Using a multisystems approach, the social worker can work directly with the family to seek to create change within this wider social context or work collaboratively with the family to link the family to resources within this context or to advocate for families.

### Level I: Individuals

Recognizing that change in one part of a family system can create changes in the larger system, coaching family members to create change represents an important treatment strategy (Hartman & Laird, 1983). Coaching includes a discussion of the change sought, problem solving regarding how to try to institute this change, and rehearsal regarding the action involved. Family members can be coached regarding ways they can try to create desired changes in terms of relationships with significant other people within the family circle. This process can be used to help family members establish more effective roles within the wider family system. Family members also need to be aware that families will exert pressure on members to retain their original roles within the family system. As a result, the coaching efforts need to include how the family members will respond to these pressures. Hartman and Laird (1983) remind counselors of the importance of making sure that clients understand that no one can guarantee what the response will be from other family members and that people can ultimately only be responsible for their own actions.

Mr. Cole might express a wish to have a better relationship with his sister from whom he has been alienated. He and his sister had once been close but there had been a falling out several years ago at the time of the divorce. His sister was very close to his wife and he did not think that she had been willing to hear his side of the story. As a result, he has shut her out of this life. Now that his wife is dead and he is struggling to raise the children alone, he is interested in reaching out to family members both for his own sake and that of his children. The counselor problem solves with Mr. Cole ways to approach his sister and what might be her possible responses. When Mr. Cole decides that he would like to begin with a phone call, the counselor role plays possible scenarios with him. They also discuss how he will handle it if his sister really is not willing to resume a relationship with him.

### Levels II and III: Family System

Exploring the nature of the immediate and wider family networks can be valuable in identifying potential solutions as well the dimensions of the problem. What the concept "family" truly means is influenced by culture and individual family patterns. In some African cultures, the word "cousin" is not used to describe the children of your siblings. They are called brother or sister and the word "cousin" is viewed as an inappropriate sign of distance. Many cultural groups have a strong sense of obligation for the extended family system, such as African American (Boyd-Franklin, 2003), Latino (Garcia-Preto, 1996), First Nations (Sutton & Broken Nose, 1996), Arabic (Abudabbeh, 1996), Italian (Giordano & McGolderick, 1996), and Indian (Almeida, 1996). Informal adoptions can take place as individuals view others as members of the family group.

Boyd-Franklin (2003) suggests exploring by using questions such as, "Who helps you with the children?" "Who lives in the house?" "Do you have a special person in your life?" "How many children live in the house or stay over often?" (pp. 244–245). She also describes the sensitive issue of discussing paternity of children in African American families. Miss White might have been reluctant to explain that her oldest daughter had another father. Boyd-Franklin suggests the importance of exploring whether grandparents might still be interested and involved in the lives of the children even if the father is no longer involved with them.

### Levels IV and V: Church, Community, and Social Service Networks

Family counselors can enable family members to access appropriate services within the community. An assessment of their current and past relationships with community services can be important in designing interventions with families in order to access appropriate resources and to avoid repeating prior ineffective efforts (Imber-Black, 1988). This issue is discussed in greater detail in Family-Focused Case Management.

As indicated, such steps can involve the counselor in various roles. The counselor might only need to link people with services by informing family members about the services and ways to access these services. The counselor might need to go further and advocate for this family with the service delivery system. In some situations, families have burned their bridges with this service in the past and the counselor needs to advocate to give them another try. Family members can also be reluctant to turn again to agencies where they did not receive services or perhaps felt demeaned by workers. Level I families can easily be victimized by people in the community. This can make them suspicious of the social worker's intentions as well as the staff of other helping groups. Helping family members in these situations can be important.

The counselor may need to play a mediator role between the family and community services because of tensions between the family and the organization. Children can be quite adept at pitting the school and their parents against each other so that two parties who need to be partners are working at cross-purposes. The counselor then serves as a mediator who tries to establish an effective partnership. Relationships between the school and the family can be especially critical because studies reveal that school performance represents the most important predictor of the child's future (Boyd-Franklin & Bry, 2000). Learning how to handle the school situation provides important coping skills for the later world of work. Confidence that one can do well in school (academic self-efficacy) buffers adolescents from other stresses (Boyd-Franklin & Bry, 2000).

The counselor may also need to serve as an educator, especially in helping community members understand more about the family in terms of its culture and unique needs. This information can enable others to respond in more appropriate ways to the family and thus make services more effective.

In other situations, the counselor might need to organize with community members to create a new set or arrangement of resources within the community to meet emerging needs. This has occurred as families from different cultural groups and with new sets of needs move into communities or in situations in which economic changes place new burdens on community families. Old arrangements for services are no longer adequate to address these new needs. Given the rapid changes occurring in many communities, this has become a rather common occurrence.

While informing families about services can be adequate for some family members, others may require more help in being able to take this step. Mr. Cole is reluctant to contact the school system because of his own bad experience as a child. His reluctance not only prevents him from addressing an important family issue but also reduces his self-efficacy as a parent. The counselor can work with Mr. Cole to help him separate his experience as a child from that of his current role as a parent. At the cognitive level, the counselor can help Mr. Cole view himself through the lens as an adult rather than the student he once was. Given his lack of confidence regarding his ability to take on this parental task, the worker might need to model this action with Mr. Cole and then role-play the respective roles of parent and teacher with Mr. Cole until he feels more comfortable with this step. The social worker identifies his interest in trying to contact the teacher as a strength and later affirms his efforts.

Exploring with families why they have not received services in the past with this agency can be helpful in identifying strategies for success. It might be that the way the family presented their situation did not fit with the agency's criteria or they did not have the necessary documentation. Miss White sought help for her family because of the chronic illness of her youngest child. She met with the agency representative and was denied the help. When the social worker explored the situation and identified the requirements for the service, she realized that Miss White did not bring proper medical documentation from the doctor. The counselor can work with families to identify ways to present their needs in a more effective manner. Sometimes the counselor learns that family members have been reluctant to state their needs or have acted in such an attacking way with the agency representatives that their needs were not recognized. Again, such efforts are useful not only because they result in the family receiving needed services, but also because they represent areas of success (for the family and the counseling endeavor) and opportunities for the family to learn how to problem solve in this area more effectively in the future. Social workers also need to be aware of services that are working at cross purposes and that sometimes end up giving families mixed messages. Workers can also use their general understanding of the community to recognize services that are especially likely to offer help or subtle barriers that limit access.

As potential resources within the community, the church family can be important for families from various religious traditions. Churches provide an array of programs for families in the community. Most religious traditions have long emphasized charitable efforts and congregations frequently offer programs for families in the community, such as Christian (Van Hook, 2001; Aguilar, 2001), Hindu (Singh, 2001) Muslim (Nadir & Dziegielewski, 2001), and Jewish (Friedman, 2001). Spirituality and the church have been strong resources for African American families over the years (Boyd-Franklin, 2003; Grant, 2001; Hines & Boyd-Franklin, 1996). Exploring whether or not this is a potential resource for the specific family can be useful. Some families may also have become alienated from the church community for a variety of reasons.

## *FAMILY PRESERVATION MODELS*

Family preservation models were developed in order to prevent children from being removed from their homes and to address the needs of families with the multiple problems that made children at risk for such placement. These models include an approach that is short-term and intensive with a combination of home and community-based interventions. The following section describes family preservation in more detail. A discussion regarding specific programs that have been identified as effective is included in the appendix.

Family preservation models share some major tenets, several of which are reflected in the previous discussion. These include

Children should remain with their families if at all possible.

Families are active agents in the change process.

Families are doing the best they can given the circumstances, but they need help in order to provide better care for their children.

Intervention should be based on family strengths.

Therapists should be nonjudgmental and accept families "as they are rather than emphasizing deficits."

Intervention takes place through engagement with a helper, who assists the family in identifying and building on inherent strengths. (Grigsby, 2003, pp. 75–76)

Family preservation models for families in crisis typically share the following characteristics while the specific details of individual programs vary. With the goal of maintaining the family unit when children are at imminent risk for out-of-home placement, the response is an immediate one. The focus of assessment and treatment is on the family unit and its community context. The goals and objectives are limited. Services include both concrete and psychological interventions and are offered on a short-term (6–12 weeks length) intensive (5–20 hours a week) basis. Services are offered in the home and the community. The family counselor is available outside traditional office hours. Case loads are small to enable the intensity of services (Grigsby, 2003).

Several core treatment elements of family preservation have been discussed in terms of multisystems therapy with families because these elements are important for counseling with crisis-prone families. The engagement process is critical and must take into consideration the family's suspicion of the counselor given the circumstances and prior experiences with the social service system. Enlisting family members in terms of what is important for them helps establish a collaborative partnership relationship with family members. Searching for the strengths of families and using these as a basis for a strength-based approach helps empower families. The counselor needs to give family members needed emotional support. This support can take the form of active involvement in the daily life of the family, helping model new ways of responding to family members, and encouraging positive changes. The counselor serves as a positive role model for the family members, especially the parents. The counselor also helps family members learn and practice more effective conflict resolution strategies. The counselor may also need to advocate for families in terms of the broader social service system as well as teaching family members ways to advocate for themselves (Grigsby, 2003).

Thomlison (2004) identifies family preservation and parent education models that have demonstrated effectiveness with at risk children and their families. These models along with a brief description and citations to obtain more information about specific models are included in the appendix.

## FAMILY-FOCUSED CASE MANAGEMENT

Family-focused case management represents an important intervention approach for families with multiple problems by connecting families with important community resources. According to Greene (2003), the purpose of the case management is to provide the family with "service options that promote group and individual functioning" (p. 95). Using a strengths-based approach, "the goals of family case management are to mobilize a family's strengths, to marshal resources, and to maximize family functioning capacity" (p. 85). As discussed in multisystems treatment with families, the case manager assumes a variety of roles in connecting families with services. These include client-focused roles (e.g., educator, enabler), coordinating roles between the family and the services (e.g., service broker, information gatherer), and advocacy roles (e.g., mediator, community organizer) (Greene, 2003).

Case management includes some of the important steps described earlier. The case manager must seek to engage the members of the family system in a relationship characterized by trust. This process includes explaining the case manager's role and nature and purpose of the information requested. The case manager assesses the family and the relevant context from appropriate sources. The case manager uses a strengths-based perspective in this assessment process. The case manager develops a case plan that is agreed upon collaboratively with the family. The next step is to link the family with relevant services using the roles described above. Service delivery must then be monitored to ensure that services are coordinated and effective. The case manager trouble-shoots as necessary to ensure that these are delivered in an appropriate manner. The case manager may need to advocate for services for individuals and for groups in the community with needs. The system of services is evaluated in terms of their effectiveness for the family. Evaluation of services includes attention to the availability and accessibility of services, the services that are available but not used by families, the needs that are going unmet, and providers that might potentially offer services to meet unmet needs (Greene, 2003). Case management can be appropriate for families facing a variety of problems that require linkage and coordination of resources within the community.

Mr. Cole and his family meet with a family case manager. The case manager explains his role in terms of helping link families with services in the community that can be helpful. Mr. Cole identifies some key problems facing the family, especially his concern about the school situation and his son, his worry about his depression and his wish to obtain better paying employment. The case manager also assesses strengths and resources within this system, including the daughter's good adjustment to school, Mr. Cole's sister, and the concern of family members for each other. The case manager helps the family identify some of the primary goals and concerns lest the family become overwhelmed with a variety of tasks and persons. The family identifies Mr. Cole's fear of relapse of his depression and the son's school programs and indicates that help in these areas is especially important. The case manager learns that Mr. Cole has discontinued his medication because he has been worried about the cost of the medication and thought that he would try to see how could do without it. The case manager offers to see if there could be some way to help with the costs of the medication if Mr. Cole's physician suggested that he resume the medication. The case manager explores whether Mr. Cole would like to meet with the school social worker who could work with the family in terms of the school situation. The case manager explains the role of school social workers and how they frequently help families in which there are problems in terms of children in school. With the agreement of the family, the case manager arranges for Mr. Cole and his son to meet with the school social worker. The case manager assures the Cole family of his ongoing interest and that he wants to make sure that the services that they need are working out for the family. He also lets the family know how to contact him if there are needs in the future or if the family later wishes to later work on some of the concerns that they identified today.

## *E*VALUATION

The families described in this chapter and other literature related to multi-systems approaches, including family preservation models and case management, need a multifaceted approach to address their multiple needs both within the family and the larger context. Multisystems family therapy has emerged as effective in improving parenting practices and changing the family environment (Thomlison, 2004) and in addressing adolescent externalizing behavior problems (Sexton, Robbins, Hollimon, Mease, & Mayorga, 2003). In families where abuse and neglect are the key issues, intervention strategies that combine a focus on improving parental skills through providing cognitive, emotional, and behavior competencies that are tailored to the specific needs of the family and their cultural values and creating collaborative partnerships with the parents and other support systems in the community are especially effective (Thomlison, 2004).

Family preservation models have been evaluated primarily in terms of prevention of out-of-home placement. Berry (1999) reviewed the outcome literature on a variety of family preservation models on this dimension. Typically the majority of children were able to remain in their homes. While the numbers ranged from 50 to 90 percent in terms of children in imminent risk of placement, definitions of imminent also differed. "Family preservation services were associated with the following changes during services: improvements in behavior, material resources, family structure, family dynamics, emotional climate, perceptions of problems, community perceptions of the family, information support network, and community involvement" (Berry, 1999, p. 212). Children also improved in terms of school adjustment, delinquency behavior, and behavior at home (Berry, 1999). Lack of control groups in most of these studies is a limitation. Berry (1999) further analyzed the service components that contribute to success: the amount of time spent in the home; the provision of concrete services "such as teaching of family care, supplemental parenting medical care, help in securing of food, and financial services" (p. 213); and being linked to formal social supports (e.g., day care, respite care, medical care). The amount of time spent in terms of these formal support services was more important than the particular service used. The ability to maintain a clean home emerged as a particularly important life skill. In evaluating these specific models of treatment, it is important to remember that poverty continues to be a problematic circumstance for families. Thomilson (2004) has identified a number of models with demonstrated effectiveness that are described in the appendix.

Despite the demonstrated effectiveness of these models with individual families, it is important not to overlook the ongoing challenges facing these families due to poverty and other environmental difficulties. As described earlier, efforts with individual families need to be paired with those at the community and social policy levels. Prevention at the community level includes addressing social and economic structures that systematically disadvantage families.

Case management has emerged as a valuable approach with families facing a variety of problems that involve negotiating complex service systems. This approach has been helpful with families and the health-care system (Greene & Kropf, 2003), older adults with a variety of needs, individuals with mental illness and issues associated with housing, employment, the mental health and social service systems. In order for case management to be effective, the case manager needs to be knowledgeable about the relevant systems, and the systems, in turn, need to have the required resources.

## SUMMARY

Models of treatment using a multisystems approach to counseling with families assume a variety of specific forms while sharing a perspective that effective help involves addressing the family and its social context. These models promote resiliency by addressing the family and its relationship to the broader social structures. Treatment models are strength based and action oriented. Social workers and other family counselors use themselves in multifaceted ways.

# 11

# *Object Relations Family Therapy*

Lewis and Emily Wilson are seeking therapy because Emily has been struggling with severe anxiety during the past year. They have been married for three years and would like to begin a family. They are seeking help to relieve Emily's suffering and because they do not think that it would be a good idea to have a baby while she is experiencing such disabling anxiety. While anti-anxiety medication has been somewhat helpful, they have also felt that there has been a strain in their relationship and do not want to risk Emily's becoming dependent on such medication. Emily wants to return to her old self, the cheerful engaging person that she was when they got married and that Lewis fell in love with. Lewis is disappointed because Emily is not the loving person that he thought he had married because her anxiety makes her withdraw from many of the activities that they used to enjoy together. Lewis works long hours as an accountant for a local business and is able to support the family adequately through his work. Sometimes he finds himself working even longer hours than necessary because he does not know how to handle the current situation at home. He then feels guilty and becomes more solicitous toward Emily. Emily has worked as a receptionist but has found it difficult to work in a steady way since her anxiety has become more severe. Both Lewis and Emily had mothers who suffered from illness (depression and cancer) and want to spare their children this pain. They met during college. Lewis was two years ahead of Emily. They married after he graduated. She found work as a receptionist and did not continue her education. Her engaging personality made her a good receptionist until she began to become so anxious.

Lewis grew up in a family in which his mother suffered from chronic depression that made her unavailable to her children. His father was burdened down with the financial responsibilities of the family and tried to meet the bills by working two jobs. Lewis was an only child and did not have siblings that would help buffer his sense of aloneness. His grandparents did not live in the area. Lewis developed internalized objects that included his anger toward his parents for their emotional unavailability and a longing for closeness along with a fear of loss and a sense of self that did not view himself as worthy of his mother's love. He coped by trying to be very mature and good (the false self) in order to try to win his parents' love and to protect himself against his own anger and longing. His appearance as a young adult in the dating

220

world was that of a pleasant and self-assured person who was attentive to the needs of others. When he met Emily in college, she was an engaging young woman who was impressed with his maturity. He in turn was impressed with her warmth and eagerness to be close to him. She was looking for a source of strength because she too had struggled with early experiences that left her feeling unsure of herself. She was the youngest of four children and the only daughter. Her mother had been ill with cancer for much of her childhood and was in and out of hospitals until she died when Emily was beginning middle school. While her mother was very loving when she was home and feeling better, her illness was very disabling for much of the time. Her father was the strong parent in the family and Emily felt safe when she was able to be with her father but his responsibilities also included financially providing for and caring for the other three children in the family. Emily grew up with internalized objects that included a fear of loss of her mother, longing for closeness and protection, and a sense that women were weak and could only be safe by being close to a strong male. While Lewis coped by appearing very mature and attentive to the needs of others, Emily coped by trying to be very engaging to her father and other men to keep them attached to her and a source of protection.

While this young couple has many protective factors in terms of adequate financial resources, their intellect, ability to cope with education and work, and commitment to each other, their relationship has become severely strained in response to Emily's anxiety and Lewis's uncertainty about how to cope with it. They are currently in a cyclical pattern. Lewis is alternating between being solicitous to Emily and distant in response to feeling overwhelmed. Emily, in turn, feels anxious when Lewis becomes distant. She is ambivalent about his solicitous response because it both sends a message that he cares and can lend her his strength but also that she is a weak person who is unable to cope and thus cannot survive without him.

Object relations family therapy addresses the interpersonal relationships within the family. From the perspective of object relations theory, relationship problems have their origin within the early life experiences of family members and are played out in the framework of current core family relationships. Family members bring to the current family aspects of earlier object relations and continue to shape their family relationships accordingly. Many of the early pioneers of family therapy had their original training and orientation in psychodynamic theory and their work grew out of this perspective. Object relations family therapy draws upon object relations theory to understand the interpersonal world occurring within the family context. From the perspective of object relations theory, relationships with others represent a core need so that life is an ongoing story of the need for connection with others as well as the need to be a separate individual. The term "object" in object relations theory has implications for the relationships between individuals; however, objects are not equivalent to other individuals. Objects represent the internalized perceptions of others and thus never truly match the reality of the other individuals. These internalized objects include not only the actual behavior of the other individuals but also how this behavior is perceived and integrated into the already existing framework (Goldstein, 1995). Such internalized objects influence subsequent relationships with others. As discussed in the following section, the child deals with frustrations in the course of development through a process of repression and splitting. Object relations family therapy seeks to reduce the need for splitting and repression and thus to modify the problematic projective systems in place within the family (Scharff & Scharff, 2003).

## *THEORETICAL BACKGROUND*

Object relations theory and family therapy come from several different theoretical approaches to human development. From the perspective of attachment theory, the infant is born both dependent upon the mother for survival as well as with the competencies to engage the mothering person (Bowlby, 1969). Research with infants has revealed that even young infants have remarkable capacities to discern the interpersonal world around them. By two to three months of age the infant appears to relate in an integrated manner suggestive of the development of a core self (Stern, 1985). Scharff and Scharff (2003) describe the infant as born "able to use relationships for survival and for the pleasure that relatedness brings" (p. 60). According to Fairbairn the child is born with a fully formed and differentiated ego that permits the child to relate to others and at the same time to be autonomous, that is, be an individual and a member of a family group. Typically the mothering person is able to respond to the child well enough so that the child can cope with the pain during times in which the mother is unable to respond. When the caregiving adult is chronically unable to able to respond or the child is constitutionally challenged, the child can become overwhelmed by the experience (Scharff & Scharff, 2003). This experience of frustration creates a differentiation within the child's ego into unconscious and conscious parts. When this sense of frustration is overwhelming, the ego deals with this by the defense of "splitting," dividing the frustrating experience into bad and the satisfying ones into good. The ego then becomes a complex internalized structure composed of three elements: (1) the *central ego* that is conscious, connected to the ideal object and feelings of satisfaction; (2) the *libidinal ego* that is unconscious, connected to the need-exciting object and feelings of emptiness, neediness, longing, and craving; and (3) the *antilibidinal ego* that is unconscious, connected to the rejecting object and filled with feelings of outrage, anger, and hurt. Although the self seeks to be whole again, the central ego continues to repress the other aspects of the self in order to protect itself from pain (Goldstein, 1995; Scharff & Scharff, 2003). As the child has ongoing interpersonal experiences, the central ego remains open to new experiences that can modify this original configuration. If the central ego has been significantly compromised because the splitting is so severe, the process of being open to new experiences and modifying in response becomes problematic.

Winnicott emphasizes the essential infant-mother bond and identifies two aspects of the mother: the environment mother who holds the infant and the object mother who engages the infant through eye contact. According to Winnicott, infants need "good enough mothering." Problematic patterns occur if mothers are too distant or do not permit their babies appropriate separation. When the infant is unable to receive mothering or experiences serious problematic patterns, the child develops "the False Self" that is erected to please others and protect the child from pain (Goldstein, 1995; Scharff & Scharff, 2003). Traumatic experiences can be especially problematic in terms of the child's attachment patterns and development of the sense of self (James, 1994).

Klein took the concept of splitting further by describing how the child projects onto the mother both the child's aggressive, death instinct (the bad mothers) and their life-affirming views (the good mother). Such a process protects the infant from his or her anger and destructive impulses. She used the term "projective identification" to describe this process (Scharff & Scharff, 2003). This process of projecting has emerged as one of the pillars of object relations family therapy. Bion (1970) viewed the infant's anxiety in terms of how the mother processes it. The mother takes the anxiety of the infant and processes it in a structured way that is manageable for the infant. As the infant identifies with the mother and her processing of anxiety, he or she develops his or her own psychic structures for coping with anxiety (Scharff & Scharff, 2003). The mother's difficulty in processing anxiety can thus be transmitted to the infant in the developmental process.

From the perspective of object relations theory, these early life experiences contribute to the relationships within the current family. The shadows of the past become incorporated into the current object relations context and individuals relate to others accordingly. Individuals whose object relations are characterized by fear of rejection bring this into their current relations and respond to others accordingly. Individuals with an anxious attachment pattern will fear loss and respond to others in ways that are governed by this fear. They might compromise other important personal needs to maintain a relationship and avoid the danger of loss. The core couple relationships consist of a union between two complex phenomena: (1) the central ego system of each individual that is characterized by a maturely functioning member of the union, and (2) the split-off and repressed internal object relationship—either the exciting or rejecting object. The process is further compounded by the process of *projective identification* identified by Klein (Nichols & Schwartz, 1998; Scharff & Scharff, 2003). In this process, the individual's conscious and unconscious internal object relationships are projected onto the spouse. Problematic patterns occur when the other partner is unable to separate from these projections and cause them to reflect reality in a more accurate manner. Scharff and Scharff (2003) describe unhealthy marriages as those in which instead of reality altering the projections, the other partner behaves in such a way to confirm these projections and both partners are unable to grow as individuals. The projective identification process is really a dance between the two partners with a joint process of projection and collusion occurring at the same time. For example, Lewis projects his anxiety and fears onto Emily who in turn accepts this projection and becomes increasingly anxious.

From the perspective of object relations family therapy, Emily and Lewis demonstrate a set of projections and identifications. As a result, their conscious needs for an adult close relationship that will allow them to become genuine partners and parents are not being met. At the unconscious level, however, this arrangement meets some important needs for both individuals that cause them to remain stuck in this pattern. Both Emily and Lewis grew up with object relations that reflected fear of loss combined with a longing for closeness. Lewis is able to project onto Emily his fear of loss and weakness that in turn fits with her own fears of loss and view of men as strong. Emily is able to project onto Lewis her fears of loss and sense of aloneness created both by her mother and her father and her insecurities about women and the parallel strength of men. Emily's anxiety keeps her safely dependent on Lewis and thus close to him. His own sense of weakness that he has defended against by his image of maturity and strength is projected onto Emily who in turn responds by becoming anxious. Emily's view of fear of loss is projected onto Lewis who in turn needs to care for her. His strength and care for her confirms her view of men as strong and herself as weak.

The challenge for this young couple is for each of them to separate their current relationship from the shadows and unmet needs of the past. Both Emily and Lewis have strengths that can contribute and needs that can be met without the cost of Emily's anxiety and Lewis's burden of the total responsibility of the family. Emily will no longer need an overall powerful man to take care of her. Lewis then can relax that Emily will not abandon him if she is able to be strong.

Scharff (2006) further describes the ongoing process that occurs within the immediate family and the wider circle in which it lives. Children and their parents both develop sets of introjected objects. Children introject objects based on their experiences with their parents. Parents in turn both project onto their children aspects of their own parents and develop internalized objects of their children. Parental projection onto children can result in children's becoming scapegoats. Parents who are struggling with their own aggressive aspects can project onto these onto their children who cooperate by acting in a delinquent manner. Other parents can project their own anxiety and sense of weakness and these children can accept these projections in the form of fear of going to school. Parents can project onto their children their own unresolved sexual needs and these children accept these projects in the form of sexual promiscuousness.

Using a family development perspective, Scharff describes family development as set within a nest of concentric circles that hold the family: the mother who holds the child and is held by the child, the father who holds both of them and is held by them, the wider nuclear family that in turn both holds and is held, that in turn is held by the extended family. This family group is then held by their relevant social circles, that in turn is held by the wider society.

## MAJOR TENETS

1. Family members bring to their current family the object relations system that was developed during their earlier life experiences.

2. Individuals project their conscious and unconscious internal object relationships upon the spouse or other family member who in turn can fit and identify with this projection.

3. Problems in the family occur when family members are unable to separate from these projections and both members of the family are unable to grow as individuals.

4. The task of the family therapist is to enable the family members to cope with their anxiety and begin to recognize and respond to people in a more open and healthy manner.

5. Transference and countertransference are important tools in the therapeutic process.

## GOAL OF TREATMENT

Object relations therapy seeks to enable family members to relate to each other in a genuine manner that fosters individual growth as well as satisfying connections within the family. The therapist seeks to do so by helping family members reduce the anxiety that keeps them bound to the types of relationships created to deal with earlier needs and conflicts. Through object relations therapy individuals are helped to move beyond the shadows cast by the previous object relationships that have been projected in a problematic way onto their current family members. Symptom relief and behavior change are viewed as byproducts of resolution of underlying conflicts.

## ROLE OF THE THERAPIST

Scharff and Scharff (2006) describe the role of the therapist as the "new attachment figure" that enables people to deal with their anxiety in a healthier manner (p. 31). Through the therapeutic relationship, the therapist seeks to enable the family to transform its anxiety into an emotional experience that can be tolerated, thought about, and thus managed differently in the future. The therapist "bears the family's anxiety, reflects on the experience of being with that family, and puts anxiety into words" (Scharff & Scharff, 2003, p. 66). Frequently family members experienced painful events that were handled either by repression or by emotional amplification by important family members in the past (Scharff & Scharff, 2006). In contrast, the therapeutic situation creates a situation in which family members can tolerate and experience painful events, past trauma, and anxiety in ways that can be integrated in a manageable way. Through this process, family members are able to develop their own ability of self-regulation by identifying with the family counselor and thus no longer need the presence of the therapist to do so (Scharff & Scharff, 2006). The emphasis is upon the therapist's relationship with the family and the members of the family with each other. Family therapists need to have a good understanding of their own personal issues to order to be helpful to the family. The family therapist behaves in a calm and helpful manner—friendly and yet professional.

### *Assessment*

Scharff and Scharff (2003) describe a structured assessment process of one to four sessions. The arrangement is carefully structured and attempts to alter this structure are explored in terms of their therapeutic meaning. The therapist seeks to hear from all concerned. The focus is on identifying any transference manifestation of treatment and exploring them in terms of anxiety about treatment. The family therapist is also attuned to his or her countertransference toward the family and uses it as a tool of understanding the family. By being aware of issues within his or her own internalized objects, the family therapist can come to a better understanding of the family (Scharff & Scharff, 1987, 2003). If the therapist begins to feel a need to protect one of the family members, it might be in response to an internalized object of weakness by a family member and the need to create relationships in which one is cared for.

The therapist focuses on the relationships among family members and between the family members and the therapist. The therapist attends to the signs of transference that take the form of resistance to treatment. As part of helping the family members begin to deal with their anxiety, the therapist brings the family's distrust of therapy into the session in a nondefensive manner that can contribute to trust.

The interview follows the family members' account of their story with attention to pauses and possible omissions that serve as clues to the unconscious of the family members. The therapist explores with the family the meaning of possible omissions. The therapist also attends to strong emotional exchanges that occur and explores with the family members if these were anything like what they had experienced in their family of origin. Intense emotions are viewed as a replay of past experiences that cannot be remembered, only reenacted. By bringing these core emotional exchanges into consciousness, family members can be helped to come to terms with them and to decrease their current toxic power (Scharff & Scharff, 2003). The calm and nonjudgemental presence of the therapist enables the family members to discuss their private life in a way that encourages understanding. As family members describe the problem, they begin to reenact family patterns that reveal their defensive patterns within the sessions in ways that can be explored within therapy. Scharff and Scharff (2003) describe transference and countertransference as the key to therapeutic action. As the therapist recognizes how the family affects her in terms of her own countertransference issues, she can begin to work with from family from this perspective.

Given the intense private nature of the content that can occur, the therapist is very conscious of appropriate family boundaries. For example, sexual relationship issues are discussed between the couple separate from their children.

The therapist begins to interpret to the family members patterns of their interactions. The family's response to these interpretations becomes a way of learning whether or not the family is interested in understanding their family problems in a psychological insightful manner or if another approach is more appropriate at this time (Scharff & Scharff, 2003). Transference and countertransference issues are critical in the ongoing treatment process and give clues in terms of the early experiences of family members.

## *TREATMENT PROCESS*

Several treatment approaches are important in object relations family therapy. Scharff and Scharff (2003), Nichols and Schwartz (1998), and Kilpatrick, Kilpatrick, and Callaway (2000) describe the following approaches.

**Interpretations** that link events and contribute to insight are valuable. These interpretations identify relationship patterns, especially those with a "because" clause. Scharff and Scharff (2003) describe these as addressing the multilayers of relationships—the relationship that is openly required, the one that is avoided, and the calamity that it fends off.

**Empathic listening** involves waiting for people to say what they want to say and imagining the situation facing them. To facilitate empathy and understanding, family members are asked to tell more, to draw a picture of the family, or to describe a dream. Empathic listening gives support to family members. As in other models of family therapy, listening includes nonverbal and well as verbal communication.

**Clarification comments** by the therapist are shared with all family members to ensure that everyone hears the views that have been expressed.

The therapist also makes "shaping comments" to bring together the process to date.

**Development of a shared narrative experience** occurs when the therapist puts conflict into words. By describing the repetitive patterns, family members can begin to face their underlying anxieties. The therapist uses countertransference to experience these conflicts.

**Identification of unconscious projections** based on the family patterns is a first step toward helping family members begin to own their projective identifications. Family members can be helped to recognize how their own repressed wishes are reflected in the "problematic" behavior of the other person.

**Use of adjunctive methods.** Object relations therapy recognizes that interpretations are not always adequate to address important patterns like substance abuse or mental illness. Therapists encourage families to seek help from programs like Alcoholics Anonymous and other appropriate forms of help.

### *Brief Object Relations Therapy*

Stadter and Scharff (2006) describe focal psychotherapy, a brief therapy approach using object relations theory with emphasis on the joint projective process within the marital relationship and a psychodynamic model of brief therapy. This approach emphasizes four key elements:

1. Each individual, family, and therapeutic relationship is unique and therapy must be tailored to this uniqueness.

2. People are helped to identify the past patterns that continue to repeat themselves so that people can be helped to create new patterns.

3. A positive therapeutic relationship is *critical* for success.

4. It is important to study the ongoing patterns within the relationship (transference and countertransference) as well as to combine them with interpretations as appropriate to enable people to develop new ways of relating.

Stadter and Scharff (2006) describe eight strategies but caution that there are two critical elements in such brief therapy efforts: (1) strategies must be set within a positive therapeutic relationship, and (2) a clear focus must be established to organize the therapeutic effort.

*Strategy 1.* Establishment of the therapeutic alliance is the critical first step and involves the therapist's emphatic understanding, nonjudgmental approach, and interactions that convey respect. It is important not to let the pressures for brief treatment force this process to proceed faster than family members are ready. This positive therapeutic relationship is fostered by several actions of the therapist: directing attention to and demonstrating understanding of the client's pain, taking a history in a way that creates a shared process of discovery, collaboratively setting a focus, and attending to the transference and countertransference reactions in ways that permit one to use the client's internal language.

*Strategy 2.* Create a dual focus on symptoms and dynamics. Ideally it is valuable to be able to link symptoms to the dynamics of the individuals. For example, "Your intense anxiety about taking your final tests seems to be linked to your ongoing fear that you will not live up to your father's expectations." "Your fear of bringing up issues with your wife/husband seems to be linked to your fear of losing someone important as occurred when your mother deserted the family when you were a child."

*Strategy 3.* Obtain historical information related to family members' object relations patterns. This process can help individuals see patterns in what previously was experienced as random, for example, understanding a history of fearing that one is not living up to one's father's expectations and a pattern of fearing to face situations in which one could be judged even if it means giving up on otherwise desired goals. Several important aspects in a history can include the following:

Family members' impression of parents and other key family members or others that influenced their personality,

Ongoing patterns of interpersonal relationships—backing away from intimacy, abuse,

Best and worst levels of functioning,

Family history of problems and dysfunction,

Previous suicidal thinking and other disturbed thinking,

Health issues,

Previous therapy. (p. 424)

*Strategy 4.* Engage family members in looking at the way in which they and the family therapist are relating. This provides family members a way of looking at their past relational patterns and ways in which they are occurring in the present. Recognizing the anxiety that this can pose for clients, the therapist can invite members by asking about their response to certain interactions.

*Strategy 5.* Interpret dynamics and patterns when possible (p. 425). The presence of transference and countertransference within the therapeutic situation provides the opportunity to look at these patterns. The therapist might notice ways in which the couple avoid dealing with painful issues by quickly changing the subject. When this occurs, the therapist can wonder if they are fearful of what might happen if they should explore this further because they sometimes appear to be fearful with each other. If previously revealed historical material might reveal trauma or other life experiences that have made such conversations anxiety producing because it makes the individual feel weak or threatened, the therapist can further link these patterns with such earlier life experiences.

*Strategy 6.* Use nonpsychodynamic techniques as appropriate. The therapist can draw upon techniques from other traditions to enhance the efforts. The therapist must be aware of the impact on the relationship of the use of other techniques and ways in which transference and countertransference issues can play out in such recommendations. Therefore it is crucial to be aware of the family member's inner world in making such recommendations.

*Strategy 7.* Therapy can be thought of in terms of segments, so that clients can return for ongoing work as needed.

*Strategy 8.* Arrange for clients to have "a new ending for an old experience" (p. 428). The therapist can offer new outcomes for old patterns of clients in order to allow them to experiment with new ways of relating. For example, a client who has always related to people who viewed her incompetent can find in the therapist a person who looks for evidence of her competence and relates to her as a competent adult rather than a child in an adult body.

Stadter and Scharff (2006) describe the following client characteristics as indicative that brief therapy would be appropriate: the ability to define a clear focus, the ability to develop quickly a positive relationship with the worker, the ability to tolerate the frustration involved in a brief treatment, the positive response to typical interventions, the history of at least one good relationship, psychological mindfulness, and motivation for more than symptom relief. Individuals facing externally imposed or developmental crises might be good candidates for brief treatment.

## *Application*

Emily and Lewis seek counseling because Emily is suffering from anxiety to the degree that they are hesitant to become parents and their marital relationship is suffering. During the session, Lewis and Emily sit close together and Lewis places his arm around Emily in a protective and caring manner. Lewis takes the lead in explaining the situation indicating that just talking about the problem makes Emily anxious. Several times Emily begins to explain what she has been feeling but then hesitates and seems unsure of herself and turn to Lewis for support. Lewis then picks up the conversation and speaks for Emily. Emily visibly seems smaller as Lewis continues to speak for her. This pattern continues as the therapist leads the couple in describing their reason for seeking help. The social worker attends to this pattern of protection by which Emily seeks strength from Lewis who in turn acts in a protective manner. The social worker also reflects on personal life experiences in childhood in which she felt overwhelmed and turned to her older siblings for help in dealing with the divorce of her parents. The therapist comments to the couple that she knows how difficult it can be to express feelings of anxiety like they are trying to do in the session.

As Emily and Lewis continue to talk about their current life and the frustration that they are feeling with the impasse that they have reached, their emotions become more intense. The therapist uses this as an opportunity to explore with them whether their current feelings are similar to any of their prior experiences as they were growing up.

The therapist comments on the pattern that she is seeing—that Emily seeks support and protection from Lewis who in turn behaves in a very protective manner. Emily finds it difficult even to describe her own feelings and turns to Lewis for strength who in turn becomes the pillar of strength in their relationship. The social worker wonders who Lewis can turn to when he needs support in dealing with problems at work and other life challenges. The couple seem receptive to an approach that helps them understand their relationship and the current situation.

Using emphatic listening and clarifying comments that are shared with the couple, the therapist continues to help the couple explore the connections between their current relationship and the family patterns growing up. The therapist is aware of the anxiety that both must be experiencing now as well as in their past and conveys a sense of calm strength. The couple describe their experiences with their own families and how important it is for them to be able to protect their children from going through what they experienced. Emily is gradually able to connect her current need for strength from Lewis as related to the little girl she once was who felt so alone and scared with the illness and subsequent death of her mother. She could only feel safe with her father by her side taking care of her. Her anxiety has kept her from being the engaging person who used to attract people and she fears even more that Lewis might leave her. When Lewis is gone she is even more frightened. Lewis is gradually able to link to his own feelings of loss and loneliness as a child because of his mother's depression and his father's absence to his way of dealing with the world—be strong and do not let yourself or others see that you have needs. He was attracted to Emily because of her warmth that made him feel loved. Her anxiety has given him an opportunity to feel strong and put behind him his own needs for protection.

As the couple is able to cope with their anxiety about these painful shadows of the past and their ties to the present, Emily is gradually able to become less anxious and dependent on Lewis. Lewis is gradually able to share more of who he is with Emily. The pain of loss and fears that they both shared in their youth has become part of their conscious connections to the present. As a result, they are able to have empathy for each other without emotionally locking their partners and themselves into these rigid roles that protected them from the shadows of the past. Initially these changes occurred primarily in the sessions with the therapist present and gradually began to permeate their life together outside of the counseling session and the presence of the therapist. Sessions were spaced farther apart to give the couple the experience of being able to maintain these new patterns with reduced support from the therapist.

## EVALUATION

The goal of object relations family therapy is more than symptom relief and behavioral change and views them as byproducts of resolution of the underlying conflicts. It seeks to accomplish reconstructive psychotherapy. The family therapist seeks to help family members relate to each other in a genuine manner that fosters individual growth as well as connections. These goals are difficult to operationalize in measurable ways that fit current outcome evaluation paradigms. Outcome studies within this model are primarily case studies (Kilpatrick, Kipatrick, & Callaway, 2000; Nichols & Schwartz, 1998) The world of managed care and expectations for brief treatment has also been problematic for object relations family therapy because of the typical length that this model entails. Implementation of this model of family treatment requires social workers and other family counselors to be very aware of their own personal issues because countertransference plays such a critical role in the treatment process. Many of the families seeking help from social workers are looking for more immediate symptomatic relief or have pressing life problems that make it difficult for them to engage in the type of lengthy insightful exploration involved in object relations family therapy.

## SUMMARY

Object relations family therapy is a model of treatment designed to address the complex interpersonal issues that have their origins in past family relationships. The treatment is intended to enable family members to reduce their anxiety so that they can reclaim portions of themselves that they have projected onto other members of the family. Family members are helped to relinquish these rigid family roles and to grow as human beings.

# 12

## *Spirituality*

Social workers and other helping professionals increasingly recognize the importance of understanding the spiritual and religious perspectives of individuals and families as part of holistic models of practice (Canda & Furman, 1999; Carlson & Erickson, 2002; Frame, 2003; Kilpatrick, Becvar, & Holland, 2003). Studies have shown that the majority of people prefer to have their spiritual practices and beliefs integrated into their counseling (Walsh, 1999). While the physical resources of life are important to people so are the aspects of the spirit, of a sense of meaning (Aponte, 1994). In a world in which people are sometimes valued by the money they earn, the possessions they have, or the work they can do, people can begin to hunger for a deeper sense of meaning and purpose and a sense of being valued for who they are rather than what they produce. Spirituality can also help provide a moral compass to guide people in making the myriad of difficult decisions in life (Aponte, 2002). This chapter on spirituality does not represent a specific model of treatment but rather an aspect of life that can emerge in various treatment approaches.

Spirituality, described both in a religious and nonreligious context, is being recognized as playing a vital role in the helping process (Aponte, 2002; Canda & Furman, 1999). Canda and Furman (1999) describe "spirituality as the heart of helping—the heart of empathy and care, the pulse of compassion, the vital flow of practice wisdom, and the driving force of action for service" (p. xv). In recognition of the important role that spirituality and religion frequently play in the lives of people, the National Association of Social Workers, in its Code of Ethics, requires that social workers be culturally competent in several areas, including those of spirituality and religion. The Council on Social Work Education has included knowledge of spirituality and religion as part of the content of the social work curriculum.

### NATURE OF SPIRITUALITY

Although spirituality refers to a specific domain of life, it permeates all aspects of life. It influences how people view and experience life events. Recognizing that spirituality can be based on a supernatural deity (typically expressed in religion) or on a philosophical nonsupernatural foundation, Aponte (2002) identifies three basic elements of spirituality: "morality, meaning, and the nature of the individual's relationship to the world" (p. 16). Spirituality shapes issues of meaning and purpose, how suffering and healing are understood, and appropriate ways to resolve life struggles. Canda (1988) identifies three aspects of spirituality: values, beliefs, and practices organized around "a person's search for meaning and purpose, developed in the context of the interdependent relationship between self, other people, and the nonhuman world, and the foundation of being itself" (p. 43). Spirituality has been linked to people's relationship with the transcendence. Religion, on the other hand, involves an institutional, organizational, and community framework with accompanying patterned belief systems and traditions. While spirituality can be separate from religion, it "takes on religious meaning when the centers of value, beliefs, images of power, practices, and master stories of one's faith—the central dynamic of one's search for meaning and purpose—are grounded in the creeds, texts of scripture, rituals, and theologies of a particular religious tradition" (Hugen, 2001, p. 11). As a result, incorporating spirituality into an assessment of families involves an understanding of the belief systems of families, their sense of values, and practices related to their sense of meaning and purpose. When family members' spirituality is grounded within religious traditions, understanding the basic beliefs and organizational nature of the faith community can also be important to understand the meaning of life events and potential resources for these families.

In terms of family counseling, spirituality is not viewed as a distinct model of counseling like structural or narrative family therapy. Instead, an appreciation of the ways in which the current and past spiritual journey of family members are influencing how people are experiencing life events and potential resources for healing can be infused in a variety of family counseling models. Such an appreciation of the potential role of spirituality and religion in the lives of families must take into consideration the complex nature of this role. While these aspects can represent a source of comfort and meaning for some people at difficult times in their lives, they can also be the source of guilt, conflict, struggle, and sense of alienation. Family members can also be in very different places in terms of their spirituality and religion and these differences can be the source of conflict or tension. Such integration can also require an understanding of how specific religious and cultural traditions shape people's spiritual experiences, their search for meaning, and their perception of appropriate strategies for addressing issues in life. Even if families are no longer affiliated with a particular tradition, earlier life experiences can cast lasting shadows in these important areas of life. For example, a family's perception of serious illness within the family could vary greatly depending on whether the family's views were shaped by their Christian Science, Catholic, Hindu, Islamic, or Buddhist traditions. Different beliefs about life after death and the rituals associated with this somber period of life can have profound meaning to families facing this difficult period of the life cycle.

Walsh (1999) describes the role of healing in family treatment as the core of a resiliency-based model of practice. Healing is the process of becoming whole or finding some way to adapt and compensate for losses. Healing in this context is "is seen as a natural response to injury or trauma" (Walsh, 1999, p. 33). It recognizes that people can heal physically but not heal emotionally. It also recognizes that "we can heal psychosocially even when we do not heal physically or when a traumatic event cannot be reversed" (Walsh, 1999, p. 33). These multiple layers of healing permit counselors to foster resiliency even in situations in which it is impossible to solve the problem or when such a problem might recur. Many families who seek help from counselors are facing current or past issues that cannot be changed, but must be faced and coped with, for example, past abuse or death in the family. Suffering is also part of the human journey. It frequently causes people to raise questions of meaning and other spiritual concerns. Healing draws upon the resources of people and their context. Incorporating spirituality into counseling with families can be instrumental in this healing process. It can address past events as well as enhance the sense of meaning, purpose, and connection that can be protective in terms of current and future life events. Recognizing the brokenness of relationships in the lives of many of the families who seek help, Walsh describes as a spiritual endeavor the work of counselors to help clients seek "reconciliation to heal wounded relationships and encourage them to forge more meaningful personal and spiritual bonds" (Walsh, 1999, p. 49).

As discussed in chapter 1, aspects of spirituality can represent important protective factors for family members. Religion in terms of beliefs, rituals, and the organizational context can be protective as well as accentuate risk factors for families and individuals (Aguilar & Van Hook, 2001; Koenig, 1999; Pargament, 1997; Van Hook & Rivera, 2004). Walsh (1999) describes spiritual beliefs and practices as strengthening "the ability to withstand and transcend adversity. Such keys to resiliency as meaning-making, hope, perseverance, and connectedness are all enhanced by spirituality" (p. 38). Further supporting resiliency is "being able to give meaning to a precarious situation, having faith that there is some greater purpose or force at work, and finding solace and strength in these outlooks" (Walsh, 1999, p. 38). Crises in people's lives can become opportunities to develop spiritual dimensions (Walsh, 1999). Understanding the nature of these risk and protective factors and enhancing the protective factors can promote healing in families.

## GOALS

This chapter is not designed to equip social workers and family counselors to be religious counselors. The goal is to enable counselors to help family members identify potential healing forces within their own spiritual and religious traditions that can be used to address their family issues and to strengthen the family as well as to identify roadblocks in the process of healing. Such family issues can be a result of the current situation facing the family members (e.g., illness of a family member, economic crisis, parent-child or marital conflict) or can be the result of emotional scars due to past life events (e.g., emotional or physical abuse, abandonment, losses) that can be coped with but cannot be changed. As discussed in chapter 1, current events can also reactivate past life events with added distress for the family members.

It is also beyond the scope of this chapter to provide information about all of the many religious traditions and the implications of social work practice in working with these families. Several resources include Van Hook, Hugen, and Aguilar (2001) that contains chapters written by social work experts regarding a variety of religious traditions, Walsh (1999) that includes chapters about various religious traditions and traditions associated with racial and ethnic groups, and Canda and Furman (1999) that describes various religious and spiritual traditions.

## *ROLE OF THE COUNSELOR*

In terms of spirituality and family counseling, the role of the counselor is one of opening the door to this important dialogue between the family members and the counselor as well as among relevant family members or some symbolic representation of them. Given the past divide between social work and other forms of family counseling and spiritual issues, family members might be reluctant to raise this issue in the counseling session because they do not think their concerns will be valued or viewed as relevant, or fear they are not being understood by the counselor. In this regard, the interview is a two-way street with family members assessing the counselor to see if they can trust the counselor with this very important aspect of themselves. One of the primary steps of the counselor is to open the door by asking appropriate questions related to potential issues related to meaning, purpose, spiritual and religious aspects of life events. This exploration helps legitimize bringing these issues to the counseling situation for those families who view spiritual as relevant. Family members thus have the choice whether or not they view these aspects as germane to the issues at hand.

In this context, Walsh (1999) describes an earlier clinical experience in which she was working with a family in which the father and husband, a beloved minister, had died in an auto accident. She counseled the widow and the children regarding their grief and loss without ever raising any issues related to spirituality. When later asked why she had not done so, she reflected on the great divide between spirituality and family counseling and its negative impact on the true effectiveness of family counselor.

Walsh (1999) describes spirituality in terms of the very fabric of the family counseling situation in ways that transcend specific treatment models. The counselors' faith in the family's potential can help restore hope. Incorporating spirituality into the counseling process requires the counselor to be able to create important and respectful connections with family members. "Valuing connections we help our clients to seek reconciliation to heal wounded relationships and encourage them to forge more meaningful personal and spiritual bonds" (Walsh, 1999, p. 49). Wright (1999) goes further to use the term "reverencing" in terms of her relationship with clients (p. 63). Reverencing involves a sense of profound awe and respect for the family members. The ensuing reciprocal connection between family members and counselors can lead to important changes in thinking behavior, and the experience of suffering. This attitude further grants dignity to people (food for the spirit).

Incorporating spirituality into the counseling process requires the counselor to have a deeper understanding of him or herself. Aponte (1994) reminds us that in order to address others about the spirit, we must first examine ourselves in terms of what gives us meaning and purpose in life and how this affects our views and relationships with others. While self-awareness is important in any counseling effort, it can be especially critical in this arena because our own spiritual and religious traditions can have a profound impact on our work with others. Without intending to, counselors can find themselves reacting in ways that impose their own beliefs on clients or at least make it uncomfortable for clients to bring up certain spiritual or religious elements. It is essential for counselors to be aware of their own spiritual beliefs and how they can influence their counseling efforts. This raises several questions. As counselors, what are our spiritual and religious beliefs and experiences? Can we appreciate other spiritual traditions and their role in the lives of families? Can we give room for people to question and doubt spiritual or religious issues that are deeply important for us?

Such self-awareness can help counselors guard against the danger of using the counseling session to proselytize or try to persuade family members to accept the counselor's spiritual or religious stance on life (Canda & Furman, 1999; Frame, 2003; Hugen, 2001; Sherwood, 2002). Sherwood (2002) stresses the importance of not using the vulnerability of a client's situation to impose one's own spiritual or religious perspective on others. Aponte (2002) describes the importance of counselors understanding their own spiritual journey in ways that permit them to use aspects of themselves to gain empathy for their client's stories and to engage in needed professional closeness without "infringing upon the boundaries of the client, and not allowing their own boundaries to be trespassed" (p. 21).

Several years ago when I was conducting workshops for social workers and mental health counselors regarding the role of spirituality and religion in working with clients, it became clear that many of the individuals in the audience were responding out of their own life experience. While general comments regarding spirituality generated positive comments, when the topic moved more specifically to the religion of family members, the comments became more heated. Some of the attendees described in great detail and with considerable emotion their own negative experiences as proof that religion could only be damaging and a source of pain for all families. Others spoke of the support they had received as something that might be valuable for all families. While social workers would be quick to realize that their personal experiences regarding marriage or divorce would not necessarily be applicable to others, it appears that it can be more difficult for people to create these appropriate boundaries between their own personal experiences and that of others in the area of religion.

The role of counselor is one of a partner rather than expert. Addressing issues related to spirituality is as a partner between the counselor and the family. Aponte (1994) further reminds us that we are "companions on a journey, their journey. We do not own expertise about the spirit. As therapists, we are not the new priesthood" (p. 246). The family counselor does not enter the arena as a spiritual or religious expert, as a religious or pastoral counselor, but as a person who can help family members identify or connect people with resources within their spiritual journey. This requires the counselor to gain an understanding of the religious and spiritual tradition of the family members. The counselor uses his or her knowledge of a spiritual or religious tradition to understand the family more effectively, and to help identify potential resources, not to guide them in terms of their belief system.

Being a partner on this journey can also means being truly with people during times of suffering, offering compassion, helping family members reach out to each other, helping family members identify their beliefs or practices that can be meaningful, and connecting them with others who can be helpful at this stage of their life. Helping people recognize the spiritual dimension of their lives can also help lend dignity and value.

## ASSESSMENT

Assessment of the family's spiritual or religious situation is an important aspect of incorporating spirituality into family counseling. Such an assessment means opening the door to this important topic as well as asking specific questions that can help understand the family. Before discussing specific ways to assess spirituality and/or religion in the lives of people, it is important to recognize that this process belongs to the arena of "knowing" rather than mere "information." Knowing pushes beyond a set of facts to the meaning of these facts in the life of another person which creates a sense of understanding. For example, a statement on a face sheet of an agency that someone is Catholic or Hindu is not the same as a series of questions that pertain to the meaning of this religion in the life of the person and how this meaning in turn relates to the current situation. If a family member is dying, issues related to important rituals prior to and following death or interpretations of the possibility and nature of life after death become extremely relevant in the knowing process. The assessment process can take the form of a guided interview (a conversation) as well some recently developed visual tools.

Social workers cannot assume that all members of racial or ethnic groups share similar religious and spiritual views because of the diversity within groups. African Americans, for example, belong to virtually every religious group in America and some have no religious perspective. At the same time, members can share a profound spiritual sense of the purpose of life despite such religious differences (Boyd-Franklin & Lockwood, 1999; Martin & Martin, 2002).

Hodge (2003) describes the guided interview—the therapeutic conversation as a spiritual anthropology. As family members describe their family, counselors can explore some relevant questions about the issues the family members are presenting as well as the solutions that they are considering. To ask about spirituality in this manner is strength based and demonstrates respect for the client's right to self-determination. These questions open the door to exploring issues of spirituality and religion in more meaningful ways than a simple notation in the record that a person is Catholic, Jewish, Hindu, nonreligious, etc. The counselor naturally needs to be sensitive to whether or not families wish to explore these issues further. Recognizing that not all issues are relevant or apropos for all families or situations, some potentially important questions could include the following.

> Are any faiths, religions, specific spiritual beliefs and practice important to the family members (both currently and in the past)?
>
> How, if at all, does the spiritual or religious tradition of the family members define and give meaning to the issues facing the family and their options for addressing them?
>
> Have the family members sought to address their current situation in part through their concept of spirituality, their religious beliefs or faith, or their religious or spiritual community, and if so, with what results? (This question can elicit potential resources, family coping strategies, and possible experiences of alienation and distress.)
>
> Are there any rituals associated with the spiritual or religious tradition that the family views as appropriate or helpful? (This can involve situations in which people have felt unable to carry out specific rituals due to their actions, their current setting, or other circumstances.)
>
> Is there a history in the family of people from different religious or spiritual traditions coming together and what had been the impact of this on the family (e.g., acceptance, cutoffs in the family)?

Are there past spiritual or religious traditions that are influencing how the current situation is being experienced?

Have there been deep wounds that have had an impact on the spiritual or religious life of the family or its members?

Are there any resources within the spiritual tradition (beliefs, practices, community) that might be helpful in coping with the current situation? Do people feel that they can avail themselves of these resources or do they feel alienated or unable to do so?

Answers to questions addressing these domains can help identify potential spiritual resources, the meaning systems that influence how life events are experienced, as well as potential tensions and burdens created by the spiritual or religious traditions. This information can help guide the counselor in drawing upon whatever sources of resiliency there are within the spiritual or religious realm of the family as well as identifying barriers in this process.

Hodge (2005) has also developed the spiritual ecogram for identifying potential strengths and issues both in earlier times and currently. This tool combines aspects of the eco map and the genogram described earlier. Prior to using this tool with families, the social worker needs to inquire if families are interested in learning more about how spirituality and or religion has played a role in their family in the past as well as their coping with current issues. The clients are the experts and decide whether or not they wish to engage in such a process.

Figure 3 represents a spiritual ecogram that links the family members' past with their current circumstances. As reflected in this ecogram, spiritual issues represent both sources of support and tension. Marilyn and Jacob N. contacted the center because Marilyn is feeling overwhelmed with the care of their five-year-old son. In this situation, she is especially feeling the pain of being cut off from her own parents. Her parents disapproved of her marriage to Jacob because he is Jewish. Jacob and his family have been very closely attached to their Jewish faith and the synagogue. For Marilyn's parents the Baptist Church and all that it represents to them in terms of faith and association is equally important. Marilyn and her husband have also been feeling alienated from her only brother. The family members are active in the synagogue and have close ties to other members. Mary is a good student and the family has good relationships to the school in terms of Mary. William is having serious learning disabilities and this has created strain between the family and the educational system. There is also tension with the health-care system as it relates to William's care.

In the spiritual ecogram, the current family situation is located within the center of the page. The earlier generations are presented similar to the genogram in which men are represented as squares and women as circles. Lines

**Figure 3.** Spiritual Ecogram

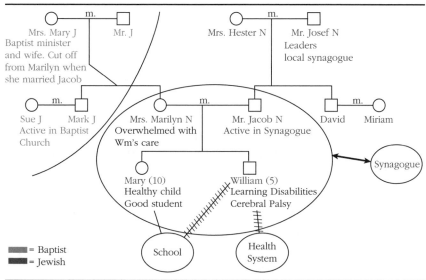

indicate relationships between people with the strength of the line representing the strength of the relationship. In this version, different religious traditions are represented by different colors. Important life events in the spiritual journey can be represented by symbols that are important for the family members. This aspect of the ecogram can reveal family legacies, potential tension, religious traditions. The second part of the ecogram represents the links between the family and relevant aspects of the current spiritual/religious life. Such aspects can include elements of the faith community, rituals, relationship with God or other transcendent relationships.

# *TREATMENT PROCESS*

Helmeke and Bischof (2002) have developed guidelines for recognizing and raising spiritual issues based on whether or not the issue is raised by the client or the counselor and if the issue is religious or spiritual in nature.

**Spiritual issues raised by the client** (Helmeke & Bischof, 2002, p. 201). Clients may raise these issues through talking about matters of purpose or meaning in life or making a comment about spirituality in a specific manner. The counselor can acknowledge with family members that they have made a comment about something related to spirituality and then explore further if this is important to them and ask if they would like to add to these thoughts. If counselors do not make this connection, family members can interpret their silence as lack of interest or willingness to discuss these issues. The counselor can further explore whether these issues related to spirituality are associated with the problem they are presenting, either in terms of potential resources or contributing factors. Understanding the client's path to spirituality can suggest other relevant issues. The counselor can also inquire how, if any, ways the family members would like spiritual issues to be part of the counseling process. Helmeke and Bischof (2002) further indicate that use of spiritual rather than religious language suggests the type of language that would be meaningful for this family.

**Religious issues raised by the client** (Helmeke & Bischof, 2002, p. 202). Members of the family can refer to something specifically related to religion. Family members might describe their anger toward God for the death of a child or how their faith made it possible for them to survive the death of a child. It is valuable for the counselor to learn about the family's religious perspective. This might mean studying the religious tradition that the family is associated with. For example, what is the meaning of death and the deity in the family's religion? If a family is close to their religious leader and feels comfortable with this individual, engaging this individual as a partner can sometimes be helpful. The leader has knowledge and expertise and can offer important support as well as identify other support systems within the faith community. Frequently the religious leader is likely to have an ongoing relationship with family members that can represent a more long-term resource than the family counselor. Referral to a religious leader depends, of course, on the comfort of the family in meeting with such individuals. While this is a resource for some families, others are struggling with such alienation that they would not be receptive to such a step.

The counselor also needs to attend to the language used by the family in order to use appropriate language that facilitates the joining process (Helmeke & Bischof, 2002). Language is used to shape reality and meaning systems. Using the language of the family helps to create an effective working relationship. Counselors also need to be aware of ways in which religion can veil other pervasive problems within the family (Helmeke & Bischof, 2002).

**Spiritual issues raised by the counselor** (Helmeke & Bischof, 2002, p. 205). The counselor can explore with clients if there may be any relevant spiritual issues in terms of the problem they are facing. The counselor then needs to respect the clients' perspective in terms of whether or not clients view these issues as relevant or useful. As Helmeke and Bischof (2002) caution, "the buried treasure that might be found may be gold to the therapist but merely dross to the client" (p. 205) and the challenge for the counselor is to respect the clients' evaluation. On the other hand, failing to explore if these issues are important can send a message that they are not germane to the counseling process and thus fail to address critical issues and miss potentially invaluable resources. Clients can be reluctant to bring up these issues because do not think that the counselor will view them as valuable, legitimate, or important. Issues related to loss and grief, serious illness, or recovery from addictions especially lend themselves to this exploration (Helmeke & Bischoff, 2002).

**Religious issues raised by the counselor** (Helmeke & Bischoff, 2002, p. 208). This situation requires the most caution and requires the greatest self-understanding of the part of the counselor. Intake forms might suggest a religious tie that can be explored with the family in terms of whether this is important for them regarding their current situation. A hospital counselor working with the parents of a severely ill child, for example, might explore what meaning, if any, their religion has for them as this time. These questions open doors and let the family decide if this is a relevant dimension for the family. Helmeke and Biscoff (2002) warn that counselors from similar religious backgrounds to the family can risk making the assumption that the family members' interpretations and experience are similar to their own and they stress the importance of exploring these issues with an open mind. Genograms are appropriate places to ask about religion. Other situations that suggest the value of exploring the relevance of religious issues include clients who have raised other related spiritual or religious issues, are addressing issues related to faith issues (e.g., life after death, interfaith marriage), or are families with strong religious community ties (Helmeke & Biscoff, 2002).

## *Application*

Family members need to have both their basic physical needs as well as spiritual issues of meaning and sense of purpose met. The needs of families can be organized around one or more of these aspects of life. Families can require various types of social support as they attempt to cope with difficult life events. They can struggle with feelings of isolation. They can be experiencing distress due to family life cycle issues or be in need of positive mentoring of family members. Relationships within families can become poisoned with the pain of anger and betrayal or profound misunderstandings. Any spiritual assessment of families is embedded within this larger assessment of the risk and protective factors of family members.

Some families are struggling to meet some of their basic needs. For these families, survival needs are primary. Counselors can explore if there are potential resources within the current spiritual or faith community of the family or the community at large that can help this family meet these essential needs. Faith communities from a wide range of religious traditions embrace the concept of charity and offer a variety of resources for their members and others in the community. Identifying such resources within the community can be part of a multisystems approach to working with families. Individual congregations also work through other community programs related to their spiritual or religious faith groups and general community organizations. Social workers can both connect families with resources as well as educate faith communities about needs within the community and ways that these communities can help in a manner that bestows to the recipients dignity and respect.

Many faith communities offer support groups for families experiencing a variety of difficult situations (e.g., grief, divorce, single parenting, caregiving). These programs can be resources for family members who are feeling alone with their problem and can benefit from supportive ties. Again, while some of these programs are for members of the group, others reach out to the community at large. Counselors can identify the services available in the community and how comfortable people are with services offered through such auspices. In addition to support, members can also gain new coping skills and encouragement to use these skills from others who are attending the group as well as from the leader.

During times of crisis, some individuals feel alienated from their faith or spiritual tradition while others can feel supported through a spiritual connection with what they view as the transcendent in their lives. Others vacillate between these responses. Alcoholics Anonymous and related self-help organizations have long identified the strength that some people draw from their higher power and have explicitly built this into their program. Pargament and Brandt (1998) suggest that religious coping is effective because it offers a response to the "problems of human insufficiency." When people are pushed beyond the limits of their own resources, they are reminded of their own basic vulnerability. At these times, religion can offer help in terms of spiritual support, answers regarding puzzling and difficult life events, and a sense of control. The longitudinal study of poor young people from a variety of ethnic groups on the island of Kauai, for example, revealed that for people from a wide variety of religious groups—including Buddhism, Catholicism, Mormonism, Jehovah's Witnesses, and others—religion "strengthened these families through times of adversity by providing a sense of purpose, mission, and salvation" (Walsh, 1999, p. 38). Counselors can explore with family members if there are any spiritual connections that can be meaningful for the family members involved at this difficult time.

In addition, what is especially important in believing that one can overcome adversity is "being able to give meaning to a precarious situation, having faith that there is some greater purpose or force at work, and finding solace and strength in these outlooks" (Walsh, 1999, p. 38). Dialogue with families in terms of spirituality and stories of faith can help elicit this sense of purpose. Discussing the family's sense that these events and their lives have a purpose in the counseling session can help support such views. During the 2005 devastating hurricanes in the U.S. Gulf Coast area, some of the resilient survivors described the greater purpose that they felt was taking place as a result of this event. Family interventions can address issues of meaning and family stories can draw upon these views of purpose in ways that give meaning and thus help counter some of the negative family stories. Counselors can explore how a sense of meaning or purpose in past life events helped them cope and explore this in addressing the current situation. Without assuming an unrealistically positive stance, counselors can explore what meaning such past events had for families. Sometimes families are able to identify ways in which the family grew and became stronger and thus begin to view the current situation as potentially having a sense of purpose and meaning in their lives.

Many families seeking help are suffering in profound ways. Wright (1999) describes from her experience that conversations about suffering frequently open the door to a discussion of spirituality if the parties involved are comfortable with this type of dialogue. Again, counselors need to be able to enter into such conversations and permit families a safe haven for their intense feelings at this time.

Rituals can be very important for families. Rituals help families deal with loss, welcome new members, mark changes in the life cycle, establish closeness to the transcendent, celebrate group ties, and many other purposes. Some community-supported rituals are tied to the spiritual or religious life of the family. Counselors can explore the role of rituals in the life of the family. Families can feel distress if they are unable to practice longstanding spiritual or religious rituals. Refugee families can be especially vulnerable here as they are torn from their previous spiritual as well as physical community. Family members can be helped to create meaningful rituals or identify ways in which they can restore important ones. These rituals can create ways to remember important family members. Sometimes just being supportive of family members' use of their important rituals to address problems can be important.

A medical social worker shared the following example of the power of drawing on the customs of culture and spirituality. An older hospitalized woman was suffering from great pain. When she refused pain medication, the social worker was urged by the medical staff to institute the process of involuntary commitment. The social worker, sensitive to possible cultural and spiritual resources within the life space of the client, engaged the family as allies. The extended family came, formed a circle around the patient, and began to sing music from their traditional religion. The effect on the woman was remarkable. The sounds of the music and the healing touch of her family helped the pain to recede. She had come from a poor Caribbean community where access to medication was very limited and where people developed rituals for healing that evoked music and the spiritual power of the community to address issues of pain and illness (Van Hook, 2007).

Social workers can identify ways in which family members are feeling unable to carry out important rituals. This can be particularly difficult for families who have left their homeland and have had difficulty carrying out their traditional spiritual rituals in their new country. Family tensions can occur if these rituals remain important for one generation and are dismissed as unimportant or irrelevant by the younger generation. People who have come from other cultural contexts might feel distress if they find it difficult to practice their old rituals. Helping family members identify ways in which they might be able to restore these rituals or at least some version of them can potentially be useful.

Other people might feel unable to carryout important rituals because of ways in which they feel they have made themselves unworthy in terms of their faith tradition. Helping link people with understanding leaders within their faith tradition can be useful here.

> Mr. K sought counseling because of severe anxiety attacks that led him to seek medical help from the emergency room. Exploration revealed that he was feeling guilty because of an affair he had several years ago. He had long ago given up this relationship and was working hard to improve his marriage. As a result of his past actions, he had not availed himself of the Sacrament of Reconciliation of the Catholic Church since that time. During this discussion, Mr. K began to see the link between his sense of anxiety and his increasing sense of distance from his faith community. He sought out an understanding priest who helped him restore his ties with the church and participate again in the sacrament. His sense of anxiety began to subside dramatically.

In this context, the social worker provided a setting in which Mr. K was able to explore his situation in ways that incorporated the spiritual dimension and in the process to draw upon the resources present within his spiritual tradition.

### *Forgiveness*

Family relationships can be distorted and hurt by anger and feelings of betrayal. Family members can find it difficult to forgive others as well as themselves. It is certainly not the right of the family counselor to make decisions regarding forgiveness for the family members (Canda & Furman, 1999) and the counselor needs to be aware of unrealistic pressure on family members to forgive that be imposed by others. At the same time, forgiveness has been shown to have great healing power (Canda & Furman, 1999; Friedman's study as cited in Frame, 2003). The concepts and obligations of forgiveness have different meanings with diverse religious traditions and it is useful for the counselor to understand the meanings of forgiveness within the family's tradition (Friedman, 2003). If family members are agreeable, it can be useful for family members to identify some of the barriers to forgiving others and themselves and to recognize the corrosive impact of their ongoing resentments.

As family members are exploring the possibility of forgiveness, they can be helped to understand that forgiveness does not necessarily mean reconciliation because reconciliation typically involves the offending party making some type of amends. Unlike reconciliation, forgiveness can occur regardless of the intentions of the other person. Family members can also be helped to understand that forgiveness does not require people to place themselves in ongoing harm's way. People who have been hurt by others certainly should not continue to put themselves in harm's way either physically or emotionally. If family members decide that they would like to build a bridge toward reconciliation, the counselor needs to help family members recognize that they are unable to control the response of the other person and can truly only be responsible for their own behavior.

Forgiveness does not mean glossing over the hurt that has occurred because part of the forgiveness process is recognizing the reality of the hurt that has occurred and the opportunity for expressing these feelings to others and experiencing validation for these feelings. As part of the process of forgiveness, people do need to give up revenge. They are helped to gain empathy for the offending party (Friedman's study as cited in Frame, 2003).

Some families have been powerful examples of the healing power of forgiveness both for the family and the larger community. A family's daughter who had gone to work with very poor people in South Africa was murdered by a member of the community. In the context of their grief, the parents established a program to reach out to these poor and alienated young people as a way of honoring her daughter and her work.

The following represents an example in which reconciliation efforts were initially rebuffed and the importance of support during this process.

> The counselor and the family pastor agreed to help a young woman try to become reconciled with her parents who disapproved of her divorce. Both the counselor and the pastor previously discussed with her the possibility that her parents might not change their minds and asked what would be her response if this occurred. Unfortunately, in the family session with the young woman, her parents, the counselor and the pastor, her angry mother could not accept her decision and instead indicated that she would rather have her daughter "dead than divorced." These words dashed the daughter's hopes for reconciliation. Her pastor continued to be strong source of support and she was able to take comfort in the fact that she had made an effort toward reconciliation. A couple of years later, her parents sought to be reconciled with her and she was able to move past these words of hurt and establish a relationship with her parents. It was, however, a reconciliation based on their acceptance of her decision about her divorce.

Family members can also feel guilty for their actions toward others in the family. While people can be struggling unrealistically with guilt and counselors need to help them lift these feelings, there are also situations in which feelings of guilt or remorse are legitimate and the appropriate response is for family members to acknowledge what they have done wrong and to make amends. Counselors can be supportive of the strength involved in taking such steps.

Counselors can also help family members access the resources of spiritual and religious leaders in their community. The specific nature of these depends on the needs and interests of the specific families. Such individuals can be helpful in addressing some of the more specific spiritual or religious issues facing family members. As indicated earlier, such referrals are the result of an assessment that families are receptive to this step.

When I was a student social worker I was counseling a woman who became very depressed following the birth of her baby, who was blind. She was convinced that this was God's punishment for getting a divorce without the sanction of the church and for remarrying. She had been waiting for her punishment. Referrals to very supportive Catholic sisters and an understanding priest were extremely valuable in her realizing that her child's problem was not God's punishment for her.

## Specific Life Issues

As indicated earlier, suffering is part of the life experience and has a profound impact on people. For some individuals, spirituality and faith become strengthened and serve as important resources, others become alienated. The following studies regarding parents who have lost children and caretakers with family members with Alzheimer's disease reflect these diverse responses.

### Loss of a Child

A variety of studies regarding how parents cope after the death of child reveal that while many parents eventually turn to their religious belief systems at this time and report a deepening of their faith, for others this is a time of loss or confusion regarding spiritual beliefs. Many parents question God's mercy and are angry with those who seek to place the death of the child within some framework of spiritual purpose of God (Brotherson & Sonderquist, 2002). For some parents, ongoing experiences of connection with their dead child serve to help parents cope with their loss. The wide variations of spiritual and religious beliefs influence how this difficult life event is experienced.

An exploratory study including qualitative interviews with white parents who had lost their children from accidents or illness revealed some important themes regarding the role of spirituality and religion in coping. Their responses were organized around four key areas: "(1) Struggle with or loss of particular beliefs, (2) spiritual beliefs and practices as a coping resource, (3) a sense of spiritual connection with their child, and (4) lack of support for or rejection of these spiritual aspects" (Brotherson & Sonderquist, 2002, pp. 62–63).

Struggles with religious doubts and a breakdown of their belief system either for a short period or on a more lasting basis were reported by some of the parents. One theme related to the fear of parents that they had done something wrong that had caused this death. Others asked how God could let something like this happen (Brotherson & Sonderquist, 2002).

On the other hand, some parents reported a deepening of their faith as the solace they found in their faith allowed them to cope with this tragic event. Beliefs that death was tied into some divine plan or that the child was alive in a better place were helpful. Parents also held to beliefs that the dead child remained as part of the family. Parents also coped through specific religious practices that permitted them to express their emotions and receive comfort (Brotherson & Sonderquist, 2002).

Spiritual connections with the child were also important. Parents continued to talk to their children and often created special places where they could feel this connection. Dreams were also ways to feel close to their child. Parents also found comfort in sensing their child as present in some special way (Brotherson & Sonderquist, 2002).

Perceived lack of support from others proved difficult for these parents. Some individuals withdrew from them because they felt uncomfortable dealing with their grief or urged parents to move beyond their grief. Parents reported that others might not validate their sense of special presence of their children. They found it difficult when their religious leaders could not offer support or could not allow them to express their spiritual struggles. It was particularly difficult if parents felt blamed in some manner (Brotherson & Sonderquist, 2002).

Addressing families struggling with these intense issues can be difficult for family counselors and requires them to be able to enter into intense and potentially painful discussions. The counseling setting can potentially be a haven for the family to reveal their pains, their doubts, their anger, and their hopes in general as well as those related to their spiritual life.

### Caregiving for Ill Family Members

Caregiving can be an extremely difficult experience. Several studies have indicated that use of spiritual and religious coping strategies can be helpful for caregiving related to a variety of health problems. A recent study conducted with caregivers of families with Alzheimer's disease revealed both ways in which spirituality and religion helped in coping as well as posed burdens (Smith & Harkness, 2002).

In terms of social support, respondents described the support they received from the clergy and their church community in mixed terms. While the majority described people as kind, a minority also revealed negative experiences. They used terms like "hypocritical" and "phony" in their descriptions of the response of others who they felt had not visited or otherwise showed an appropriate interest. Caretakers reported finding support from their spiritual life and their relationship to God even though some had gone through times of anger. Creating a sense of meaning of this experience was also important to respondents. Part of this sense of meaning was carrying out the legacy of the family member who was ill (Smith & Harkness, 2002).

Based on these findings, Smith and Harkness (2002) reiterate some of the themes described earlier in terms of drawing upon spirituality in a holistic approach to care. Counselors should be aware of their own spiritual and religious stance in this regard. Counselors also need to learn from the family if including spirituality into the model of helping the family fits with the family's view of what is useful. The family counselor gains information and counsels the family from the perspective of one who learns from the family its sense of meaning rather than the counselor's own expertise. The counselor can sometimes work in partnership with the religious or spiritual leader of the family. Social workers and other family counselors also need to recognize their professional limitations of expertise in addressing these areas with the accompanying need for a referral of such is viewed as appropriate for the family.

## SUMMARY

Incorporating spirituality and religion can enrich the counseling experience with families by identifying potential protective and risk factors related to these dimensions of life. Life events can raise issues of meaning and purpose in life. Opening the door to spirituality can enable some family members to discuss issues of profound importance to them and to identify potential resources. Such an approach requires family counselors to have a thorough self-understanding and to recognize that the family members are the experts on this journey. Counselors need to learn about the traditions of the family members in order to understand how life events are experienced. The specific ways in which these elements are incorporated into counseling depend on the family and its views of what is helpful, their religious and spiritual traditions, and the situation facing the family. Partnerships with spiritual and religious leaders can potentially be useful in helping some families. Spirituality also involves a genuine valuing of family members by the counselor.

# Part III

# *Resiliency-Based Practice Framework*

# 13

# *Families Coping with Difficult Life Events*

Families seeking help from social workers are frequently contending with one or more difficult events in the life of the family. A few of the many circumstances include a family member who has lost a job with consequent economic problems for the family or a family struggling with the burden of a chronically ill family member. Other families are referred for problems related to their children—perhaps behavior problems in school or suspicion of child neglect or abuse. Some families are coping with difficult transitions to a new culture and country. For many families, there is a pileup of life events. The preceding chapters contained examples of families struggling with one or more difficult life events.

This chapter addresses these struggles from a resiliency perspective by describing potential risk and protective factors that have been identified in terms of specific life circumstances. Understanding the patterns of risk and protective factors associated with life events can help social workers and other family counselors in their search for sources of resiliency as they seek to enhance and support the ability of families to cope. This information can also help in the ongoing process of clinical judgment, especially in terms of the useful intervention approaches with a particular family facing a unique set of problems within a current context. While information in this chapter is organized in terms of specific problem areas, it is important to assess individual families and their members to identify the unique combination of risk and protective factors present within this family and how the family is interpreting this life event. As a result, while this chapter includes a discussion regarding links between the research literature of risk and protective factors and treatment models, it is done with the caveat that in practice situations such information must be set within the context of the characteristics of the individual family in making any treatment decisions. Assessment is always an ongoing process and decisions regarding appropriate intervention approaches may need to be revised accordingly. The nature of these risk and protective factors highlights the need to expand the perspective used for assessment and treatment to include the wider community and social context.

# ILLNESS

The entire family experiences stress when a member becomes ill, especially if the illness is disabling or fatal. As discussed in chapter 4, Lillian's and Bradley's situations illustrate how the illness of a family member ripples throughout the family system. Chronic illness creates an ongoing source of stress for families that presents the family with a number of additive stressors over the years in ways that particularly challenge the coping ability of families. The ability of family members to cope is strongly influenced by how family members interpret the illness, including the cause and consequences of the illness, as well as the skills that the family members possess to deal with the situation.

## Children with Chronic Illness

Studies have identified coping strategies that enhance protective factors in the face of this difficult experience. Families coped by seeking information and turning to their social support systems. They also addressed family organizational issues by seeking to maintain the integration of the family. Parents sought to be aware of the needs of both the ill child and others within the family circle. They also encouraged communication among family members. Resilient families demonstrated a combination of family togetherness (cohesion) and the ability to be flexible regarding family responsibilities (Kliewer, 1997; Patterson & McCubbin, 1983).

## HIV/AIDS

The AIDS crisis has had a devastating impact on millions of people and their families. Recognizing that families with a member suffering from AIDS vary widely on many dimensions, a review of the literature reveals that mothers in general have tended to be the most likely to accept and to provide care for the ill person (Thompson, 1999).

The AIDS epidemic has had an especially harsh impact on African American families. Rates of HIV/AIDS among African American women are twenty-five times that of white women and HIV/AIDS has been a leading cause of death among African American women between twenty-five and forty-four years, a period during which women typically have major responsibilities for the family (Centers for Disease Control, 2005a, 2005b).

The combination of risk and protective factors for many of these women is compounded by long-term poverty, along with drug addiction, and the accompanying stressors that are frequently part of their lives in addition to their illness. Reflecting this context, African American women who are HIV positive tend to report the stress of lack of financial resources, lack of support from their community, violence and crime, stigma regarding the illness, and tension within the family circle (Center for Disease Control, 2005a; Greenwood et al., 1996).

Protective factors include family support by members of the immediate, extended, and "fictive kin" as well reliance upon religion. A treatment approach (structural ecosystems therapy, SET) is based on a systems approach has been effective in empowering individuals and their families. Key components include skills to negotiate more effectively with the environment and to improve family interaction and communication (Greenwood et al., 1996).

The AIDS epidemic has further created 80,000 orphaned children and adolescents with at least 80 percent of these African Americans or Hispanics in the United States. Grandmothers care for the majority of these children within the African American community (Winston, 2003). A recent qualitative study including African American grandmothers who are caring for their grandchildren who have been orphaned by AIDS revealed the following risk and resiliency factors in dealing with their pain and added responsibilities.

In terms of risk factors, the further loss of grandchildren compounds the stress experienced. These grandmothers suffered strong feelings of anxiety, guilt, and loss in the context of the physical suffering of their children as well as the impending and present death. The stigma of AIDS reduced their support systems because they were reluctant to discuss the circumstances of the illness and death with nonfamily members. Assuming primary care for their grandchildren was also stressful. It meant relinquishing the pleasure of grandparenthood to assume parental roles and often involved major changes in their lives. These included remaining in employment longer or moving away from their communities and support systems. They also experienced a variety of health problems as they assumed these new responsibilities (Winston, 2003).

The women found the strength to cope through a variety of sources that reflected supportive relationships and beliefs. Cultural beliefs within the African American community of the primacy of the family with its strong extended kinship structure supported their new roles. The presence of the children helped them turn from loss and death to life. Their spiritual relationship with God was a major source of resiliency. They viewed the death of their child as part of the will of God. While they had initially prayed for healing, they later asked that their child be released from suffering. Their religion also provided a support system through religious services and inspirational reading or programs. They worked to keep the memory of their child alive through pictures, rituals, and conversation. Caring for their grandchildren became part of sustaining the continuity of the family (Winston, 2003).

In a study including white mothers of family members with AIDS, the unpredictable nature of the illness shaped the nature of their successful coping efforts. These included "taking one day at a time" and managing their emotions on a daily basis by addressing issues as they arose. They sought to maintain a sense of normalcy by focusing on daily living and emphasized living in the moment. They remained flexible to meet the various needs that arose which served as an active coping style given the reality of the illness (Thompson, 1999). They sought support in terms of relevant information and emotional support from professionals, other family members, and others who were also facing the illness. Mothers worked closely with the health-care system to cope with the medical complexities of AIDS. As a reflection of family cohesion and flexibility, other family members joined forces to offer the mother support in her caring role (Thompson, 1999).

Appraisal strategies were also valuable. Despite the sadness and sense of loss, many mothers were able to see positive aspects in terms of increased connectedness with the ill family member, renewal of strained relationships between the ill family members and others within the family, and personal growth (Thompson, 1999).

Families also used issues of family organization to help cope. Family members either defined family boundaries to temporarily exclude members who contributed to stress and conflict or expanded boundaries to include others outside the family who offered support. Spirituality and religion emerged as valuable coping strategies. Participants also coped by politicizing the issue through becoming engaged in advocacy and education efforts (Thompson, 1999).

## Diabetes

Diabetes represents another growing health problem for both children and adults. Based on a series of studies conducted with families living with noninsulin dependent family members, the following helpful coping skills emerged: family organization and relationship skills and effective family communication and cohesiveness. Control of diabetes requires specific coping skills, including monitoring food intake. Knowledge of the dietary demands was only the first and easiest step. Changes in long-term dietary habits required critical negotiation and problem-solving skills on the part of both partners (Chesla, 1999).

## Mental Illness

Mental illness can represent major responsibilities for family members. Such family responsibilities are typically long term and require different approaches depending on the current state of the illness. Parents worry about who will care for the ill family member when they are no longer able to do so. As discussed in chapter 4, Gregg's parents typify family members who are frightened about the impact of this illness on their family members and are confused regarding what to do. In terms of risk factors, regardless of culture, the most difficult sources of strain for families were the level of behavioral problems of the ill family member combined with uncertainty about how to handle them. Contextual issues related to problems in the service delivery system also contributed to this distress (Lefley, 1998).

Cultural backgrounds influence how families cope. Families that belong to cultures that are more collectivist with an emphasis on interdependence are more likely to include family members in the basic healing process and to provide support for the individuals involved (Lefley, 1998). In a study comparing African American and white families, African American families with a member with a psychiatric disability tended to experience this situation as less of a burden than did white families. African American parents were more likely to score higher on the dimensions of mastery and self-esteem with greater ability to adjust expectations levels appropriate to the disability. White parents found it more difficult to accommodate to lower levels of expectations (Lefley, 1998).

A study including primarily women caretakers who are members of Latino and African American families revealed some sources of strength that echo that of other studies. Family appraisals of the situation, self-efficacy, and social supports emerged as important protective factors. Appraisals influenced both the nature of the illness and the caretaker role. These family members avoided the blame that has sometimes burdened families. African American parents attributed the illness of the family member to hardship in life or traumatic events, for example, the death or abandonment of the father. Latino families blamed external factors or events or the intrinsic weakness of the ill person that prevented the person from dealing with the difficulties of life. They used the concept of *nervios* in contrast to *locura,* which refers to enduring madness. Their concepts of the illness engendered hope. Their religious beliefs in the power of God gave them faith that one could be cured. They viewed mental illness along a continuum of severity. While family members did not necessarily expect a complete cure, they were hopeful that the person might be able to function independently. They were also able to take a strengths-based perspective by identifying the strengths of the ill person and nourishing these strengths. Cultural appraisals of caregiving also helped. Caregiving was viewed as "this is what one does for family or the ill." Those who provided care were able to take a sense of pride in being able to care for an ill family member rather than viewing it as burden. They also developed important skills that helped them be more effective caregivers. They became knowledgeable about the illness of the person and were able to recognize when the ill person needed additional help. Social support systems were important in terms of other members of the family, church, and the neighborhood. They also sought and received help from the mental health services. Latino caregivers also received help from traditional healers (Parra & Guarnaccia, 1998). While the preceding discussion reflects general patterns, it is always essential for family counselors to assess individual members of any group in terms of their perspectives and coping resources.

## *Dementia*

Caretakers of family members with dementia must also contend with long-term and emotionally draining responsibilities that frequently lead to the distress of caregivers. Such responsibilities are replete with the additive stressors identified in the risk and resiliency literature. This distress can contribute to anger and depression. A study of the role of psychoeducational programs for female caretakers identified several key protective factors. Caretakers' self-efficacy for controlling upsetting thoughts and their perceived competence to deal with the situation helped to reduce both hostility and depression. (Coon, Thompson, Steffen, Sorocco, & Gallagher-Thompson, 2003).

## *Assessment and Treatment*

Although the specific illnesses and treatments in the preceding discussion vary widely, some important themes regarding risk and protective factors support the value of psychoeducational models in helping families. These programs offer a combination of information about the specific illness and types of treatment. They also help family members develop more effective coping strategies that in turn enhance their sense of self-efficacy. Such programs further provide information about the impact of the illness on family to help members address the needs of the family members as a whole. Social workers also need to help family members establish links to key health-care providers as well as others within the ongoing support system of family members. Identifying the meaning of this illness for the families is important. Views that give family members a sense of meaning and purpose as they cope are especially valuable. For some families, spirituality has been valuable in offering this sense of meaning and support. Families may need support to maintain effective leadership in coping with the illness and changes within the family organization.

Multisystems models that address both the functioning of the individual family as well as available resources within the larger context in which families operate can be useful for families in which the structure of the family is challenged and the need for external resources becomes especially critical. Exploring spiritual resources can also be valuable.

# SEX ABUSE

Tragically, approximately 16 to 34 percent of girls and 10 to 20 percent of boys are sexually abused in some way during their childhood. These life events can create scars that pose ongoing pain and suffering for those involved (American Psychological Association Task Force on Violence and the Family, 1996). Several studies of women who were abused as children have sought to discover the sources of resiliency that have helped survivors succeed in creating rewarding lives.

In one study including adults who had experienced sex abuse as children, participants were primarily white and members of the Church of the Latter-day Saints. For these women, religion was important in their lives (Valentine & Feinauer, 1993). Although the women in this study had suffered from the pain of sexual abuse in the form of struggling with feelings of guilt, depression, and low self-worth, and difficulty in having honest relationships with others, they were gradually able to overcome these experiences and create satisfying adult lives.

The women identified the following themes as the protective factors that helped them cope with the abuse and move beyond this experience. These themes echo earlier identified ones related to interpersonal support, the nature of attributions, and self-efficacy. There was at least one caretaker with whom the women could establish a bond. The ability to find supportive relationships outside of the family was very important. "Good relationships and support from others has been the most important thing in helping me to overcome the experience of sexual abuse" (Valentin & Feinauer, 1993, p. 218). Another woman spoke in terms of her marriage, "Having someone who believes in me has made all the difference" (p. 218). They were able to forge self-regard, believe in their self and in their own self-worth. Religion was helpful in several ways for these women. The support network of the church community gave them a group of people with which to interact in a positive manner and their religion enabled them to create a meaning of the experience that freed them of guilt and blame and gave them a sense of value, meaning, and purpose in their lives. Their attributions about the abuse were also helpful, especially in viewing a future without abuse and recognizing there was something wrong with the person who was abusing them. Similar to a concept of self-efficacy, gaining a sense of their own power in terms of being able take control of their lives was also important (Valentin & Feinauer, 1993).

Another study, involving primarily (86%) African American women, offers further insights, gives support to these findings, and demonstrates the complex interaction of life events that influence resiliency. In comparing women who were identified as resilient (functioning well in the domains of psychological well-being, health, interpersonal relationships, lack of adult arrest records, and economic situation) with those who were demonstrated poor resilience (as indicated on the previously cited dimensions), their childhood family situation, their educational achievement levels, and the presence or absence of experience of violence as an adult emerged as important risk and protective factors. Resilient women were less likely to have been abused by family members and to have generally stable families in which physical abuse did not occur. These women were also more likely to have

.ced from high school. Other behaviors on their part were also associ-
.d with resiliency—lack of an arrest record, not becoming pregnant during
.neir teenage years. Resilient women were less likely to have experienced
violence again as adults. For some women sexual abuse as a child was part
of a larger problematic picture that set in motion yet another series of troubling life events that in turn compromised their ability to function compe-
tently in areas that promote competency and resiliency (Hyman & Williams,
2001). Sexual abuse is thus part of a troubling foundation for the future.

## Assessment and Treatment

The prevalence of sexual abuse means that family counselors rather frequently in the course of their work with families will encounter individuals
who have been sexually abused. These can be situations in which the abuse
occurred relatively recently and the goal is to protect the child from future
abuse as well as to reduce the scars of this life event. Removal of the abusing family member and support for the child and other family members (as
occurred in the James family, Narrative Family Therapy) is critical here to
prevent future abuse and to give the child a sense of safety necessary for
the healing process. As discussed in chapter 4, the James family illustrates
that sexual abuse can have long shadows on all the members of the family.
In addition to protecting the child from the risk of future abuse, the profile
of risk and protective factors also indicates the need to address potential
problematic family interactions and other types of violence that can reinforce
the trauma of sexual abuse. Intensive multisystems approaches to address
such a range of problems and enlist needed external supports can be useful
for some of these families.

In other families, one of the members was abused earlier by someone
outside the family with whom they are living with currently. Women who
had been abused earlier reported being helped by life experiences that gave
them a sense of their ability to take control of their own lives, to absolve
them of blame and guilt, and to feel loved and cared for in their current family relationships. This helped women gain trust that while the abuse was part
of their past, it did not have to be part of their future. While the literature
cited above refers to sexual abuse of women, it is important to remember
that boys can also be sexually abused by family members or others with
very painful consequences.

Several family models can potentially be useful depending on the unique
family situation. Solution-focused therapy specifically places the control of
the direction of treatment in the hands of the family members and reinforces
this sense of control that can be very healing for those who experienced lack
of control in a very painful manner. The narrative approaches help people
distinguish between themselves and the events that have happened to them
and to replace problem-saturated stories and identities with more empowering

ones. Family members can thus begin the process of editing their story in ways that look at their strengths in terms of survival and the new possibilities in their present context. This was an important step for the James family where the cloud of "damaged goods" hangs over the family. Psychoeducational approaches can be useful by educating people about the potential impact that sexual abuse can have on the parties involved. This information can be valuable not only for the individual who was abused but also for the partner in order to realize that her or his reactions in certain situations are the consequence of previous life experiences. Both individuals can be helped to identify ways to help the abused partner recapture a sense of control and to feel loved and cared for in their current relationship in ways that meet the needs of both partners. For individuals who were abused in the past with ongoing shadows in terms of their current relationships, object relations family therapy can be a means of altering the destructive patterns that have been brought from past problematic relationships into the present family life in order to help individuals experience the potential reality of feeling loved and cared for.

## DIVORCE

Current high rates of divorce mean that many families consist of divorced parents and their children. These families must deal with the sometimes painful aftermath of the problems that led to the divorce as well as circumstances of the divorce itself. As discussed in chapter 4, the King family's past experiences with divorce can have a lingering impact on the current family situation. Studies of mothers raising their children following a divorce reveal greater problems in terms of communication with children, less consistent and less affectionate relationships with children, and less effectiveness in enlisting cooperation from their children (Golby & Bretherton, 1999). According to Golby and Bretherton, use of the concept of resiliency developed by Garmezy and Rutter as "competence functioning in the face of emotional stressors" fits the situation of divorced families. Divorce typically brings pain to all the members of the family as well as new meanings and the challenge of adjusting to new relationships and structures (1999). As a result, the social worker must understand resiliency not in terms of lack of difficulties, but how families negotiate these adaptations and forge effective new meanings.

In terms of protective factors, studies of divorced parents and their children also reveal family patterns that promote resiliency within this context, especially two years after divorce (Golby & Bretherton, 1999). It is important for parents to reorganize in an adaptive way in their postdivorce lives. This enables parents again to "respond sensitively to their children's needs and to manage discipline issues effectively" (Hetherington, 1989, p. 238).

Drawing on the narrative account of mothers who were raising young children at least two years postdivorce, a series of protectors factors emerged. As in other studies, sense of effectiveness as a parent (self-efficacy) was an important factor in promoting positive adjustment. While resilient mothers frequently faced situations similar to those facing other mothers, their interpretations of events helped them to cope in a more effective manner rather than become caught up in destructive and hurtful power struggles or abdicate their parental control. These mothers recognized the existence of problems and were confident in their ability to address them and generally felt in charge of the family situation. They were able to communicate sensitively with their children and to modulate their own demands on the children. They were able to place firm demands on their children in a flexible manner depending on the situation. These mothers were able to be empathic and to view the situation from the child's perspective as well as their own. At the same time they had expectations of their children. For many of these mothers, the process of parenting postdivorce has required them to adapt their parenting methods to fit with their new situation as a single parent.

In contrast, in families that reflected a poor adaptation, mothers described their sense of ineffectiveness and inflexibility in dealing with their children. They felt overwhelmed and seemed insensitive in communicating with their children. Many of these mothers felt unable to negotiate with their children and instead placed themselves in ultimatum and power struggle situations. Other mothers felt unable or reluctant to place demands on their children and used giving in as a typical strategy. These mothers also found it difficult to let their children express their sadness or anger for the situation and to be sensitive to their children's feelings (Golby & Bretherton, 1999).

Parents can also vary in terms of their support they received from others in coping with their new role. Risk and resiliency factors thus reside in the family's context as well as within the family circle itself (Golby & Bretherton, 1999).

These findings regarding divorce echo family resiliency themes in general of self-efficacy, effective communication and leadership, flexibility, parental coping skills, social support, and meaning systems that support the process of adaptation.

The perspective of children on the divorce process is also critical in understanding and working with families. Grych and Fincham (1997) reviewed risk and protective factors from the children's perspective. Although children from a divorced family are more likely to demonstrate emotional difficulties, most of these children are as well-adjusted as children from intact families. Recognizing that all children will experience distress in the short term following the parent's divorce and many will continue to do so for the first one to two years, the issue is what influences the long-term adjustment of children.

In terms of risk factors, children described the most stressful aspects of divorce as including their being blamed for the divorce, conflict between the parents, loss of relationship with one of the parents, and changes in their daily living arrangement. Postdivorce conflicts between the parents and situations in which children feel drawn into this conflict in ways that require them to demonstrate loyalty to one rather than both of the parents also create distress for children. Distance from the noncustodial parent emerged as a risk factor. Problems in parenting by the custodial parent due to her or his own emotional distress also were problematic. Changes in the living environment and economic problems were also risk factors (Grych & Fincham, 1997).

Protective factors included strong relationships with parents, preferably with both parents, and extended family members. Unfortunately, siblings were typically so involved in their own reactions that they provided limited support to each other. Peers also played a limited role until the teenage years (Grych & Fincham, 1997). Children who demonstrated better adaptation were also more likely to use active behavioral or cognitive coping strategies to understand or solve the problem and distraction by engaging in other activities. Children's sense of control over events was also protective. Avoidance (trying not to think about it) was linked with more problematic responses. The nature of the support that children could enlist from their parents and others in the environment was in turn influenced by the behavior of the child. Tempermentally easy children were better able to cope under conditions of stress (Grych & Fincham, 1997).

## *Assessment and Treatment*

Studies regarding risk and protective factors have implications for family treatment with families that are dealing with divorce. These families vary widely so that the selection and implementation of specific treatment models must be tailored to the individual family and their social context. The following identifies themes that emerge in the research in terms of ways in which several models can address important risk and protective factors. Parental effectiveness that enables parents to respond with appropriate empathy and firmness is helpful to the children involved. Such effectiveness in turn promotes self-efficacy by parents in their parental roles. Separation and divorce frequently require parents to assume new parental roles as well as to deal with their own emotional pain and interpretation.

Social learning models combined with cognitive approaches can be useful in helping parents learn and apply new parenting skills as well as identifying and addressing their beliefs. As parents become more effective in their parenting role, they are better able to meet the needs of family members and to gain confidence in their new parental responsibilities. Structural models can be helpful in enabling parents to establish more effective parental structures that in turn give children a sense of security. Parents and children can also benefit from solution-focused approaches that enable both parents and children to identify which steps can help the family adapt in a more effective manner. Since issues of control and divided loyalty are important for children in coping, children can be given the opportunity to indicate the steps that are important to them in creating a new family arrangement. In discussing such steps, children have the opportunity to express their concerns about important issues such as divided loyalties and specific ways in which parents can give permission for their children to show their love for both parents. For some families, divorce is accompanied by serious economic and other social needs that require linkage with resources within the community. Family members can also identify members of the extended family or family of choice who can participate in the family sessions to support the family's adaptation.

# TRAUMA

## Refugee Trauma

Millions of families are refugees from political turmoil, war, natural disasters, and political and religious persecution. They have experienced or feared for violence in their homeland and are now trying to establish new lives in a new setting, sometimes in the context of resentment of their presence (Barwick, Beiser, & Edwards, 2002; Mayadas, Elliott, & Ramanthan, 1999). As discussed in chapter 1, the Lo family's experience of the traumas of the past can carry over to the present life of the family in ways that can potentially limit their view of realistic options. Many of these families come from cultures that are organized around the family and view both trauma and coping through the lens of the family.

A recent study with refugee Bosnian families currently living in Chicago identified both sources of distress and resiliency. These families had experienced a degree of trauma to the extent that at least one member met the criteria for post-trauma stress disorder. Weine et al. (2004) identified issues related to family organization (roles and obligations), communication, social support involving the family and the broader ethnic community, and family belief systems that emerged as sources of pain and resiliency. Families reported negative changes regarding family roles and obligations in several areas: greater dependence on the children by the parents and grandparents, decreased time to spend with the family because of pressures to provide financially for the family, and challenges to traditional patriarchal customs. Men have lost their traditional control over the family as women and teenagers are working and female family members have observed gender patterns in America (Weine et al., 2004).

Families described the following strategies as promoting resiliency, although some are two-edged swords because they carry both the potential for healing as well as distress. First, children represent the hope for the future for the family. Seeing their children doing well is restorative for parents. At the same time, it is extremely difficult for parents to see their children having difficulties. Second, families have developed greater flexibility in terms of family roles. Third, family togetherness has become a primary goal of the families as they band together to survive. Fourth, when grandparents are part of the extended family scene, they assume more central roles to meet the family needs left by parents' extensive work demands. This change has kept grandparents from becoming isolated and permits sharing across generational lines (Weine et al., 2004).

Family communication and related memories bring pain as well as help rebuild the life of the family. Memories of the past bring pain to family members. Adults avoid talking about the past because they are seeking to forget this painful time. The children are overwhelmed by the trauma of the past and also do not want these events to be talked about. Family members are also reluctant to talk about the past out of fear of burdening others. Families reported the following strategies for rebuilding their lives. They sought to share the good memories from the past. Talking with children helps parents look at the positive aspects of life. Unfortunately, some of the problems facing children, especially violence, remind them of past traumas. Despite the pain of communicating about the past, family members also find healing through expressing their emotions about the past and sharing with other family members to create a climate of trust (Weine et al., 2004).

Family relationships with their extended family have frequently experienced major disruptions and loss. Many families left important family members behind with the sense of loss and guilt involved. Others have had to contend with the scattering of family members who once lived close to them. Some families have members with special physical or mental health needs that need extra care. Women who lost their husbands under traumatic conditions must now care for their families without this support. Families contend with these separations by hoping for a return someday to their old community and by working to reunite their family members. Single mothers seek to rebuild some type of family network. Family members also try to give financial help to their family members who were unable to leave (Weine et al., 2004).

Families also contend with changes in their connections with the extended ethnic community. Many felt that they were losing their way of life in a new world. Children who no longer used their original language and adapted to American culture have compounded this fear. Families coped with these changes by teaching their children their history and language. They also sought to return to their religious traditions to promote continuity, to retain their culture, and to gain spiritual support. Retaining their culture was an important source of resiliency (Weine et al., 2004).

A review of research of refugee children with an emphasis on South-eastern Asian families revealed sources of resiliency as well as risks within children (Barwick et al., 2002; Kinzie & Sack, 2002). Patterns of assimilation influenced the resiliency process. A bicultural orientation (ethnic resilience) that permitted children and family members to retain their language and tradition while also learning the new language and cultural ways was associated with a better adjustment than families that insisted on only maintaining their traditional cultural ways or became totally assimilated (Barwick et al., 2002). The support of parents, members of the extended family, as well as others within the ethnic community is an important source of resiliency. In the absence of members of the ethnic community, supportive friendships with other community members can help reduce loneliness and isolation during the adjustment period. Problems in reuniting families, however, can be a major source of distress for families. Although living in areas of concentrated poverty emerges as a risk factor generally and refugee families typically are poorer than their counterparts, they also experience less subjective stress because they hold out hope for a better future (Barwick et al., 2002). A combination of stressful family and community issues, including family distress, hostility from the community, and academic problems in the school is an important risk factor (Barwick et al., 2002).

### Assessment and Treatment

Research reveals a wide range of potentially difficult issues facing refugee families in adapting to life in their new world. In addition to adapting to a new culture, many families have experienced major traumas that cast shadows over family members. Supportive ties within the immediate and extended family and hopes for a better future help to sustain families. Interventions for families include efforts at the community level to create sustaining connections and to educate concerned community groups about the specific needs and cultural issues pertaining to the group in question so that appropriate services and programs can be designed. Case management interventions to connect families with needed services within the community can be vital for some families. In working with refugee families, it is important to assess cultural prescriptions regarding family roles and the extent to which these have been disrupted by the move. Many refugee families come from cultural settings in which the authority of the parents is important and these cultural prescriptions need to be recognized in work with families. Solution-focused efforts can also be used to help families look at their strengths and ways in which the family members can jointly take steps to create a viable adaptation in this new world. Such interventions can tap the family's hopes for a better life in this new world.

## *Natural Disaster Trauma*

Natural disasters can also be sources of trauma and create major disruptions for families. Tornados, hurricanes, and floods destroy homes and communities and leave dazed survivors who must find a way to move on with their lives. Disasters are described as "'collective traumas' that test assumptions, plus the adaptive responses of individuals, families, and communities beyond their capacities, and lead, at least temporarily, to major disruptions of functioning" (Gordon, 2003, p. 4). As has been tragically evident in several of the recent natural disasters globally, such disasters frequently represent community-wide problems that leave large segments of the community struggling to restore normalcy to family life for a long period of time. Consequently, community resources are also severely reduced and communities are fractured. Families must address issues in the external world as well as their own feelings about this traumatic situation. Studies have examined what contributes to resiliency in this context.

A study of families who were forced to abandon their homes in response to a major flood followed by evidence of serious toxicity levels revealed important themes. Men evidenced more signs of distress than women, probably in response to the disruption of their roles as providers. The role of social support was a complex one. Mid levels of support were protective but higher levels posed burdens of reciprocity that people were unable to meet. Interpretations of events mediated levels of distress. Self-blame increased distress and reduced the help-seeking by people who had suffered the effects of the disaster (Solomon & Smith, 1994).

Problems in social functioning emerged in a study of a community that experienced periodic major flooding in Kentucky. People experienced personal losses, increased sense of danger, and reductions in the social fabric due to the high demands placed on many within the community. Older adults with experience in dealing with past floods were more able to cope than middle-aged adults possibly as a result of their longer-term experience in coping with such events (Norris, Phifer & Kaniasty, 1994) and consequent sense of self-efficacy described earlier in the resiliency literature.

The impact of events on the community and families is influenced by the phases involved in this process. These phases reflect the emotional state of the people involved: (1) Honeymoon phase lasts from one to six weeks. During this time, the victims feel sense a community through their common experience and loss. Buoyed by the hope of help, they begin the task of cleaning up. The response of community groups is very important during this time; (2) Disillusionment phase lasts from two months to two years. If promised help is not forthcoming, people begin to feel disappointed, angry, and resentful. The sense of community of the Honeymoon stage diminishes as people focus on rebuilding the lives of their own families. Outside agencies stop providing help; and (3) Reconstruction phase occurs in the several years after the disaster. Families recognize that they will need to assume primary responsibility for restoring their lives and either move forward or emotional problems may appear (Smith, 1983).

Perceptions of events are important, especially whether they are viewed as crisis provoking or challenging. Protective family characteristics include problem-solving skills, family organizational patterns, and extended family resources. The ability to solve problematic life events in general translates into coping with such disasters. The family's ability to work together as a team to solve the problems facing them is valuable. Family leadership is also important, especially in being able to restore family life to normalcy as much as possible. Families need to be attuned to the emotional needs and responses of family members, including supporting the use of outside resources as needed to deal with the emotional trauma involved. Strong extended family ties are another important resource (Smith, 1983). Studies of children experiencing disasters also reveal the importance of supportive resources within the family in reducing distress (Saylor, Belter, & Stokes, 1997). The nature of community resources is also critical in terms of the impact on families.

### *Assessment and Treatment*

Recent events in the United States, for example, Hurricane Katrina that devastated New Orleans and many coastal communities along the Gulf of Mexico, as well as natural disasters globally, reveal the ongoing distress that can created by natural disasters. Stories regarding New Orleans and other communities in the area point out the extreme difficulty and length of time involved in restoring life to normal for families as well as for their communities. Interventions with families must be set within the context of social efforts to restore homes and communities. The initial response with families addresses the crisis needs of the family—helping families meet their basic survival needs through case management and community efforts. The recent storms demonstrated the importance as well as the difficulty of these steps and the need for community preparedness as a community and broader social scale. Crisis models recognize the need to help persons identify their strengths. Even after these needs are met, the upheaval experienced by families can disrupt old patterns that enabled families to survive or reveal ongoing family patterns that pose difficulties. Strength-based efforts are critical for such families who have become demoralized by the major changes and losses that they have experienced. Multisystems models that address the family's struggles with adapting to change, link family to potential resources, and address the resource base within the community can fit with these needs. Case management can be essential in negotiating complex systems. Solution-focused treatment can help families identify realistic goals in their current situation, steps that family members can take to help meet them, and ways in which the family is currently managing to survive despite this realistically difficult time.

# CHILDHOOD ISSUES
## Delinquency and Conduct Disorders of Youth

Many families are referred to social workers because of behavior problems of their children. Williams, Ayers, Van Dorn, and Arthur (2004) reviewed research regarding risk and protective factors in terms of this critical issue.

They divided risk factors into the two categories of contextual/community (structure and values within the social environment and peer group) and interpersonal/individual (family, peers, school, genetic) risk factors. Community-level risk factors included community violence, poverty, limited access to services, high mobility within neighborhoods, and community disorganization. Family risk factors included family management problems, family conflict, family disruption, and parental modeling of inappropriate and illicit behaviors. In terms of parenting, the strongest predictors of problems were poor parental supervision and lack of parental involvement in the lives of their children. School risk factors, especially for males and white youth, were low academic achievement, lack of commitment to school, and discipline problems. Peer relationships that supported delinquent behavior were additional risk factors.

Four major types of family protective factors emerged from longitudinal studies. These echo themes identified earlier in terms of families and youth are: "(1) supportive parent-child relationships and family environment, (2) positive discipline techniques, (3) monitoring and supervision, and (4) family advocacy (seeking information and support for the benefit of their children" (Williams, Ayers, Van Dorn, & Arthur, 2004, p. 224). In the absence of supportive relationships with parents, peer support can have negative consequences by making youth more vulnerable to high-risk behaviors, including substance abuse (Sandler, Wolchik, MacKinnon, Auyers, & Roosa, 1997). In terms of African American families in this context, important protective factors include "a strong economic base, a strong orientation to achievement, strong spiritual values, racial pride, extended family bonds, community involvement, and commitment to family" (Williams et al., 2004, p. 224). The combination of risk and protective factors supports efforts to strengthen family coping efforts and the community as well as interventions targeted to youth alone.

## Maltreatment of Children

Many families are referred for social work services, frequently on an involuntary basis, because children in the family have been mistreated.

Maltreatment leads to children dying each day in the United States. Maltreatment in the form of neglect and physical or sexual abuse can have profound negative implications for the children in terms of problematic behavior as children and adults, poor academic achievement, and health problems (Thomlison, 2004).

A key risk factor for maltreatment is the contextual issue of poverty and the related social conditions. As Thomlison (2004) describes, "the poorest of the poor are at highest risk" (p. 93). Differences in child maltreatment rates in various racial/ethnic groups are closely linked with poverty and community violence. In terms of the impact of additive sources of stress, longitudinal studies indicate that "the number of risk factors to which a child is exposed is the most salient predictor of maltreatment and the negative development outcomes" (Thomlison, 2004, p. 98). The combination of risk factors has a greater effect than the sum of effects of each risk factor (Fatusso, McDermott, & Lutz, 1999).

In terms of family issues, distress of the parent-caregiver is the primary individual risk factor. Parental problems emerged in terms of "parental affective disturbances, such as depression, withdrawal, anger, and aggression, low self-esteem, immaturity, rigid or unrealistic expectations, and undue reliance so that the parent's needs conflict with the child's needs" (Thomlison, 2004, p. 98). In terms of relevant skills, lack of knowledge regarding parenting and the associated skills contribute to poor parenting through inappropriate expectations, poor problem-solving skills, and harsh and/or inconsistent parenting. Current or past substance abuse by parents is an important risk factor. Parental problems in turn are exacerbated by behavioral characteristics of children (impulsiveness, disruptive temperament) and environmental stresses. A key issue for physical abuse is the parent's own history of maltreatment. A weak social support system for parents substantially increases the risk of neglect (Thomlison, 2004).

Protective factors that protect families from maltreating their children reveal the importance of contextual factors. Such factors include "economic stability and access to health, education, and employment" (Thomlison, 2004, p. 100). External social supports both help protect parents from maltreating their children and serve as sources of resiliency for the children themselves. In contrast to fragmented communities, those that are stable and cohesive offer needed support for families through employment, schools, and community members who are appropriate role models help reduce child maltreatment (Thomlison, 2004).

Life circumstances that protect by reducing distress or inhibiting aggression include the presence "of a supportive spouse, socioeconomic stability, success at work and school, social supports, and positive adult role models" (Thomlison, 2004, p. 100). Parents are also enabled to manage crises more effectively (ability to cope with stress) and to reduce their arousal and aggressive behavior with family members (improved ability to regulate moods and reduce anger) (Thomlison, 2004).

Individual parental factors that protect include high self-esteem and self-efficacy and the ability to operate within normal boundaries and to demonstrate social competence. Easygoing temperaments that help parents show warmth and satisfaction in relationships with others also contribute (Thomlison, 2004).

### *Assessment and Treatment*

As a result of these risk and resiliency patterns, a combination of approaches offers the most promise for families. These include those that help parents gain effective parental skills, enable parents to cope more effectively with stress and anger, and strengthen the support system for families through collaborative relationships with parents, teachers, and others in the community (Thomlison, 2004).

Addressing childhood behavior problems and child maltreatment are frequently linked because children from families who are at greatest risk for maltreatment are also the most likely to demonstrate behavioral problems. A dual approach that addresses the environment as well as the ability of family members to parent more effectively and relate to each other in a less toxic manner is appropriate for many of these families. The multisystems model of family interventions incorporates this dual perspective by helping families develop more effective ways of relating to its members and by improving the social context. As discussed in chapter 10, many specific programs incorporate multisystems models. Recognizing that these families are also demoralized by their many problems, these models take an explicit strengths-based approach.

## SUMMARY

Families seek help as a result of a variety of life circumstances that create distress for family members. While some of the specific risk and protective factors vary depending on these situations, some key resiliency factors identified in the general research on resiliency continue to emerge as themes. Experiencing caring and validation from a social and spiritual support network is an important resource that appears to decrease distress and increase self-esteem. Such support networks often provide valuable role models. A community context that provides a sense of coherence, access to services, and appropriate economic and other opportunities also supports resiliency.

Appropriate skills to cope with the situation at hand are also important, for example, parenting effectively, caring for ill family members, advocating for services, and dealing with new cultural expectations. Families need appropriate information to guide their coping efforts. Families need to be able to communicate effectively to deal with stressors without resorting to undue conflict and to meet the emotional needs of family members. These resiliency factors are aided by self-perceptions of self-efficacy and views of situations as challenging but not impossible. The process is a cyclical one as demonstrating appropriate skills and effectively solving problems in turn enhances the self-efficacy of family members.

The resiliency framework thus serves as a valuable framework for assessing families and developing and implementing strategies for helping families. It provides a respective, collaborative model that supports strengths-based and culturally competent social work practice with families.

# 14

## *Conclusion*

The resiliency framework with the accompanying major themes of risk and resiliency described in preceding chapters represents a useful way to organize the assessment and design of interventions with families. It provides a framework for analyzing the information about families that highlights the resources both within the family and its context as well as the challenges the family faces. The resiliency perspective can also help guide the counselor in creating a therapeutic relationship that highlights the strengths of families. Such an approach fits well with the social work value stance of respect for persons. The framework of resiliency enables the social worker, family therapist, and family counselor to take a strengths-based approach while at the same time being realistic about the challenges facing the family and its current needs. This dual focus is critical in gaining an accurate understanding of the family and in identifying possible ways to strengthen the resources available to the family and the barriers that families face in meeting the needs of their members.

A resiliency perspective helps the family counselor look beyond the family to incorporate the social, economic, and physical contexts of the family that can be sources of resources as well as challenges. These contexts further influence how events, potential resources, and challenges are viewed by family members and key members of their support system. Such a perspective is thus compatible with a culturally competent way of working with families.

While studies can identify the characteristics that generally challenge and support resiliency, each individual family has its unique set that interact throughout the life span of the family and are embedded within a particular contextual and historical environment. The assessment process must thus move beyond any generalizations to understand the specific set of risk and protective factors at work with this family. It is also important to individualize what these mean in the life of an individual family and its members. Such information paired with research regarding the effectiveness of treatment approaches thus becomes the basis for professional judgment regarding the design of the intervention. Studies regarding resiliency in general can represent a valuable first step but must always be viewed through the lens of specific families and their members. Social constructionist perspectives remind us that the meaning of life events and thus of potential solutions is mediated by life experiences and appraisals of individuals and their families. The hovering behavior by parents that in one context might be viewed as unrealistic overprotection, in another more dangerous setting might be viewed as essential protection.

The outcomes of the family's attempts to deal with the challenges facing them have important current and future implications for the family. Families are strengthened by their successful attempts to deal with adversity but can become demoralized by their inability to do so. Unfortunately, many of the families who seek help from social workers have reached the point that they have become discouraged by their inability to address a problem or have been given the message by others that they have not been able to do so appropriately. As a result, they can become demoralized about their ability to cope as a family. The process becomes a cyclical one as some of their cognitive or behavioral responses further impede their ability to cope effectively and thus increase their sense of demoralization. In response, they can fall into patterns of blaming specific family members or others in the environment or become discouraged by past efforts. They can find it even more difficult to develop realistic coping strategies. The problems facing them can come to be viewed as insurmountable. They can come to expect blame and criticism from counselors and in turn become defensive or guarded.

In this context, the use of a resiliency perspective can be helpful in several ways. During the establishment of the working alliance and the assessment process, the search for strengths within the family (e.g., evidence of success in coping with the past or in other areas of life, concern for family members) and the community can help engender hope and begin to reduce some of these problematic responses. Throughout the counseling process and more specifically toward termination, the social worker can help the family take ownership of their enhanced ability to cope as well as to identify what steps the family has taken that have helped make this difference so they can draw upon these when they face some inevitable future challenges. The goal is to enable families to increase their ability to face the challenges as well as their self-efficacy in being able to do so.

The use of the resiliency framework does not limit the family counselor to the use of a single theoretical model. Rather it suggests the value of being able to consider a variety of intervention models and strategies based on the assessment of the needs of the family as well as the protective factors that can be capitalized on and strengthened. These resources can be present within the family (beliefs, coping skills, relationships among the members, characteristics of individual family members), the links between the family and other social contexts (extended family, friends, community), and the nature of the community (employment patterns, access to health care, educational systems). On the other side of the equation are the risks created by the combination of the characteristics of family members, the family as a unit, the context, and the developmental stages of the family. Based on the assessment of the situation facing the family and the unique combination of risks and protective factors, the social worker can identify treatment models and accompanying strategies that can draw upon and strengthen these protective factors and seek to make the changes that can reduce the risk factors. For one family the emphasis might be upon the need to expand specific community resources, while another family might need to learn new coping skills in dealing with a new cultural setting, or to enhance the leadership of the family, or to replace problem-saturated stories with more empowering ones. The key here is emphasis. An essential part of the assessment process is to identify what are the most pressing or amenable to change factors and what combination of specific strategies seems most appropriate at this time in the life of the family. The way in which the therapy model is implemented, of course, will depend on the family, the counselor, and the unique settings.

Efforts have been made to identify the aspects of family counseling that enhance effectiveness. These efforts reflect the complex nature of counseling with families with all of the difficulties in identifying what works with what family. Friedlander reviewed a large number of studies to identify the themes related to effectiveness in terms of the actions of the therapist with families. These included studies examining the process of family therapy from a variety of theoretical perspectives. Successful approaches incorporated both intrapersonal and interpersonal aspects. The collaborative nature of the therapist relationship characterized by a resiliency approach emerged as essential. While the specific techniques used by the counselor may vary, effective therapy "needs to be conducted in a warm, nonthreatening atmosphere in which there is a sense of mutual respect and collaboration" (Friedlander, 1998, p. 526). Effective family therapists also tended to be active and to take charge of the sessions in ways that involved the emotional, cognitive, and behavioral realms of experience (Friedlander, 1999). Interventions that are positive and nonblaming, that highlight the positive aspects of the family (asking about exceptions, selectively attending to positive statements) and include positive reframing can reduce conflict and negativity within families (Sexton, Robbins, Hollimons, Mease, & Mayorga, 2003). These findings support the themes inherent in a resiliency perspective on social work practice with families.

The resiliency-based approach to working with families recognizes the complex nature of families and the world in which they attempt to meet the needs of their members. It sets the stage for a collaborative working relationship between the family and the social worker. Recognition of the family's struggles as well as their strengths and protective factors helps identify which specific approach can be most effective for this specific family at this time in its life cycle. Together the family members and the social worker continue to evaluate whether the approach selected is the best choice for the family at this stage in their development.

# Appendix:
# Family Preservation Models

**The Homebuilders** (see Kinney, Haapala, & Booth, 1991). A home-based program in which the entire family receives family-based intervention. It is intensive and brief (about six weeks). Specific treatment goals and activities vary depending on the family. It focuses on parenting skills and anger management.

**Parent-Child Educaton Program for Physically Abusive Parents** (see Wolfe, Sandler, & Kaufman, 1981). Includes intensive (two hours a week) home-based parent education on a weekly basis for eight weeks. With the goal of reducing power assertive discipline methods and child abuse, parents receive skill training that includes modeling in positive parenting strategies.

***The Incredible Years Training Service*** (see Webster-Stratton, 2000; Juvenile Justice Bulletin. Washington, DC: Office of Juvenile Justice and Delinquency Prevention). Program helps parents replace negative parenting techniques with positive, nonviolent discipline methods, and support parent approaches that promote children's self-confidence, prosocial behavior and academic success. The program is custom-tailored to parents of children of different ages and is designed to help parents learn positive parenting strategies appropriate for that age.

**Multisystemic Family Treatment (MST)** (see Henggeler, Schoewald, Borduin, & Rowland, & Cunningham, 1998; Sheidow, Henggeler, & Schenwalk, 2003). Incorporates many of the components described earlier. It provides in-home services that include parent education, information about parent-child expectations, marital therapy, advocacy, coaching, and emotional support. This model has been effectively used in a variety of community settings to address serious child behavior problems. Interventions include reframing, joining, and actions to assist in family restructuring. The MST provides for a flexible protocol within the parameters of nine basic treatment principles.

Principle 1. The primary purpose of assessment is to understand the fit between the identified problems and their broader context.

Principle 2. Therapeutic contacts emphasize the positive and use systemic strengths as levers for change.

Principle 3. Interventions are designed to promote responsible behavior and decrease irresponsible behavior among family members.

Principle 4. Interventions are present focused and action oriented, targeting specific and well-defined problems.

Principle 5. Interventions target sequences of behavior within and among multiple systems that maintain the identified problems.

Principle 6. Interventions are developmentally appropriate and fit the developmental needs of the youth.

Principle 7. Interventions are designed to require daily or weekly effort by family members.

Principle 8. Intervention effectiveness is evaluated continuously from multiple perspectives with providers assuming accountability for overcoming barriers to successful outcomes.

Principle 9. Interventions are designed to promote treatment generalization and long-term maintenance of therapeutic change by empowering caregivers to address family members' needs across multiple systemic contexts. (p. 23)

**Project 12 Ways** (see Lutzker et al., 1998). Focuses on enhancing environments and social support for families in three areas: child health, home safety, and parent-child interactions. Activities include parent education and planned parenting activities. Paraprofessionals or volunteers are used to provide the following as needed: marital counseling, financial planning, and home health. Referrals are made to appropriate community services.

**Social Support Network Interventions** (see Gaudin, Wodarski, Arkinson, & Avery, 1990–1991). Designed to strengthen the informal support network of families in order to reduce family isolation. It includes social skills training from volunteers or neighbor-to-neighbor connection.

# References

Abudabbeh, N. (1996). Arab families. In M. McGolderick, J. Giordano, & J. Pearce (Eds.), *Ethnicity and family therapy* (2nd ed., pp. 333–346). New York: Guilford.

Albom, M. (1997). *Tuesdays with Morrie.* New York: Doubleday.

Almeida, R. (1996). Hindu, Christian, and Muslim families. In M. McGolderick, J. Giordano, & J. Pearce (Eds.), *Ethnicity and family therapy* (2nd ed., pp. 395–426). New York: Guilford.

American Psychological Association Task Force on Violence and the Family. (1996). *Violence and the family.* Washington, DC: American Psychological Association.

Anderson, T. (1991). The context and history of the reflecting team. In T. Anderson (Ed.), *The reflecting team: Dialogues and dialogues about the dialogues* (pp. 1–14). New York: Norton.

Anderson, B. J., Brackett, J., Ho, J., & Laffel, L. M. (1999). An office-based intervention to maintain parent adolescent teamwork in diabetes management. *Diabetes Care, 22,* 713–721.

Antonovsky, A. (1998). The structure and properties of the Sense of Coherence Scale. In H. I. McCubbin, E. Thompson, A. Thompson, & J. Fromer (Eds.), *Stress, coping, and health in families: Sense of coherence and resiliency* (pp. 21–40). Resiliency in families series. Thousand Oaks, CA: Sage.

Aponte, H. (1994). *Bread and spirit: Therapy with the new poor.* New York: Norton.

Aponte, H. (1999). The stresses of poverty and the comfort of spirituality. In F. Walsh (Ed.), *Spiritual resources in family therapy* (pp. 76–89). New York: Guilford.

Aponte, H. (2002). Spirituality: The heart of therapy. In T. Carlson & M. Erikson (Eds.), *Spirituality and family therapy* (pp. 13–27). New York: Haworth.

Aponte, H. (2003). Structural family interventions. In A. Kilpatrick & T. Holland (Eds.), *Working with families: An integrative model by level of needs* (pp. 104–115). Boston: Allyn & Bacon.

Ariel, J., & McPherson, D. (2000) Therapy with lesbian gay parents and their children. *Journal of Marital and Family Therapy, 26*(4), 421–432.

Bagley, C., & Carroll, J. (1998). Healing forces in African American families. In H. I. McCubbin, E. Thompson, A. Thompson, & J. Futrell (Eds.), *Resiliency in African American families* (pp. 117–142). Thousand Oaks, CA: Sage.

Bandura, A. (1978). The self-system in reciprocal determinism. *American Psychologist, 33,* 344–358.

Bandura, A. (1977). *Social learning theory.* Englewood Cliffs, NJ: Prentice-Hall.

Barwick, C., Beiser, M., & Edwards, G. (2002). Refugee children and their families: Exploring mental health risks and protective factors. In F. Azima & N. Grizenko (Eds.), *Immigrant and refugee children and their families: Clinical, research, and training issues* (pp. 37–63). Madison, CT: International Universities Press.

Beardslee, W. (1989). The role of self-understanding in resilient individuals: The development of a perspective. *American Journal of Orthopsychiatry, 59*(2), 266–278.

Beardslee, W., Salt, P., Porterfield, K., Rothberg, P., Van de Velde, P., Swatling, S., et al. (1993). Comparison of preventive interventions for families with parental affective disorder. *Journal of American Academy of Child and Adolescent Psychiatry, 32*(2), 254–263. Retrieved August 24, 2005, from Expanded Academic.

Beavers, W. (1986). *Successful marriages.* New York: Norton.

Beavers, W., & Hampson, R. (1990). *Successful families: Assessment and interventions.* New York: Norton.

Beck, A. (1976). *Cognitive therapy and the emotional disorders.* New York: International Universities Press.

Berg, I., & Miller, S. (1992). *Working with the problem drinker: A solution-focused approach.* New York: Norton.

Berg, I., & Dolan, Y. (2001). *Tales of solutions: A collection of hope-inspiring stories.* New York: Norton.

Bernal, G., & Shapiro, E. (1996). Cuban families. In M. McGolderick, J. Giordanoa, & J. Pearce (Eds.), *Ethnicity and family therapy* (pp. 155–168). New York: Guilford.

Berry, M. (1999). Family preservation practice. In C. Franklin & C. Jordan (Eds.), *Family practice: Brief systems methods for social work* (pp. 199–224). Pacific Grove, CA: Brooks/Cole.

Besa, D. (1994). Evaluating narrative family therapy using single-system research designs. *Research on Social Work Practice, 43*(3), 309–325.

Biever, J., Gardner, G., & Bobele, M. (1999). Social construction and narrative family practice. In C. Franklin & C. Jordan (Eds.), *Family practice: Brief systems methods for social work* (pp. 143–174). Pacific Grove, CA: Brooks/Cole.

Bigner, J. (1996). Working with gay fathers: Developmental, post divorce parenting, and therapeutic issues. In J. Laird & R. Green (Eds.), *Lesbians and gays in couples and families* (pp. 370–403). San Francisco: Jossey-Bass.

Bion, W. (1970). *Attention and interpretation.* London: Heinemann.

Blundo, R. (2002). Mental health: A shift in perspective. In R. Greene (Ed.), *Resiliency: An integrated approach to practice, policy, and research* (pp. 133–152). Washington, DC: NASW Press.

Bos, H., Van Balen, F., & Van den Boom, D. (2005). Lesbian families and family functioning: An overview. *Patient Education and Counseling, 59*(3), 263–275.

Boss, P. (2006). *Loss, trauma, and resilience.* New York: Norton.

Bowen, D. (1995). Honoring the elders: Interviews with two Lakota men. *Journal of Sociology and Social Welfare, 32*(1), 125–134.

Bowen, G. & Othner, D. (1993). Family adaptation of single parents in the United States Army: An empirical analysis of work stressor and adaptive resources. *Family Relations, 42*(3), 293–304.

Bowlby, J. (1969). *Attachment.* New York: Basic Books.

Bowlby, J. (1973). *Separation: Anxiety and anger.* New York: Basic Books.

Boyd-Franklin, N. (2003). *Black families in therapy* (2nd ed.). New York: Guilford.

Boyd-Franklin, N., & Bry, H. (2000). *Reaching out in family therapy: Home-based, school, and community interventions.* New York: Guilford.

Boyd-Franklin, N., & Lockwood, T. (1999). Spirituality and religion: Implications for psychotherapy with African American clients and families. In F. Walsh (Ed.), *Spiritual resources in family therapy* (pp. 90–104). New York: Guilford.

Brennan, J. (1995). A short-term psychoeducational multi-group for bipolar patients and their families. *Social Work, 40*(6), 737–743.

Brock, G., & Barnard, C. (1999) *Procedures in marriage and family therapy* (3rd ed.). Boston: Allyn & Bacon.

Brody, G., Kim, S., Murry, V., Brown, A. (2004). Protective longitudinal paths: Linking child competence to behavioral problems among African American siblings. *Child Development, 75*(2), 455–467.

Brody, G., Dorsey, S., Forehand, R., & Armisted, L. (2002). Unique and protective contributions of parenting and classroom processes to the adjustment of African American children living in single-parent families. *Child Development, 73*(1), 274–286.

Bronfenbrenner, U. (1979). *The ecology of human development.* Cambridge, MA: Harvard University Press.

Brotherson, S., & Soderquist, J. (2002). Coping with a child's death: Spiritual issues and therapeutic implications. In T. Carlson & M. Erikson (Eds.), *Spirituality and family therapy* (pp. 53–86). New York: Haworth.

Bushy, A. (2002). *National Rural Health Association Rural Minority Health Resource Book.* Kansas City: National Rural Health Association.

Butler, W., & Powers, K. (1996). Solution-focused grief therapy. In S. Miller, M. Hubble, & B. Duncan (Eds.), *Handbook of solution focused brief therapy* (pp. 228–247). San Francisco: Jossey.

Campbell, C., & Demi, A. (2000). Adult children of fathers missing in action (MIA): An examination of emotional distress, grief, and family hardiness. *Family Relations, 49*(3), pp. 267–276.

Canda, E., & Furman, E. (1999). *Spiritual diversity in social work practice: The heart of healing.* New York: Free Press.

Capers, M. (2003). From subsistence to sustainability: Treating drug abuse in Alaska. *Substance Abuse and Mental Health Services News, 11*(4), 1, 8–10.

Carlson, T., & Erikson, M. (Eds.). (2002). *Spirituality and family therapy.* New York: Haworth.

Caspi, A., Elder, G., Jr., & Berm, D. (1987). Moving against the world: Life course patterns of explosive children. *Developmental Psychology, 23,* 308–313.

Centers for Disease Control. (2005a). HIV/AIDS among women. Retrieved October 25, 2005, from http://www.cdc.gov/hiv/pubs/facts/women.htm

Centers for Disease Control. (2005b). HIV/AIDS among African Americans. Retrieved October 25, 2005, from http://www.cdc.gov/hiv/pubs/Facts/afam.htm

Chavez, N., & Gonzalez, J. (2000). *Mexican immigrant youth and resiliency: Research and promoting programs.* ERIC U.S. Department of Government Educational Research Center.

Chazin, R., Kaplan, S., & Terio, S. (2000). Introducing a strengths/resiliency mode in mental health organizations. In E. Norman (Ed.), *Resiliency enhancement: Putting the strengths perspective into social work practice* (pp. 192–210). New York: Columbia University Press.

Chesla, C. (1999). Becoming resilient: Skill development in couples living with non-insulin dependent diabetes. In H. I. McCubbin, E. Thompson, A. Thompson, J. Futrell (Eds.), *The dynamics of resiliency families* (pp. 99–133). Resiliency in Families series. Thousand Oaks, CA: Sage.

Coles, R. (1964). *Children of crisis: A study of courage and fear.* New York: Dell.

Conger, R., & Elder, G. (1994). *Families in troubled times: Adapting to change in rural America.* New York: Aldine De Gruyter.

Conger, R., Wallace, L., Sun, Y., Simons, R., McLoyd, V., & Brody, G. (2002). Economic pressure in African American families: A replication and extension of the model. *Developmental Psychology, 38*(2), 179–193.

Conner, M. (1998). Level of satisfaction in African-American marriages: A preliminary investigation. In H. I. McCubbin, E. Thompson, A. Thompson, & J. Futrell (Eds.), *Resiliency in African-American families* (pp. 159–178). Thousand Oaks, CA: Sage.

Coon, D., Thompson, K., Steffen, A., Sorocco, K., & Gallagher-Thompson, D. (2002). Anger and depression management: Psychoeducational skill training interventions for women caretakers of a relative with dementia. *Gerontologist, 43*(5), 678–689.

Coulehan, R., Friedlander, M., & Heatherington, L. (1998). Transforming narratives: A change event in constructivist family therapy. *Family Process, 37,* 17–33.

Cross, T. (1999). Understanding family resiliency from a relational world view. In H. I. McCubbin, E. Thompson, A. Thompson, & J. Fromer (Eds.), *Resiliency in na-*

*tive American and immigrant families* (pp. 143–157). Resiliency in Families series. Thousand Oaks, CA: Sage.

DeJong, P., & Berg, I. (1998). *Interviewing for solutions.* Pacific Grove, CA: Brooks/Cole.

deShazer, S. (1994). *Words were originally magic.* New York: Norton.

DiNitto, D., & Gustavsson, N. (1999) The interface between family practice and family policy. In C. Franklin & C. Jordon (Eds.), *Family practice: Brief systems models for social work* (pp. 341–393). Pacific Grove, CA: Brooks/Cole.

Dixon, L., McFarlane, W., Lefley, H., Lucksted, A., Cohen, M., Falloon, I., et al. (2001). Evidenced-based practices for services to families of people with psychiatric disabilities. *Psychiatric Services, 52*(7), 903–910.

Drummet, A. R., Coleman, M., & Cable, S. (2003). Military families under stress: Implications for family life education. *Family Relations, 52*(3), 279–287.

Elder, G., & Conger, R. (2000). *Children of the land.* Chicago: University of Chicago Press.

Epstein, N., Balwin, L., & Bisho, D. (1983). The McMaster Family Assessment Devise. *Journal of Marital and Family Therapy, 9,* 171–180.

Falicov, C. (1996). Mexican families. In M. McGolderick, J. Giordano, & J. Pearce (Eds.), *Ethnicity and family therapy* (pp. 169–182). New York: Guilford.

Falicov, C. (1998). *Latino families in therapy: A guide to multicultural practice.* New York: Guilford.

Falicov, C. (1999). Religion and spiritual folk traditions in immigrant families: Therapeutic resources for Latinos. In F. Walsh (Ed.), *Spiritual resources in family therapy* (pp. 104–135). New York: Guilford.

Fatusso, L., McDermott, P., & Lutz, M. (1999). Clinical issues in the assessment of family violence involving children. In R. Ammerman & M. Hersen (Eds.), *Assessment of family violence: A clinical and legal sourcebook* (2nd ed., pp. 10–24). New York: Wiley.

Fellenberg, S. (2004). The contribution of enactments to structural family therapy: A process study. *Dissertation Abstracts International* Section B. The Sciences and Engineering, Vol. 64 (11B) 2004, p. 5780.S.

Felsman, J. (1989). Risk and resilience in childhood: The lives of street children. In T. Dugan and R. Coles (Eds.), *The child in our times* (pp. 56–79). New York: Bruner-Mazel.

Fisher, L., & Weihs, K. L. (2000). Can addressing family relationships improve chronic disease? *Journal of Family Practice, 49*(6), 561–566.

Frame, M. (2003). *Integrating religion and spirituality into counseling: A comprehensive approach.* Pacific Grove, CA: Thompson.

Fraser, M., Kirby, L., & Smokowski, P. (2004). Risk and resiliency in childhood. In M. Fraser (Ed.), *Risk and resilience in childhood: An ecological approach* (pp. 13–66). Washington, DC: NASW Press.

Fraser, M., & Galinsky, M. (2004). Risk and resilience in childhood: Toward an evidence-based model of practice. In M. Fraser (Ed.), *Risk and resilience in childhood: An ecological approach* (pp. 385–402). Washington, DC: NASW Press.

Fraser, M., Richman, J., & Galinsky, M. (1999). Risk protection, and resiliency: Toward a conceptual framework for social work practice. *Social Work Research, 23,* 129–208.

Freedman, J., & Combs, G. (1996). *Narrative therapy: The social construction of preferred realities.* New York: Norton.

Friedlander, M. (1998) Family therapy research: Science into practice, practice into science. In M. Nichols & R. Schwartz (Eds.), *Family therapy: Concepts and methods* (4th ed., pp. 503–553). Boston: Allyn & Bacon.

Friedman, B. (2001). Judaism. In M. Van Hook, B. Hugen, & M. Aguilar (Eds.), *Spirituality within religious traditions and social work practice* (pp. 98–119). Pacific Grove, CA: Brooks/Cole.

Friedman, E. (1986). Resources for healing and survival in families. In M. Karpel (Ed.), *Family resources: The hidden partner in family therapy* (pp. 65–92). New York: Guilford.

Garcia-Preto, N. (1996). Puerto Rican families. In M. McGolderick, J. Giordano, & J. Pearce (Eds.), *Ethnicity and family therapy* (pp. 183–199). New York: Guilford.

Garcia-Preto, N. (1996b). Latino families: An overview. In M. McGolderick, J. Giordano, & J. Pearce (Eds.), *Ethnicity and family therapy* (2nd ed., pp. 141–154). New York: Guilford.

Garmezy, N. (1985). Stress-resistant children: The search for protective factors. In J. Stevenson (Ed.), Recent research in developmental psychopathology. *Journal of Child Psychology and Psychiatry* (Book Supplement No. 4, 213–233). Oxford: Pergamon.

Garmezy, N. (1993). Children in poverty: Resilience despite risk. *Psychiatry, 56,* 127–136.

Gaudin, J., Wodarski, J., Arkinson, M., & Avery, L. (1990–1991). Remedying child neglect: Effectiveness of social network interventions. *Journal of Applied Social Sciences, 15,* 97–123.

Genero, N. (1998). Culture, resiliency, and mutual psychological development. In H. I. McCubbin, E. Thompson, A. Thompson, & J. Futrell (Eds.), *Resiliency in African-American families* (pp. 31–48). Thousand Oaks, CA: Sage.

Gibbon, F., Gerrard, M., Cleveland, M., Wills, T., & Brody, G. (2004). Perceived discrimination and substance use in African American parents and their children: A panel study. *Journal of Personality and Social Psychology, 86*(4), 517–529.

Gingerich, W., & Eisengart, S. (2000). Solution focused brief therapy: A review of the outcomes research. *Family Process, 39*(4), 477–498.

Giordana, J., & McGolderick, M. (1996). Italian families. In M. McGolderick, J. Giordano, & J. Pearce. (Eds.), *Ethnicity and family therapy* (2nd ed., pp. 427–441). New York: Guilford.

Golby, B., & Bretherton, I. (1999). Resilience in postdivorce mother-child relationships. In H. I. McCubbin, E. Thompson, A. Thompson, & J. Futrell (Eds.), *The dynamics of resiliency families* (pp. 238–269). Resiliency in Families series. Thousand Oaks, CA: Sage.

Goldberg-Arnold, J., Fristad, M., & Gavazzi, S. (1999). Family psychoeducation: Giving caretakers what they want and need. *Family Relations, 48,* 411–417.

Goldenberg, I., & Goldenberg, H. (1996). *Family therapy: An overview* (4th ed.). Pacific Grove, CA: Brooks/Cole.

Goldenberg, I., & Goldenberg, H. (1998). *Counseling today's families* (3rd ed.). Pacific Grove, CA: Brooks/Cole.

Goldenberg, I., & Goldenberg, H. (2000). *Family therapy: An overview* (5th ed.). Pacific Grove, CA: Brooks/Cole.

Goldstein, E. (1995). *Ego psychology and social work practice* (2nd ed.). New York: Free Press.

Gonzales, J. (2003). Cesar Chavez: A Case study of a resilient children's adaptation to adulthood. Retrieved March 2, 2004. ERIC U.S. Department of Government Educational Research Center.

Gonzales, N., & Kim, L. (1997). Stress and coping in an ethnic minority context: Children's cultural ecologies. In S. Wolchik & I. Sandler (Eds.), *Handbook of children's coping: Integration theory and practice* (pp. 481–511). New York: Plenum.

Gordon, J. (2003). What makes a tragedy public? In M. Lattanzi-Licht & K. Doka (Eds.), *Living with grief: Coping with public tragedy* (pp. 3–13). New York: Brunner-Routlege.

Gordon, K. (1996). Resilient Hispanic youths' self-concept and motivational patterns. *Hispanic Journal of Behavioral Social Sciences, 18*(1), 63–73.

Gordon, W. E., & Song, L. D. (1994). Variations in the experience of resilience. In M. Wang & W. Gordon (Eds.), *Educational resiliency in inner-city America: Challenges and prospects* (pp. 27–40). Hillsdale, NJ: Erlbaum.

Grant, D. (1999). Effective therapeutic approaches with ethnic families. In C. Franklin & C. Jordan (Eds.), *Family practice: Brief systems methods for social work* (pp. 259–297). Pacific Grove, CA: Brooks/Cole.

Grant, D. (2001). The African-American Baptist tradition. In M. Van Hook, B. Hugen, & M. Aguilar (Eds.), *Spirituality within religious traditions and social work practice* (pp. 205–227). Pacific Grove, CA: Brooks/Cole.

Granvold, D., & Martin, J. (1999). Family therapy with gay and lesbian clients. In C. Franklin & C. Jordan (Eds.), *Family practice: Brief systems methods for social work* (pp. 299–320). Pacific Grove, CA: Brooks/Cole.

Green, J. (2003). *Introduction to family theory and therapy: Exploring an evolving field.* Pacific Grove, CA: Thompson.

Greene, R., & Conrad, A. (2002). Basic assumptions and terms. In R. Greene (Ed.), *Resiliency: An integrated approach to practice, policy, and research* (pp. 29–62). Washington, DC: NASW Press.

Greene, R., & Kropf, N. (2003). A family case management approach for Level I needs. In A. Kilpatrick & T. Holland (Eds.), *Working with families: An integrated model by level of need* (3rd ed., pp. 85–103). Boston: Allyn & Bacon.

Greenwood, D., Szapocznik, J., McIntosh, S., Antoni, M., Ironson, G., Tejeda, M., et al. (1996). African American women, their families, and HIV/AIDS. In R. Resnick & R. Rozensky (Eds.), *Health psychology through the lifespan: Practice and research opportunities* (pp. 349–359). Washington, DC: American Psychological Association.

Grigsby, R. (2003). Interventions to meet basic needs of high-risk families with children. In A. Kilpatrick & T. Holland (Eds.), *Working with families: An integrated model by level of need* (3rd ed., pp. 69–84). Boston: Allyn & Bacon.

Grych, J., & Fincham, F. (1997). Children's adaptation to divorce: From description to explanation. In W. Wolchik & I. Sandler (Eds.), *Handbook of children's coping: Linking theory and intervention* (pp. 159–193). New York: Plenum.

Guarnaccia, P. (1998). Multicultural experiences of family caregiving: A study of African American, European American, and Hispanic American families. In H. Lefley (Ed.), *Family coping with mental illness: The cultural context* (pp. 45–61). San Francisco: Jossey-Bass.

Gunderson, J., Berkowitz, C., & Ruiz-Sancho, A. (1997). Families of borderline patients: A psychoeducational approach. *Bulletin of the Menninger Clinic, 61*(4), 446–458. Retrieved August 24, 2005, from Academic Search Premier.

Gutheil, I., & Congress, E. (2000). Resiliency in older people: A paradigm for practice. In E. Norman (Ed.), *Resiliency enhancement: Putting the strengths perspective into practice* (pp. 40–52). New York: Columbia University Press.

Hartman, A. (1999). The long road to equality: Lesbians and social policy. In J. Laird (Ed.), *Lesbians and lesbian families: Reflections on theory and practice* (pp. 91–122). New York: Columbia University Press.

Hartman, A., & Laird, J. (1983). *Family centered social work practice.* New York: Free Press.

Helmeke, K., & Bischof, G. (2002). Recognizing and raising spiritual and religious issues in therapy: Guidelines for the timid (pp. 195–214). In T. Carlson & M. Erikson (Eds.), *Spirituality and family therapy.* New York: Haworth.

Henggeler, S., Schoenwald, S., Borduin, C., & Rowland, M., & Cunningham, P. (1998). *Multisystemic treatment of antisocial behavior of children and adolescents.* New York: Guilford.

Hetherington, E. M. (1989). Coping with family transitions: Winners, losers, and survivors. *Child Development, 60,* 1–14.

Hill, R. (1949). *Families under stress.* New York: Harper & Row.

Hill, R. (1999). *The strengths of African American Families: Twenty-five years later.* New York: University Press of America.

Hines, P., & Boyd-Franklin, C. (1996). African-American families. In M. McGolderick, J. Giordano, & J. Pearce. *Ethnicity and family therapy* (2nd ed., pp. 66–84). New York: Guilford.

Hodge, D. (2003). *Spiritual assessment: Handbook for helping professionals.* Botsford. CT: North American Association for Christians in Social Work.

Hodge, D. (2005). Spiritual ecograms: A new assessment instrument for identifying clients' strengths in space and across time. *Families in Society. 86*(2) 287–296.

Hoffman, L. (1993). *Exchanging voices: A collaborative approach to family therapy.* London: Karnac Books.

Homrich, A., & Horne, A. (2000). Brief family therapy. In A. M. Horne (Ed.), *Family counseling and therapy* (3rd ed., pp. 243–270). Itasca, IL: Peacock.

Horne, A. & Sayger, T. (2000). Behavioral approaches to couple and family therapy. In A. Horne (Ed.), *Family counseling and therapy* (3rd ed., pp. 454–488). Itasca, IL: Peacock.

Horne, A. & Sayger, T. (2003). Social learning family interventions. In A. Kilpatrick & T. Holland (Eds.), *Working with families: An integrative model by level of need* (pp. 116–130). New York: Allyn & Bacon.

Hudson, W., & McMurtry, S. (1997). Comprehensive assessment in social work practice: The Multi-Problem Screening Inventory. *Research on Social Work Practice, 7,* 79–98.

Hugen, B. (2001). Spirituality and religion in social work practice: A conceptual model. pp. 9–17. In M. Van Hook, B. Hugen, & M. Aguilar (Eds.) *Spirituality within religious traditions in social work practice.* Pacific Grove, CA: Thompson.

Hyman, B., & Williams, L. (2001). Resiliency among women survivors of child sexual abuse. *Affilia, 16*(2), 198–219.

Imber-Black, E. (1988). *Families and larger systems.* New York: Guilford.

James, B. (1994). *Handbook for treatment of attachment-trauma problems in children.* New York; Lexington Books/Free Press.

Johnson, C., & Johnson, D. (1998). Working with Native American families. In H. Lefley (Ed.), *Families coping with mental illness: The cultural context* (pp. 89–96). San Francisco: Jossey-Bass.

Jones, D., Forehand, R., Brody, G., Armistead, L. (2002). Psychosocial adjustment of African American children in single-mother families: A test of three risk models. *Journal of Marriage and Family, 64*(1).

Jones, T. & Schmidt, H. (1960). *The Fantastiks.*

Jordan, C., Cobb, N. H., & Franklin, C. (1999). Behavioral and cognitive-behavior family therapy. In C. Franklin & C. Jordan (Eds.), *Family practice: Brief systems methods for social work* (pp. 73–103). Pacific Grove, CA: Brooks/Cole.

Jordan, C., & Franklin, C. (1999). Structural family therapy. In C. Jordan & C. Franklin (Eds.), *Family practice: Brief systems methods for social work* (pp. 23–44). Pacific Grove, CA: Brooks/Cole.

Jordan, C., Lewellen, A., & Vandiver, V. (1995). Psychoeducation for minority families: A social work perspective. *International Journal of Mental Health, 23*(4), 27–43.

Kantor, D. & Kupferman, W. (1985). The client's interview of the therapist. *Journal of Marital and Family Therapy, 11*(3), 225–244.

Karpel, M. A. (1986). Testing, promoting, and preserving family resources: Beyond pathology and power. In M. Karpel (Ed.), *Family resources: The hidden partner in family therapy* (pp. 175–232). New York: Guilford.

Kilpatrick, A. (2003). Levels of family need. In A. Kilpatrick & T. Holland (Eds.), *Working with families: An integrative model by levels of need* (3rd ed., pp. 1–13). Boston: Allyn & Bacon.

Kilpatrick, A., Becvar, D., & Holland, T. (2003). Ethically and spiritually sensitive practice. (pp. 49–67). In A. Kilpatrick & T. Holland (Eds.), *Working with families: An integrative model by level of need.* Boston: Allyn & Bacon.

Kilpatrick, A., Kilpatrick, Jr., E., & Callaway, J. (2000). Object relations family therapy. In A. Horne (Ed.), *Family counseling and therapy* (3rd ed., pp. 300–329). Itasca, IL: Peacock.

Kinney, J., Haapala, D., & Booth, C. (1991). *Keeping families together: The homebuilders model.* New York: Aldine De Gruyter.

Kinsie, J., & Sack, W. (2002). The psychiatric disorders among Canadian adolescents: The effects of severe trauma. In F. Azima & N. Grizenko (Eds.), *Immigrant and refugee children and their families: Clinical, research, and training issues* (pp. 95–112). Madison, CT: International Universities Press.

Kliewer, W. (1997). Children's coping with chronic illness. In W. Wolchik & I. Sandler (Eds.), *Handbook of children's coping: Linking theory and intervention* (pp. 275–300). New York: Plenum.

Koenig, H. (1999). *The healing power of faith: Science explores medicine's last great frontier.* New York; Simon & Schuster.

Koob, J. (2003). Solution-focused family interventions. In A. Kilpatrick & T. Holland (Eds.), *Working with families: An integrative model by level of functioning* (3rd ed., pp. 131–150). Boston: Allyn & Bacon.

Krasner, B. (1986). Trustworthiness: The primary family resource. In M. Karpel (Ed.), *Family resources: The hidden partner in family therapy* (pp. 116–147). New York: Guilford.

Kurtines, W., & Szapocznik, J. (1996). Family interaction patterns: Structural family therapy within context of cultural diversity. In E. Hibbs & P. Jensen (Eds.), *Psychosocial treatments for child and adolescent disorders: Empirically based strategies for clinical practice* (pp. 671–697). Washington, DC: American Psychological Association.

Laird, J. (2000). Culture and narratives as metaphors for clinical practice with families. In D. Demo, K. Allen, & M. Fine (Eds.), *Handbook of family diversity* (pp. 338–358). New York: Oxford University Press.

Lau, A., & Takeuchi, D. (2001). Cultural factors in help-seeking for child behavior problems: Value orientation, affective responding, and severity appraisals among Chinese-American families. *Journal of Community Psychology, 29*(6), 675–692.

Lee, E. (1996). Asian American families: An overview. In M., McGolderick, J. Giordano, & J. Pearce (Eds.), *Ethnicity and family therapy* (2nd ed., pp. 227–248). New York: Guilford.

Lefley, H. P. (1998). *Families coping with mental illness: The cultural context.* San Francisco: Jossey-Bass.

Lopez, M., Toprac, M., Crismon, M. L. (2005). Psychoeducational program for children with ADHD or depression and their families: Results from the CMAP feasibility study. *Community Mental Health Journal, 41*(1), 51–66.

Lott-Whitehead, L., & Tully, C. (1999). The family lives of lesbian mothers. In J. Laird (Ed.), *Lesbians and lesbian families: Reflections on theory and practice* (pp. 243–260). New York: Columbia University Press.

Lutzker, J., Bigelow, K., Doctor, R. & Kessler, M. (1998). Safety, health care, and bonding within an ecobehavioral approach to treating and preventing child abuse and neglect. *Journal of Family Violence, 2,* 283–290.

Marsella, A., Oliveira, J., Plummer, C., & Crabbe, K. (1998). Native Hawaiian (Kanoka Maoli) culture, mind, and well-being. In H. I. McCubbin, E. Thompson, A. Thompson, & J. Fromer (Eds.), *Resiliency in Native American and immigrant families* (pp. 93–131). Thousand Oaks, CA: Sage.

Martin. E., & Martin, J. (2002). *Spirituality and the black helping tradition in social work.* Washington, DC: NASW Press.

Masten, A. (1994). Resilience in individual development: Successful adaptation despite risk and adversity. In M. Wang & E. Gordon (Eds.), *Educational resilience in inner-city America: Challenges and prospects* (pp. 3–25). Hillsdale, NJ: Erlbaum.

Masten, A., & Coatsworth, J. (1998). The development of competence in favorable and unfavorable environments: Lessons from research of successful children. *American Psychologist, 53* (2), 205–220.

Masten, A., & Garmezny, N. (1983). Risk, vulnerability, and protective factors in developmental psychopathology. In B. Lahey & A. Kazdin (Eds.), *Advances in clinical child psychology* (Vol. 8, pp. 1–51). New York: Plenum.

Masten, A., Best, K., & Garmezny, N. (1990). Resilience and development: Contributions from the study of children who overcome adversity. *Development and Psychopathology, 2,* 425–444.

Mayadas, N., Elliott, D., & Ramanathan, S. (1999). A global model of ethnic diversity conflict: Implications for social work with populations at risk. In S. Ramanathan & R. Link (Eds.), *All our futures: Principles and resources for social work practice in a global era* (pp. 138–155). Belmont, CA: Brooks/Cole.

McAdoo, H. (1998). African-American families: Strengths and realities. In H. I. McCubbin, E. Thompson, A. Thompson, & J. Futrell (Eds.), *Resiliency in African-American families* (pp. 17–30). Thousand Oaks, CA: Sage.

McCubbin, H. I. (1998). Resiliency in African-American families: Military families in foreign environments. In H. I. McCubbin & E. Thompson, A. Thompson & J. Futrell (Eds.), *Resiliency in African American families* (pp. 67–97). Thousand Oaks, CA: Sage.

McCubbin, H. I., Dahl, B., & Hunter, E. (1976). *Families in the military system.* Thousand Oaks, CA: Sage.

McCubbin, H. I., Futrell, J., Thompson, E., & Thompson, A. (1998). Resilient families in an ethnic and cultural context. In H. McCubbin, E. Thompson, A. Thompson, & J. Futrell (Eds.), *Resiliency in African American families* (pp. 329–353). Thousand Oaks, CA: Sage.

McCubbin, M., & McCubbin, H. (1996). Resiliency in families: A conceptual model of family adjustment and adaptation in response to stress and crisis. In H. I. McCubbin, A. Thompson, & M. McCubbin (Eds.), *Family assessment: resiliency, coping, and adaptation: Inventories for research and practice* (pp. 1–64). Madison: University of Wisconsin Press.

McCubbin, H. I., McCubbin, M., Thompson, A., & Thompson, E. (1999). Resiliency in ethnic families. In H. I. McCubbin, E. Thompson, A. Thompson, & J. Fromer (Eds.), *Resiliency in Native American and immigrant families* (pp. 3–48). Thousand Oaks, CA: Sage.

McCubbin, H., Thompson, E., Thompson, A., & Futrell, J. (1999). *The dynamics of resilient families.* Thousand Oaks, CA: Sage.

McCubbin, H. E., & Patterson, J. (1983). Family transitions: Adaptation to stress. In H. I. McCubbin & C. Figley (Eds.), *Stress and the family: Coping with normative transitions. I.* New York: Bruner-Mazel.

McCubbin, H. I., Thompson, A., McCubbin, M. (1996). *Family assessment: Resiliency, coping, and adaptation: Inventories for research and practice.* Madison: University of Wisconsin Press.

McCubbin, H. I., Thompson, E., Thompson, A., & Fromer, J. (1998). Preface. In H. I. McCubbin, E. Thompson, A. Thompson, & J. Fromer (Eds.), *Resiliency in Native American and immigrant families* (pp. xvi–xvii). Thousand Oaks, CA: Sage.

McCubbin, H. I., Thompson, E., Thompson, A., Elver, K., & McCubbin, M. (1998). Ethnicity, schema, and coherence: Appraisal processes for families in crisis. In H. I. McCubbin, A. Thompson, E. Thompson, & J. Fromer (Eds.), *Stress, coping, and health in families: Sense of coherence and resiliency* (pp. 41–67). Resiliency in Families series. Thousand Oaks, CA: Sage.

McFarlene, W., Link, B., Dushay, R., Marchal, J., & Crilly, J. (1995). Psychoeducational multiple family groups: Four-year relapse outcome in schizophrenia. *Family Process, 34,* 127–144.

McGolderick, M., & Gerson, R. (1985). *Genograms in family assessment.* New York: Norton.

McGolderick, M., & Giordaro, J. (1986). Overview: Ethnicity and family therapy. In M. McGolderick, J. Giordano, & J. Pearce (Eds.), *Ethnicity and family therapy* (2nd ed., pp. 1–27). New York: Guilford.

McQuaide, Sharon. (2000). Women's resiliency at midlife: What is it? How do you mobilize it? In E. Norman (Ed.), *Resiliency enhancement: Putting the strengths perspective into social work practice* (pp. 70–82). New York: Columbia University Press.

McWhirter, J., & Ryan, C. (1991). Counseling the Navajo: Cultural understanding. *Journal of Multicultural Counseling and Development, 19*(2).

Mederer, H. (1999). Surviving the demise of a way of life: Stress and resilience in Northeastern commercial fishing families. In H. I. McCubbin, E. Thompson, A. Thompson, & J. Futrell (Eds.), *The dynamics of resilient families* (pp. 203–235). Thousand Oaks, CA: Sage.

Miguel, K., Morrison, G., & Weissglass, T. (1998). The relationship of sources of support and service needs. In E. I. McCubin, E. Thompson, A. Thompson, & J. Fromer (Eds.), *Resiliency in Native American and immigrant families* (pp. 385–400). Thousand Oaks, CA: Sage.

Miller, J., Kabacoff, R., Bishop, D., Epstein, N., & Keitner, G. (1994). The development of the McMaster Clinical Rating Scale. *Family Process, 33,* 53–69.

Miller, J., Ryan, C. Keitner, G., Bishop, D., & Epstein, N. (1999). The McMaster Approach to Families: Theory, assessment., treatment, and research. *Journal of Family Therapy, 22,* 169–189.

Minuchin, S. (1974). *Families and family therapy.* Cambridge, MA: Harvard University Press.

Minuchin, S., & Fishman, H. (1981). *Family therapy techniques.* Cambridge, MA: Harvard University Press.

Minuchin, S., & Nichols, M. (1991). *Family healing: Strategies for hope and understanding.* New York: Simon & Schuster.

Minuchin, S., Rosman, B., & Baker, L. (1978). *Psychosomatic families.* Cambridge, MA: Harvard University Press.

Mittelman, M., Ferris, S., Shulman, G., & Levin, B. (1996). A family intervention to delay nursing home placement of patients with Alzheimer disease: Randomized control trial. *Journal of the American Medical Association, 276*(21), 1725–1731.

Morales, E. (2000). A contextual understanding of the process of educational resilience: High achieving Dominican American students and the "Resilience Cycle." *Innovative Higher Education, 25*(1), 7–22.

Moskowitz, S. (1983). *Love despite hate.* New York: Schocken.

Murry, V., Bynum, M., Brody, G., Willert, A., & Stephens, D. (2001). African American single mothers and children in context: A review of studies on risk and resilience. *Clinical Child and Family Psychology Review, 4*(2), 133–154.

Muzio, C. (199). Lesbian co-parenting: On being/being with the invisible (M)other. In J. Laird (Ed.), *Lesbians and lesbian families: Reflections on theory and practice* (pp. 197–212). New York: Columbia University Press.

Nadir, A., & Dziegielewski, S. (2001). Islam. In M. Van Hook, B. Hugen, & M. Aguilar (Eds.), *Spirituality within religious traditions and social work practice* (pp. 146–166). Pacific Grove, CA: Brooks/Cole.

Nichols, M., & Schwartz, R. (1998). *Family therapy: Concepts and methods* (4th ed.). Boston: Allyn & Bacon.

Nichols, M., & Schwartz, R. (2001). *Family therapy: Concepts and methods* (5th ed.). New York: Allyn & Bacon.

Nichols, M., & Schwartz, R. (2005). *The essentials of family therapy.* New York: Allyn & Bacon.

Norman, E. (2000). Introduction: The strengths perspective and resiliency enhancement—a natural partnership. In E. Norman (Ed.), *Resiliency enhancement: Putting the strengths perspective into social work practice* (pp. 1–16) New York: Columbia University Press.

Norris, F., Phifer, J., & Kaniasty, K. (1994). Individual and community reactions to the Kentucky floods: Findings from a longitudinal study of older adults. In R. Ursano, B. McCughey, & C. Fullerton (Eds.), *Individual and community responses to trauma and disaster: The structure of human chaos* (pp. 378–400). Cambridge UK: Cambridge University Press.

O'Connell, B. (1998). *Solution-focused therapy.* Thousand Oaks, CA: Sage.

O'Connor, T., Meakes, E., Pickering, R., & Schuman, M. (1997). On the right track: Clients' experience of narrative therapy. *Contemporary Family Therapy, 19,* 479–496.

O'Hanlon, W., & Weiner-Davis, M. (1989). *In search of solutions: A new direction in psychotherapy.* New York: Norton.

Olsen, N. (2001). *Albania: The background, the issues, the people.* Oxford UK: Oxfam.

Olson, D. (1993). Circumplex model of marital and family systems. In F. Walsh (Ed.), *Normal family processes* (2nd ed.). New York: Guilford.

Orthner, D., Jones-Sanpei, H., & Williamson, S. (2004). The resilience and strengths of low-income families. *Family Relations, 53,* 159–167.

Pang, E., Jordan-Marsh, M., Silverstein, M., & Cody, M. (2003). Health-seeking behaviors of elderly Chinese Americans: Shifts in expectations. *Gerontologist, 43*(6), 864–874.

Papalos, D. (2002). *The family psychoeducational approach.* Retrieved August 31, 2005, from http://www.pendlum.org.articles/articles_bipolar.psychoed.html

Pargament, K. (1997). *The psychology of religion and coping: Theory, research, and practice.* New York: Guilford.

Pargament, K., & Brandt, C. (1998). Religion in coping. In H. Koenig (Ed.), *Handbook of religion and mental health* (pp. 111–128). New York: Academic.

Parra, P., & Guarnacia, P. (1998). Ethnicity, culture, and resiliency in caregivers of a seriously mentally ill family member. In H. I. McCubbin, E. Thompson, A. Thompson, and J. Futrell (Eds.), *The dynamics of resilient families: The dynamics of resilient families.* (pp. 431–450). Thousand Oaks, CA: Sage.

Patterson, J., & McCubbin, H. I. (1983). Chronic illness: Family stress and coping. In C. Figley & H. I. McCubbin (Eds), *Stress and the family.* Vol. 2, *Coping with catastrophe* (pp. 21–36). New York: Bruner-Mazel.

Perez-Koenig, R. (2000). The Unitas extended family circle: Developing resiliency in Hispanic youngsters. In E. Norman (Ed.), *Resiliency enhancement: Putting the strengths perspective into social work practice* (pp. 143–153). New York: Columbia University Press.

Pittman, J., Kerpelman, J., & McFadyem, J. (2004). Internal and external adaptation in army families: Lesson from Operation Desert Shield and Desert Storm. *Family Relations, 53*(3), 249–260.

Prochaska, J., DiClementi, C., & Norcross, J. (1992). In search of how people change: Applications to addictive behaviors. *American Psychologist, 47*(9), 1102–1114.

Reiss, D. (1981). *The family's construction of reality.* Cambridge, MA: Harvard University Press.

Rivera, C. (1988, Spring). Culturally sensitive aftercare services for chronically mentally ill Hispanics: The case of the psychoeducational treatment model. *Research Bulletin, Hispanic Research Center. 11*(1). New York: Fordham University Press.

Robinson, Harold. (2000). Enhancing couple resiliency. In E. Norman (Ed.), *Resiliency enhancement: Putting the strength perspective into social work practice* (pp. 102–127). New York: Columbia University Press.

Roen, T. (2004, July 8). Founder's family carries on. *Orlando Sentinel,* H1, H3.

Romeo, I. (2000). A multisystematic look at Mexican American gangs: Adolescents at risk. In M. Flores & G. Carey (Eds.), *Family therapy with Hispanics: Toward appreciating diversity* (pp. 265–280). Boston: Allyn & Bacon.

Rutter, M. (1984). Resilient children. *Psychology Today.* March 57–65.

Saleebey, D. (2000). *The strengths perspective in social work practice* (2nd ed.). New York: Longman.

Sandler, I., Wolchik, S., MacKinnon, D., Aers, T., & Roosa, M. (1997). Developing linkages between theory and intervention in stress and coping. In S. Wolchik & I. Sandler (Eds.), *Handbook of children's coping* (pp. 3–40) New York: Plenum.

Saylor, C., Belter, R., & Stokes, S. (1997). Children and families coping with disaster. In S. Wolchik & I. Sandler (Eds.), *Handbook of children's coping: Linking theory and intervention* (pp. 361–383). New York: Plenum.

Scharff, D. (2006). Models of the mind for couple and family therapy. In J. Scharff & D. Scharff (Eds.), *New paradigms for treating relationships* (pp. 7–17). New York: Aronson.

Scharff, D., & Scharff, J. (1987). *Object relations family therapy.* Northvale, NJ: Aronson.

Scharff, J., & Scharff, D. (2003). Object-relations and psychodynamic approaches to couple and family therapy. In T. Sexton; G. Weeks, & M. Robbins (Eds.), *Handbook of family therapy* (pp. 59–81). New York: Brunner-Routledge.

Scharff, J., & Scharff, D. (2006). New paradigms for treating relationships. In J. Scarff & D. Scarff (Eds.), *New paradigms for treating relationships* (pp. 19–32). New York: Aronson.

Schreiner, A., & Morimoto, T. (2003). The relationship between mastery and depression among Japanese family caregivers. *International Journal of Aging and Human Development, 56*(4), 307–321.

Seligman, M. (1990). *Learned optimism.* New York: Random House.

Sexton, T., Robbins, M., Hollimon, A., Mease, A., & Mayorga, C. (2003). Efficacy, effectiveness, and change mechanisms in couple and family therapy. In T. Sexton, G. Weeks, & M. Robbins (Eds.), *Handbook of family therapy* (pp. 229–261). New York: Brunner-Routledge.

Sheidow, A., Henggeler, S., & Schoenwald, S. (2003). Multisystemic therapy. In T. Sexton, G. Weeks, & M. Robbins (Eds.), *Handbook of family therapy* (pp. 303–322). New York: Brunner-Routledge.

Sherwood, D. (2002). Ethical integration of faith and social work practice: Evangelism. *Social Work and Christianity, 29*(1), 1–12.

Shonkoff, J. (2005, April). *The science of early childhood development: Closing the gap between what we know and what we do.* Paper presented at the 15th National Conference on Child Abuse and Neglect, Boston, MA.

Simmons, T., Franks, J., Peters, C., & Burham, V. (2003, July). *Development of a cultural grounded system of care for Alaska Native Children.* Paper presented at the National Association for Rural Mental Health, Orlando, FL.

Simon, C., McNeil, J., Franklin, C., & Cooperman, A. (1991). The family and schizophrenia: Toward a psychoeducational approach. *Families in Society, 72*(6), 323–333.

Simons, L., Simons, R., Conger, R., & Brody, G. (2004). Collective socialization and child conduct problems: A multilevel analysis with an African American sample. *Youth & Society, 35*(3), 267–292.

Singh, R. (2001). Hinduism. In M. Van Hook, B. Hugen, & M. Aguilar (Eds.), *Spirituality within religious traditions and social work practice* (pp. 34–52). Pacific Grove, CA: Brooks/Cole.

Sirin, S., & Rogers-Sirin, L. (2004). Exploring school engagement of middle-class African-American adolescents. *Youth & Society, 35*(3), 323–340.

Smith, A., & Harkness, J. (2002). Spirituality and meaning: A qualitative inquiry with caregivers of Alzheimer's disease. In T. Carlson & M. Erikson (Eds.), *Spirituality and family therapy* (pp. 87–108). New York: Haworth.

Solomon, P. (1996). Moving from psychoeducation to family education for families of adults with serious mental illness. *Psychiatric Services, 47*(12), 1364–1370.

Solomon, P. (1998). The cultural context of interventions for family members with a seriously mental ill relative. In H. Lefley (Ed.), *Families coping with mental illness: The cultural context* (pp. 5–16). San Francisco: Jossey-Bass.

Solomon, S., & Smith, E. (1994). Social support and perceived control as moderators of responses to dioxin and flood exposure. In R. Ursano, B. McCughey, & C. Fullerton (Eds.), *Individual and community responses to trauma and disaster: The structure of human chaos* (pp. 179–200). Cambridge UK: Cambridge University Press.

Stadter, M. & Scharff, D. (2006). Brief therapy with couples and individuals. In J. Scharff and D. Scharff (Eds.), *New paradigms for treating relationships* (pp. 419–446). Lanham, MD: Aronson.

Stern, D. (1985). *The interpersonal world of the infant: A view from psychoanalysis and developmental psychology.* New York: Basic Books.

Stewart, M., Reid, G., & Mangham, C. (1997). Fostering children's resilience. *Journal of Pediatric Nursing, 12,* 21–31.

Strumpf, N., Glicksman, A., Goldberg-Glen, R., Fox, R., & Logue, E. (2001). Caregiver and elder experiences of Cambodian, Vietnamese, Soviet Jewish, and Ukrainian refugees. *International Journal of Aging and Human Development, 53*(3), 233–252.

Sutton, C., & Broken Nose, M. (1996). American Indian families: An overview. In M. McGolderick, J. Giordano, & J. Pearce (Eds.), *Ethnicity and family therapy* (2nd ed., pp. 31–44). New York: Guilford.

Tam, V., & Detzner, D. (1998). Grandparents as a family resource in Chinese-American families. In H. I. McCubbin, E. Thompson, A. Thompson, & J. Fromer (Eds.), *Resiliency in Native American and immigrant families* (pp. 243–263). Thousand Oaks, CA: Sage.

Thomlison, B. (2004). Child maltreatment: A risk and protective factor perspective. In M. Fraser (Ed.), *Risk and resilience in childhood: An ecological perspective* (pp. 89–132). Washington, DC: NASW Press.

Thompson, E. (1999). Resiliency in family members facing AIDS. In H. I. McCubbin, E. Thompson, A. Thompson & J. Futrell, (Eds.), *The dynamics of resilient families.* (pp. 135–164). Thousand Oaks, CA: Sage.

Thompson, E., McCubbin, H. I., Thompson, A., & Elver, K. (1998). Vulnerability and resiliency in Native Hawaiian families under stress. In H. I. McCubbin, E. Thompson, A. Thompson, & J. Fromer (Eds.), *Resiliency in Naïve American and immigrant families* (pp. 115–131). Resiliency in Families series. Thousand Oaks, CA: Sage.

Thornton, M. (1998). Indigenous resources and strategies of resistance: Informal caregiving and racial socialization in black communities. In H. I. McCubbin, E. Thompson, A. Thompson, & J. Futrell (Eds.), *Resiliency in African-American families* (pp. 49–66). Thousand Oaks, CA: Sage

Valentine, L., & Feinauer, L. (1993). Resilience factors associated with female survivors of childhood sexual abuse. *American Journal of Family Therapy, 21*(3), 216–224.

Vandiver, V., & Keopraseuth, K. (1998). Family wisdom and clinical support: Culturally relevant practice strategies for working with Indochinese families who care for a relative with mental illness. In H. Lefley (Ed.), *Families coping with mental illness: The cultural context* (pp. 75–88). San Francisco: Jossey-Bass.

Van Hook, M. (in press). Spirituality. In A. Strozier & J. Carpenter (Eds.), *An introduction to alternative and complementary therapies.* New York: Haworth.

Van Hook, M. (1990a). The Iowa farm crisis: Perceptions, interpretations, and family patterns. In V. McLyold & C. Flannagan (Eds.), *New Directions for Child Development, 46,* 71–86.

Van Hook, M. (1990b). Family response to the farm crisis: A study in coping. *Social Work, 35*(5), 425–431.

Van Hook, M., & Aguilar, M. (2001). Health, religion and spirituality. In M. Van Hook, B. Hugen, & M. Aguilar (Eds.), *Spirituality within religious traditions in social work practice* (pp. 273–289). Pacific Grove, CA: Thompson.

Van Hook, M., Hugen, B., & Aguilar, M. (2001). *Spirituality within religious traditions and social work practice.* Pacific Grove, CA: Brooks/Cole.

Van Hook, M., & Rivera, O. (2004). Coping with difficult life transitions by older adults: The role of religion. *Christianity and Social Work, 31*(3), 233–253.

Vega, W. (1995). The study of Latino families: A point of departure. In R. Zambrana (Ed.), *Understanding Latino families: Scholarship, policy, and practice* (pp. 1–17). Thousand Oaks, CA: Sage.

Walsh, F. (1998). *Strengthening family resilience.* New York: Guilford.

Walsh, F. (1999). Opening family therapy to spirituality. In F. Walsh (Ed.), *Spiritual resources in family therapy* (pp. 28–58). New York: Guilford.

Walter, J., & Peller, J. (1996). Rethinking our assumptions: Assuming anew in a post modern world. In S. Miller, M. Hubble, & B. Duncan (Eds.), *Handbook of solution-focused brief therapy*. San Francisco: Jossey-Bass.

Weine, S., Muzurovic, N., Kulauzovic, Y., Besic, S., Lezic, A., Mujagic, A., et al. (2004). Family consequences of refugee trauma. *Family Process, 43*(2), 147–160.

Weiner-Davis, M. (1993). Pro-constructured reality. In S. Gilligan & R. Price (Eds.), *Therapeutic conversations*. New York: Norton.

Werner, E., & Smith, R. (1992). *Overcoming the odds: High risk children from birth to adulthood*. Ithaca, NY: Cornell University Press.

Whitaker, C. (1989, April). *Family therapy*. Paper presented at the Iowa National Association for Social Workers Conference, Des Moines, IA.

White, M., & Epston, D. (1990). *Narrative means to therapeutic ends*. New York: Norton.

Williams, J., Ayers, C., Van Dorn, R., & Arthur, M. (2004). Risk and protective factors in the development of delinquency and conduct disorder. In M. W. Fraser (Ed.), *Risk and resiliency in childhood* (pp. 209–250). Washington, DC: NASW Press.

Williams, N., & Kurtz, P. (2003). Narrative family interventions. In A. Kilpatrick & T. Holland (Eds.), *Working with families: An integrative model by level of need* (3rd ed., pp. 174–195). Boston: Allyn & Bacon.

Winston, C. (2003). African American grandmothers parenting AIDS orphans: Concomitant grief and loss. *American Journal of Orthopsychiatry, 73*(1), 91–100.

Wolfe, D., & Sandler, J. (1981). Training abusive parents in effective child management. *Behavior Modification, 5,* 320–335.

Wolfe, D., & Sandler, J., & Kaufman, K. (1981). A competency-based parent training program for child abusers. *Journal of Consulting and Clinical Psychology Review, 49,* 6333–6340.

Worden, M. (2003). *Family therapy basics* (3rd ed.). Pacific Grove, CA: Brooks/Cole.

Wright, L. (1999). Spirituality, suffering, and beliefs: The soul of healing with families. In F. Walsh (Ed.), *Spiritual resources in family therapy* (pp. 61–75). New York: Guilford.

Yellow-Horse Brave Heart, M. (2001). Lakota-Native People's spirituality. In M. Van Hook, B. Hugen, & M. Aguilar (Eds.), *Spirituality within religious traditions and social work* (pp. 18–33). Pacific Grove, CA: Brooks/Cole.

Zimmerman, J., & Dickerson, V. (1994). Using a narrative metaphor: Implications for theory and clinical practice. *Family Process, 33,* 233–245.

Zimmerman, J., & Dickerson, V. (1996). *If problems talked: Adventures in narrative therapy.* New York: Guilford.

Zimmerman, M., Ramirez, J., Washienko, K., Walter, B., & Dyer, S. (1998). Enculturation hypothesis: Exploring direct and protective effects among Native American youth. In H. I. McCubbin, E. Thompson, A. Thompson, & J. Fromer (Eds.), *Resiliency in Native American and immigrant families* (pp. 199–220). Resiliency in Families Series. Thousand Oaks, CA: Sage.

# Index

*Page numbers in italics refer to figures and tables.*

# Practice Essentials for your Professional Library

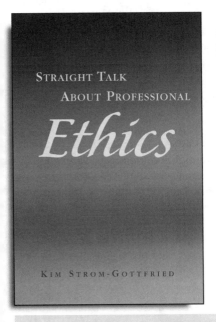

**STRAIGHT TALK ABOUT PROFESSIONAL ETHICS**

Kim Strom-Gottfried,
*University of North Carolina, Chapel Hill*
*ISBN 978-0-933478-0-36,*
*Price $28.95, 2007, Paper, 256 Pages*

Ethics is a complex and high-stakes area of professional practice. Too often, though, ethical discussion is separated from the realities of everyday life. Strom-Gottfried offers a clear and accessible approach to incorporating ethical behavior into professional practice and examines the ethical standards governing social service practice as they might be applied in a variety of situations.

## CONTENTS

### SAVE 15% WHEN YOU ORDER FROM OUR WEB SITE!

Visit www.lyceumbooks.com/shop and use coupon code **vanhook** when ordering.

LYCEUM
B O O K S ,   I N C .
5758 S. Blackstone, Chicago, IL 60637

**4 EASY WAYS TO ORDER**
Call: 1-773-643-1902
Fax: 1-773-643-1903
Email: lyceum@lyceumbooks.com
Web: www.lyceumbooks.com/shop

# Practice Essentials for your Professional Library

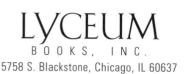